Climbing Colorado's Mountains

Susan Joy Paul

FALCON GUIDES

GUILFORD, CONNECTICUT
HELENA, MONTANA

To the men who loved the mountains, and made me love them, too:

Avrim Cantor (July 20, 1948–August 29, 2010),
Bill Boyle (February 20, 1950–June 2, 2014),
Bill Brown, Bob Mouner, Dan Anderson,
Doug Hatfield, Eric Hunter, Greg Long, Kevin Baker,
Patrick Niedringhaus (May 5, 1987–December 22, 2005),
Spencer Swanger (May 15, 1940–July 20, 2010),
and Stewart Green;

and to those who climbed ahead and still owe me a peak:

Jim DiNapoli (November 9, 1954–March 28, 2014),
Steve Gladbach (June 6, 1961–June 23, 2013),
Adam Helman (July 12, 1960–January 9, 2015),
and Terry Mathews (September 20, 1974–July 13, 2013).

FALCONGUIDES®

An imprint of Rowman & Littlefield
Falcon, FalconGuides, and Outfit Your Mind are registered trademarks of Rowman & Littlefield.

Distributed by NATIONAL BOOK NETWORK

Copyright © 2015 by Rowman & Littlefield
Maps: Nord Compo © Rowman & Littlefield

British Library Cataloguing-in-Publication Information available

Library of Congress Cataloging-in-Publication Data available

ISBN 978-0-7627-8495-0 (paperback)
ISBN 978-1-4930-1436-1 (e-book)

∞™ The paper used in this publication meets the minimum requirements of American National Standard for Information Sciences—Permanence of Paper for Printed Library Materials, ANSI/NISO Z39.48-1992.

Contents

Overview

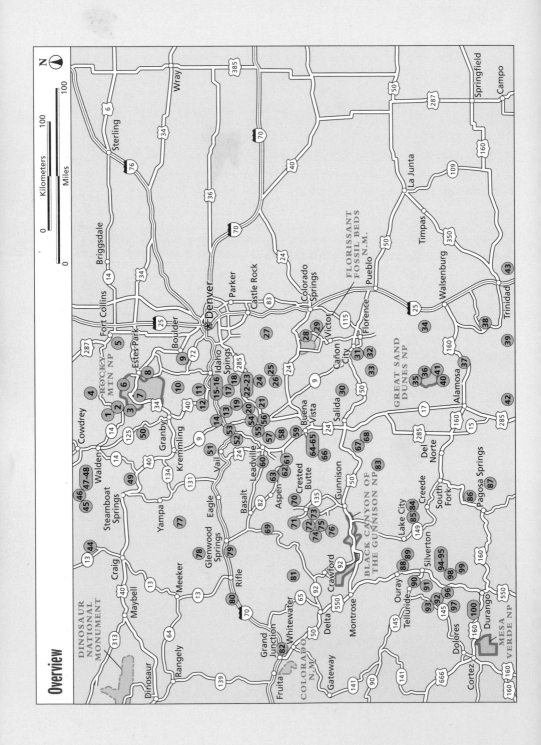

Acknowledgments

This book was written with the support and kindness of friends and strangers on and off the peaks. Many thanks to Stewart Green and Doug Hatfield for climbing a lot of peaks with me over the years. To steal a phrase from Cathy McKeen: "I'd hike to hell and back with you guys."

Muchos gracias to Bill Middlebrook, John Kirk, Stewart Green, Kevin Baker, Doug Hatfield, Brian Miller, Erik Packard, David Goldstein, Teresa Gergen, Sarah Meiser, and Kiefer Thomas for providing peak photographs and beta, and for proofing some of the chapters in this book; to Mike Rodenak for proofing many chapters in this book and providing generous feedback; to Chris Rudnick for proofreading the mountain geology information and providing feedback; and to Morgan Kiger, James McNally, Kait Orme, and Trevor Smith for giving me free copies of my notes and maps whenever my printer ran out of ink. Thanks, Eric Hunter, for that great lead on the Third Flatiron; thank you, Ian Green, for letting me pitch my tent in your backyard; and thank you, Jeff and Keith Huck, for hauling me out of the snow on Michigan Creek Road.

Thank you to my acquisitions editor, Katie Benoit; production editor, Lauren Brancato; map manager, Melissa Baker; copy editor, Elissa Curcio; layout artist, Sue Murray; and publisher, FalconGuides / Globe Pequot / Rowman & Littlefield, for all your hard work and support.

Thanks for being such great company on some peaks in this book, intentionally or incidentally: Lisa Heckel, David Dietz, Eric Hunter, Chris Gilsdorf, Uwe Sartori, Darin Baker, Scott Patterson, Alberto Pizzato, William "Clint" Cochrane, Jill Cunningham, Nela Lewis, Erica Burgon, the "Old Brown Hermit," and Kim and Fred DeVore.

Oodles of gratitude to the fine people who always have a kind word to outweigh the harsh ones: Timothy Best, Cindi Carter, Ben Conners, Kathleen Cook, Jay Dahl, Jim Davies, Catie Deines, Valerie Deneau, Matt Ellis, Scott Farish, Greg Fisching, Stephen Gallagher, Tall Grass, Kristi Harshbarger, Mindy Carson Hatcher, Doug Hempel, Andy Hixson, Beauvais Jeanmard, Barry Johnson, Britt Jones, Sally Krenz, Ryan Kushner, Kent Loar, Ian MacDonald, Mike McElhaney, Doug Melton, Darlene Michaelis, Shae Noble, Doug Norris, Bill Nosko, Mark Obmascik, Cassie Olson, Julie Peters, Stephanie Pugh, Senad Rizvanovic, Robin Robinson, Ryan Schilling, Tyree Terry, Brent Thompson, Tory Wells, and Jared Workman.

And a big hug to my divine family of women, for raising me up: Jane Clifford, Priscilla Paul, Carolyn McNeil, Alison Milligan, Melissa Clifford, Janina Botchis, Diane Castillo, Michelle Leon, Elaine Duchaineau, Mary Castillo, and Kimberly Flack; and to my sons, Joshua Levesque and Garrett Schaller, for never letting me down.

Welcome!

A Message from Your Mountain Guide

Mountains define our Colorado landscape. They're as familiar to us as the sun, the moon, and the stars above them, and the foothills, forests, and prairies below, all members of our natural family on this earthly place that we call home. For the Colorado mountain climber, they're a destination and a calling, each one named, numbered, and categorized, and there are as many reasons to climb them as there are mountaineers. Colorado has the highest mean elevation, at 6,800', and the highest low point, at 3,315', of any state in the country. It has more land mass above 10,000' and more mountains with summits above 14,000'—including 53 ranked 14ers—than any other state. It's the only state that lies entirely above 1,000 meters (3,281'). About 40 percent of Colorado is public land, including much of the higher elevations, allowing for mostly free and unfettered access to the state's multitude of peaks. This dynamic and

Mountain goats are a common sight on Colorado's highest peaks. PHOTO BY BILL MIDDLEBROOK

legally accessible topography provides a wondrous land of climbing adventure for the Colorado mountaineer.

The hikes and climbs in this book lead to more than 100 of Colorado's summits and represent a cross section of elevations, prominence, distances, terrain, geography, and technical difficulty. Most of the hikes have a path from the trailhead to the top, or most of the way to the top. Each peak falls into one of three categories:

The legally accessible highpoints of every major mountain range and subrange, major hills, mesas, plateaus, and sand dunes are represented, totaling 58 highpoints and comprising the first category.

In the second category, major mountain passes are represented, with high trail-heads and short approaches to the surrounding peaks. Some of Colorado's mountain passes lie on roadways that connect cities and mountain towns and lead to Colorado's ski resorts. They are plowed and open all year, with only occasional closures during winter storms, giving you access to the nearby peaks. With consideration for road safety, wind, weather, snowpack, and avalanche conditions, passes allow the Colorado mountaineer to climb year-round. After you have climbed a peak from a pass in this book, you can do more research and climb the rest of the peaks at that pass. Note that there are many *more* passes through Colorado's mountains—not included in this book and accessed by rough road and trail—for you to discover as you expand your travel among the peaks.

A handful of local favorites comprise the third category. These are popular peaks, climbed often by local residents, and representative of the diversity of Colorado summits.

While this book provides lots of information about the mountains and how to reach their summits, it does not take the place of training and experience. Moun-taineering as a hobby or as a way of life requires ongoing education and practice. As you begin your journey to the summits of Colorado, supplement your learning with formal coursework and fieldwork, and training guidebooks specific to each skill. Find an experienced mentor, hook up with a group of climbing friends, and put in some time on the peaks. Take care of each other. I'll see you out there.

How to Use This Book

This book includes 100 adventures and you may be tempted to jump right in and hit the trail, but understanding how to use this book will help you make better choices and have a safer and more enjoyable time in the mountains.

The **overview map** shows all the peaks in this book, so you can see their loca-tions in Colorado. The **introductory chapters** offer general guidelines for staying safe, being respectful to the areas you visit, and packing and planning for your adven-tures, along with information about the mountains that will expand your knowledge beyond just getting from point A to point B. The **appendices** at the end of this book include reference materials for planning more mountaineering adventures and land-use contact information. The land-use areas listed cover all the hikes and climbs in this book and do not represent every national forest or wilderness area in the state.

Each hike or climb in this book is organized as follows:

Name: The name of the peak or peaks, prefaced by its categorization within this book. The categorization denotes if it's a range highpoint, a peak at a pass, or a local favorite. The name of the peak is what you will find on most maps, designated by the United States Board on Geographic Names, or USBGN. When the name is unofficial, it is shown in quotation marks.

Elevation: The elevation of the highest point of the mountain, in feet above sea level. Currently, United States Geological Survey (USGS) maps show elevations based on vertical datum defined by the National Geodetic Vertical Datum of 1929, or NGVD29. However, the more recent North America Vertical Datum of 1988, or NAVD88, found that Colorado's summits were as much as 7' higher above sea level than previously thought. This book uses NGVD29 elevations, to match available maps, and where the new elevations are known, they are presented as well, in parentheses. For example, Pikes Peak is shown as **Elevation:** 14,110' (NAVD88 14,115'). The NAVD88 elevation is then referenced for the summit only throughout each chapter, while the NGVD29 elevations are used for points along the route, to allow for easier route-finding with a map.

Distinctions: Features that align the peak within particular categories. There are many features that make a peak distinct, but the ones noted within this book include: (a) mountain range highpoint; (b) county highpoint; (c) wilderness area highpoint; (d) elevation designation within the highest 300 in the state, noted as "Centennial" if the peak is among the highest 100, "Bicentennial" if the peak is among the highest 200, and "Tricentennial" if the peak is among the highest 300; (e) prominence designation within the most prominent 300 peaks in the state, noted as "Prominence 100" if the peak is among the 100 most prominent, "Prominence 200" if the peak is among the most prominent 200, and "Prominence 300" if the peak is among the most prominent 300 (not to be confused with "P300," which denotes 300' of prominence); (f) prominence designations of 1-, 2-, 3-, or 4,000' or more, noted as "P1K," "P2K," "P3K," and "P4K," respectively, and 5,000' or more, or "Ultra-prominence"; (g) noting if the peak is ranked, unranked, or soft-ranked (see "Mountain Ranges, Rankings, and Ratings") along with elevation above sea level to 1,000', for example "ranked 12er," "unranked 13er," etc.; and (h) special designations such as being listed on the National Register of Historic Places or as a Historic Natural Landmark.

Class: The highest technical class that occurs for the route provided, based on the most difficult move, followed by details of other classes that exist along the route. Easier and more difficult class routes may exist for each peak, but the classes listed in each chapter reflect those of *that specific route only*.

Difficulty and skill level: Difficulty ratings include Easy, Moderate, Strenuous, and Very Strenuous, and skill levels include Beginner, Intermediate, and Advanced, depending on the distance, elevation gain, altitude, terrain, and class of the peak. Generally speaking: *Easy* climbs are 0–4 miles long or have less than 1,500' of elevation gain; *Moderate* climbs are 4–8 miles long or have 1,500–2,500' of elevation gain;

Strenuous climbs are 8–12 miles long or have 2,500–3,500' of elevation gain; and *Very Strenuous* climbs are greater than 12 miles or have more than 3,500' of elevation gain, round-trip. *Beginner* climbs are Class 1 on a marked trail; *Intermediate* climbs are Class 1 to Class 2 and may require some route-finding due to a faint trail or no trail; and *Advanced* climbs are Class 3 or higher, or may demand crossing terrain that is exposed, or where there is rockfall danger. All peaks above 14,000' are also classified as Advanced due to sudden and dramatic weather events common to those peaks. *Difficulty and skill levels are highly subjective, based on the mountaineer, the season, and existing conditions on the peak.*

Approximate moving time: The time it takes an average climber to summit the peak and complete the route, trailhead to trailhead. This does not take into account rests, bathroom stops, clothing adjustment, or snack breaks along the trail, or time spent on the summit, which may increase your own time considerably. Especially fit or fast, or unfit or slow, climbers may experience widely varied moving times. Use this as a rule of thumb only and adjust your own expectations after a few climbs.

Distance: The distance in tenths of a mile round-trip, from trailhead to trailhead.

Elevation trailhead to summit: The net gain in elevation from the trailhead to the summit. When there is a substantial loss of elevation on the ascent, an overall round-trip elevation gain is also listed, rounded to hundreds of feet.

Terrain: The ground conditions encountered along the route in summer, such as paved road, dirt trail, duff, rocks, boulders, talus, scree, slabs, grass, tundra, ledges, and sand. Creek crossings, exposure, and risk of rockfall are also noted. Terrain conditions will be different under snow, and avalanche danger is *not* noted within this section but should be considered on every route where snow exists on or above your path.

Recommended extra gear: Additional items that may be required for a safe ascent, in addition to your standard mountaineering clothing and gear. These are recommendations only, and you should always use your best judgment or seek out the advice of an expert for a specific climb on a specific day, under specific conditions.

Restrictions: Special considerations and precautions beyond the general guidelines for backcountry travel, including fees, seasonal access, and whether or not dogs are allowed on the route, and if they are required to be leashed. If the route travels within a wilderness area, that is also noted, and additional restrictions apply.

Amenities: Amenities include access to toilets; picnic areas; backcountry, primitive, dispersed, campsite, or campground camping; visitor centers; and services such as grocers, gas, and lodging.

Trailhead: The name of the trailhead where the route begins. Unofficial trailheads appear in quotation marks, and if there is no trailhead, the location where the climb begins is described.

Trails: The names and numbers, where applicable, of the trails utilized from trailhead to summit. Unofficial trail names appear in quotation marks, and off-trail travel is generalized with terms such as "off-trail South Slope" or "off-trail West Ridge."

Maps: The page(s) and grid number(s) in the DeLorme map guide 10th edition (2011), and the name of the United States Geological Survey map(s) where the route exists, ordered from summit to trailhead, for example: Delorme Page 39 B5, C5, Page 38 C4; USGS Empire, Berthoud Pass. Although maps—with routes and important features shown—are included in this book, you should obtain full-size topographical maps of the area for greater detail and portability. You can download maps for free from the USGS Map Locator and Downloader site (www.store.usgs.gov), or purchase hard copies from the site or from many other online sites. You can also create your own maps with a good topo program, and plug in the waypoints listed in the "Miles and Directions" section of each climb, for greater accuracy. Carry your maps and directions in a ziplock bag on the trail, along with a pencil to mark your progress, and reference them often so you can identify your location as you go.

County: The county or counties where the summit of the peak sits. The entire mountain from saddles to summit may cross several county lines, but if you are climbing all the peaks in a particular county, you only need to focus on where the highest point of each peak sits to complete the county.

Land status: The land's designation as a national or state forest or park, wilderness area, Bureau of Land Management land, or state wildlife area and contact information for learning more about the area is shown here, for further research and to obtain the latest information on conditions, access, and closures. Although your first source of information about a wilderness area should be the local ranger district, the University of Montana's website Wilderness.net is also listed, as a well-organized online resource for finding lots of information about each area.

Finding the trailhead: Driving directions from the closest town or major highway, along with the GPS waypoint of the trailhead. If you have a GPS in your car, you can input the waypoints before you leave for the trailhead.

The Peak: General information about the peak, such as historical data and general views from the summit. Websites and apps like PeakFinder.org are useful for providing more detailed 360-degree information on the summits in view from each peak.

The Climb: Special precautions and recommendations, and suggested alternate routes and other peaks that may be added to your outing. Seasonal information is provided in some chapters, but will vary from year to year and should be further researched and considered before a climb.

Miles and Directions: The mileage from trailhead to summit and back, in tenths of a mile, with descriptions of each section and GPS waypoints for most entries. The GPS waypoints coincide with the location at the mileage noted in each entry—and where the descriptions begin—but are placed at the end of each description for clarity. If you have a GPS, you can plug in the waypoints for easier route-finding. If you have created your own map from a topo program, you can export the waypoints from your map to your GPS. Cardinal (N, E, S, W), intercardinal (NE, SE, SW, NW), and secondary-intercardinal (NNE, ENE, ESE, SSE, SSW, WSW, WNW, NNW)

East Beckwith Mountain rises above Lost Lake Slough near Kebler Pass in the West Elk Mountains. PHOTO BY STEWART M. GREEN

directions are also noted within the miles and directions, and are especially helpful if you do not have a GPS and are relying solely on a map and compass for route-finding.

Note that the route defined within the "Miles and Directions" is, by default, a summer route and does not take into account snow or other conditions that may render the route susceptible to avalanche danger or otherwise unsafe. In winter and during the shoulder seasons of late fall and early spring, further research may be required to ensure the route is safe for foot travel.

In addition, a **map** is included for each climb, showing the route, and **photographs** provide a visual of the peak or views from the peak. Now that you know a little bit about this book, let's learn about the peaks!

Colorado Mountains: What They Are and How They Got Here

Three major provinces comprise Colorado's topography: the plains or prairies of the east, the plateaus of the west, and the mountains—specifically, the **Rocky Mountains**—that split the state from north to south, between the prairies and plateaus. The Rocky Mountain system is composed of many smaller mountain ranges and subranges, most running north–south, with a few running east–west. The mountains, or *peaks*, of Colorado are as varied as the forces that created and defined them. Our mountains began their slow development about 1.8 billion years ago, when the shifting of tectonic plates—sections of the earth's outer crust, or lithosphere—movement of molten rock or magma within the earth's crust, and volcanic eruptions all served to thrust the landscape of our state upward. At the same time, wind, rain, ice, lava, and rockfall pummeled the terrain, eroding the uplifted earth away to a lower, smoother playing ground. It is these two forces, uplift and erosion, that formed the mountains of Colorado we see and climb today.

Generally speaking, the major ranges of Colorado can trace their origins back to uplift in the form of *batholiths* and *faulted anticlines*. Batholiths formed when an *igneous intrusion*—molten rock that intruded the lithosphere but did not break through to the surface—solidified as a large mass beneath the earth. This mass was later exposed due to volcanic activity that pushed it up, and by erosion that cleared sediment from the surface. Underground pressure forced softer rock upward into tentlike folds, or *anticlines*, and *faults* were created as the rock—under tremendous stress—split and the sections shifted apart. Erupted volcanoes and layers of eroded and erupted rock, or *sediments*, topped some of the mountain ranges as well, forming newer ranges. Mountain building, or *orogeny*, is not isolated to Colorado, and in fact the Rocky Mountains extend north into Canada and south into New Mexico and are part of a larger system known as the **North American Cordillera,** a subrange of the **American Cordillera** that stretches from Alaska to South America.

The many types of rocks created by uplift and erosion add to the variety in our peaks. Colorado's mountains are composed mainly of *igneous* rocks like basalt, breccia, gabbro, granite, pegmatite, porphyry, and tuff; *sedimentary* rocks like conglomerate, dolomite, limestone, sandstone, and shale; and *metamorphic* rocks like gneiss, hornfels, migmatite, schist, and quartzite.

It may seem strange that the mountains of landlocked Colorado consist of such a wide variety of rocks and minerals, until you examine the geologic evolution of our state. The geologic record tells us the earth's crust stabilized 4.5 billion years ago, and the uplift and erosion that formed Colorado's landscape occurred within roughly the last 2 billion years. The mountains may not have been here since the beginning of time, but they have been in development for a very, *very* long time.

Colorado's mountains continue to evolve, shaped by forces of nature like uplift, erosion, precipitation, rockslides, mudslides, flash floods, and changing temperatures, and by human intrusion with mining, road-building, and, of course, mountaineering. This creates an ever-changing and unpredictable environment for the Colorado mountaineer, and a demand for vigilance on every outing.

Colorado Mountain Ranges, Rankings, and Ratings

There are many ways to categorize mountains. In general, *ranges* tell you where they are, *rankings* tell how high and how prominent they are, and *ratings* tell you how difficult they are to climb.

Mountain ranges are distinct and somewhat discrete groups of mountains that generally share the same geologic origin. The mountains within a range are linked by ridges, slopes, and saddles and tend to line up along the same cardinal bearing, trending in a north–south or east–west direction, although there are exceptions that

State highpoint Mount Elbert tops the Sawatch Range near Leadville. PHOTO BY BILL MIDDLEBROOK

start off on one bearing and then head off on another. Ranges may include subranges and hills, subsets of uplift which can branch off from a mountain range, lie parallel alongside its main ridge, or line up within the range. Mountain ranges may comprise several ranges within the range proper, such as the many subranges that lie within the Front Range. The major ranges in Colorado—the Front Range, Sangre de Cristo Range, Park Ranges, Sawatch Range, Elk Range, and San Juan Mountains—are all part of the Rocky Mountains.

Mountain ranges are separated by highlands, valleys, parks, and passes. Understanding the mountain ranges—their geographic locations, geology, and main access points—is instrumental in determining your mountain-climbing plans, for each presents a unique set of challenges and rewards. This guidebook will introduce you to all six ranges within the Rocky Mountains in Colorado and their respective subranges. Also included are the major southern and western plateaus and mesas, including the Flat Tops, White River Plateau, Roan Plateau, Grand Mesa, and Raton Mesa, as well as the prominent hills and sand dunes of the San Luis Valley.

A discussion of Colorado's mountains would not be complete without mention of the Continental Divide. Stretching more than 6,700 miles from the Bering Strait at Cape Prince of Wales, Alaska, to the Strait of Magellan at Tierra del Fuego, South

America, the Continental Divide, or "Great Divide," is an area of uplift separating the western and eastern watersheds of the Americas. In the United States, river systems lying west of the divide drain into the Pacific Ocean, while those to the east flow into the Arctic Ocean, the Atlantic Ocean, and the Gulf of Mexico. The Continental Divide splits Colorado into the western slope and the eastern slope, from the Sierra Madre Range to the South San Juans, and many peaks in this book lie on or near the Divide.

Mountain rankings and elevations define the *prominence* of a peak and its height above sea level. A *ranked* (P300) peak in Colorado has at least 300' of prominence—or vertical rise—between its summit and the highest adjoining saddle between it and a higher, ranked peak. An *unranked* peak has less than 300' of prominence, and a *soft-ranked* peak is one whose prominence and status is estimated yet not firmly established as ranked because the elevation of the summit, the connecting saddle, or both have not been surveyed, but rather have been determined by interpolation between known contour lines. The elevation of a peak is highly regarded by Colorado mountaineers, as it separates the coveted list of peaks higher than 14,000' from other peaks in the state. Peaks are categorized many ways along elevation and prominence limits, and climbers will often focus their attention on limited criteria in their mountain-climbing attempts. Popular "peakbagging lists" include:

14ers: Peaks 14,000' or higher above sea level, including ranked (with at least 300' of prominence) and unranked (with less than 300' of prominence)

Centennials: The highest 100 ranked peaks in the state

P2K peaks: Peaks with 2,000' or more of prominence

Ultra-prominence peaks: Peaks with 1,500 meters (roughly 5,000') or more of prominence

Peakbagging lists may also be based on locations or official naming of the peaks, such as wilderness area ranked peaks or highpoints; county ranked peaks, unranked peaks, or highpoints; national park highpoints; named peaks; etc. While some climbers eschew lists, they are a great way to get you out to many different parts of the state, and the desire to "finish a list" may motivate you to keep climbing.

Mountain ratings define the technical difficulty of a climb. There are many complicated descriptions of the different classes of climbs, but to help you understand the specific ratings within this guidebook, they are simplified as follows:

Class 1: A hike on a defined trail or road.

Class 2: A hike off-trail, which may require route-finding but does not require the use of your hands. Class 1 and Class 2 "climbs" gain elevation by walking, not by climbing in the traditional sense, with hands and feet.

Class 3: A hike on off-camber, rocky, or unstable terrain that requires the use of your hands for balance, or for light climbing, with solid handholds and footholds. Class 3 climbing does not require edging on narrow ledges or smearing (friction climbing) on rock, is not executed over exposed areas with potentially harmful or fatal drop-off, and may be comfortably accomplished both facing in and facing out.

Class 4: Climbing with hands and feet that may not be accomplished facing out but requires facing in, and may be over an exposed area with the risk of injury or death in the event of a fall, but otherwise comfortably accomplished with solid handholds and without a rope for protection. A rope may be used for Class 4 terrain if the rock is questionable, or if the consequences of a potential fall render the climber uncomfortable with unroped travel.

Class 5: Climbing that entails smearing, edging, or using tiny finger or toe holds, which cannot be accomplished facing out and for which a rope for protection is necessary for the safety of the climber. Although some climbers do not use ropes for Class 5 terrain, the practice presents great danger and is not recommended. There are many classes of technical difficulty within the Class 5 rating, and if you enjoy alpine mountain climbing on Class 5 terrain, you will want to learn more about them with proper guidance and training. There are just two Class 5 routes in this book—the Third Flatiron and Coxcomb Peak—and if you are not experienced, you should seek out a leader or hire a guide to take you to those summits.

Mountain Climbing Skills, Safety, and Protocol

The mountains were not designed with our safety or comfort in mind. For all their beauty, they are inherently dangerous and inhospitable places for humans, and people die on them every year. That's why we prepare for our climbs and keep our visits to the summits short: to increase our chances of a successful ascent and descent without injury or death. There are many skills required to becoming a mountaineer and books, classes, clubs, and websites devoted to each one. This book is not a comprehensive guide to becoming a Colorado mountain climber, and there is no one book that encompasses everything you need to know to be safe and self-sufficient in the mountains.

Following is some general information you need to know now, and an overview of the skills you will need to master over time, in order to be a responsible mountaineer. Seek out other resources to build on your knowledge and experience as you advance from beginner to more advanced climbs. Read books and take coursework specific to land navigation and route-finding, weather, mountain travel, wilderness first aid, camping, backpacking, snow travel, self-arrest, backcountry group dynamics and leadership, and avalanche safety. Then add AIARE (American Institute for Avalanche Research and Education) Level 1 and Level 2 classes and Wilderness First Responder (WFR), and take courses that include fieldwork in roped glacier travel, rock climbing, and ice climbing, so you can expand your climbs into more difficult territory. There are numerous licensed and insured organizations in Colorado that offer these resources.

What to Wear

Comfortable layers are the rule of thumb on the mountain. You may be hiking and climbing for many hours, so you don't want to wear clothes that are uncomfortable in any way. Layering allows you to adjust your clothing to match the varying temperatures and changing weather conditions that you will encounter. You may arrive at the trailhead in a T-shirt and sandals, but you'll need to have the following items in a duffle bag in your car to put on at the trailhead, or already packed away in your backpack to carry on the mountain:

A pair of shoes or boots made for the terrain. If you're sticking to Class 1 climbs on trails, trail runners will do, but if you're going to be scrambling through talus and boulders, you may want something sturdier, with support and protection for your ankles. Do not go cheap on your hiking boots or shoes. You may be able to skimp on other items, but your choice of footwear is critical and will determine your basic level of comfort—and possibly even your success—on a peak. They need to have good support, a grippy sole, and a comfortable footbed. Try them on with the socks you will wear with them so you get the right fit. Wear them around the store, and if the store has multiple levels or a ramp, run up and down the stairs and walk the ramp a few times to see if they "slip," or crush your toes. You don't want to have your feet moving around in the boots while you're hiking, or you will get blisters, and you don't want to crush your toes for thousands of steps on a descent, or you will lose toenails. You can buy inserts for more heel stabilization, but you will still want a comfortable footbed. If you will be traveling in wet terrain, you can get waterproof boots, and reapply waterproofing solution regularly. In winter, you'll want a stiffer boot that holds a crampon or microspikes.

A pair of sock liners to keep your feet clean and dry, and a pair of heavier socks to keep your feet warm. Do not wear cotton socks, which hold moisture and lose their insulating ability when wet.

Three layers for your torso, and layers for your bottom. A thin, wicking base layer, thick insulating layer, and wind- and waterproof top layer will keep you warm and dry.

You may already have clothing for other sports specially made to wick moisture away from your skin, and you can wear those as your base layers until you have the money for mountaineering base layers. Summer and winter base layer weights and materials vary, so buy what you need based on when you will be climbing. A long-sleeve, light-colored base layer is a good idea in summer, to protect your arms from the sun. Short-sleeve shirts may be more comfortable and are OK below timberline, but remember to add layers (or sunscreen) when you're out of the trees. Hiking pants will do for your bottom layer in the summer, and zip-off legs make it easy to adjust for changing temps and terrain. You will want to do some layering in colder months.

Your insulating layer should fit comfortably over your base layer. A fleece-type shirt with a quarter-zip makes a nice insulating layer, and you can adjust the zipper up or down to suit your body temperature. For your legs, rain pants will keep you dry in summer storms, and insulated, waterproof mountaineering pants provide two layers in winter, and you can wear them over a base layer for very cold days. Look for clothing with zippered "vents" that you can open and close so you can quickly adjust to changing temperatures without stopping.

Your top layer jacket should be waterproof, fit over everything, and have a hood, too. For winter climbs, you will want another, warmer "puffy" jacket with a hood to fit over everything. This is the jacket that will sit in the bottom of your pack nearly all the time, but that you will truly appreciate on the summit.

Over time you may want to pick up other layers, such as a light, windproof jacket and a light insulating jacket. Again, start on easy peaks in good weather, and buy gear and clothing as you need it. If you get into a situation where you are not prepared, head back to the trailhead.

A hat with a brim to protect your face from the sun. In winter, you'll also need a warm, snug-fitting cap, a headband or earflaps for your ears, and a buff to protect your face from the wind and cold. The buff also prevents cold air from entering your lungs, which accelerates dehydration and can chill you from the inside out. In extreme weather, be sure to seal off all gaps with other layers, such as a fabric facemask, so there is no skin exposed to the elements. Windburn and frostbite are common, painful ailments in winter mountaineering. Cover up.

Thin, warm **glove liners** for your hands, plus a **thicker glove** that fits over the liners for colder weather, and a **windproof mitt** that fits over both layers for extreme wind and cold. The layers you need depend on the temperature and weather, but the liners should be warm enough to keep your hands from going numb, while allowing you to manipulate zippers and other small items so you're not tempted to remove them during clothing adjustments or bathroom breaks. If you cannot zip closures with your liners on, tie some cord to each zipper pull.

Short gaiters will keep rocks out of your shoes in the summer, and knee-high **winter gaiters** will keep the snow out of your boots while keeping the bottoms of your pants dry, and will also help to protect your calves from accidental "stabbings" with your crampons.

Sunglasses or wraparound glacier glasses for sun and wind, and goggles for extreme winter cold and wind. Sun protection for your eyes is even more important in winter, when the sun is reflecting off the snow and can cause painful and debilitating snowblindness.

Wear a rock-climbing helmet on any Class 3 or higher terrain and on any route where there is risk of rockfall, especially on popular routes where there will likely be climbers above you, kicking down debris. You can carry your helmet inside your pack or attach it to the outside with a carabiner until you need it.

What to Carry

Mountaineering gear can be expensive, so start with easier hikes in good weather that require less gear. Repurpose items to save cash, and save weight in your pack, and if you're traveling with friends, share camping gear like tents and stoves, and split the weight in your packs. Here are some tips to get you started:

Get a pack that fits everything. You may have a "day pack" for trips you can do in one day and a larger pack for backpacking trips, to fit all your camping and cooking gear and extra food. Try on the pack in the store, fill it up, and make sure it's comfortable. Ideally your pack should have an interior pocket for a water bladder; outside loops for attaching items like ice axes, crampons, and a helmet; and outer pockets for trekking poles, food, and a bathroom kit. There should be a zippered compartment at the bottom so you can stash your rain jacket and get it out quickly in sudden storms, without having to dig through your pack. Consider a waterproof cover for your pack, too. A large "lawn size" garbage bag will do as a pack cover in a pinch. The bag, split lengthwise, also works well as a ground cover under your tent.

Start with the 10 essentials: (1) first-aid kit; (2) fire starter; (3) extra clothing layers; (4) headlamp with extra batteries; (5) map and compass, and a GPS (and extra batteries); (6) plenty of food; (7) sun protection such as a hat, sunglasses, and SPF 30 or higher sunscreen and lip balm; (8) emergency shelter, such as a tarp; (9) water and electrolyte drink; and (10) any tools you might need for gear repairs, such as a small knife, duct tape, cord, and zip ties. You don't need to break the bank to acquire these items. For example, your first aid kit may be as simple as bandages and pain reliever, and your fire starter may be a book of waterproof matches in a plastic bag. Add items as you can afford them. You don't need to make a large upfront financial investment to enjoy the outdoors.

Carry plenty of water. A general rule of thumb for a full day of mountain climbing is to carry 2 liters of water and 2 liters of electrolyte drink, but this will vary among climbs and climbers. Water bladders with tubes for sipping on the go are wonderful in warm weather, but when the temperatures dip below freezing, leave them at home and carry all your drinks in bottles. An insulated bottle "parka" hooked to your pack will keep water from freezing, and if it's really cold out, turn the bottle upside-down in the parka to prevent freezing at the top. Store extra bottles in your pack, and consider a thermos full of hot cocoa, tea, or soup for the summit.

For food, bring items that travel well and will not get crushed in your pack. In winter, pack foods that won't freeze or become too hard to chew. You should have a good combination of foods that supply energy and nutrition. Sweet and salty foods taste especially good in the mountains, where your appetite may be diminished by the altitude. You need to eat to climb, so carry foods that you will want to eat.

Tuck a card into your first-aid kit with your personal information on it and the contact information of a trusted friend. If you are in an accident, your climbing partners can use the card to communicate that information to first responders, who will want to know how tall you are and how much you weigh, and what medications you are on. You can also keep your Colorado Outdoor Recreation Search and Rescue (CORSAR) card in the kit. The purchase of a CORSAR card supports local search-and-rescue teams that assist climbers in distress; they can be purchased online or at your local outdoor recreation shop. Also pack a pencil and some paper so that if there is an accident, you can note important information such as the location and condition of the victim, and get accurate information to rescuers. Use proper precautions to ensure a safe, unassisted ascent and descent of your peak, but know that if you are ever injured or incapacitated, SAR is your best bet for emergency assistance in the mountains. 911 operators will contact SAR for you, if needed.

Carry a small mirror and a whistle to signal for help in the event of an emergency. Use the mirror to reflect sunlight as a signal to search helicopters passing overhead, and blow the whistle to help searchers on the ground locate you. A foil emergency blanket may also be used to reflect sunlight.

Devise a system for storing your items in your pack and stick to it. Over time you'll figure out which items are coming out of your pack most often. Make them readily accessible. In general, store heavy items like extra water bottles and thermoses in the bottom of your pack and food and clothing on top. Store batteries together, and if it's cold out, store them in a pocket on your body, as the cold will deplete them. Having a storage "system" is helpful so you can retrieve items quickly, without standing around in the wind and cold.

If you are traveling in winter or spring, you will need special gear and training in snow travel and avalanche safety. Additional gear may include snowshoes, skis, an ice axe, traction for your boots such as crampons or microspikes, and extra clothing layers. Buy the right-size ice axe for your height, and wrap some insulation—such as a bit of foam padding and duct tape—around the handle near the head to protect your hands from the cold metal. In addition to learning about avalanche safety, snow travel, and self-arrest with an ice axe, you will need to purchase and learn how to use an avalanche beacon, a probe, and a shovel, and you should practice using these items every year so you are able to react quickly in the event that they are needed.

Special gear presents special storage challenges. While your beacon is worn under your clothing and over your base layer, other avalanche gear should be packed inside your pack. It may look cool to be climbing with a shovel on your pack, but an avalanche will tear it off, so store it, and your probe, inside your pack. Ice axes may be stored outside your pack, and most large packs have a loop on the bottom for sliding the axe down through, and then you can flip it up and secure the handle with a side strap on your pack. Strap your snowshoes to the outside of your pack with the pack straps, or add some webbing and carabiners to secure them tightly. There should be nothing "swinging" off your pack when you move.

Although ice axes and microspikes are typical gear for snow travel, they also come in handy year-round on steep scree and on icy patches and lingering snow. Consider carrying them any time of year if you have them.

A bathroom kit is necessary for breaks along the trail. A large ziplock bag and paper or wet wipes, plus feminine items for women and an anti-chafing stick for men, will do. Include a second bag to carry out all used items. Do not leave toilet paper behind. Women should carry a female urinary diversion device, or FUDD, so they can pee without dropping their drawers. It can be difficult to find a private spot above treeline, and getting out of a rope on steep, exposed rock or snow is dangerous. The FUD prevents this. Women can also skip the paper when taking a pee and just wear a pantiliner to absorb excess moisture. A small plastic trowel comes in handy to dig a cat hole for solid waste, or just use your ice axe. Bathroom breaks should be taken at least 200' from lakes, streams, and other water sources, and solid waste should be buried at least 6" below the ground. Do not contaminate outdoor water sources.

Trekking poles are good for balance and will take some of the weight off your joints, especially while descending steep slopes. They should not be used for glissading steep terrain. If you're going to be on Class 3 or higher terrain, make sure you have pockets on the sides of your pack to stash them in and clip them to the gear loops with a carabiner, or buy collapsible poles.

If you are camping, you will need a sleeping bag, pad, tent, footprint for the tent, water filter and/or water purification tablets, stove, fuel, cook pot, and eating utensils, and you will also need to know how to set up the tent, filter water, and prepare a meal. In winter, you will have to melt snow for water, so carry extra fuel. You'll also need more food and clothing, including sandals or booties and a warm jacket to wear around camp.

Personal locator beacons and SPOT devices are used to alert others to your location in the event of an accident. While cell phones, satellite phones, and electronic messenger devices can be useful for search-and-rescue operations, they are not a substitute for training, skills, and good decision making. Also, you will not always have reception in the backcountry, especially if you are in an especially remote area or in a canyon.

Before You Go

Mountain climbing requires planning. Depending on the season and the peak you are doing, you may need to plan your hikes and climbs days, weeks, or even months in advance.

Be prepared with the appropriate clothing, gear, and supplies you'll need for a safe climb.

Carry a written plan of your expected route, with directions to the trailhead and the summit, and the name of the trailhead and the peak.

Share a copy of your plan with someone you trust, along with the make, model, and license plate number of the vehicle you will be leaving at the trailhead, and a "latest time to call" so that—in the event of an accident—someone will know where you are and can contact first responders with that information. "First responders" are *always* 911, where the operator will connect you with rescue personnel. Your "latest time" should be realistic. For example, it may take you two hours to drive to the trailhead, three hours to get up the mountain, two hours to get down, plus two hours of breaks and time on the summit, and another hour to drive from the trailhead to a place where you have cell phone service. The more climbs you do, the better you will get at estimating your own "climb times."

Check the Colorado Department of Transportation (CDOT) site for road conditions and closures.

Call the ranger district of the national forest or wilderness area where you will be traveling for information on access and closures on roads not covered by CDOT.

Check the National Oceanic and Atmospheric Administration (NOAA) site for weather conditions, and be sure that you won't be hiking through open areas or above treeline in extreme wind or if there's a danger of lightning. Lightning storms above treeline occur almost daily in the mountains, especially in the summer, and can move in very quickly. Note the temperature, wind speed and direction, precipitation, and lightning danger expectations for the day, and expect them all to be worse.

In snow, check the Colorado Avalanche Information Center (CAIC) site for avalanche conditions. Even if you have all the gear and the training to survive an avalanche, do not underestimate the danger. A beacon *may* save you, but more likely it will only be useful to retrieve your body. A good rule of thumb is, if you will not feel safe doing a climb *without* a beacon, probe, and shovel, then don't do the climb with them.

Check the National Operational Hydrologic Remote Sensing Center (NOHRSC) site for information on precipitation and snow depths. Even if avalanche danger is low or nonexistent, you will want to know how much snow exists so you are prepared with appropriate gear. Expect a much longer day snowshoeing or post-holing in deep snow. The Open Snow website also offers lots of winter weather and snow accumulation information. See Appendix A for URLs to each website.

If you plan on camping at a campground, check recreation.gov for availability and reservations. For backcountry camping, identify water sources along the route so you'll have water to filter for drinking and cooking. Some areas also require permits and that you camp in designated sites only, so check before you go.

Check with your climbing friends, or on your favorite climbing website, for the latest trailhead conditions, or call the local ranger district.

Be aware of the hunting calendar in Colorado, and wear blaze orange if you will be hiking in an area where hunters are active. Check the Colorado Parks & Wildlife website for calendar dates (www.cpw.state.co.us).

Gas up before you go and especially before getting on a long dirt road, so you don't get stranded.

Clip your fingernails and toenails a day or two before the climb, and hydrate with plenty of water and electrolyte drinks.

On the Road

Sometimes the most dangerous part of a climb is just getting from your home to the trailhead and back. Colorado's busy highways are filled with drivers on their way to work, or the ski slopes, or out to the mountains, just like you.

Mountain climbing usually requires a very early start, and the general rule of thumb is to be off the summit by noon to avoid lightning and precipitation. Plan your climbs with this in mind, and be on the road in time to drive to the trailhead, gear up, and get to the summit before noon. Traffic on the major roadways is busier than you might expect in the early hours, especially on I-25, I-70, and CO 470, and ski traffic can bring you to a halt. CO 115 and US 24, 50, 160, and 550 are generally not as busy, but there are long stretches of single-lane road where you are at the mercy of drivers ahead of you. Leave early, or head to the trailhead the night prior and camp or get a room.

A *DeLorme Colorado Atlas & Gazetteer* in your car will come in handy for identifying roads for your route, and alternate roads in the event of a detour. Know the page number and grid of your home and the page number and grid of the trailhead (listed in each climb in this book), and bookmark them so you can figure this out quickly in your vehicle.

Pack an emergency kit for your trunk, with food and water to sustain you for a couple of days in case you are stranded. Also pack a shovel for digging out of snow and a small handsaw to cut tree branches that can fall across back roads and block your path. It is not a bad idea to have a tent, sleeping bag, and pillow in the trunk, even if you are not camping. Cars get very cold very quickly overnight. In winter and spring, bring your snowshoes and ice axe even if you don't plan on using them on the peak, in case you need them to get from your car to a gas station.

Pack a cooler full of food and drinks for the drive, and for after the climb, a recovery drink. Some people crave salt after a climb, so you may want to add a tasty snack like pretzels, nuts, or chips. Bring trash bags for your recyclables and compost, and small bills so you can pick up extra items along the way, and use the restrooms at gas stations and convenience stores.

If there is a fee and a self-serve kiosk at the trailhead or campground, bring your checkbook and a pen or the exact amount in cash. Some kiosks accept credit cards, but don't count on it.

When driving to the trailhead, be aware of changing conditions, especially during inclement weather or disasters. Rainfall, snowfall, rockfall, mudslides, and wildfires can impact your route, so be prepared to turn around if conditions become unsafe.

Watch for runners, bicyclists, and motorcyclists, and yield to all of them. Also watch for wild animals on the road. Deer, elk, bighorn sheep, antelope, and moose are especially active along the roadways at dusk and dawn, when the lighting is bad and you are en route to the trailhead or on your way home.

On steep, narrow back roads, yield to uphill-driving traffic (traffic that is *below* and heading *up*). If you are approaching a flat, single-lane stretch and you have a convenient place to pull over, pull off and let other drivers pass.

Don't overestimate your ability, or the ability of your vehicle, to make it to a trailhead. When in doubt, pull over and park completely off the road or turn around, and walk to the trailhead. Tows in the backcountry are very expensive.

After a climb, assess your ability to drive safely, without "nodding off." Mountain climbing can be exhausting, so if you need a nap, take a nap in your tent or car. Don't drive home drowsy.

At the Trailhead

You may feel pressured to push off from the trailhead quickly, but take a moment to ensure you are properly geared up and prepared for the long day ahead.

Put on sunscreen, and dress for the first couple of miles so you can minimize clothing adjustment stops. Being slightly cold at the trailhead will probably have you feeling just right when you're hiking uphill. Unzip armpit zippers, and push sleeves and pull zippers and buffs up and down to adjust your body temperature, instead of constantly stopping. If you're bashing your way through a mosquito-infested area, put a light jacket on to protect your arms and cover your face. If the terrain begins in wet grass, put on your rain pants to keep your hiking pants dry.

Don't leave valuables or your garage door opener in sight in your car at the trailhead. Lock them in the trunk or glove box, or take them with you. If you have an extra car key, give it to one of your climbing buddies in case you lose yours.

Signs at the trailhead provide information on access and restrictions. Read them. Don't assume you can camp or have a campfire at a trailhead, as the rules vary.

On the Trail

Vigilance is as important on the trail as it is on the roadways and on the peak. If you follow the trail or others in your group "blindly," you may get lost. Use every hike and climb as an opportunity to hone your land navigation skills.

Learn route-finding skills, how to use a map and compass, and also how to use a GPS, if you have one. Keep your map and compass handy and track your location along the route. Do this every time on good trails, in good conditions, until you are able to do it off-trail, in bad conditions.

Travel in small groups to lessen impact in the backcountry. In wilderness areas, there is a limit on the number of people allowed to hike together. The website Wilderness.net has complete listings of wilderness regulations and maps, too. Contact the local ranger district for more information.

Keep dogs on leash or under voice command, and do not allow them to chase wildlife, which can stress the animals, causing death. Animals in the wild may be responsible for feeding young ones, so killing a single adult can wipe out an entire family.

Do not approach wildlife. Although attacks are rare, they can happen, and are more likely when an animal feels threatened. Even small animals carry diseases, so don't try to pet or feed them.

Leave berries and other native foods for the animals. They rely on these foods for their nutrition and survival. Eat your own food.

You may be sharing the trail with others, and a right-of-way protocol should be followed. Bikers should yield to hikers and horses, and hikers should yield to horses. Descending hikers should yield to those traveling uphill. However, use your common sense here. If you are a single hiker climbing up a trail and you see a large group heading down toward you, step off the trail and let them pass. Likewise, if you see a biker barreling toward you, it's probably a good idea to move to the side of the trail and allow them to pass safely. Bikers who are coming up behind you will usually let you know they are coming, so you don't accidentally step out in front of them.

Take extreme care when crossing streams. Use dry rocks and tree limbs to step across, or take off your shoes and wade. If you have to cross something deep, unfasten your pack straps so that if you are pulled in, the weight of the pack does not carry you downstream, but if you are concerned about being carried away at all, find a shallower place to cross, string a safety line of rope and tie in to it, or turn around. If you anticipate a deep crossing, pack some water shoes. Snowmelt and rain during the day can turn an early morning babbling creek into a roaring torrent later in the day, so be prepared for more difficult crossings on the way out.

Pack out all trash and personal items, including toilet paper. In some areas you are also required to pack out solid waste, so be prepared with a suitable container.

Keep to established trails and avoid traveling off-trail or on social trails. Where the use of off-trail travel is required to summit a peak, adhere to the Leave No Trace principles to lessen your impact and prevent resource damage. The Leave No Trace (lnt.org) principles are easy to follow and ensure a clean and pristine environment for inhabitants and future visitors to the peaks.

Do not cut "switchbacks," which destroys vegetation and causes erosion.

Leave everything on the trail as you found it. Do not remove rocks, plants, wildflowers, live trees, or historical artifacts from the wilderness, but leave them for others to enjoy. Per the Antiquities Act of 1906, removing artifacts is illegal and punishable with fines and jail time.

Tread lightly above timberline. Unlike alpine tundra in northern lands, Colorado tundra drains continuously, preventing the development of protective permafrost. High-altitude plant life has a short growing season, so regrowth of damaged areas takes a very long time.

Purify creek water before you drink it, and if you're traveling around a mining area, don't use the water at all.

Rocks, tree roots, and even dirt are very slippery when wet. Try to keep your boots dry, but if that's not possible, use trekking poles for balance and traction to help keep you upright.

Stay dry. Clothing adjustments are time-consuming, but if it starts to rain or snow, cover up immediately, before your clothing gets wet and you get chilled.

Lightning, exposure, sunstroke, hypothermia, dehydration, and altitude sickness are killers. If a storm threatens, or if you get very cold or overheated, or if you are feeling sick, take action immediately. Remedy your situation by descending, drinking fluids, eating, adjusting clothing layers, or taking medication, and then reassess your condition and the situation, and make the decision to continue on or to descend. Check in with your partners regularly to make sure they're OK, too.

Apply sunscreen before and during your climb. Don't neglect your ears and the inside of your nose. Reflected sun off snow will burn your nasal passages and the roof of your mouth, and you will likely not even realize it's happening until much later, when you get home and the inside of your nose starts peeling and your mouth is sore. Use sunscreen and a buff to protect these sensitive areas.

Eat and drink *regularly*, even if you're not hungry or thirsty, to stay hydrated, energized, and warm. If you wait until you feel thirsty, you may already be dehydrated.

Don't separate from your climbing buddies. It's inconsiderate and can put all of you in an unsafe situation.

At Camp

Camping can be a very rewarding experience, especially if you enjoy socializing with your climbing buddies. It's also the best way to get an early start on your climb.

Carry everything you need in your pack, including a tent, sleeping pad, and sleeping bag, plus cooking gear, including a stove, fuel, cooking pot, supper and breakfast foods, and eating utensils, such as an insulated mug for tea and soup and a spork.

In summer, bring a water filter to ensure fresh drinking water from nearby streams, and in winter, carry extra fuel to melt snow. Put some water in your pot before melting snow or it will just burn the bottom of the pot. Prepare your water for the next day before you go to bed, so you don't delay your alpine start in the morning.

Do not camp within 200' of lakes, streams, or trails, but camp close enough to them so that you can get to a water source for cooking meals.

Stay clear of mountain beetle–killed trees, which can fall on your tent.

Do not camp in a low area that can flood overnight, or in a high area that is susceptible to extreme winds and lightning strikes.

Seek out durable surfaces or sites that have already been established, to lessen your impact.

Respect campfire restrictions, and if you do have one, make sure you put it out completely before you leave camp.

Hang your food in a bear-proof bag to keep animals away from your camp. Do not eat or store food in your tent, which can attract wild animals.

Designate a bathroom area beyond your camp, and far from water sources. In snow, stomp out a track to it while it's still light out, so you can find it in the dark. Designate an area on the opposite side of your camp for collecting snow to melt for drinking and cooking.

Winter camping presents special challenges, with short days and long, very cold nights. You'll want to set up camp quickly and keep everything except "hard items" like ice axes and crampons with you in your tent. Cold fuel will take forever to warm up, and cold batteries for your camera, avalanche beacon, or GPS will die quickly. Keep these items in the tent, in a bag, stowed with you in your sleeping bag, to take advantage of your body heat. Water should also be stored in the tent, and you can put the bottles in a plastic bag at the bottom of your sleeping bag. A snug sleeping bag will keep you warm, but you will want to have some room at the bottom of your winter bag to store items and prevent them from freezing. In general, bag up water, batteries, fuel, clothing, your headlamp, GPS, any electronics, and your boots, and stow them in your sleeping bag.

A small candle made just for tent camping can be very comforting on long winter nights, and may raise the temperature a few degrees, too.

Nights at altitude are cold. If you don't want to leave the tent to go to the bathroom, get comfortable using a "pee bottle" in the tent. Mark the bottle with some tape to differentiate it from your drinking bottles in the dark. Women should practice using a FUD as well, kneeling or lying down. If you have to leave the tent, insulated "booties" are easier to slip on than trying to squeeze back into your cold boots.

Camping is easier if everyone pitches in to get the tent up, the water filtered or snow melted, and the meals cooked. Work together to make it happen.

If you are camping at altitude, you may have trouble sleeping. This is normal, and sometimes it takes a few nights for your body to adjust. Caffeine and alcohol can make it even harder to get a good night's sleep, so avoid them. Sleep aids should also be avoided, as they may interfere with your breathing and cause more serious issues. A hot cup of soup, a good book, and earplugs are safer alternatives for inducing sleep at altitude.

On the Peak

People die every year on Colorado's mountains. Injury and death is sometimes caused by a climber's inexperience and bad decisions, and sometimes it happens even when an experienced mountaineer has done everything within his or her power to be safe. We can minimize the odds of an accident with good mountaineering education, training, and experience.

Safe mountain travel demands vigilance at all times. The greatest dangers are unstable terrain, weather, poor judgment, and bad decisions. Loose rocks can fall on you or give way under your feet. Snow can bury you in an avalanche, cornices can break away beneath you, and slick, icy terrain can cause you to slip and fall. Lightning is common in the mountains and can maim or kill you. Exposure to heat, sun, cold, wind, and altitude can bring on many illnesses, and even death. If you are new to mountaineering, find a mentor or a small group of more experienced climbers willing to join you on your forays to the summits, while you embark on a personal mission to get a thorough education on safe mountain travel.

Keep an eye on the weather so you're not caught in a storm. Lightning, rain, and snowstorms can come at any time of day, and in any month of the year. Make a habit of checking the sky for incoming weather.

Winds on Colorado mountains and passes can be ferocious, knocking you to your feet. Plan to descend immediately if the wind suddenly picks up.

Don't throw rocks, or anything else, from a peak. You could start a rockslide and kill someone, or the velocity of the thrown rock, in a long descent, could kill someone.

Do not climb over others on loose terrain. You could dislodge a rock that might kill someone below. If you do accidentally dislodge a rock, yell "Rock!" loudly so anyone below you will know it's coming.

Some peaks have registers at the trailheads and on the summits—scrolls of paper, logs, or notebooks to sign, in waterproof containers—and this information is useful for those who track trail usage and maintain the trails, and may come in handy for rescue personnel, too. It's OK to sign a register, but do not sign your name on rocks or anything else on a peak, and do not leave signs, water bottles, or anything else behind on the summit. There are no paid garbage men in the mountains, so you have to clean up after yourself.

Be very wary of shortcuts off peaks. In particular, stay out of loose gullies, and don't climb down anything that you can't climb back up, or up anything that you can't climb back down. That's how climbers get "cliffed out" and have to get rescued.

Don't let "summit fever" or the herd mentality that often accompanies group hikes cloud your judgment. If the terrain or weather conditions are unsafe, or if you are not mentally or physically prepared to summit a peak, turn around. Your peak, your climb, your life: Don't hand that responsibility off to anyone else in the mountains.

Beyond This Book

This book is a good start for planning your adventures, but you will want to expand your knowledge with more resources. Lucky for you, the Colorado mountaineering community is rife with guidebooks, websites, and organizations to help you with your education.

Take some classes with formal outdoor-education service providers, and hire them to take you out and teach you the basics of mountaineering. Nonprofit organizations like the Colorado Mountain Club also offer classes to members, for a fee.

If you are going to be climbing in the spring or winter, take an avalanche safety course and invest in a probe, shovel, and beacon, and learn how to use them. Make avalanche safety coursework and self-arrest practice with an ice axe part of your annual training. Don't take chances with snow, period. Nonprofit organizations like Friends of Berthoud Pass also offer avalanche awareness and safety instruction.

Recreational shops like REI and local gear shops offer workshops and presentations on hiking and climbing. These are a good introduction and a refresher for formal coursework.

If you find that you are interested in a particular group of peaks, read guidebooks and websites that provide comprehensive information on the peaks in that set, or location. Appendix A lists a few books and sites, written and managed by Colorado climbers and mountaineers, to help you get started.

If you do some technical climbs in the mountains and decide that Class 5 climbing is for you, climber and FalconGuides author Stewart M. Green has written a number of excellent guidebooks to the best climbing areas in the state, including his comprehensive book *Rock Climbing Colorado* (2010). You can also stay up to date with climbing trends and techniques by following his posts on About.com, where he is the climbing expert and content provider for the climbing section on that site.

If you prefer to descend the mountains on skis rather than on foot, ensure a thorough education in snow travel and avalanche safety, and refer to *Climbing and Skiing Colorado's Mountains* (2014) by FalconGuides authors Ben Conners and Brian Miller.

Websites 14ers.com and 13ers.com have amassed and organized volumes of information about the highest peaks in the state. Colorado mountaineer and site administrator Bill Middlebrook's websites are free, but you may be compelled to make an annual offering for his generosity in providing access to everything you need to plan a 14er climb. This is a great place to get up-to-the-minute route and conditions information from other climbers, and much more. It's also a good place to make climbing friends.

Lists of John, a website developed and maintained by Colorado mountaineer John Kirk, is a database of all the mountains in Colorado, and in the country. You can discover at a glance which peaks are located in a particular county, or are of a particular elevation or steepness, or are on a number of other "lists." The basics on this site are free, while additional services require an annual fee. Lists of John users are also a great resource for learning more about the peaks and for finding climbing partners.

Other sites like Summitpost and Peakbagger are useful for discovering historical and route information about the mountains of Colorado and beyond.

Finally, develop a network of friends who share your interest in mountain climbing so that you will have other people to climb with and assist with planning, driving, and shared gear. Climbing friends will also motivate you to take mountaineering courses, read mountaineering books, and climb!

Now that you know what it takes to become a Colorado mountaineer, let's take a look at some of the peaks. The mountain chapters are next. Pick a peak, make a plan. This is the exciting part.

Map Legend

Municipal

≡⟨70⟩≡	Interstate Highway
≡⟨24⟩≡	US Highway
≡⟨83⟩≡	State Road
≡⟨263⟩≡	Local/County Road
≡⟨FR 356⟩≡	Forest Road
≡≡≡≡	Gravel Road
≡≡≡≡	Unpaved Road
⊢—⊢—⊢	Railroad
··········	Continental Divide
—·—·—··	State Lines

Trails

-------	Featured Trail
═══════	Featured Trail Under Road
------	Trail

Water Features

⬭	Body of Water
	Marsh/Swamp
∿	River/Creek
	Intermittent Stream
	Waterfall
⌐	Spring

Symbols

≍	Bridge
■	Building/Point of Interest
⛺	Campground
×	Elevation
▲	Mountain/Peak
🅿	Parking
≍	Pass/Gap
⊞	Picnic Area
⛷	Ski Area
🏠	Ranger Station/Park Office
🚻	Restroom
👁	Scenic View/Viewpoint
○	Town
✹	Capital
⊢—⊣	Tunnel
①	Trailhead
❓	Visitor/Information Center

Land Management

▭	National Park/Forest
▭	National Monument/Wilderness Area
▭	State/County Park

The Front Range

The Front Range defines the eastern edge of the Rocky Mountains in the state, trending north–south through central Colorado from the Wyoming border to Cañon City. The Rawah Range, Laramie Mountains, Never Summer Range, Mummy Range, Indian Peaks, Vasquez Mountains, Williams Fork Mountains, Platte River Mountains, Kenosha Mountains, Tarryall Mountains, Puma Hills, Rampart Range, and even the lowly South Park Hills, Gorge Hills, Grand Canyon Hills, and McIntyre Hills all lie within the Front Range, making it the longest continuous uplift in the state. The mountains rise as a formidable front between North Park, Middle Park, and South Park, west of the range, and the Great Plains, to the east. The Continental Divide follows the Front Range from the Never Summers at Cameron Pass south to Hoosier Pass. The Divide reaches its North American highpoint at the summit of Front Range highpoint 14,276' Grays Peak. Roads cross the Divide in the Front Range at Cameron Pass, Milner Pass, Berthoud Pass, Loveland Pass, Georgia Pass, Boreas Pass, Hoosier Pass, and at the Eisenhower Tunnel. Wilderness areas within the Front Range include the Platte River, Rawah, Comanche Peak, Cache la Poudre, Neota, Never Summer, Rocky Mountain National Park, Indian Peaks, James Peak, Vasquez Peak, Byers Peak, Ptarmigan Peak, Mount Evans, and Lost Creek Wildernesses. Finally, six ranked 14ers lie within the Front Range, and due to their proximity to the populated areas of Fort Collins, Denver, and Colorado Springs, they are among the most popular in the state. The Front Range offers many more accessible peaks, and is where most Colorado mountain climbers get their start on the peaks.

Pikes Peak defines the skyline in the Front Range west of Colorado Springs.
PHOTO BY STEWART M. GREEN

1 Rawah Range Highpoint: Clark Peak B

Elevation: 12,951' (NAVD88 12,956')
Distinctions: Rawah Range Highpoint, Jackson County Highpoint, Rawah Wilderness Highpoint, Prominence 100, P2K, Ranked 12er
Class: 2; Class 1 to Ruby Jewel Lake, Class 2 to summit
Difficulty and skill level: Strenuous; Intermediate
Approximate moving time: 5 hours
Distance: 6.8 miles round-trip
Elevation trailhead to summit: 9,665' to 12,956' (+3,291')
Terrain: Dirt road and trail, talus, grass, and scree; minor creek crossings
Restrictions: Day-use fee area, payable by cash or check at self-serve kiosk; trail closed to motorized vehicles; pets must be on leash; follow wilderness regulations

Amenities: Toilets at camping areas; overnight parking and camping in Colorado State Forest State Park by permit, payable at self-serve kiosk; yurts and cabins available by reservation; seasonal campgrounds along CO 14; services in Walden
Trailhead: 2WD parking area on Ruby Jewel Road
Trails: Ruby Jewel 4WD Road, Ruby Jewel Trail, off-trail South Slopes and West Ridge
Maps: DeLorme Page 18 E3; USGS Clark Peak
Counties: Jackson, Larimer
Land status: Colorado State Forest State Park, (970) 723-8366, www.parks.state.co.us; Medicine Bow–Routt National Forest, (307) 745-2300, www.fs.usda.gov/mbr; Parks Ranger District, (970) 723-2700; Rawah Wilderness, www.wilderness.net

Finding the trailhead: From Fort Collins, go north on US 287 for about 10 miles and turn left onto CO 14 West. Drive 69.3 miles and turn right at the KOA, onto unpaved CR 41. This turn is 18.7 miles east of Walden. Drive 5 miles on CR 41 and bear left at the split for Bockman and Montgomery Pass. Follow signs for Ruby Jewel Lake Trailhead, turn right onto Ruby Jewel Road, and drive 2 miles. Although designated a 2WD road, a high-clearance 4WD vehicle is recommended. Park at the 2WD parking area (GPS: N40 35.029' / W105 57.690').

The Peak

The Rawah Range, a 40-mile-long southern extension of Wyoming's Medicine Bow Mountains, forms the northwest border of Colorado's Front Range. *Medicine Bow* refers to the legend of American natives gathering to make wooden bows graced with "good medicine" from the gods, and *Rawah* is the native term for "wild place," or "wilderness." Clark Peak (*B*, as it is the second-highest Clark Peak in the state) is named for William Clark of the Lewis and Clark Expedition, the 19th-century exploration of the western United States. The two men are credited with naming the state's major mountain system, the Rocky Mountains. From atop Clark Peak, you will have views of the Medicine Bow Mountains and Laramie Mountains to the north,

Clark Peak offers views of North Park to the west, the Lake District to the east, the Never Summers to the south, and the Medicine Bow Mountains to the north. PHOTO BY SUSAN JOY PAUL

the Mummy Range to the east, the Never Summer Range and Rabbit Ears Range to the south, and the Park Range to the west.

The Climb

The approach to Clark Peak is in Colorado State Forest State Park, a self-serve fee area, so bring your checkbook and a pen. To add in ranked 12er "Lewis Peak," descend to the Clark–Lewis saddle from Clark Peak and make the Class 2 northwest ascent to the summit (N40 36.577' / W105 56.348'), then return to the saddle, adding about 0.6 mile and 400' of elevation, round-trip.

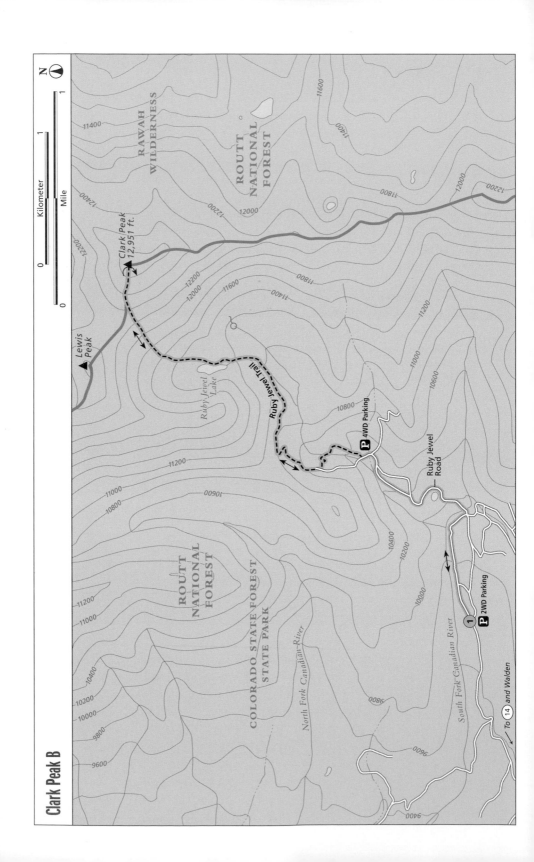

Clark Peak B

N

0 Kilometer 1

0 Mile 1

Lewis Peak

Clark Peak
12,951 ft.

RAWAH
WILDERNESS

ROUTT
NATIONAL
FOREST

Ruby Jewel Lake

Ruby Jewel Trail

4WD Parking

Ruby Jewel
Road

ROUTT
NATIONAL
FOREST

COLORADO STATE FOREST
STATE PARK

North Fork Canadian River

South Fork Canadian River

2WD Parking

To 14 and Walden

Miles and Directions

0.0 Begin at the 2WD parking area (9,665') and hike east, then north, on the road.

1.3 At the 4WD parking area and the Ruby Jewel Lake Trailhead, go north to cross the South Fork of the Canadian River on a split log, then cross the river again on a footbridge over a swampy area on logs and planks (N40 35.437' / W105 56.798').

1.9 At the Kelly Lake Trail junction, continue straight (right) and northeast on the Ruby Jewel Trail (N40 35.774' / W105 56.798').

2.0 Cross the boulder field on a talus trail and hike east into the meadow. Contour the mountainside, cross the river on rocks, and climb north into the basin (N40 35.815' / W105 56.744').

2.7 The trail ends at Ruby Jewel Lake (11,240'). Ranked "Lewis Peak" is north, and Clark Peak rises to the northeast. Go around the east side of the lake and north-northeast up steep grass and talus slopes to the Clark-Lewis saddle (12,250') or to a point to the right of the saddle on Clark Peak's west ridge (N40 36.051' / W105 56.309').

3.3 Gain the west ridge (12,600') and climb east to the summit (N40 36.431' / W105 55.957').

3.4 Arrive at ranked 12,956' Clark Peak. Return the way you came (N40 36.414' / W105 55.815').

6.8 Arrive back at the 2WD parking area (N40 35.029' / W105 57.69').

2 Cameron Pass Peaks: The Diamond Peaks

Elevations: 11,852' (NAVD88 11,857') North Diamond Peak; 11,701' South Diamond Peak
Distinctions: Ranked 11er (North Diamond Peak); Unranked 11er (South Diamond Peak)
Class: 2; Class 1 to basin, Class 2 to summits
Difficulty and skill level: Moderate; Intermediate
Approximate moving time: 3 hours
Distance: 3.0 miles round-trip
Elevation trailhead to summit: 10,276' to 11,857' (+1,581') for North Diamond Peak; about 1,900' round-trip for both peaks
Terrain: Dirt trail, off-trail talus, grass, and scree
Restrictions: No overnight parking or camping at trailhead; no bicycles or horses allowed on trail; pets must be on leash

Amenities: Trailhead toilets and picnic area; backcountry camping; campground and dispersed camping at nearby Crags Campground and Colorado State Forest State Park by permit only, payable at self-serve kiosk; seasonal campgrounds along CO 14; services in Walden and Fort Collins
Trailhead: Cameron Pass
Trail: Unofficial "Joe Wright Trail," off-trail East Slopes
Maps: DeLorme Page 28 A3; USGS Clark Peak
Counties: Jackson, Larimer
Land status: Roosevelt National Forest, (970) 295-6600, www.fs.usda.gov/arp; Canyon Lakes Ranger District, (970) 295-6700

Finding the trailhead: From Fort Collins, go north on US 287 for about 10 miles and turn left (at "Ted's Place") onto CO 14 West / Poudre Canyon Highway. Drive 58 miles and turn right to parking at Cameron Pass. If coming from Walden, get on CO 14 East and drive 30 miles to Cameron Pass, on left (GPS: N40 31.220' / W105 53.626').

The Peaks

North Diamond Peak and South Diamond Peak (the Diamond Peaks) are located north and west of CO 14 at 10,276' Cameron Pass. The pass, named for General Robert A. Cameron, founder of Fort Collins, divides the Rawah Range to the north and the Never Summer Range to the south. The summits provide views north of Clark Peak and the Rawahs, and south of the Mummy, Never Summer, and Rabbit Ears Ranges. Views of the Nokhu Crags are particularly spectacular from the Diamonds.

The Climb

The Diamond Peaks are accessible from the paved highway at Cameron Pass year-round, making them a favorite among snowshoers and backcountry skiers under safe spring snow conditions. The east face may become heavily loaded, presenting a high avalanche danger in winter.

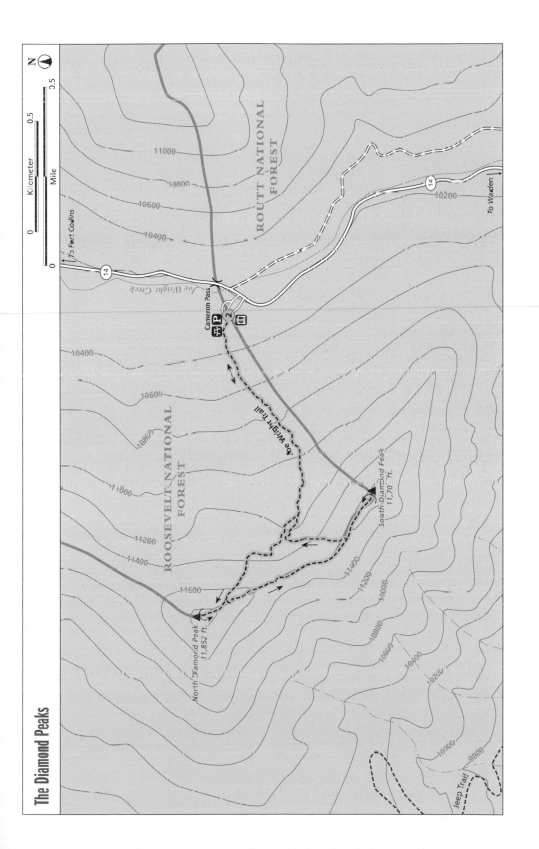

The Diamond Peaks

N

Kilometer
0   0.5

Mile
0   0.5

To Fort Collins

To Walden

ROUTT NATIONAL FOREST

ROOSEVELT NATIONAL FOREST

Joe Wright Creek

Cameron Pass

Joe Wright Trail

North Diamond Peak
11,852 ft.

South Diamond Peak
11,70_ ft.

Jeep Trail

14

Looking south from North Diamond Peak to South Diamond Peak, the Nokhu Crags and Mount Richthofen appear beyond. PHOTO BY SUSAN JOY PAUL

Miles and Directions

0.0   Hike west-southwest from the parking area (10,276') on a trail that follows the left side of Joe Wright Creek.

0.5   At timberline (10,980'), hike northwest across a large bowl below the peaks, aiming for the obvious northernmost saddle between the summits. Follow the ridge north-northwest to the highpoint (N40 31.044' / W105 54.094').

1.1   Arrive at ranked 11,857' North Diamond Peak. Depart the summit and hike south-southeast on the ridge crest (N40 31.292' / W105 54.650').

1.4   Reach the first saddle (11,500') and continue over the false summit, down to the next saddle and up to the true summit (N40 31.086' / W105 54.516').

1.7   Arrive at unranked 11,701' South Diamond Peak. Return to the saddle, and descend back to the bowl. Hike east to the trail at timberline, and continue down to the pass (N40 30.856' / W105 54.239').

3.0   Arrive back at the trailhead (N40 31.220' / W105 53.626').

3 Never Summer Range Highpoint: Mount Richthofen

Elevation: 12,940' (NAVD88 12,945')

Distinctions: Never Summer Range Highpoint, Prominence 100, P2K, Ranked 12er

Class: 4; Class 1 to Lake Agnes, mixed Class 2, 3, and 4 to summit

Difficulty and skill level: Strenuous; Advanced

Approximate moving time: 5 hours

Distance: 4.6 miles round-trip

Elevation trailhead to summit: 10,250' to 12,945' (+2,695')

Terrain: Dirt trail, talus, grass, scree, and boulders; exposure, risk of rockfall

Recommended extra gear: Helmet

Restrictions: Day-use fee area, payable by cash or check at self-serve kiosk; no overnight parking or camping at trailhead; no bicycles allowed on trail; pets must be on leash; follow wilderness regulations

Amenities: Trailhead toilets; campground and dispersed camping in Crags Campground and Colorado State Forest State Park by permit, payable at self-serve kiosk; seasonal campgrounds along CO 14; services in Walden and Fort Collins

Trailhead: Lake Agnes Trailhead

Trail: Lake Agnes Trail, off-trail North Slopes and West Ridge

Maps: DeLorme Page 28 A3; USGS Mount Richthofen

Counties: Grand, Jackson

Land status: Colorado State Forest State Park, (970) 723-8366, www.parks.state.co.us; Medicine Bow–Routt National Forest, (307) 745-2300, www.fs.usda.gov/mbr; Parks Ranger District, (970) 723-2700; Rocky Mountain National Park, (970) 586-1206, www.nps.gov/romo; Rocky Mountain National Park Wilderness, www.wilderness.net

Finding the trailhead: From Fort Collins, go north on US 287 for about 10 miles and turn left onto CO 14 West. Drive 60.3 miles and make a hard left onto CR 62, toward Lake Agnes. The turn is 27.7 miles east of Walden and 2.3 miles west of Cameron Pass. Continue 0.7 mile and turn right on FR 170. Cross the single-lane bridge and drive up the rough road for 1.2 miles to the trailhead (GPS: N40 29.394' / E105 54.199').

The Peak

Mount Richthofen sits on the Continental Divide, south of Cameron Pass and with its summit in the northwest corner of Rocky Mountain National Park. The peak is named for 19th-century German geologist and geographer Baron Ferdinand von Richthofen, and the 10-mile-long Never Summer Range gets its name from the Arapaho *Ni-chebe-chii*, or "never no summer." From the summit, the Divide continues west through the Rabbit Ears Range and north over Static Peak, then south, through the Never Summers and Rocky Mountain National Park. Mountain range highpoints in view include the Rabbit Ears Range's Parkview Mountain to the southwest, Mummy Range's Hagues Peak to the east, and Rawah Range's Clark Peak to the north.

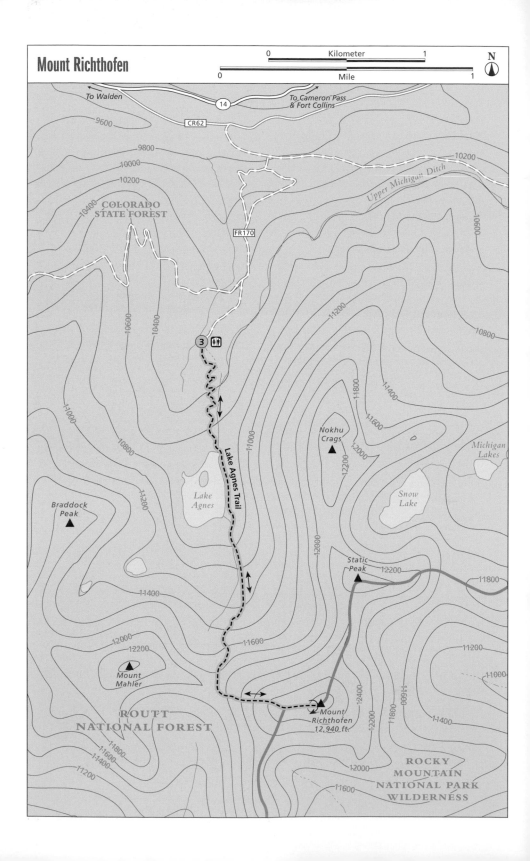

Mount Richthofen

0   Kilometer   1

0   Mile   1

N

To Walden

14

To Cameron Pass
& Fort Collins

CR62

9600

9800

10000

10200

10400

COLORADO
STATE FOREST

Upper Michigan Ditch

10200

FR170

10600

10200

10800

11200

3

10600

10400

11800

11400

11000

Nokhu
Crags

11600

Michigan
Lakes

11000

10800

Lake Agnes Trail

12200

Braddock
Peak

11200

Lake
Agnes

Snow
Lake

12000

Static
Peak

12200

11800

11400

11600

11200

12000

12200

11000

Mount
Mahler

11600

Mount
Richthofen
12,940 ft.

12400

ROUTT
NATIONAL FOREST

11800

11600

11400

11200

11800

12000

11600

ROCKY
MOUNTAIN
NATIONAL PARK
WILDERNESS

The Richthofen-Mahler saddle provides views north of Lake Agnes, the Nokhu Crags, the Diamond Peaks, and Clark Peak. PHOTO BY SUSAN JOY PAUL

The Climb

Mount Richthofen is a short climb with a variety of challenging terrain. This is the kind of peak that you'll want to repeat with friends. It's short, sweet, and very, very steep.

Miles and Directions

0.0 Begin at the trailhead (10,250') and hike south on Lake Agnes Trail.

0.7 Go left around the east side of the lake (10,663') on dirt, talus, and boulders (N40 29.056' / W105 54.155').

0.9 At the southeast edge of the lake, hike south up steep grass slopes, left of a creek drainage (N40 28.833' / W105 54.074').

1.5 At about 11,300', go right (south-southwest) and cross a talus field to the base of a scree slope below the Richthofen-Mahler saddle (N40 28.463' / W105 54.071').

1.8 Hike south up the scree trail to the saddle, or climb the Class 3 rock gully to the right of the scree slope. The rock makes for an easy climb up, while the scree trail makes for a speedy descent (N40 28.291' / W105 54.137').

1.9 At the saddle (12,000'), turn left and hike east upslope. Bear to the right of the loose center, where you'll find more solid terrain. About halfway up, cross to the right over a rocky rib, and scramble up to the ridge (N40 28.214' / W105 54.117').

2.1 Hit the ridge at 12,600' and turn left to follow it east (N40 28.186' / W105 53.908').

2.2 Hike over a false summit and continue on a climber's trail left of the crest. The final pitch is exposed Class 4 rock, to the left of a loose talus gully. Test your holds and note your exit point at the top (N40 28.159' / W105 53.839').

2.3 Arrive at ranked 12,945' Mount Richthofen. A summit marker is erroneously stamped with an elevation of 12,951'. Return the way you came (N40 28.170' / W105 53.687').

4.6 Arrive back at the trailhead (N40 29.394' / E105 54.199').

4 Laramie Mountains Highpoint: Laramie Mountains Highpoint

Elevation: 11,020'
Distinctions: Laramie Mountains Highpoint, Prominence 100, P1K, Ranked 11er
Class: 2; Class 1 for first 3.5 miles, Class 2 to summit
Difficulty and skill level: Moderate; Beginner
Approximate moving time: 4 hours
Distance: 7.4 miles round-trip
Elevation trailhead to summit: 9,163' to 11,020' (+1,857')
Terrain: Dirt trail, grass, and duff; creek crossings
Recommended extra gear: GPS

Restrictions: Trailhead is closed mid-June through Nov; no camping at trailhead; dogs must be under voice command
Amenities: Backcountry camping; seasonal camping at North Fork Poudre Campground; services in Fort Collins
Trailhead: Killpecker Trailhead #52
Trail: Killpecker Trail #956, off-trail South Slope
Maps: DeLorme Page 19 C5; USGS South Bald Mountain
County: Larimer
Land status: Roosevelt National Forest, (970) 295-6600, www.fs.usda.gov/arp; Canyon Lakes Ranger District, (970) 295-6700

Finding the trailhead: From Fort Collins, go north on US 287 for about 21 miles and turn left onto CR 74E / Red Feather Lakes Road. Drive 24.1 miles and turn left onto unpaved CR 86 / Deadman Road. Continue 6.8 miles to a small pullout and the trailhead, on left (GPS: N40 48.808' / W105 42.568').

The Peak

The Laramie Mountains form the 30-mile-long northeast border of the Front Range in Colorado, paralleling the Rawahs and trending north from the Mummy Range across the state line to Powder River Basin, in Wyoming. Wyoming's Laramie Peak is the highpoint of the range in that state, but the actual highpoint of the Laramie Mountains lies at the southern end of the range, in Colorado. The Laramie Mountains were named for 19th-century fur trapper Jacques La Ramie. A unique geologic feature of the range is kimberlite, an igneous rock which forms vertically from the earth's mantle. Kimberlite pipes, as they are known, drive other rocks to the surface, and the kimberlites of the Laramie Mountains are the likely source of billion-year-old diamonds that have been discovered in the range. With the highest point of the range barely scraping 11,000', hikes here lie below timberline and in the shade, with views afforded only from the summits of the highest peaks. You'll have nice views west of the Rawahs from the summit of Laramie Mountains Highpoint.

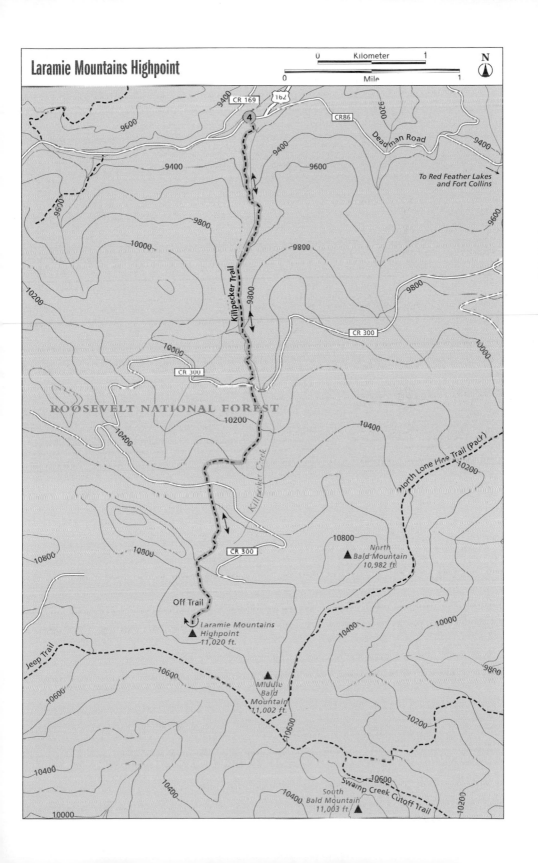

Laramie Mountains Highpoint

Kilometer

Mile

N

CR 169

162

CR86

Deadman Road

To Red Feather Lakes
and Fort Collins

9400

9600

9200

9400

9600

9800

9800

10000

10200

9600

9800

Killpecker Trail

9800

CR 300

CR 300

ROOSEVELT NATIONAL FOREST

10200

Killpecker Creek

North Lone Pine Trail (Pack)

10400

10200

10000

10400

CR 300

Off Trail

10800

North
Bald Mountain
10,982 ft.

10800

10900

10800

10600

Laramie Mountains
Highpoint
11,020 ft.

10400

10000

9800

Jeep Trail

10600

10600

Middle
Bald
Mountain
11,002 ft.

10600

10200

10400

Swamp Creek Cutoff Trail

10600

10200

10400

10000

10400

South
Bald Mountain
11,003 ft.

The Laramie Mountains Highpoint, seen here from Middle Bald Mountain, rises in Roosevelt National Forest near Red Feather Lakes. PHOTO BY SUSAN JOY PAUL

The Climb

Killpecker Trail crosses several forest roads, and you can shorten your hike by driving up Killpecker Road or Elkhorn Baldy Road and pulling off at any of the trail intersections, but then you'd miss out on a nice hike. The last bit is off-trail and hidden in the forest, but you will know it when you see it: It's a big bald bump in the woods. You can add three more peaks by returning to the trail from Laramie Mountains Highpoint and continuing south to unranked 12er Middle Bald Mountain. Get out your map and compass or GPS to add ranked 12ers South Bald Mountain, to the south, and North Bald Mountain, to the north, for a roughly 12-mile round-trip outing on mixed trail and off-trail terrain.

Miles and Directions

0.0 Begin at the trailhead (9,163') and hike south, crossing Killpecker Creek on logs at 0.5 and 1.4 miles.

1.7 Cross Killpecker Road and head east (left) on the road to pick up the signed trail on the other side. Cross the road two more times, at 2.6 and 3.2 miles.

3.5 Depart the trail on the right and hike southwest through the forest, over a rise, and toward a large mound to the south (N40 46.305' / E105 42.844').

3.7 Arrive at ranked 11,020' Laramie Mountains Highpoint. Return the way you came (N40 46.167' / W105 42.959').

7.4 Arrive back at the trailhead (N40 48.808' / W105 42.568').

5 Fort Collins Local Favorite: Horsetooth Mountain

Elevation: 7,255' (NAVD88 7,258')
Distinction: Ranked 7er
Class: 4; mixed Class 1 and 2 to base, mixed Class 3 and 4 to highpoint
Difficulty and skill level: Moderate; Beginner to base and Intermediate to summit
Approximate moving time: 3 hours
Distance: 5.0 miles round trip
Elevation trailhead to summit: 5,800' to 7,258' (+1,458')
Terrain: Dirt trail, wood steps, and rock slabs; exposure
Restrictions: Fee area, payable by cash or check at self-serve kiosk and by credit card at manned pay station during business hours; no camping at trailhead or in parking lot; trail closed to bicycles and motor vehicles (bicycles allowed on South Ridge Trail); pets must be on leash; see regulations brochure at trailhead

Amenities: Toilets, potable water, and covered picnic area at trailhead; backcountry camping with ranger check-in; seasonal campgrounds at Horsetooth Reservoir; services in Fort Collins
Trailhead: Horsetooth Mountain Open Space Trailhead
Trail: Horsetooth Rock Trail, off-trail South Ridge
Maps: DeLorme Page 20 E1; USGS Horsetooth Reservoir
County: Larimer
Land status: Larimer County Department of Natural Resources, Larimer County Parks and Open Lands, Horsetooth Mountain Open Space, Horsetooth Mountain Park, (970) 679-4570, www.co.larimer.co.us/naturalresources/htmp.ofm

Finding the trailhead: From I-25 north of Denver, take exit 265 for Harmony Road in Fort Collins. Turn left onto Harmony Road / CR 38 and drive 7 miles to the Taft Hill Road intersection. Bear left onto CR 38E and drive 6.5 miles, past the South Bay and Inlet Bay entrances to Horsetooth Reservoir, and turn right into Horsetooth Mountain Open Space (GPS: N40 31.441' / W105 10.869').

The Peak

Horsetooth Mountain's rocky top, with its three jagged summits, is named for its resemblance to a horse's tooth. According to Native American legend, the summits were once a single rock—the heart of a giant—slashed into their current, broken state by Chief Maununmoku. From the top of Horsetooth Mountain you can see north to Wyoming, east to Fort Collins, south to the Front Range, and west to the Mummy Range.

The Climb

Horsetooth Mountain Open Space is open 24 hours a day, year-round. The trailhead is located at the paved parking area, with two trails leading to the peak: the multiuse South Ridge Trail and the hikers-only Horsetooth Rock Trail. You may return the way you came up, or take the South Ridge Trail back to the trailhead, adding in the Audra Culver Trail section for variety. The South Ridge Trail has open views southwest of Mount Meeker and Longs Peak.

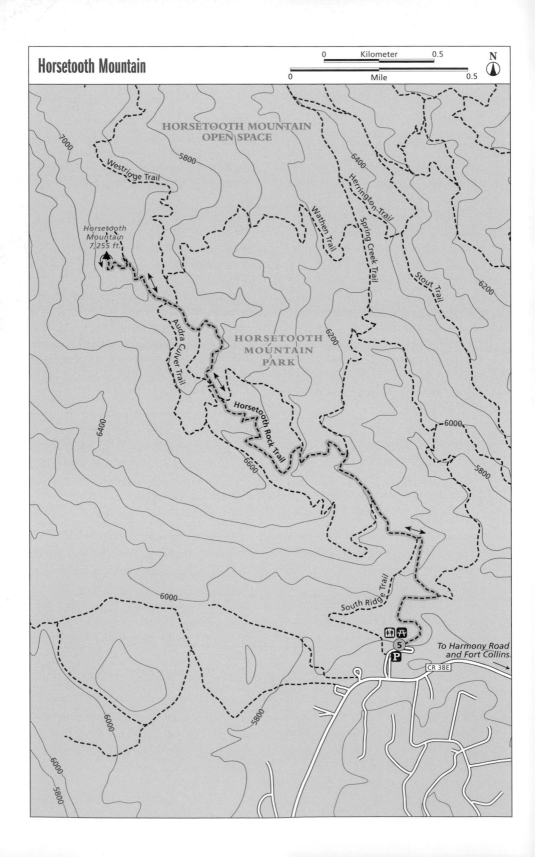

Horsetooth Mountain

0 | Kilometer | 0.5
0 | Mile | 0.5

N

HORSETOOTH MOUNTAIN
OPEN SPACE

7000

5800

Westridge Trail

6400

Herrington Trail

Wathen Trail

Spring Creek Trail

Stout Trail

6200

*Horsetooth
Mountain
7,255 ft.*

Audra Culver Trail

HORSETOOTH
MOUNTAIN
PARK

6200

Horsetooth Rock Trail

6000

5800

6600

6000

South Ridge Trail

5

P

To Harmony Road
and Fort Collins

CR 38E

6000

5800

6000

5800

Climbers take in views of Horsetooth Reservoir from the south summit of Horsetooth Mountain.
PHOTO BY SUSAN JOY PAUL

Miles and Directions

0.0 Begin at the trailhead (5,800') and hike northeast on the Horsetooth Rock Trail.

0.3 Pass the junction with the Horsetooth Falls Trail to the right, and continue straight (west) on the Horsetooth Rock Trail.

0.5 The South Ridge Trail joins your trail, from the left. Continue straight, northwest.

0.7 The South Ridge Trail departs your trail, to the left. Continue straight.

0.9 At the trail junction with the Soderberg Trail, stay left on the Horsetooth Rock Trail.

1.7 The South Ridge Trail joins your trail and goes left. Continue straight on the Horsetooth Rock Trail.

2.0 At the trail intersection with a cairn and memorial, bear right to stay on the Horsetooth Rock Trail (N40 32.202' / W105 11.512').

2.1 The Wathen Trail drops to the right. Stay straight and cross rocky slabs, then go up steps cut into the rock, on left.

2.3 At the trail junction with the Audra Culver Trail, turn right and contour across the rock slab, then climb up to the left.

2.4 The standard trail goes right at 7,020', up Class 3 rock to the north summit. To reach the south summit and highpoint of Horsetooth Mountain, go left on a climber's trail toward the east wall of the south "tooth." Locate a wide crack system and scramble up to the ridge, then follow the ridge north to the summit.

2.5 Arrive at ranked 7,258' Horsetooth Mountain. Return the way you came (N40 32.373' / W105 11.805').

5.0 Arrive back at the trailhead (N40 31.441' / W105 10.860').

6 Mummy Range Highpoint: Hagues Peak

Elevation: 13,560' (NAVD88 13,566')
Distinctions: Mummy Range Highpoint, Larimer County Highpoint, Tricentennial, Prominence 100, P2K, Ranked 13er
Class: 4; Class 1 to saddle, mixed Class 2, 3, and 4 to summit
Difficulty and skill level: Very Strenuous; Advanced
Approximate moving time: 10 hours
Distance: 18.4 miles round-trip
Elevation trailhead to summit: 8,540' to 13,566' (+5,026')
Terrain: Dirt trail, grass, tundra, talus, scree, and boulders; minor creek crossings; exposure, risk of rockfall
Recommended extra gear: Helmet
Restrictions: Rocky Mountain National Park is a fee area; no bicycles or dogs allowed on trail; follow wilderness regulations

Amenities: Trailhead toilets; overnight parking and backcountry camping in Rocky Mountain National Park by permit; seasonal campgrounds by reservation; concessions available seasonally at various locations in park; services in Estes Park
Trailhead: Lawn Lake Trailhead
Trails: Lawn Lake Trail, Black Canyon Trail, off-trail Southwest Slopes
Maps: DeLorme Page 29 A5, A6, B6; USGS Trail Ridge
County: Larimer
Land status: Rocky Mountain National Park, (970) 586-1206, www.nps.gov/romo; Rocky Mountain National Park Wilderness, www.wilderness.net

Finding the trailhead: From Estes Park, take US 34 West / Fall River Road for 4.7 miles to the Fall River Entrance of Rocky Mountain National Park. Continue 2.1 miles on US 34 and turn right onto Old Fall River Road, toward the Endovalley Picnic Area. Drive 0.1 mile to the parking area on the right (GPS: N40 24.446' / W105 37.568').

The Peak

Hagues Peak is the northernmost ranked 13er in Colorado and the highpoint of the 21-mile-long Mummy Range, a spur of the Front Range near Estes Park. The Mummy Range is named for its resemblance to a reclining Egyptian mummy, with Hagues Peak at the head, ranked 13ers Fairchild Mountain and Ypsilon Mountain as the knees and feet, and ranked 12er Mount Chapin and unranked 13er Chiquita representing the mummy's footstools. The peak is named for Boston geologists James and Arnold Hague, who surveyed the area in the late 1800s. From the summit, enjoy views of the surrounding Mummy Range, the Never Summer Range to the west, Rawah Range to the northwest, and Front Range to the south. Rowe Glacier is also in view along the western slopes of unranked Rowe Peak, to the north. Melt-off feeds a tarn below, at 13,100', one of the highest lakes in the country and a source of the North Fork of the Big Thompson River.

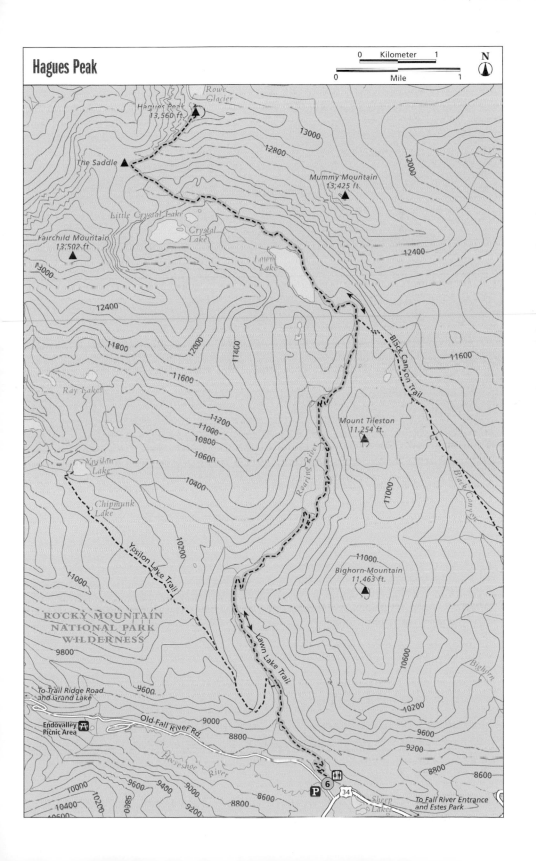

Hagues Peak

0 Kilometer 1

0 Mile 1

N

Rowe Glacier

Hagues Peak 13,560 ft.

13000

12800

The Saddle

Mummy Mountain 13,425 ft.

12000

Little Crystal Lake

Crystal Lake

Fairchild Mountain 13,502 ft.

12400

Lawn Lake

13000

12400

Black Canyon Trail

11600

11800

12000

11400

11600

Ray Lakes

Mount Tileston 11,254 ft.

Roaring River

Black Canyon

11200

11000

10800

10600

Ypsilon Lake

10400

Chipmunk Lake

11000

Bighorn Mountain 11,463 ft.

Ypsilon Lake Trail

10200

10000

11000

ROCKY MOUNTAIN NATIONAL PARK WILDERNESS

9800

Lawn Lake Trail

10600

10200

9600

9000

Bighorn

To Trail Ridge Road and Grand Lake

Endovalley Picnic Area

Old Fall River Rd.

9000

8800

9600

9200

Horseshoe River

10000

9600 9400 9000

9200

8800

6

34

8800

8600

P

Sheep Lakes

To Fall River Entrance and Estes Park

10400 10200 9800 8800 8600

10600

From the Hagues-Fairchild saddle, the vertical west face of Hagues Peak rises in sharp contrast to the gentler south slopes. PHOTO BY SUSAN JOY PAUL

The Climb

Hagues Peak is in Rocky Mountain National Park, so bring a card or a checkbook, and if you like the area, consider getting an annual pass. For the descent, you can backtrack your route, or skip the Hagues-Fairchild saddle and choose a more direct line, down the loose south slopes on a steep scree gully, to the trail. Hagues Peak is also climbed with a traverse of the six major peaks of the Mummy Range, known as "Mummy Madness." The route runs from the Lawn Lake Trailhead to Chapin Pass, in either direction, and with a car shuttle.

Miles and Directions

0.0 Begin at the trailhead (8,540') and follow signs northwest for Lawn Lake.

1.4 Bear right at trail junction to stay north-northeast on the Lawn Lake Trail (N40 25.204' / W105 38.088').

5.6 Continue straight at trail junction (10,800') to join the Black Canyon Trail (N40 27.652' / W105 37.295').

6.3 At Lawn Lake, at about 11,000', take the left fork at a three-way trail junction on Black Canyon Trail (N40 27.929' / W105 37.704').

7.3 Go right at the signed trail junction and ascend the steep trail west-northwest toward the Hagues-Fairchild saddle, "The Saddle." The trail crosses the creek on rocks, to the left, and then back to the right, with cairns to mark your path (N40 28.390' / W105 38.388').

8.4 Arrive at The Saddle at about 12,360' and hike northeast, up the grassy slope. The vertical west face of Hagues Peak appears ahead. Contour around to the southeast side of the ridge (N40 28.740' / W105 39.350').

9.0 Scramble northeast through Class 3 boulders. Skirt the ridge on boulders and a faint scree trail, to a point below the ridge and east of the summit (N40 29.017' / W105 38.821').

9.1 Climb straight up the Class 4 section, choosing the most solid rock. At the summit area, hike southwest to the highpoint (N40 29.077' / W105 38.760').

9.2 Arrive at ranked 13,560' Hagues Peak. Return the way you came (N40 29.071' / W105 38.784').

18.4 Arrive back at the trailhead (N40 24.446' / W105 37.568').

7 Milner Pass Peak: Mount Ida

Elevation: 12,900'

Distinction: Ranked 12er

Class: 2; Class 1 for most of route, Class 2 to summit

Difficulty and skill level: Moderate; Intermediate

Approximate moving time: 5 hours

Distance: 9.4 miles round-trip

Elevation trailhead to summit: 10,758' to 12,900' (+2,142'); about 2,400' round-trip

Terrain: Dirt trail, talus, and tundra

Restrictions: Trail Ridge Road is open seasonally from the Fri before Memorial Day until the 3rd week in Oct, conditions permitting; Rocky Mountain National Park is a fee area; follow wilderness regulations

Amenities: Trailhead toilets; overnight parking and backcountry camping in Rocky Mountain National Park by permit; seasonal campgrounds by reservation; concessions available seasonally at various locations in park; services in Grand Lake and Estes Park

Trailhead: Milner Pass Trailhead

Trails: Ute Trail, Mount Ida Trail, off-trail Northwest Ridge

Maps: DeLorme Page 28 B4; USGS Grand Lake

Counties: Grand, Larimer

Land status: Rocky Mountain National Park, (970) 586-1206, www.nps.gov/romo; Rocky Mountain National Park Wilderness, www.wilderness.net

Finding the trailhead: From Estes Park, take US 34 West / Fall River Road for 4.7 miles to the Fall River Entrance of Rocky Mountain National Park. Drive 3 miles on US 34 to Deer Ridge Junction, and continue on US 34 / Trail Ridge Road West for 21.7 miles, past the Alpine Visitor Center, to Milner Pass, on left (GPS: N40 25.218' / W105 48.685').

The Peak

Trail Ridge Road is the highest continuous paved road in the country and crosses the Continental Divide at 10,758' Milner Pass in Rocky Mountain National Park. Overlooks along Trail Ridge Road afford excellent views of Mount Ida and other peaks above the Gorge Lakes cirque on the east side of the peak. Milner Pass was named for T. J. Milner, who surveyed the area while in search of a route between Salt Lake City and Denver. Mount Ida, "The Mountain of the Goddess," was likely named after the Mount Idas of Greek mythology. Views from the peak are never-ending, with the Never Summer Mountains to the west, the Mummy Range to the north, and the Front Range to the south. Bighorn sheep are common on the upper slopes, and marmots scamper through the rocks at the summit.

The Climb

Most of this hike is above timberline and open to the elements, contouring the mountainside along the Continental Divide. The route fades toward the summit, so if you lose your way, head east to the Divide and follow it until you pick up the trail. If you are an experienced mountaineer, you can add six 12ers to your day, beyond

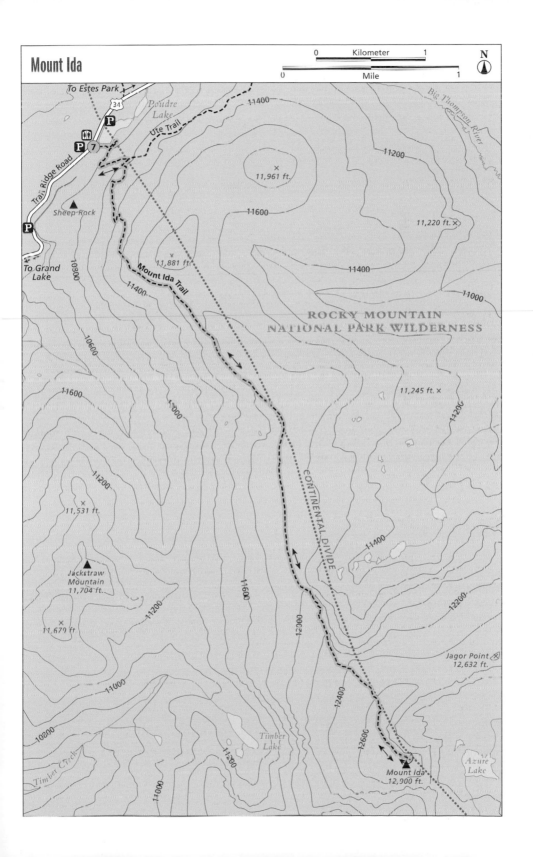

Mount Ida

0 Kilometer 1

0 Mile 1

N

To Estes Park

34

Poudre Lake

Ute Trail

11400

Big Thompson River

11200

P

P 7

11,961 ft.

11600

11,220 ft. ×

Trail Ridge Road

Sheep Rock

P

11,881 ft.

Mount Ida Trail

11400

11400

ROCKY MOUNTAIN
NATIONAL PARK WILDERNESS

11000

To Grand Lake

10300

10600

11600

11400

11600

11200

11200

11,531 ft. ×

Jackstraw Mountain 11,704 ft.

11,679 ft ×

CONTINENTAL DIVIDE

11400

11,245 ft. ×

11200

12200

Jagor Point 12,632 ft.

12400

11000

Timber Lake

11600

12000

12600

12400

10200

Timber Creek

11200

11400

Mount Ida 12,900 ft.

Azure Lake

Overlooks on Trail Ridge Road afford views of Mount Ida above the Gorge Lakes cirque in Rocky Mountain National Park. PHOTO BY SUSAN JOY PAUL

Mount Ida: unranked Chief Cheley Peak, ranked Point 12820, unranked Cracktop, ranked Mount Julian, and unranked Terra Tomah Mountain from south to east, and unranked "Jagor Point" to the northeast. The terrain is exposed Class 2 and 3, and there is no trail.

Miles and Directions

0.0 Begin at the trailhead (10,758') and hike east and south up switchbacks.

0.6 Pass a signed cutoff to Fall River Pass on the left, and continue south-southeast toward Mount Ida. Contour the mountainside under unranked Points 11881 and 12150.

2.7 Bear right at a cairn to stay on the correct trail. The upper trail is a social trail that peters out. The lower trail descends to a saddle (N40 23.736' / W105 47.537').

3.3 Reach the saddle (12,000') and hike upslope south-southeast on trail (N40 23.240' / W105 47.465').

3.6 Gain the ridge and continue along the rim of the cirque, as the trail fades to a cairned mix of dirt, talus, and tundra. Left of the trail, Trail Ridge Road is visible in the distance, with ranked 12er Sundance Mountain beyond (N40 23.020' / W105 47.301').

3.9 Hike upslope southeast and follow the rim of the next cirque, overlooking Gorge Lakes. The rocky summit of Mount Ida is just ahead (N40 22.822' / W105 47.202').

4.7 Arrive at ranked 12,900' Mount Ida. Return the way you came (N40 22.327' / W105 46.732').

9.4 Arrive back at the trailhead (N40 25.218' / W105 48.685').

8 Wind River Pass Peaks: Twin Sisters Peaks

Elevations: 11,428' (NAVD88 11,433') Twin Sisters Peaks East; 11,413' (NAVD88 11,418') Twin Sisters Peaks West

Distinctions: Prominence 100, P2K, Ranked 11er (Twin Sisters Peak East); Unranked 11er (Twin Sisters Peak West)

Class: 2+; Class 1 to saddle, Class 2 to west summit, and Class 2+ to east summit

Difficulty and skill level: Moderate; Intermediate

Approximate moving time: 5 hours

Distance: 6.8 miles round-trip

Elevation trailhead to summit: 9,200' to 11,433' (+2,233'); about 2,500' round-trip

Terrain: Dirt trail and talus

Restrictions: Serenity Lane is closed seasonally, but you can park at visitor center at bottom of road or across road at Lily Lake; no dogs or bicycles allowed on trail; follow wilderness regulations

Amenities: Toilet across road at Lily Lake Trailhead; overnight parking and backcountry camping in Rocky Mountain National Park by permit only; campsites at nearby Longs Peak Campground and Meeker Park Campground; services in Estes Park

Trailhead: Twin Sisters Trailhead

Trail: Twin Sisters Trail #998

Maps: DeLorme Page 29 C7, C6; USGS Longs Peak

County: Larimer

Land status: Roosevelt National Forest, (970) 295-6600, www.fs.usda.gov/arp; Canyon Lakes Ranger District, (970) 295-6700; Rocky Mountain National Park, (970) 586-1206, www.nps.gov/romo; Rocky Mountain National Park Wilderness, www.wilderness.net

Finding the trailhead: From CO 36 in Estes Park, take CO 7 East for 6.3 miles, or from Allenspark, take CO 7 West for about 11 miles, and turn east onto unpaved Serenity Lane. Drive 0.4 mile and park on the right side of the road, then walk up the road to the trailhead, on left (GPS: N40 18.186' / W105 32.112').

The Peak

Wind River Pass rises to 9,150' on the paved highway between Estes Park and Allenspark. The popular East Longs Peak Trail lies west of the pass, and a trail across the road from Lily Lake leads to the summits of Twin Sisters Peaks. In autumn, aspens along the west slopes of the peak form the "Butterfly Burn," with gold and orange hues in the shape of a mountain fritillary, or passion butterfly. "Twin Sisters" is a biblical reference to Aclima and Jumella, twin sisters of Cain and Abel, respectively. Each woman was promised to her non-twin brother, but Cain preferred his own twin and murdered Abel in a jealous rage. On your climb of Twin Sisters Peaks, you can enjoy both summits, Aclima to the east and Jumella to the west. You'll have views west of ranked peaks including 13er Mount Meeker, 14er Longs Peak, 13er Mount Lady Washington, 11er Estes Cone, and 10ers "Lightning Peak" and "Thunder Peak."

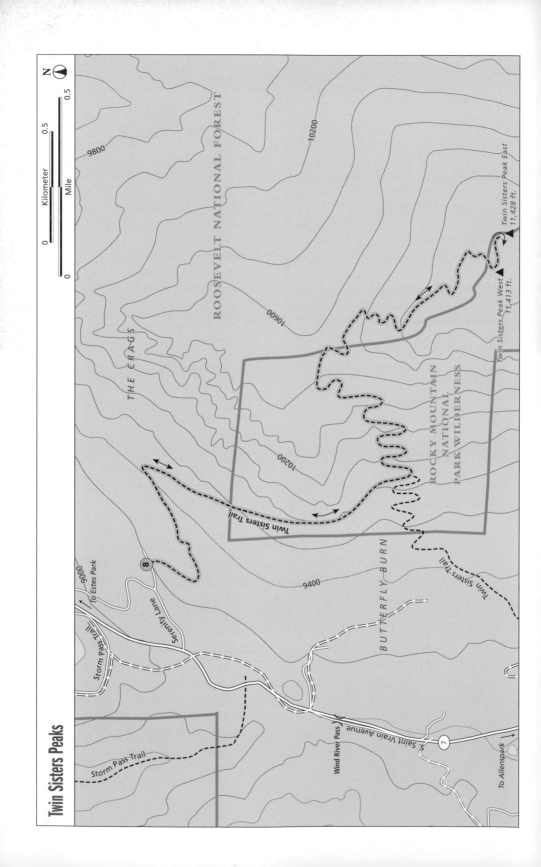

Twin Sisters Peaks

The eastern summit is the highest point of Twin Sisters Peaks near Wind River Pass.
PHOTO BY JOHN KIRK

The Climb

Twin Sisters Peaks are climbed in all seasons, thanks to a maintained trail in Rocky Mountain National Park. You can add ranked 11er Twin Sisters Mountain to your hike by descending south off the peaks to a saddle at 11,000' and ascending 400' to the 11,381' summit. This will add about 2 round-trip miles.

Miles and Directions

0.0 Begin at the pullout (9,200'), hike south up the road, and get on the trail on the left side of the road. The trail climbs east, then switches south at about half a mile.

1.3 Reach a slide area at 9,840' and continue south. Follow cairned switchbacks east, along the steep south edge of the washed-out area (N40 17.595' / W105 31.848').

2.3 The trail eases, leaves Rocky Mountain National Park, and heads southeast into national forest lands at 10,640' (N40 17.757' / W105 31.444').

2.8 Leave the forest at 11,040' and continue southeast on mixed dirt and talus, and up switchbacks to the saddle (N40 17.547' / W105 31.313').

3.2 Gain the 12,400' saddle and then go right to the west summit (N40 17.352' / W105 31.124').

3.3 Arrive at unranked 11,418' Twin Sisters Peak West. Drop back to the saddle, and climb the loose dirt trail to the east summit (N40 17.347' / W105 31.163').

3.4 Arrive at ranked 11,433' Twin Sisters Peak East. Return to the saddle and hike out the way you came in (N40 17.322' / W105 31.053').

6.8 Arrive back at the trailhead (N40 18.186' / W105 32.112').

9 Boulder Local Favorite: Third Flatiron

Elevation: 7,220'

Distinction: Unranked 7er

Class: 5.4; Class 1 to East Bench, mixed Class 4 to 5.4 to summit, rappels, Class 2 and 1 back to trailhead

Difficulty and skill level: Moderate; Advanced

Approximate moving time: 4 hours (varies depending on crowds on crag and at rappels)

Distance: 3.0 miles round-trip

Elevation trailhead to summit: 5,697' to 7,220' (+1,523')

Terrain: Dirt and talus trail, rock slab; exposure, risk of rockfall

Recommended extra gear: Backpack to carry gear, food, water, sports drink, extra clothing, plus your hiking shoes/boots; rock-climbing shoes, helmet, harness, personal anchor system (PAS) with locking carabiner, belay device (ATC) with locking carabiner, 200' (60 m) rope, set of wired stoppers, cams to 2", webbing for belay anchor, and slings

Restrictions: Closed Feb 1 through July 31 for nesting falcons; no camping; trail closed to bicycles and motor vehicles; dogs on trail must be on leash or display a Boulder Voice & Sight Control tag

Amenities: Trailhead toilets; services in Boulder

Trailhead: Chatauqua Trailhead

Trails: Bluebell Road / Mesa Trail, Royal Arch Trail, Third Flatiron Trail, and off-trail East Face

Maps: DeLorme Page 39 A8, Page 40 A1; USGS Eldorado Springs

County: Boulder

Land status: City of Boulder Open Space & Mountain Parks, (303) 441-3440, www.bouldercolorado.gov

Finding the trailhead: From US 36 in Boulder, go west on Baseline Road for 1.4 miles to Chatauqua Park. Turn south (left) to parking at Grant Place (GPS: N39 59.932' / W105 16.968').

The Peak

The Third Flatiron, or "The Third," as it is referred to locally, was the first technical rock climb in Colorado and is still the most popular climb in the state. It's one of five summits known collectively as "The Flatirons." The dramatic escarpments rise west of Boulder, and a trail system allows easy access to the Flatirons and many other technical climbs in the area. The Third Flatiron has been targeted for many antics over the years: It was climbed naked, roller-skated, and partially skied. Climbers scale The Third in moonlight with headlamps, free climb it with no gear, and speed climb it in an effort to break the fastest known time, or their own personal best. College students have painted logos on it, and some of the paint still remains. You are reminded to practice Leave No Trace principles on your own climb, and to leave it as pristine as you found it for future generations of climbers.

The Climb

This climb demands technical skills and gear, and so if you are not an experienced rock climber, you'll need to enlist the services of a trusted lead climber and rent some

Eight pitches take you to the summit of the Third Flatiron in the Flatirons west of Boulder.
PHOTO BY STEWART M. GREEN

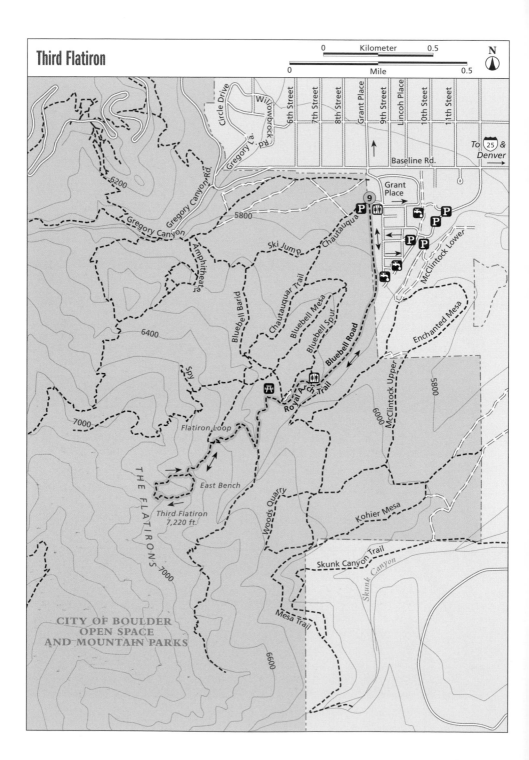

Third Flatiron

Kilometer
0   0.5

Mile
0   0.5

N

Circle Drive
Willowbrook Rd
Gregory La.
6th Street
7th Street
8th Street
Grant Place
9th Street
Lincoln Place
10th Steet
11th Steet

To 25 &
Denver

Gregory Canyon Rd
Gregory La.
Baseline Rd.

6200

Gregory Canyon

5800

Grant
Place

9

P

McClintock Lower

Amphitheater

Ski Jump

Chautauqua Trail

Chautauqua

Bluebell Barid

Bluebell Mesa

Bluebell Spur

Bluebell Road

Enchanted Mesa

6400

Spy

5800

Royal Arch Trail

McClintock Upper

6000

Flatiron Loop

7000

East Bench

THE FLATIRONS

Third Flatiron
7,220 ft.

Woods Quarry

Kohier Mesa

7000

Skunk Canyon Trail

Skunk Canyon

CITY OF BOULDER
OPEN SPACE
AND MOUNTAIN PARKS

Mesa Trail

6600

gear, or hire a professional guide to lead you on the Third Flatiron. If you are not comfortable with the final pitch, you can bail at the "Gash," located at the top of the 7th pitch to the left of the climbing route, and scramble over rock to the bottom of the first rappel.

Miles and Directions

0.0 From the trailhead, hike south on Bluebell Road onto the Mesa Trail, and bear right toward the Bluebell Shelter. Pass an outhouse and bear left onto the Royal Arch Trail, then right to signed Second and Third Flatiron Access. Get on the Second and Third Flatiron Loop, and go right toward the Third Flatiron Climbing Access.

1.2 Turn left toward Third Flatiron East Bench. Note that this is the junction where you will rejoin the trail after you descend the Third Flatiron (N39 59.289' / W105 17.512').

1.3 Arrive at the East Bench and begin Class 5 climbing. Each pitch is 100 to 140' (N39 59.259' / W105 17.505').

Pitch 1: Climb up and left for 100', past a bolt, over a water trough, and 40' up a rib to an eyebolt.

Pitch 2: Climb 120' up and right to the next eyebolt.

Pitch 3: Climb 120' up, bearing left to another eyebolt.

Pitch 4: Climb 140' up to another eyebolt below the painted letter C.

Pitch 5: Climb 120' up to the last eyebolt at the top right corner of the C.

Pitch 6: Climb 100' up and left of a large gully and set up a belay.

Pitch 7: Climb another 100' to the next belay, to the left of a large chockstone.

Pitch 8: Cross the chockstone, continue onto a ledge, then climb 100' up, over a horizontal crack, then left and up to the summit.

1.5 Arrive at unranked 7,220' Third Flatiron. Complete three rappels off the west side of the summit (N39 59.236' / W105 17.588').

Rappel 1: From 3 eyebolts 45' down to the South Bowl.

Rappel 2: From 2 eyebolts 50' down to Friday's Folly Ledge. It is 140' down to the base of the cliff from the first set of bolts that you see. Instead, go left (west) along the exposed ledge for 10' to the next set of bolts.

Rappel 3: From 2 eyebolts at the west end of the ledge, 72' down to the West Bench. Scramble north down to a climber's trail and hike east, through the talus and down to the trail. Signs note "3rd Flatiron Descent."

1.8 Rejoin the Flatiron Loop and turn left to return to the trailhead.

3.0 Arrive back at the trailhead (N39 59.932' / W105 16.968').

10 Indian Peaks Highpoint: North Arapaho Peak

Elevations: 13,502' (NAVD88 13,508') North Arapaho Peak; 13,397' (NAVD88 13,403') South Arapaho Peak
Distinctions: Indian Peaks Highpoint, Indian Peaks Wilderness Highpoint, Tricentennial, Prominence 200, P1K, Ranked 13er (North Arapaho Peak); unranked 13er (South Arapaho Peak)
Class: 4; Class 1 to South Arapaho–Old Baldy saddle; Class 2 to South Arapaho Peak; mixed Class 2, 3, and 4 to North Arapaho Peak
Difficulty and skill level: Very Strenuous; Advanced
Approximate moving time: 8 hours
Distance: 9.2 miles round-trip
Elevation trailhead to summit: 10,120' to 13,508' (+3,388'); about 4,200' round-trip
Terrain: Dirt trail, scree, talus, and boulders; creek crossings; exposure, risk of rockfall
Recommended extra gear: Helmet

Restrictions: Road subject to winter closure from mid-Sept until June; trail closed to bicycles and motorized vehicles; pets must be on leash; permit required for organized hiking groups (free); follow wilderness regulations
Amenities: Trailhead toilets; backcountry camping by permit (for a fee) between June 1 and Sept 15; first-come, first-served Buckingham Campground located at trailhead; services in Nederland
Trailhead: Fourth of July Trailhead
Trails: Arapaho Pass Trail, Arapaho Glacier Trail, off-trail South Ridge
Maps: DeLorme Page 29 E5, Page 39 A5; USGS Monarch Lake
Counties: Boulder, Grand
Land status: Roosevelt National Forest, (970) 295-6600, www.fs.usda.gov/arp; Boulder Ranger District, (303) 541-2500; Indian Peaks Wilderness, www.wilderness.net

Finding the trailhead: From Boulder, take CO 119 West for 16 miles, and drive through the traffic circle in Nederland onto North Bridge Street / CO 119. Drive 0.6 mile and turn right onto CR 130 / Eldora Road. Continue 2.5 miles, turn right onto Eldora Avenue, and bear right at 0.9 mile onto unpaved CR 111 / 4th of July Road. Drive 4 miles to the trailhead, on right (GPS: N39 59.710' / W105 38.057').

The Peak

North Arapaho Peak tops the Indian Peaks Range west of Boulder in the Indian Peaks Wilderness. The mountain range follows the Continental Divide from Cony Pass to Rollins Pass, with six ranked 13ers in its domain. North Arapaho Peak is the southernmost and highest ranked 13er in the Indian Peaks, with its summit on the Divide. The Arapaho Peaks were named in the 1870s for Native American tribes, the North Arapaho and South Arapaho, and the name is a distortion of the Crow *aa-raxpé-ahu*, or "tattoo." From the summits looking west, Middle Park stretches from north to south, with the Rabbit Ears Range, the Gore Range, and the Williams Fork

A climber starts the ridge traverse to North Arapaho Peak with his poles tucked in his pack.
PHOTO BY KEVIN BAKER

Mountains beyond. North and south of the peak the Front Range continues, with 14er Longs Peak in view at Rocky Mountain National Park. The Arapaho Glacier lies just below the peaks, to the east.

The Climb

The Indian Peaks Wilderness is one of the busiest wilderness areas in the state, so a weekday climb is recommended. The South to North Arapaho Peak traverse is above timberline on a ridge with no bailouts, and it will take several hours to cover the distance from the south peak to the north peak and back. Don't get caught on this ridge in a storm or in the dark. In consolidated snow, the Arapaho Peaks may be accessed via Skywalker Couloir and Streetwalker Couloir on South Arapaho's southwest face and North Star Couloir on North Arapaho's west face, requiring skill with steep snow climbing, snow gear, and a proper education in self-arrest and avalanche safety. The crux of the Skywalker climb is one of three finishes, "Princess Leia," "Han Solo," and the "Escape" exit, offering a range of technical difficulty.

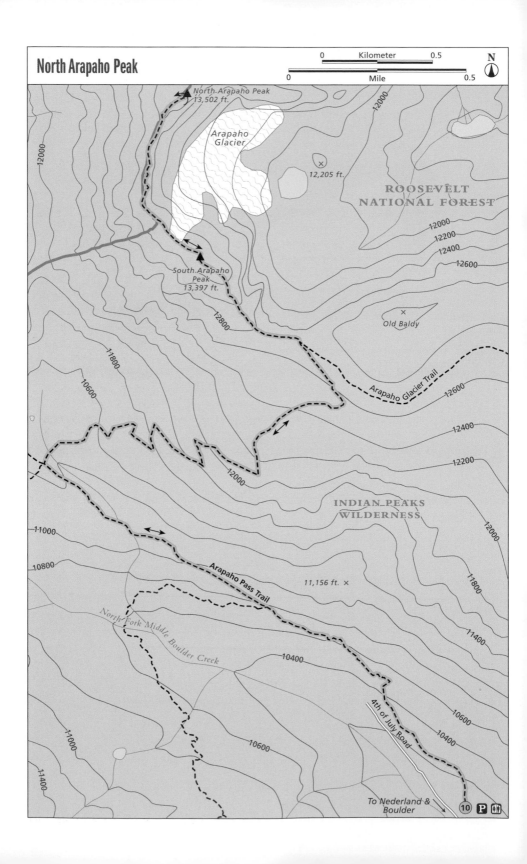

North Arapaho Peak

0 Kilometer 0.5

0 Mile 0.5

N

North Arapaho Peak
13,502 ft.

Arapaho
Glacier

12000

12205 ft.

ROOSEVELT
NATIONAL FOREST

12000
12200
12400
12600

South Arapaho
Peak
13,397 ft.

12800

Old Baldy

11800

Arapaho Glacier Trail

12600

10600

12400

12200

12000

INDIAN PEAKS
WILDERNESS

11,156 ft. ×

12000

11000

11800

10800

Arapaho Pass Trail

North Fork Middle Boulder Creek

11400

10400

10600

4th of July Road

10600

11000

10400

10600

11400

To Nederland &
Boulder

10 P

Miles and Directions

0.0 From the trailhead (10,120'), hike north-northwest on switchbacks and cross a creek.

1.0 Pass the Diamond Lake Trail junction on the left and continue northwest on the Arapaho Pass Trail, over open terrain and through willows (N40 0.253' / W105 38.759').

1.8 At the Fourth of July Mine (11,240'), turn right onto the Arapaho Glacier Trail, then cross a creek and some marshes. Continue east, through more willows and above treeline, where views open to South Arapaho Peak. The trail switches back to the northwest and rises to the Arapaho Glacier Overlook (N40 0.625' / W105 39.511').

3.5 At the overlook and South Arapaho–Old Baldy saddle (12,720'), depart the Arapaho Glacier Trail and go west-northwest on a climber's trail along the southeast ridge of South Arapaho Peak. Stick to the ridge or just west (left) of the ridge on scree, talus, and boulders, following the use trail and cairns past a false summit (N40 0.950' / W105 38.633').

4.0 Arrive at unranked 13,403' South Arapaho Peak. Descend west-northwest on scree, down to exciting views of the Arapaho Glacier. Climb a short Class 3 section, then traverse exposed ledges west of the ridge, veering left of some rocky bumps, without losing too much elevation (N40 1.176' / W105 38.970').

4.3 Follow orange arrows up a steep Class 4 section on the ridge, "The Block," starting on ledges and then climbing straight up the slab and left to exit. The difficult moves involve latching onto cracks and hauling yourself onto a ledge, then scrambling up to the top of the block. From the top, bear left on the narrow ridge and downclimb exposed ledges. Traverse north, up and through an obvious notch. Follow arrows and cairns, staying clear of the exposed east face. Downclimb a long slab to avoid the next vertical section, then regain your elevation and continue north, around the left side of the final ridge ahead, and up a steep, exposed gully. Move right to the next gully, and head up to the summit (N40 1.350' / W105 39.150').

4.6 Arrive at ranked 13,508' North Arapaho Peak. Return the way you came (N40 01.598' / W105 39.014').

9.2 Arrive back at the trailhead (N39 59.710' / W105 38.057').

11 Berthoud Pass Peaks: Mount Flora, Mount Eva, and Parry Peak

Elevations: 13,146' (NAVD88 13,152') Mount Flora; 13,130' (NAVD88 13,136') Mount Eva; 13,391' (NAVD88 13,397') Parry Peak
Distinctions: Prominence 200, P1K (Parry Peak); Ranked 13ers (all three peaks)
Class: 2; Class 1 to first (false) summit of Mount Flora, Class 2 for rest of hike
Difficulty and skill level: Moderate and Beginner for Mount Flora only; Strenuous and Intermediate for Mount Eva; Very Strenuous and Intermediate for Parry Peak
Approximate moving time: 4 hours for Mount Flora only; 6 hours for Mount Flora and Mount Eva; 8 hours for all 3 peaks
Distance: 6.8 miles round-trip for Mount Flora only; 10.6 miles round-trip for Mount Flora and Mount Eva; 11.8 miles round-trip for all 3 peaks
Elevations trailhead to summits: 11,307' to 13,152' (+1,845') for Mount Flora, to 13,136' (+1,829') for Mount Eva, and to 13,397' (+2,090') for Parry Peak; about 2,000' for Mount Flora round-trip, 3,100' for Mount Flora and Mount Eva round-trip, and 4,100' for all 3 peaks round-trip
Terrain: Dirt trail, talus, and tundra
Restrictions: Trail closed to bicycles and motor vehicles; dogs must be on leash or under voice command
Amenities: Trailhead toilets and warming hut; seasonal camping south on US 40 at Mizpah Campground and at campgrounds north in Winter Park; services in Empire and Winter Park
Trailhead: Berthoud Pass Trailhead
Trail: Continental Divide National Scenic Trail, off-trail Southwest Ridges
Maps: DeLorme Page 39 B5, C5, Page 38 C4; USGS Empire, Berthoud Pass
Counties: Grand, Clear Creek
Land status: Arapaho National Forest, (970) 295-6600, www.fs.usda.gov/arp; Clear Creek Ranger District, (303) 567-3000

Finding the trailhead: From I-70, about 29 miles west of Denver and 26 miles east of Silverthorne, take exit 232 to US 40 for Empire/Granby. Drive 15.1 miles, through the towns of Empire and Berthoud Falls, to the top of Berthoud Pass and a large paved parking area on the right (GPS: N39 47.902' / W105 46.561').

The Peaks

Three ranked 13ers follow the Continental Divide northeast of 11,315' Berthoud Pass. The route overlooks the Vasquez and Williams Fork Mountains to the west, the Indian Peaks to the north, and the peaks at Loveland Pass and Guanella Pass to the south. The pass was named for Captain Edward L. Berthoud, who discovered it while looking for a railroad route, and in 1938 US 40 over Berthoud Pass became the first paved road to cross the Continental Divide in Colorado.

The Climb

The peaks at Berthoud Pass are climbed year-round, with the crux on the steep back-side of Mount Eva. Ranked 12er "Colorado Mines Peak" lies at the top of the service

Mount Flora, Mount Eva and Parry Peak

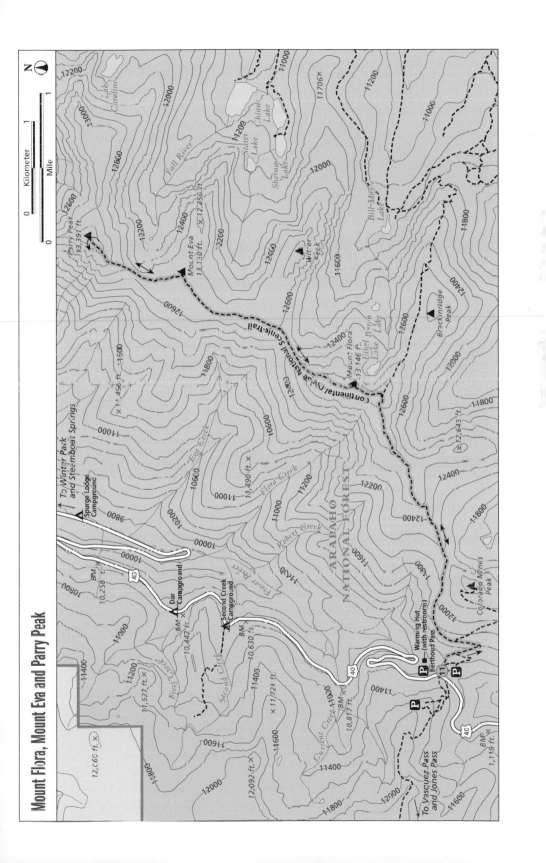

The tiny summit of Mount Flora, with Mount Eva's snowy south face and Parry Peak beyond, line up along the Continental Divide at Berthoud Pass. PHOTO BY SUSAN JOY PAUL

road and can be picked up on the way out or back, with a short detour. You can also extend your climb past Parry Peak, east to unranked 13er Mount Bancroft, and then north to ranked 13er James Peak, where a car shuttle at the Saint Mary's Glacier Trailhead makes a lot more sense than retracing your steps back to Berthoud Pass.

Miles and Directions

- **0.0** Begin at the trailhead (11,307') and hike east on trail to a service road that switches back up the mountainside. The alternative, a steep direct ascent from the trailhead on trail, leads to a highpoint on the service road and shaves off some distance, but is not suitable for groups.
- **0.9** Depart the road on the left at the signed trail to Mount Flora. Contour north and east below "Colorado Mines Peak," and follow the ridge northeast (N39 47.797' / W105 46.323').
- **3.2** Arrive at the lower summit of Mount Flora. Leave the trail and head north to the highpoint (N39 48.297' / W105 44.141').
- **3.4** Arrive at ranked 13,152' Mount Flora. Continue north along the ridge (N39 48.459' / W105 44.110').
- **3.7** Contour left around a bump on the ridge, and descend the northeast ridge to the Eva-Flora saddle. Stay away from the loose gullies and cornices to the east. Climbing back up this slope after hitting the next two peaks will be the toughest part of the day. At the saddle, contour left past the fallen tower debris (N39 48.694' / W105 43.998').
- **5.3** Arrive at ranked 13,136' Mount Eva. Follow the ridge north on a use trail through talus, about 10' in from the ridge. At the Parry-Eva saddle, head northeast in an ascending traverse on talus, over a false bump and up the final slope. Look for ptarmigan on the easy summit stroll (N39 49.653' / W105 43.108').
- **5.9** Arrive at ranked 13,397' Parry Peak. Return the way you came (N39 50.287' / W105 42.783').
- **11.8** Arrive back at the trailhead (N39 47.902' / W105 46.561').

12 Vasquez Mountains Highpoint: Vasquez Peak

Elevation: 12,947' (NAVD88 12,953')

Distinctions: Vasquez Mountains Highpoint, Vasquez Peak Wilderness Highpoint, P1K, Ranked 12er

Class: 2+; Class 1 for first 3 miles, Class 2 and 2+ to highpoint

Difficulty and skill level: Strenuous; Intermediate

Approximate moving time: 5 hours

Distance: 7.4 miles round-trip

Elevation trailhead to summit: 10,434' to 12,953' (+2,519')

Terrain: Dirt trail, grass, tundra, talus, and boulders

Restrictions: Summer route; road closed to vehicle traffic (except snowmobiles) at Henderson Mine in winter; trail closed to bicycles and motorized vehicles; dogs must be on leash or under voice command; follow wilderness regulations

Amenities: Backcountry camping; seasonal picnic area with toilets at nearby Big Bend Picnic Ground; seasonal camping at nearby Mizpah Campground; services in Empire and Winter Park

Trailhead: Henderson Trailhead

Trails: Henderson Trail, Continental Divide Trail, off-trail South Slopes

Maps: DeLorme Page 38 C4; USGS Berthoud Pass

Counties: Clear Creek, Grand

Land status: Arapaho National Forest, (970) 295-6600, www.fs.usda.gov/arp; Clear Creek Ranger District, (303) 567-3000; Vasquez Peak Wilderness, www.wilderness.net

Finding the trailhead: From I-70, about 40 miles west of Denver and 26 miles east of Silverthorne, take exit 232 to US 40 for Empire/Granby. Drive 9.3 miles, through Empire and Berthoud Falls, and turn left onto CR 202 / Henderson Mine Road, signed for Jones Pass. Go 1.8 miles and turn right, onto unpaved FR 144 toward Jones Pass. Continue for 0.5 mile to a pullout on the left side of the road and the trailhead on the right (GPS: N39 46.259' / W105 51.222').

The Peak

Vasquez Peak is located on the Continental Divide between Jones Pass to the southwest and Vasquez Pass and Berthoud Pass to the east. The Vasquez Mountains, a western spur of the Front Range, are named for Pierre Luis (Louis) Vasquez (1798–1868), a Missouri fur trapper and trader who established an early trading post, Fort Vasquez. Views from Vasquez Peak are spectacular, with the high 13ers of Berthoud Pass to the east, the Indian Peaks to the north, and the Williams Fork Mountains and Gore Range to the west.

The Climb

The road to the trailhead of Vasquez Peak is popular year-round, providing access to nearby Butler Gulch Trail, Jones Pass, and the Continental Divide Trail. Skiers and snowshoers frequent the area in snow, but Vasquez Peak should be avoided in winter and spring and during summer monsoons, due to avalanche and rockslide danger above the trail. The peak may also be approached from Jones Pass and the west ridge,

Vasquez Peak

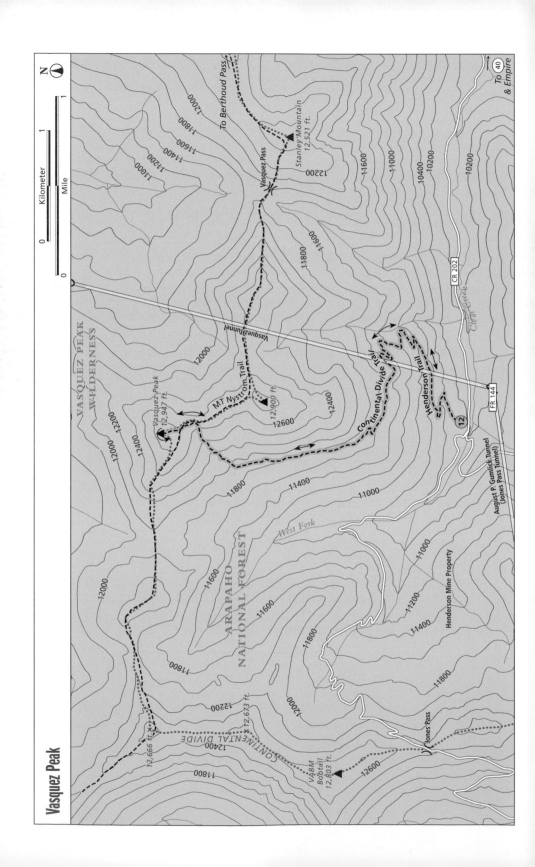

Kilometer

Mile

VASQUEZ PEAK WILDERNESS

Vasquez Peak
12,947 ft.

MT Nystrom Trail

12,900 ft.

12,666 ft.

CONTINENTAL DIVIDE

12,673 ft.

VABM Bobtail
12,803 ft.

ARAPAHO
NATIONAL FOREST

West Fork

Continental Divide Trail

Henderson Trail

Henderson Mine Property

August P. Gumlick Tunnel
(Jones Pass Tunnel)

Jones Pass

Vasquez Pass

Vasquez tunnel

To Berthoud Pass

Stanley Mountain
12,521 ft.

Clear Creek

CR 202

FR 144

To 40
& Empire

Vasquez Peak tops the Vasquez Mountains in the Vasquez Peak Wilderness near Jones Pass.
PHOTO BY JOHN KIRK

or from the east at Berthoud Pass, by climbing over several unranked 12ers and dropping into Vasquez Pass, then climbing over two more unranked 12ers and up to Vasquez Peak. The south approach, described here, begins on property owned by the Henderson Mine Company with access granted to the US Forest Service.

Miles and Directions

0.0 Begin at the trailhead on the north side of FR 144 (10,434') and follow switchbacks northeast on the Henderson Trail.

1.4 Reach the Continental Divide Trail junction (11,260') with Stanley Mountain and Berthoud Pass to the right. Go left (west) toward Jones Pass, contouring north below the steep west slopes of unranked Point 12900 (N39 46.684' / W105 50.694').

3.1 Depart trail to the right. Ascend steep grass and tundra slopes northeast, to the right of the rock slide and scree, to the Vasquez–Point 12900 saddle (N39 47.396' / W105 51.526').

3.5 Arrive at the saddle marked by a pile of white quartz. Head north-northwest on tundra, talus, and over a boulder pile (N39 47.614' / W105 51.230').

3.7 Arrive at ranked 12,953' Vasquez Peak. Return the way you came (N39 47.772' / W105 51.307').

7.4 Arrive back at the trailhead (N39 46.259' / W105 51.222').

13 Williams Fork Mountains Highpoint: Coon Hill

Elevation: 12,757' (NAVD88 12,763')
Distinctions: Williams Fork Mountains Highpoint, Ptarmigan Peak Wilderness Highpoint, Ranked 12er
Class: 2
Difficulty and skill level: Moderate; Intermediate
Approximate moving time: 2 hours
Distance: 2.8 miles round-trip
Elevation trailhead to summit: 11,160' to 12,763' (+1,603')
Terrain: Grass, tundra, and talus

Restrictions: Trailhead may be closed during road construction; follow wilderness regulations
Amenities: Services in Dillon and Georgetown
Trailhead: Rest area at west end of Eisenhower Memorial Tunnel
Trail: Off-trail South Ridge
Maps: DeLorme Page 38 D3; USGS Loveland Pass
Counties: Grand, Summit
Land status: White River National Forest, (970) 945-2521, www.fs.usda.gov/whiteriver; Dillon Ranger District, (970) 468-5400; Ptarmigan Peak Wilderness, www.wilderness.net

Finding the trailhead: From Denver, take I-70 West for about 46 miles, through the Eisenhower Memorial Tunnel, and park at the rest area immediately past the west end of the tunnel, on the north (right) side of the road. If coming from the west, from Dillon, take I-70 East for about 10 miles and take exit 216 for Loveland Pass, turn left onto US 6, then take the ramp to get onto I-70 West and drive through the tunnel (GPS: N39 40.727' / W105 56.274').

The Peak

The Williams Fork Mountains branch west from the Continental Divide north of Loveland Pass, paralleling I-70 over highpoint Coon Hill and bending northwest at Ptarmigan Peak. Your route to Coon Hill begins at a rest stop on the west end of the Eisenhower–Johnson Memorial Tunnel. The tunnel, at 11,158', is the highpoint of an interstate highway system that stretches from Utah to Maryland. The Williams Fork Mountains are named for William Sherley Williams, "Ol' Bill Williams," 19th-century trapper and mountain guide. From the top of Coon Hill, the rest of the Williams Fork Mountains stretch west and north, framed by the Gore Range. To the east, the long ridge connecting the Williams Fork Mountains to the Continental Divide is in view, marked by ranked 13ers "Golden Bear Peak," Hagar Mountain, "The Citadel," and Pettingell Peak. The 13ers at Loveland Pass and 14ers Grays Peak and Torreys Peak rise southeast.

The Climb

Coon Hill is climbed year-round, with regard for potential avalanche danger from winter to early spring. The most difficult part of the climb is making the turnoff to the rest area, where your hike begins. Be in the right lane in the tunnel, and put on

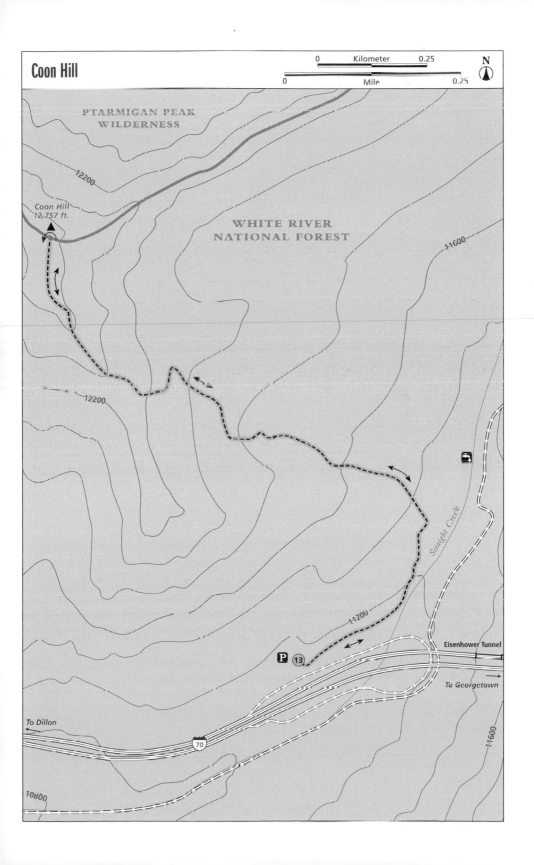

Coon Hill

0   Kilometer   0.25

0   Mile   0.25

N

PTARMIGAN PEAK
WILDERNESS

12200

Coon Hill
12,757 ft.

WHITE RIVER
NATIONAL FOREST

11600

12200

Straight Creek

11200

P (13)

Eisenhower Tunnel

To Georgetown

To Dillon

70

11600

10800

Looking southwest to Coon Hill from the Golden Bear–Coon Hill saddle, the southeast ridge route is in view left of the summit. PHOTO BY SUSAN JOY PAUL

your signal light early so other drivers know you're pulling off. At the rest area, park to the left of the "Trailhead Parking" sign, and stay off the service road and away from the CDOT building.

Miles and Directions

0.0 Begin at the trailhead (11,160') and hike northeast on a faint trail left of the service road.

0.2 Contour north up the drainage, then west up the grass slope.

0.4 From the top of the bench, continue west-northwest up a series of slopes and benches (N39 40.959' / W105 56.065').

0.7 Hike around a huge rock and past a talus slope, then go west up steep slopes and contour northwest toward the ridge. Do not head up to the ridge too early, or you will end up on cliffs (N39 41.053' / W105 56.325').

1.1 Top out on the ridge (12,400') and go north-northwest. Go over one false bump, then upslope to another and the summit just ahead (N39 41.145' / W105 56.646').

1.4 Arrive at ranked 12,763' Coon Hill. There are two markers, and you should tag them both. Return the way you came (N39 41.336' / W105 56.738').

2.8 Arrive back at the trailhead (N39 40.727' / W105 56.274').

14 Silverthorne Local Favorite: Ptarmigan Peak B

Elevation: 12,498' (NAVD88 12,504')
Distinction: Ranked 12er
Class: 1
Difficulty and skill level: Very Strenuous;
Intermediate
Approximate moving time: 7 hours
Distance: 11.8 miles round-trip
Elevation trailhead to summit: 8,927' to
12,504' (+3,577'); about 3,700' round trip
Terrain: Dirt trail, minor creek crossings
Restrictions: Trail closed to bicycles and motor
vehicles; pets must be on leash of maximum 6'
length; follow wilderness regulations

Amenities: Backcountry camping; services in
Silverthorne
Trailhead: Ptarmigan Peak Trailhead
Trail: Ptarmigan Peak Trail #69
Maps: DeLorme Page 38 D2; USGS Dillon
Counties: Grand, Summit
Land status: White River National Forest, (970)
945-2521, www.fs.usda.gov/whiteriver; Dillon
Ranger District, (970) 468-5400; Ptarmigan
Peak Wilderness, www.wilderness.net

Finding the trailhead: From I-70, about 55 miles west of Denver and 30 miles east of Vail,
take exit 205 (Dillon/Silverthorne) onto CO 9. Drive north for 0.5 mile and turn right onto Rainbow
Drive, then go 0.2 mile and turn right onto Tanglewood Lane. Continue 0.2 mile and turn right onto
unpaved Ptarmigan Trail, then drive 0.5 mile to the parking area on the right. The trailhead is on
the left side of the road (GPS: N39 38.112' / W106 3.208').

The Peak

The Williams Fork mountain range is L-shaped, and if you imagine it as a long leg with a
foot turned to the right, or east, Coon Hill—the range's highpoint—is situated at the toe,
near the Eisenhower Tunnel, and Ptarmigan Peak sits at the heel, above Silverthorne. It's
not the highest Ptarmigan Peak in the state—an unranked 13er at Weston Pass is higher—
but it is the highest ranked one. Ptarmigan Peak is named for the white-tailed grouse, or
ptarmigan, a bird common to Colorado's alpine zone. Ptarmigans may be hard to spot, as
they molt with the seasons in varying tones of gray, to brown, and finally winter-white.
You may not see any birds on Ptarmigan Peak, but you will see many mountains. From
the top of the peak, the Williams Fork Mountains continue north over ranked Point
12358, Ute Peak, Prairie Mountain, Williams Benchmark, Williams Peak, Points 11204
and 10881, and unranked 10er Copper Mountain; and east over ranked Points 12429
and 12346 and Coon Hill. To the west, the Gore Range lines the sky, and to the east the
Continental Divide provides a steady stream of 13,000' and 14,000' Front Range peaks.

The Climb

Ptarmigan Peak is accessible year-round, with southern access and a good trail all the
way up. Point 12358 and Ute Peak can be added to the hike, north on the Ute Peak

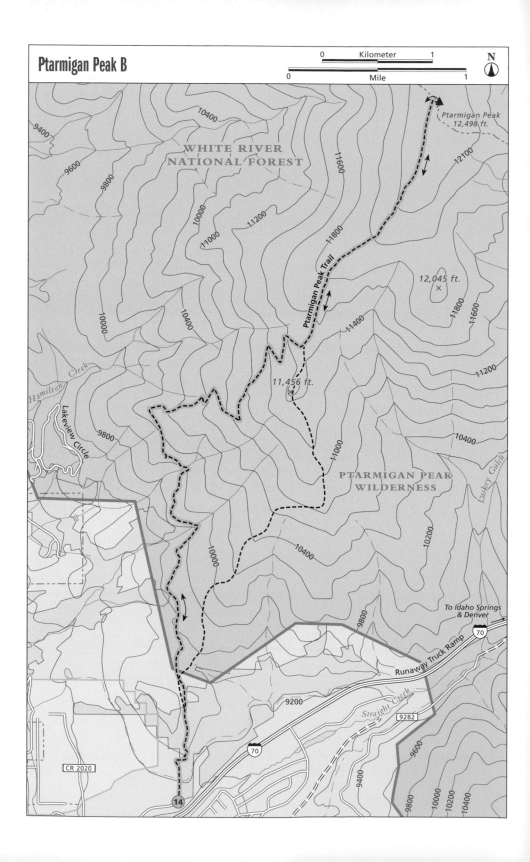

Ptarmigan Peak B

0 — Kilometer — 1

0 — Mile — 1

N

10400

9400

9600

9800

WHITE RIVER
NATIONAL FOREST

11600

10000

11000

11200

11800

12100

Ptarmigan Peak
12,498 ft.

Ptarmigan Peak Trail

12,045 ft.
×

11800

11600

11400

Hamilton Creek

Lakeview Circle

9800

11,456 ft.

11000

11200

10400

10000

10400

PTARMIGAN PEAK
WILDERNESS

Laskey Gulch

10400

10000

10200

9800

To Idaho Springs
& Denver

70

Runaway Truck Ramp

9200

Straight Creek

9282

70

9400

9600

9800

10000

10200

10400

CR 2020

14

A beautiful trail leads north above Lake Dillon to Ptarmigan Peak, in the Williams Fork Mountains near Silverthorne. PHOTO BY SUSAN JOY PAUL

Trail which continues to Ute Pass. Williams Fork Mountains east of Ptarmigan Peak may be climbed with a descent to Ptarmigan Pass on the Ptarmigan Pass Trail, or via more direct routes at Laskey Gulch from the south, the South Park Trail from the north, or from the pullout east, at the Eisenhower Tunnel.

Miles and Directions

0.0 Begin at the 8,927' trailhead. Hike north on the trail and a private road on an easement.

0.2 Rejoin Ptarmigan Peak Trail, on right. The trail climbs the meadow with views of Lake Dillon to the south.

0.6 Pass a large information sign (9,600') and descend into the forest (N39 38.579' / W106 3.172').

1.8 Cross a small creek to your left and contour west and north along the hillside.

1.9 Pass a junction with a trail that switches back left and continue straight (N39 39.472' / W106 3.235').

2.2 Cross another small stream (10,000'), and after another 0.25 mile, you can rest on a log to the left of the trail, with views of the Tenmile Range and Gore Range. Continue north, then northeast up switchbacks through the forest.

4.3 Out of the trees (11,500'), enter the Ptarmigan Peak Wilderness (N39 40.296' / W106 2.437').

4.8 At 11,850' pass the junction with Ptarmigan Pass Trail #35, to the east, and continue northeast over open tundra on the Ptarmigan Peak Trail (N39 40.687' / W106 2.234').

5.9 Turn right to the obvious summit cairn, in view. Ute Peak Trail #24 continues north, but you'll hike east to the top of ranked 12,504' Ptarmigan Peak. Return the way you came (N39 41.453' / W106 1.584').

11.8 Arrive back at the trailhead (N39 38.112' / W106 3.208').

15 Loveland Pass Northeast Peak: Mount Sniktau

Elevation: 13,234' (NAVD88 13,240')
Distinction: Ranked 13er
Class: 2; Class 1 to Point 12915, mixed Class 1 and 2 to summit
Difficulty and skill level: Easy; Beginner
Approximate moving time: 3 hours
Distance: 3.6 miles round-trip
Elevation trailhead to summit: 11,990' to 13,240' (+1,250'); about 1,500' round-trip
Terrain: Dirt trail, talus, and tundra
Restrictions: Trail closed to bicycles and motor vehicles; dogs must be on leash or under voice command

Amenities: Services in Keystone and Georgetown
Trailhead: Loveland Pass Trailhead
Trail: Unofficial "Mount Sniktau Trail," off-trail Southwest Ridge
Maps: DeLorme Page 38 D4; USGS Grays Peak, Loveland Pass
County: Clear Creek
Land status: Arapaho National Forest, (970) 295-6600, www.fs.usda.gov/arp; Clear Creek Ranger District, (303) 567-3000

Finding the trailhead: From I-70, about 40 miles west of Denver and 85 miles east of Vail, take exit 216 onto US 6 West and drive 4.7 miles to the top of Loveland Pass. Parking and the trailhead are located on the left (east) side of the road (GPS: N39 39.817' / W105 52.721').

The Peak

Loveland Pass, at 11,990', is the highest paved mountain pass in the state that's open year-round. Situated on the Continental Divide between Loveland Ski Area and Arapaho Basin, the pass is a busy place in the summer, and even busier in the winter, so come early to get a parking spot. Loveland Pass was named for William A. H. Loveland, president of the Colorado Central Railroad and lieutenant governor of Colorado during the 1800s. "Sniktau" was the pen name of Edwin H. N. Patterson, a journalist and editor of the local newspaper, and friend to writer Edgar Allan Poe. Mount Sniktau offers views in all directions. From the summit, looking north and turning clockwise, the following peaks are visible: 12ers Mount Bethel and Woods Mountain, and 13ers Mount Parnassus and Bard Peak; 13er Kelso Mountain and 14er Torreys Peak to the east and southeast, respectively; 13ers Grizzly Peak and "Cupid" to the south; unnamed 12ers on the other side of the pass, and 12ers of the Williams Fork Mountains to the west; and 13ers "Golden Bear Peak," Hagar Mountain, and "The Citadel" to the northwest. Beyond these peaks, many more summits border the horizon, with the Front Range to the east; Sawatch, Tenmile and Mosquito Ranges to the south; and Gore Range to the west.

The Climb

Mount Sniktau is climbed year-round, with a high ridge that's subject to lightning in the summer, on a pass that's notorious for high winds in winter. Still the peak and

Mount Sniktau, "Cupid" and Grizzly Peak

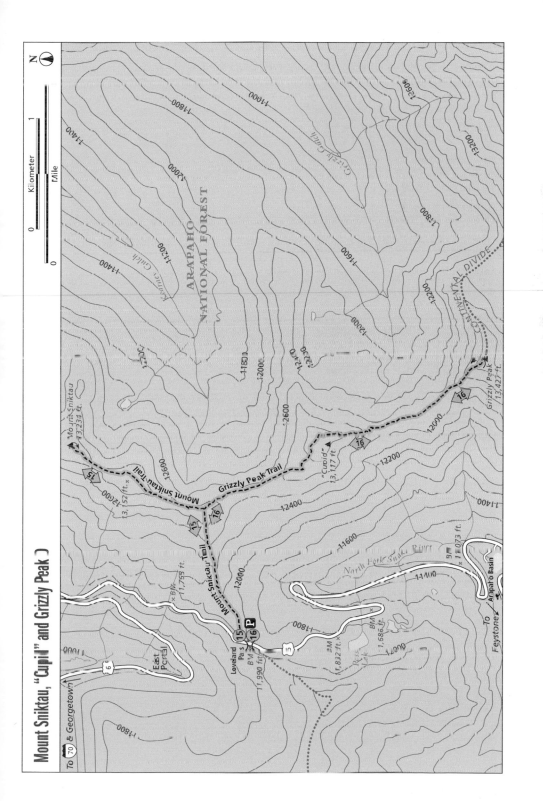

Mount Sniktau is a ranked 13er with year-round access and low avalanche danger along the southwest ridge. PHOTO BY SUSAN JOY PAUL

the route—visible from the trailhead—present an easy ranked 13er, barring weather events. Mount Sniktau can be combined with ranked 13ers "Cupid" and Grizzly Peak by retreating to Point 12915 and continuing south along the ridge. That hike is described in the next climb.

Miles and Directions

0.0 Begin at the trailhead (11,990'), marked by a wooden post on the east side of the road, and hike east-northeast up the trail to a highpoint on the ridge.

0.8 At unranked Point 12915, the summit of Mount Sniktau is hidden from view. Turn left (north) and hike to the next unnamed point (N39 40.037' / W105 51.875').

1.4 From unranked Point 13152, continue north-northeast, dropping to the saddle and then climbing Mount Sniktau's easy southwest ridge. Stay clear of the sheer east face and cornices that can give way (N39 40.424' / W105 51.637').

1.8 Arrive at ranked 13,240' Mount Sniktau. Return the way you came (N39 40.700' / W105 51.454').

3.6 Arrive back at the trailhead (N39 39.817' / W105 52.721').

16 Loveland Pass Southeast Peaks: "Cupid" and Grizzly Peak D

See map on page 73.

Elevations: 13,427' (NAVD88 13,433') Grizzly Peak; 13,117' (NAVD88 13,123') "Cupid"

Distinction: Ranked 13ers (both peaks)

Class: 2; Class 1 to Point 12915, mixed Class 1 and 2 to summits

Difficulty and skill level: Strenuous; Intermediate

Approximate moving time: 5 hours

Distance: 5.8 miles round-trip

Elevation trailhead to summit: 11,990' to 13,433' (+1,443'); about 3,000' round-trip

Terrain: Dirt trail, rocks, and talus

Restrictions: Trail closed to bicycles and motor vehicles; dogs must be on leash or under voice command

Amenities: Services in Keystone and Georgetown

Trailhead: Loveland Pass Trailhead

Trails: Unofficial "Mount Sniktau Trail" and "Grizzly Peak Trail," off-trail Northwest Ridge

Maps: DeLorme Page 38 D4; USGS Grays Peak, Loveland Pass

Counties: Clear Creek, Summit

Land status: Arapaho National Forest, (970) 205 6600, www.fs.usda.gov/arp; Clear Creek Ranger District, (303) 567-3000

Finding the trailhead: From I-70, about 40 miles west of Denver and 85 miles east of Vail, take exit 216 onto US 6 West and drive 4.7 miles to the top of Loveland Pass. Parking and the trailhead are located on the left (east) side of the road (GPS: N39 39.817' / W105 52.721').

The Peaks

Grizzly Peak and "Cupid" lie on the Continental Divide at Loveland Pass. The origination of the name Cupid is not known, but the peak makes for an easy summit on Valentine's Day, provided the road is open and the winds don't blow you off the ridge. Grizzly Peak is named for the bears that once roamed the state, now gone. There are five "Grizzly Peaks" in Colorado, all ranked 13ers, and while this one is not the highest, it affords some of the best views. 14ers Torreys Peak and Grays Peak are particularly prominent to the east.

The Climb

"Cupid," Grizzly Peak, and most of the route are visible from the trailhead. There are a lot of bumps along the ridge to get up and over or around, making for a tougher and longer day out than you might anticipate. Stay clear of the edges and cornices, as a slip off the ridge will send you careening more than a thousand feet down into Grizzly Gulch to the east or Arapaho Basin to the west. In snow, microspikes for your feet and an ice axe in your hand are required gear for the north side of Grizzly. Climbers may continue east from Grizzly, for an alternate route to 14ers Torreys Peak and Grays Peak. If you want to add another, easier peak, return to Point 12915 and

Ranked 13ers "Cupid" and Grizzly Peak ride the Continental Divide at Loveland Pass.
PHOTO BY SUSAN JOY PAUL

go north to Mount Sniktau for a 13er trifecta. This will add 2.8 miles and 600' of elevation to your day, for a total of three ranked peaks in 8.6 miles and about 3,600' of elevation gain.

Miles and Directions

0.0 Begin at the trailhead (11,990'), marked by a wooden post on the east side of the road, and hike east to an obvious highpoint on the ridge.

0.8 At unranked Point 12915, turn right (south-southeast) and descend about 200', then hike up to the next point (N39 40.037' / W105 51.875').

1.1 From unranked Point 12714, the trail curves left and climbs 400' to the southeast (N39 39.803' / W105 51.738').

1.7 Arrive at ranked 13,123' "Cupid." Descend the south side of the peak. The ridge narrows dramatically to the next point, approached from the left (N39 39.468' / W105 51.395').

2.1 From unranked Point 12756, the rest of the route is in view. Continue south-southeast to the next unnamed summit (N39 39.184' / W105 51.360').

2.4 At unranked Point 12936, head southeast up the final, steep slope (N39 38.950' / W105 51.248').

2.9 Arrive at ranked 13,433' Grizzly Peak. The summit is the first highpoint you reach and is marked with a rock cairn. Return the way you came (N39 38.653' / W105 50.903').

5.8 Arrive back at the trailhead (N39 39.817' / W105 52.721').

17 Front Range Highpoint: Grays Peak

Elevation: 14,270' (NAVD88 14,276')
Distinctions: Front Range Highpoint, Clear Creek County Highpoint, Summit County Highpoint, Centennial, Prominence 100, P2K, Ranked 14er
Class: 1
Difficulty and skill level: Strenuous; Advanced
Approximate moving time: 5 hours
Distance: 7.2 miles round-trip
Elevation trailhead to summit: 11,200' to 14,276' (+3,076')
Terrain: Dirt, talus, and tundra trail
Recommended extra gear: Crampons or microspikes and ice axe if snow exists

Restrictions: Stevens Gulch Road is impassable by vehicle in winter through late spring, high clearance 4WD vehicle is recommended other seasons; trail closed to bicycles and motor vehicles; dogs must be on leash
Amenities: Trailhead toilets; backcountry camping; services in Georgetown
Trailhead: Grays Peak Trailhead
Trail: Grays Peak National Recreation Trail #54
Maps: DeLorme Page 38 D4; USGS Grays Peak
Counties: Summit, Clear Creek
Land status: Arapaho National Forest, (970) 295-6600, www.fs.usda.gov/arp; Clear Creek Ranger District, (303) 567-3000

Finding the trailhead: From Denver, take I-70 West for about 40 miles, then take exit 221 toward Bakerville. Drive 0.2 mile and turn left onto East Bakerville Road / Stevens Gulch Road, which becomes unpaved CR 321 / Stevens Gulch Road. Continue 3.1 miles to the trailhead (GPS: N39 39.645' / W105 47.082').

The Peak

Grays Peak and nearby Torreys Peak lie west of Denver in the Front Range, and are the only 14,000' peaks in Colorado with summits on the Continental Divide. Like many of the state's highest peaks, the mountains rise along the Mineral Belt, an ore-rich area trending from the La Plata Mountains of the San Juans, northeast to the Front Range at Boulder. The Mineral Belt defined the state's 19th-century mining boom, drove the development of the railroad system, and is responsible for many of the current roads and trails to Colorado's mountains. Grays Peak and Torreys Peak were climbed in 1861 by Charles C. Parry, a surgeon and mountaineer who studied botany under Asa Gray and John Torrey, for whom he named the peaks. Parry is credited with being the first to determine the elevations of many of Colorado's mountains by barometric measurement. From the top of Grays Peak, you'll have views of the Front Range as far south as Pikes Peak at Colorado Springs, and north to Longs Peak in Rocky Mountain National Park. The Gores, Tenmiles, and Mosquitos are also in view, along with the northern tip of the Sawatch, west.

The Climb

Grays Peak is best climbed in summer and fall, due to a road that's impassable by car under snow, adding miles to your hike. Extreme avalanche danger also exists

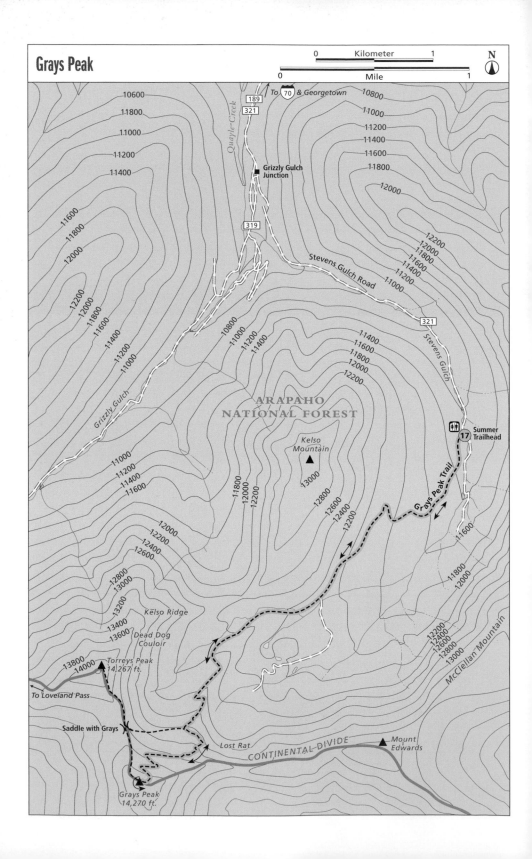

Grays Peak

0   Kilometer   1

0   Mile   1

N

10600

11800

To 70 & Georgetown

189
321

10800

11000

11000

11200

11400

11200

11600

11400

Grizzly Gulch Junction

11800

Quayle Creek

12000

319

11600

11800

Stevens Gulch Road

12200

12000

12000

11800

11600

11400

11000

12200

11200

Grizzly Gulch

10800

11000

11200

11400

321

Stevens Gulch

11400

11600

11800

12000

12200

ARAPAHO
NATIONAL FOREST

Summer
Trailhead

17

Kelso
Mountain

11000

11200

11400

11600

13000

11800

12000

12200

12800

12600

12400

12200

Grays Peak Trail

11600

11800

12000

12000

12200

12400

12600

12800

13000

13200

Kelso Ridge

13400

13600

Dead Dog
Couloir

12200

12600

12800

13000

McClellan Mountain

13800

14000

Torreys Peak
14,267 ft.

To Loveland Pass

Saddle with Grays

Lost Rat

Mount
Edwards

CONTINENTAL DIVIDE

Grays Peak
14,270 ft.

Grays Peak tops the Front Range and the Continental Divide in Colorado.
PHOTO BY BILL MIDDLEBROOK

on the road and on the trail. If you go in winter or spring, keep a wide berth below Kelso Mountain, to the west (right) of the road and trail, which slides often and has taken lives. In summer, a midweek climb is recommended to ensure a parking spot and primitive campsite at the popular trailhead. Weather and time permitting, you can add Torreys Peak by departing Grays to the north on a steep, rocky trail that descends to the 13,700' saddle in about 0.4 mile, then gains about 570' in 0.4 mile on a loose path to the summit. Descend back to the saddle and locate the trail back to Grays Peak National Recreation Trail for your hike out. This will add about a mile and a couple of hours to your day. In consolidated snow, Grays Peak may be climbed via Lost Rat Couloir on the north side of the peak. You may also climb the peak by summiting Torreys Peak first, accessed from either Loveland Pass, the Grays–Torreys saddle, or via Class 3 Kelso Ridge. Research the weather and snow conditions before attempting any of these routes.

Miles and Directions

0.0 Begin at the trailhead (11,200'), cross the footbridge over Quayle Creek, and hike south-southwest into Stevens Gulch, with unranked 13er McClellan Mountain to your left (east) and ranked 13er Kelso Mountain to your right. Grays and Torreys are quickly in sight, and after 1.5 miles pass an information sign at about 12,100'. The trail levels out, then curves left (east) around a ridge, and gains the ridge at about 12,600'.

2.8 At about 13,270', bear left (southeast) at the split for Grays Peak and the Grays-Torreys saddle, and continue on dirt, scree, and talus to the summit (N39 38.272' / W105 48.795').

3.6 Arrive at ranked 14,276' Grays Peak. Return the way you came (N39 38.028' / W105 49.050').

7.2 Arrive back at the trailhead (N39 39.645' / W105 47.082').

18　Guanella Pass Peak: Square Top Mountain

Elevation: 13,794' (NAVD88 13,800')
Distinctions: Bicentennial, Ranked 13er
Class: 2; Class 1 for first 2.1 miles, Class 2 to summit
Difficulty and skill level: Moderate; Intermediate
Approximate moving time: 4 hours
Distance: 6.8 miles round-trip
Elevation trailhead to summit: 11,720' to 13,800' (+2,080'); about 2,400' round-trip
Terrain: Dirt trail, grass, tundra, and talus; minor creek crossing
Restrictions: Guanella Pass is open year-round but may be impassable under snow; no bicycles or motor vehicles allowed on trail; dogs must be on leash
Amenities: Trailhead toilet; backcountry camping; seasonal campgrounds along Guanella Pass Road; services in Grant and Georgetown
Trailhead: Guanella Pass Trailhead
Trail: South Park Trail #600, off-trail East Ridge
Maps: Page 38 E4, Page 39 E5; USGS Montezuma, Mount Evans
County: Clear Creek
Land status: Pike National Forest, (719) 553-1400, www.fs.usda.gov/psicc; South Park Ranger District, (719) 836-2031

Finding the trailhead: From Fairplay, take US 285 North for 27.8 miles, turn left at Grant onto CR 62 / Guanella Pass Road, and drive 12.9 miles to Guanella Pass, then turn left and go 0.2 mile to park in the upper parking area. Or, from I-70 about 33 miles west of Denver, take exit 228 towards Georgetown and follow signs onto CR 381 for about 12.1 miles to Guanella Pass, then turn right and go 0.2 mile to park at the upper parking area on the west side of the pass. The trailhead is located at the west end of the lot near the vault toilet (GPS: N39 35.830' / W105 42.778').

The Peak

Guanella Pass rises to 11,669' on the Guanella Pass Scenic and Historic Byway. The route was developed in the 1800s as a wagon road in Colorado's mineral belt, connecting mining towns Georgetown and Grant, and the pass is named for Byron Guanella, a Clear Creek County commissioner and road superintendent who planned the permanent route over the pass in the 1950s. Guanella Pass is a popular trailhead in Colorado, with approaches to a lot of peaks, including ranked 14ers Mount Evans and Mount Bierstadt. Square Top Mountain lies west of the pass, its angular profile and long flat ridge to the summit giving it a squared-off appearance. The spacious summit affords views of the Mount Evans Wilderness to the east, including the Sawtooth, a jagged ridge connecting Mounts Evans and Bierstadt. To the north, ranked 13er Mount Wilcox rises above Silver Dollar Lake, and west, the Continental Divide stretches north to south in an array of high peaks, including 14ers Torreys Peak and Grays Peak, ranked 13ers Mount Edwards and Argentine Peak, ranked 12ers Decatur Mountain and Revenue Mountain, and ranked 13ers Santa Fe Peak, Geneva Peak, Whale Peak, and Mount Guyot.

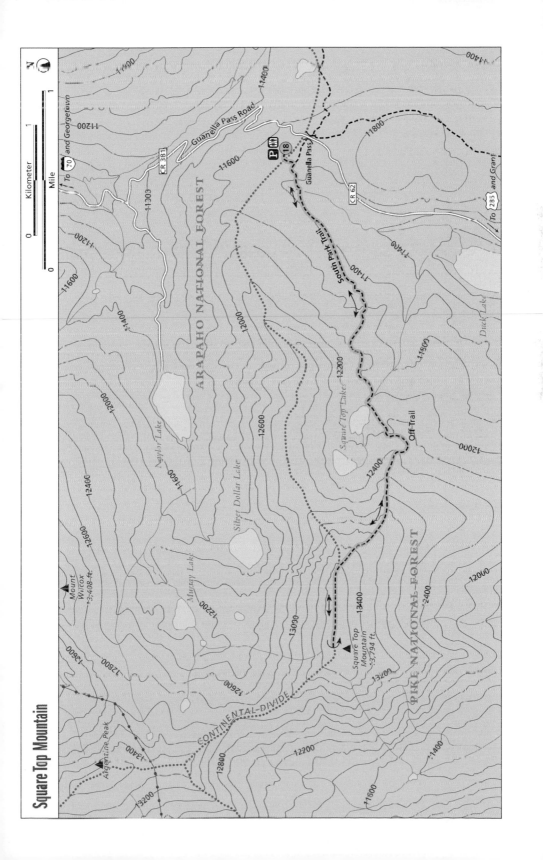

Square Top Mountain

To 70 and Georgetown

CR 381

Guanella Pass Road

ARAPAHO NATIONAL FOREST

P 18

Guanella Pass

CR 62

To 283 and Grant

South Park Trail

Duck Lake

Naylor Lake

Silver Dollar Lake

Square Top Lakes

Off-Trail

Murray Lake

Mount Wilcox
13,408 ft.

PIKE NATIONAL FOREST

Square Top Mountain
13,794 ft.

Argentine Peak

CONTINENTAL DIVIDE

N

Kilometer

Mile

Square Top Mountain rises west of Guanella Pass in the Pike National Forest.
PHOTO BY SUSAN JOY PAUL

The Climb

There are three popular trails at the top of the pass. The Rosalie Trail goes south into the Pike National Forest, and the Bierstadt Trail heads east into the Arapaho National Forest and Mount Evans Wilderness. Park at the upper parking area on the northwest side of the pass, and locate the South Park / Square Top Lakes Trail for this hike.

Miles and Directions

0.0 Begin at the trailhead (11,720') and hike southwest. Turn right (the trail continues straight to an overlook) and descend west-southwest over footbridges above the marshes and willows, and hike up to a saddle, where the peak is in view. Descend and cross the creek between Square Top Lakes and Duck Lake, then head up to another rise and past lower Square Top Lake.

2.0 Turn left at the sign for Square Top Lakes (12,200') and continue south on the fainter South Park Trail (N39 35.335' / W105 44.495').

2.1 Turn right at the sign for South Park Trail to leave the trail, and hike northwest up the steep slope. Go over several rocky bumps and continue west-northwest upslope toward the east ridge of Square Top Mountain (N39 35.231' / W105 44.545').

3.0 Gain the ridge (13,650') and go west on talus and tundra, over and around several false bumps (N39 35.583' / W105 45.350').

3.4 Arrive at ranked 13,800' Square Top Mountain. Return the way you came (N39 35.597' / W105 45.795').

6.8 Arrive back at the trailhead (N39 35.830' / W105 42.778').

19 Georgia Pass Peak: Mount Guyot

Elevation: 13,370' (NAVD88 13,376')
Distinctions: Prominence 300, P1K,
Ranked 13er
Class: 2+; Class 1 for first 0.5 mile, Class 2+
to summit
Difficulty and skill level: Moderate;
Intermediate
Approximate moving time: 4 hours
Distance: 2.5 miles round-trip
Elevation trailhead to summit: 11,598' to
13,376' (+1,778')
Terrain: Dirt trail, grass, tundra, and talus
Restrictions: Summer route; high-clearance
4WD vehicle is highly recommended; road may
not be passable in winter

Amenities: Backcountry camping; seasonal
camping at nearby Michigan Creek Camp-
ground; services in Jefferson and Fairplay
Trailhead: Georgia Pass
Trail: Unnamed miner's trail, off trail
East Ridge
Maps: DeLorme Page 48 A3; USGS
Boreas Pass
Counties: Park, Summit
Land status: Pike National Forest, (719)
553-1400, www.fs.usda.gov/psicc; South Park
Ranger District, (719) 836-2031

Finding the trailhead: From Jefferson, located 16 miles north of Fairplay and 12 miles south of Grant on US 285, turn west onto CR 35. Drive 3.6 miles and bear left onto unpaved CR 54 (Michigan Creek Road). Drive 2.5 miles, entering the Pike National Forest, and turn left toward Georgia Pass and Michigan Creek Campground. Continue 6.8 miles to Georgia Pass and the trailhead (GPS: N39 27.469' / W105 55.000').

The Peak

Mount Guyot sits on the Continental Divide at 11,598' Georgia Pass, the first pass you cross on the Divide hiking the Colorado Trail from Denver. Although topographically part of the Front Range, Mount Guyot's geologic evolution occurred much later, during volcanic activity that produced an igneous intrusion. Great blocks of tumbled granite rest uneasily atop one another along its slopes and make for a tedious, uneven climb. Mount Guyot (pronounced "GEE oh") was named for geologist, geographer, author, and college professor Arnold Henry Guyot (1807–1884), whose work in meteorology led to the founding of the US Weather Bureau. Climbing the peak is a Rocky Mountain high that offers a visual panorama of peaks. To the north, the Williams Fork Mountains and peaks of the Front Range at Loveland Pass and Guanella Pass appear; to the south, the peaks of Boreas Pass and Hoosier Pass stand tall; and to the east, the Tarryalls, Kenosha Mountains, and Platte River Mountains at Kenosha Pass roll along. At the summit of Mount Guyot, the peaks to the west are in view, with 13er Bald Mountain front and center at Boreas Pass, and the Gore, Tenmile, and Mosquito Ranges lined up, north to south, with the Sawatch Range beyond.

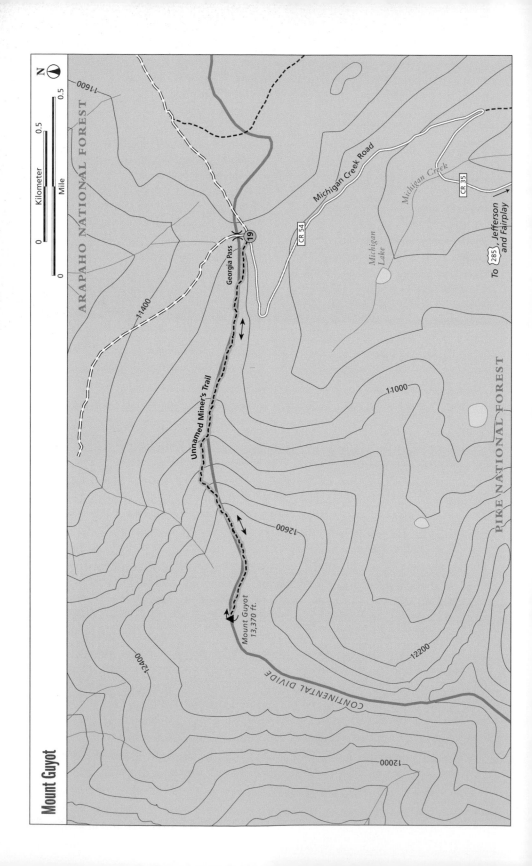

Mount Guyot

ARAPAHO NATIONAL FOREST

PIKE NATIONAL FOREST

CONTIENENTAL DIVIDE

Georgia Pass

Unnamed Miner's Trail

Mount Guyot
13,370 ft.

Michigan Creek Road

CR 54

CR 35

Michigan Creek

Michigan Lake

To 285 Jefferson
and Fairplay

19

11600

11400

12400

12000

12600

12200

11000

N

Kilometer
0   0.5

Mile
0   0.5

From the top of Mount Guyot, the high peaks at Boreas Pass, including Bald Mountain, appear over French Gulch, to the west. PHOTO BY SUSAN JOY PAUL

The Climb

Mount Guyot from Georgia Pass is a summer route and should not be attempted under snow. The danger appears just below the summit, where the ridge narrows, rises abruptly, and takes a sudden turn to the northwest. This final section forces you onto a steep snow slab over a sheer and rocky north face, where a slip would likely be fatal. Unfortunately, this final section is not obvious until you are nearly at the top, with the summit cairn in view. The steep, loose jumble of rocks that make up the east ridge of Mount Guyot provide plenty of excitement and challenges on the driest of sunny summer days. If you prefer to do the peak in snow, a winter route exists from a northwest side, at Breckenridge.

Miles and Directions

0.0 Begin at the trailhead (11,598') and hike west on an unsigned use trail.

0.5 At the end of the trail, cross a broad, flat area and hike up the grassy slopes and through a short section of krummholz (N39 27.540' / W105 55.464').

0.6 Gain a bench at the top of the slope (11,950') and begin the steep ascent on loose talus. Angle up toward the ridge crest as the north slopes steepen, and follow a line along the north side of the ridge (N39 27.575' / W105 55.641').

1.2 Gain the ridge proper and continue west-northwest to the summit area (N39 27.479' / W105 56.109').

1.3 Arrive at ranked 13,376' Mount Guyot. Return the way you came (N39 27.516' / W105 56.263').

2.5 Arrive back at the trailhead (N39 27.469' / W105 55.000').

20 Boreas Pass Peak: Bald Mountain

Elevation: 13,684' (NAVD88 13,690')

Distinctions: Bicentennial, Prominence 100, P2K, Ranked 13er

Class: 2+; Class 1 to Black Powder Pass, mixed Class 2 and 2+ to summit

Difficulty and skill level: Strenuous; Intermediate

Approximate moving time: 5 hours

Distance: 6.0 miles round-trip

Elevation trailhead to summit: 11,482' to 13,690' (+2,208'); about 2,800' round-trip

Terrain: Dirt, grass, scree, talus, tundra, and boulders

Restrictions: Boreas Pass is closed at winter gates seasonally Nov through mid-June, adding many miles to your climb; no bicycles or motor vehicles allowed on trail

Amenities: Trailhead toilet; backcountry camping; seasonal campgrounds on Boreas Pass Road; services in Fairplay and Breckenridge

Trailhead: Black Powder Pass Trailhead

Trail: Black Powder Pass Trail #9188, off-trail Southeast Ridge

Maps: DeLorme Page 48 A3; USGS Boreas Pass

County: Summit

Land status: White River National Forest, (970) 945-2521, www.fs.usda.gov/whiteriver; Dillon Ranger District, (970) 468-5400

Finding the trailhead: From the intersection of CO 9 and US 285 in Fairplay, take US 285 North for 9.3 miles and turn left (west) onto CR 33 / Boreas Pass Road. Continue 11 miles to Boreas Pass, and park on the left side of the road. You will drive through the town of Como, and the road becomes unpaved at 0.9 mile, switches back to the right at 3.8 miles, passes through a winter gate, and becomes increasingly steep, rocky, and exposed for a mile. From Breckenridge, take Boreas Pass Road for 9 miles to Boreas Pass (GPS: N39 24.619' / W105 58.093').

The Peak

Bald Mountain (A) rises north of 11,482' Boreas Pass between Como and Breckenridge. The road over the pass was the route of the Denver, South Park & Pacific Railroad, and an interpretive site details its history. Ken's Cabin is also here, an 1860s section house built on the original wagon road, in current, regular use as a winter ski hut. Boreas Pass is named for the Greek god of the North Wind, and Bald Mountain is so-named for its bare, rocky summit. From the top of the peak, you'll have views of the Williams Fork Mountains north and, clockwise, nearby 13er Mount Guyot to the east, the Front Range and Mosquito peaks at Hoosier Pass, and the Mosquito and Tenmile Ranges to the southwest.

The Climb

Bald Mountain is climbed year-round, with off-season climbs beginning at the winter gates on the standard approach, or from French Gulch to access couloirs on the northeast and southeast. Under snow, give serious consideration to steep slopes that rise and fall along the ridge. This is a great summer climb, but expect slow progress

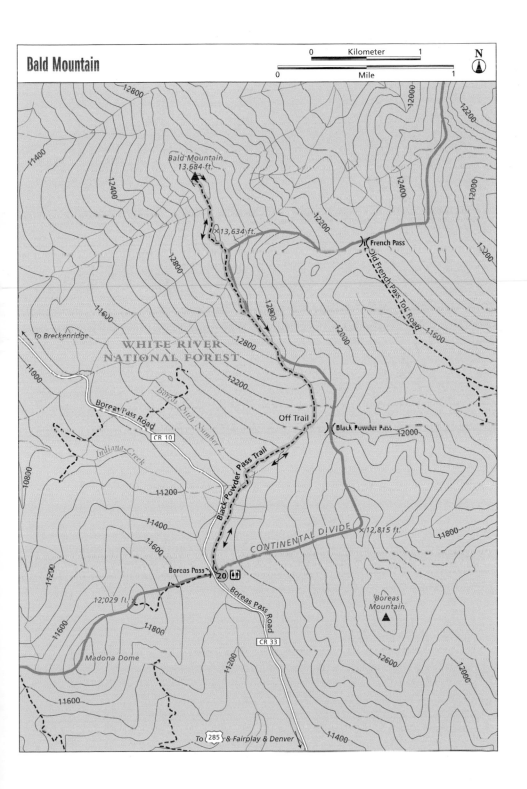

Bald Mountain

0   Kilometer   1

0   Mile   1

N

12800

12000

12200

11400

12400

Bald Mountain
13,684 ft.

12200

12400

12000

X 13,634 ft.

)(French Pass

12800

Old French Pass Toll Road

11600

12000

To Breckenridge

WHITE RIVER
NATIONAL FOREST

12800

12200

Boreas Ditch Number 2

11600

11000

12200

Off Trail

)(Black Powder Pass

12000

Boreas Pass Road

CR 10

Indiana Creek

Black Powder Pass Trail

10800

11200

11400

CONTINENTAL DIVIDE

X 12,815 ft.

11800

11600

Boreas Pass

20

12,029 ft. X

11200

11800

Boreas Pass Road

Boreas
Mountain

Madona Dome

CR 33

12200

12600

12000

11600

11400

To 285 & Fairplay & Denver

Boulders and talus make for slow progress along Bald Mountain's southeast ridge.
PHOTO BY SUSAN JOY PAUL

along the large boulders and loose talus on the ridge. Other peaks located at Boreas Pass include ranked 13ers Boreas Mountain and "Madonna Dome."

Miles and Directions

0.0 Begin at the trailhead (11,482') about 100' from parking on the northeast side of the pass. Follow the trail northeast along Indiana Creek and the Boreas Ditch, toward the Bald-Boreas saddle at Black Powder Pass.

1.2 Depart the trail short of the pass and hike north up the grassy slope, following the drainage toward talus at the base of the mountain's southeast ridge (N39 25.406' / W105 57.435').

1.5 Hike northwest up scree and talus at 12,480', following cairns and a scree trail to the ridge (N39 25.650' / W105 57.507').

1.8 Unranked Point 13679 comes into view to the northeast. Continue northwest on the ridge, across tundra (N39 25.817' / W105 57.707').

2.0 Climb over a series of false summits along the ridge, sticking to the crest or just to the left (west) of the ridge. The rest of the route is scree, talus, and boulders, and some of it is loose. Do not drop too far west onto the looser, steeper rock and scree (N39 25.967' / W105 57.868').

3.0 Arrive at ranked 13,690' Bald Mountain. Return the way you came (N39 26.682' / W105 58.232').

6.0 Arrive back at the trailhead (N39 24.619' / W105 58.093').

21　Hoosier Pass East Peak: Hoosier Ridge

Elevation: 13,352' (NAVD88 13,358')

Distinction: Ranked 13er

Class: 2; Class 1 for first 0.5 mile, Class 2 for rest of climb

Difficulty and skill level: Strenuous; Intermediate

Approximate moving time: 6 hours

Distance: 8.8 miles round-trip

Elevation trailhead to summit: 11,542' to 13,358' (+1,816'); about 3,200' round-trip

Terrain: Dirt road and trail, tundra, and talus

Restrictions: Trail closed to bicycles and motor vehicles; dogs must be on leash or under voice command

Amenities: Backcountry camping; services in Alma, Fairplay, and Breckenridge

Trailhead: Hoosier Pass, Bemrose Creek Ski Circus

Trail: White River National Forest Service Road 848, off trail South Ridge

Maps: DeLorme Page 48 B2; USGS Breckenridge, Alma

Counties: Park, Summit

Land status: White River National Forest, (970) 945-2521, www.fs.usda.gov/whiteriver; Dillon Ranger District, (970) 468-5400; Pike National Forest, (719) 553-1400, www.fs.usda.gov/psicc; South Park Ranger District, (719) 836-2031

Finding the trailhead: Take CO 9 to the top of Hoosier Pass, located about 10 miles south of Breckenridge and 11 miles north of Fairplay. The parking lot is located on the west side of the highway, and the trailhead is on the east side. Carefully cross the highway to the trailhead (GPS: N39 21.681' / W106 3.753').

The Peak

Hoosier Ridge is a long, undulating ridge located east of 11,541' Hoosier Pass, on the Continental Divide. The pass divides the Front Range to the east, the Mosquito Range to the southwest, and the Tenmile Range to the northwest. The pass and the ridge were named by 19th-century gold prospectors from Indiana, the "Hoosier State." Peaks in view along your hike include Tenmile Range highpoint Quandary Peak to the northwest, Mosquito Range highpoint Mount Lincoln to the southwest, and ranked 13er Mount Silverheels to the south. From the summit, the high peaks of Boreas Pass appear to the northeast, while to the southeast, across South Park, the southern Front Range, including 14er Pikes Peak, are in view on the horizon.

The Climb

Hoosier Pass provides year-round access to several ranked 13ers. Most of the route to Hoosier Ridge is above treeline, subjecting you to the elements, which may quickly fluctuate from pleasant, to uncomfortable, to severe and dangerous. Avalanche danger is generally low, making this a go-to peak for winter mountaineers. From the summit, ranked 13,229' Red Mountain is located 0.75 mile northwest, and unranked 13er

Hoosier Ridge

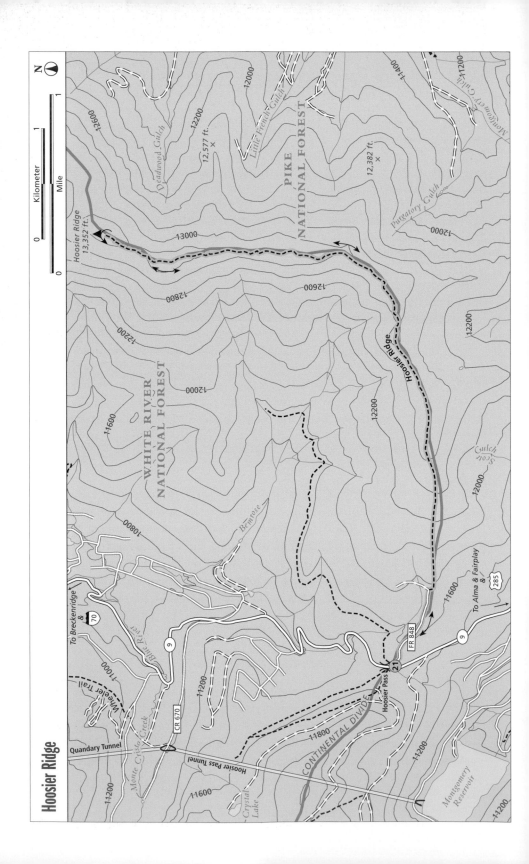

N

Kilometer

0   1

0   1
Mile

Hoosier Ridge
13,352 ft.

12600

12200

13000

12800

12200

WHITE RIVER
NATIONAL FOREST

12000

11600

10800

Benrose

Deadwood Gulch

12200

12000

12,577 ft.
×

Little French Gulch

PIKE
NATIONAL FOREST

12,382 ft.
×

Purgatory Gulch

12000

11400

Montgomery Gulch

11200

12600

Hoosier Ridge

12200

Scott Gulch

12000

12200

11600

FR 848

9

To Alma & Fairplay

285

21

Hoosier Pass

CONTINENTAL DIVIDE

11800

11200

11200

Montgomery
Reservoir

11600

Crystal
Lake

Hoosier Pass Tunnel

Quandary Tunnel

Monte Cristo Creek

Blue River

CR 670

11200

11000

Wheeler Trail

To Breckenridge
&

70

9

11600

11200

The undulating ridge and multiple sub-summits add a lot of elevation loss and regain to your Hoosier Ridge climb PHOTO BY SUSAN JOY PAUL

Red Peak lies 0.75 mile northeast. You can add them both if conditions permit, but Red Mountain is prone to avalanche danger on the southeast slopes, directly in your path to the summit.

Miles and Directions

0.0 From the east side of the pass (11,542'), hike past the gate and up the dirt road, and past the information sign. Continue east on the road for half a mile, where it curves north.

0.5 Depart the road and go east, up a short rise and onto a use trail. Hike through the forest and into an open area, then up the slope toward a highpoint (N39 21.510' / W106 3.245').

1.5 Arrive at the first of many cairned points on the ridge. Continue hiking along the ridge as it bends northeast, across unranked Point 12814 and up to the next point (N39 21.509' / W106 2.166').

2.4 At unranked Point 12953, hike northeast on the ridge (N39 21.730' / W106 1.281').

2.7 Arrive at the next point and go north on the ridge (N39 21.930' / W106 1.053').

3.0 Hike up a steep talus slope to unranked Point 13201. Descend the steep talus slope on the other side. The highpoint of Hoosier Ridge is beyond the bumps ahead, tucked away to the right (northeast). Continue to follow the ridge, north, over more bumps (N39 22.172' / W106 1.045').

4.1 Climb the final unranked rise directly to the north. This may also be skirted on the right (east) side. Descend the other side, cross the saddle, and hike northeast up the talus slope.

4.4 Arrive at ranked 13,358' Hoosier Ridge. Return the way you came (N39 23.148' / W106 0.921').

8.8 Arrive back at the trailhead (N39 21.681' / W106 3.753').

22 Kenosha Pass Peak: North Twin Cone Peak

Elevation: 12,323' (NAVD88 12,328')
Distinction: Ranked 12er
Class: 1
Difficulty and skill level: Easy; Beginner
Approximate moving time: 2 hours
Distance: 3.6 miles round-trip
Elevation trailhead to summit: 11,100' to 12,328' (+1,228')
Terrain: Dirt road
Restrictions: Kenosha Pass is open year-round, with access to trailhead limited in winter; high-clearance 4WD vehicle is recommended all year

Amenities: Toilets, seasonal camping, and picnic area at Kenosha Pass Campground; backcountry camping; services in Fairplay and Bailey
Trailhead: FR 126, east of Kenosha Pass
Trail: FR 126
Maps: DeLorme Page 49 A5; USGS Mount Logan
County: Park
Land status: Pike National Forest, (719) 553-1400, www.fs.usda.gov/psicc; South Platte Ranger District, (303) 275-5610

Finding the trailhead: From Denver, take US 285 South for 37 miles to Bailey, then continue another 32.3 miles and turn left onto unpaved CR 845, signed for Pike National Forest, Kenosha Pass, and the Colorado Trail. If traveling from Fairplay, go 20.3 miles north on US 285, through Jefferson, and turn right onto CR 845. Go 0.3 mile, past the Kenosha Pass (Colorado Trail) East Trailhead, toilets, and Kenosha Pass (East) Campground, and turn right onto FR 126. The trailhead is 5.5 miles from this point, and the road gets increasingly rougher. Pass through a gate and enter private property at 0.8 mile, pass through a second gate to enter the national forest at 2.1 miles, pass an Adopt-a-Trail sign at 3.3 miles, and reach a yellow Adopt-a-Road sign at 5.5 miles, where there is a pullout on the right side of the road. This is your trailhead, and your hike continues up the road (GPS: N39 24.883' / W105 42.077').

The Peak

Kenosha Pass is named for the city in Wisconsin, derived from the Algonquian word for "pike," or "fish." A railroad once crossed the 10,001' pass, but the area now serves as a base for campers, all-terrain vehicle enthusiasts, and hikers on the Colorado Trail, which crosses here. An interpretive center and a historic section of the Denver, South Park & Pacific Railroad, laid in a meadow by the Forest Service, draws tourists, too. If the road is not passable to the trailhead, park here and enjoy a 14-mile round-trip hike to North Twin Cone Peak. The route is a dirt road, and a communication tower sits at the summit, but views west and north to the Continental Divide and east to Lost Creek Wilderness make for a scenic trip.

The Climb

From North Twin Cone Peak, you can add unranked 12,308' Mount Blaine and ranked 12,345' South Twin Cone Peak—the highpoint of the Platte River Mountains—to your day. To get to these peaks, hike 0.4 mile back down to the North Twin Cone–Blaine

North Twin Cone Peak and South Twin Cone Peak

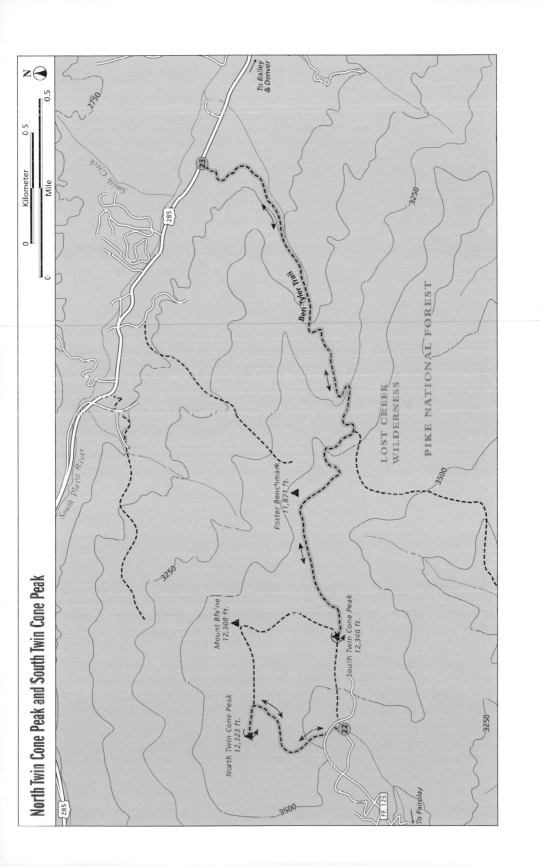

North Twin Cone Peak
12,323 ft.

Mount Blaine
12,308 ft.

South Twin Cone Peak
12,340 ft.

Foster Benchmark
11,871 ft.

Ben Tyler Trail

LOST CREEK
WILDERNESS

PIKE NATIONAL FOREST

South Platte River

Smith Creek

To Bailey
& Denver

To Fairplay

FR 126

285

285

23

22

3250

3250

3250

3500

3500

3250

N

0   .5   Kilometer
0   .5   Mile

A dirt road leads to the top of ranked 12er North Twin Cone Peak in the Pike National Forest.
PHOTO BY SUSAN JOY PAUL

saddle and go off-trail east 0.9 mile to Mount Blaine (N39 25.821' / W105 40.818'), an obvious rock pile with a Class 3 move to the summit. From Mount Blaine, head south for 1.2 miles to South Twin Cone Peak (N39 24.899' / W105 40.933'), and west 1.1 miles back to the trailhead, for a 5-mile loop of all three peaks. The saddle between Mount Blaine and South Twin Cone Peak is marshy, so waterproof boots are a must, but you can pick a game trail through the worst of it. The descent off South Twin Cone Peak is a talus slope; once you are below it, follow the east side of the creek to a crossing near the trailhead. South Twin Cone Peak is in the Lost Creek Wilderness, so abide by wilderness rules. An alternate route is described in the next climb.

Miles and Directions

0.0 Begin at the trailhead (11,100') and hike north up the dirt road.

0.5 Bear to the right on the 4WD road, with views west of the Front Range.

1.4 Cross the North Twin Cone-Blaine saddle with views to Guanella Pass north, and continue west, past a post, and on to the highpoint beyond (N39 25.672' / W105 41.788').

1.8 Arrive at ranked 12,328' North Twin Cone Peak, where a summit marker from 1981 denotes "Twin Cone." Return the way you came (N39 25.706' / W105 42.133').

3.6 Arrive back at the trailhead (N39 24.883' / W105 42.077').

23 Platte River Mountains Highpoint: South Twin Cone Peak

See map on page 93.

Elevations: 12,340' (NAVD88 12,345') South Twin Cone Peak; 11,871' (NAVD88 11,876') Foster Benchmark

Distinctions: Platte River Mountains Highpoint, Ranked 12er (South Twin Cone Peak); Unranked 11er (Foster Benchmark)

Class: 2; Class 1 for first 5.9 miles, Class 2 to summit

Difficulty and skill level: Very Strenuous; Intermediate

Approximate moving time: 8 hours

Distance: 16.0 miles round-trip

Elevations trailhead to summit: 8,260' to 12,345' (+4,085') for South Twin Cone Peak only; adding Foster Benchmark one way is about 4,400' round-trip

Terrain: Dirt trail, talus, boulders, willows, and marshes; creek crossings

Restrictions: Limited parking at the small trailhead; trail closed to bicycles and motorized vehicles; dogs must be on leash; follow wilderness regulations

Amenities: Backcountry camping; seasonal campgrounds along US 285; services in Bailey and Fairplay

Trailhead: Ben Tyler–North Trailhead

Trail: Ben Tyler Trail #606, off-trail East Slopes

Maps: DeLorme Page 49 A5, A6; USGS Shawnee, Mount Logan

County: Park

Land status: Pike National Forest, (719) 553-1400, www.fs.usda.gov/psicc; South Platte Ranger District, (303) 275-5610; Lost Creek Wilderness, www.wilderness.net

Finding the trailhead: From Denver, take US 285 South and travel about 37 miles to Bailey. Continue another 6.8 miles to a pullout on the left side of the road and the trailhead. If traveling from Fairplay, go 32.3 miles north on US 285 to the trailhead, on the right (GPS: N39 26.159' / W105 35.450').

The Peak

The Platte River Mountains are the northernmost of three Front Range subranges in the Lost Creek Wilderness. The range lies south of US 285 and trends southeast, bordered by South Park to the west and the Rampart Range to the east. The Platte River Mountains are named for the river, whose headwaters originate as the North Platte River in North Park and the South Platte River in South Park. Summit views include the Kenosha and Tarryall Mountains to the south and the peaks of Kenosha Pass to the west, with the Continental Divide providing a long line of peaks in sight, from Hoosier Pass northeast to Guanella Pass.

The Climb

The Ben Tyler Trail is a long route, providing other peakbagging opportunities in the nearby Kenosha Mountains, plus unranked Foster Benchmark. To skip Foster

Unranked 11er Foster Benchmark is a short detour on your way to South Twin Cone Peak.
PHOTO BY SUSAN JOY PAUL

Benchmark, you can continue west on the trail, past the cutoff to Foster. As the trail thins out, angle up to the South Twin Cone–Foster saddle and locate a use trail to the east slopes of the peak. From South Twin Cone Peak, a trip north to unranked 12er Mount Blaine, then west to ranked 12er North Twin Cone Peak and back, will add about 6 round-trip miles.

Miles and Directions

0.0 Begin at the trailhead (8,260') and hike east then south on switchbacks.

1.4 Enter Lost Creek Wilderness. The trail eases and trends southwest, through Ben Tyler Gulch (N39 25.572' / W105 35.780').

1.6 Pass a junction and log crossing on the left and stay straight on the trail, then cross a creek at 2 miles.

3.1 Pass a trail marker, and cross the creek again at 3.5 miles. Rising from the trees, the Platte River Mountains appear south (N39 25.160' / W105 37.435').

4.0 Switchback left (east) at 10,550', and follow switchbacks for the next mile.

5.0 At the junction with Craig Park Trail, stay right on the Ben Tyler Trail. Continue west and leave the forest with views of ranked 12er "Kenosha Peak" (N39 24.778' / W105 38.468').

5.9 Reach a large flat area and a post at 11,650', the north end of the Kenosha Mountains. Leave the trail and head northwest upslope to the first summit (N39 24.893' / W105 39.063').

6.4 Arrive at unranked 11,876' Foster Benchmark. Descend the west side and head southwest. Cross marshes and willows, and climb through boulders and over talus to the next summit (N39 25.260' / W105 39.444').

8.0 Arrive at ranked 12,345' South Twin Cone Peak. Return the way you came, or skip Foster Benchmark and drop off the south side of the saddle between the peaks and head straight back to the trail, taking about 0.2 mile off the route (N39 24.899' / W105 40.933').

16.0 Arrive back at the trailhead (N39 26.159' / W105 35.450').

24 Kenosha Mountains Highpoint: "Peak X"

Elevation: 12,429' (NAVD88 12,434')

Distinctions: Kenosha Mountains Highpoint, Prominence 200, P1K, Ranked 12er

Class: 2+; Class 1 for first 0.7 mile, Class 2 and 2+ to summit

Difficulty and skill level: Moderate; Intermediate

Approximate moving time: 3 hours

Distance: 4.4 miles round-trip

Elevation trailhead to summit: 10,078' to 12,434' (+2,356')

Terrain: Dirt trail, bushwhack, and talus; creek crossing

Recommended extra gear: GPS

Restrictions: Road is rough, not maintained in winter, and may require high-clearance 4WD all year; limited parking at trailhead; trail closed to bicycles and motorized vehicles; dogs must be on leash; follow wilderness regulations

Amenities: Backcountry camping; seasonal camping at nearby Lost Park Campground; services in Fairplay and Bailey

Trailhead: Long Gulch Trailhead

Trails: Colorado Trail (Section 4), Hooper Trail, off-trail South Slopes

Maps: DeLorme Page 49 B6; USGS Topaz Mountain

County: Park

Land status: Pike National Forest, (719) 553-1400, www.fs.usda.gov/psicc; South Park Ranger District, (719) 836-2031; Lost Creek Wilderness, www.wilderness.net

Finding the trailhead: From Denver, take US 285 South for about 37 miles to Bailey. Drive another 35.4 miles and turn left onto unpaved CR 56. If traveling from Fairplay, go 17.2 miles north on US 285, through Jefferson, and turn right onto CR 56. Continue 10.8 miles on CR 56, past turnoffs for Tarryall Road on the right and Rock Creek Trailhead and Ben Tyler Trailhead on the left. Bear left onto FR 817, and go 0.1 mile to the trailhead (GPS: N39 20.844' / W105 37.140').

The Peak

"Peak X" in the Kenosha Mountains is the second-highest peak in the Lost Creek Wilderness, just 2' lower than the Tarryall Mountains' Bison Peak. The Kenosha Mountains are wedged between the Platte River Mountains to the north and the Tarryalls to the south. The range and nearby Kenosha Pass were named by a stagecoach driver from Kenosha, Wisconsin. With 36 ranked peaks, the Kenosha Mountains provide the peak-bagger with opportunities for tagging a lot of summits in a short time.

The Climb

This is the most direct route to the top of the Kenosha Mountains, involving a bit of bushwhacking, but it gets you above treeline fast, where you can add more peaks. Soft-ranked, 12,105' "X Prime" (N39 22.452' / W105 37.110') lies less than a mile to the northwest and is a Class 2, off-trail hike. Or you can continue southeast from "Peak X" and take in ranked 12,279' "Peak Y" (N39 21.648' / W105 35.400'); 12,249' "Peak Z" and with a Class 3 boulder on top (N39 21.294' / W105 34.770'); and 12,072' "Zephyr" (N39 20.832' / W105 33.864'). "Peak X" to "Zephyr" is about

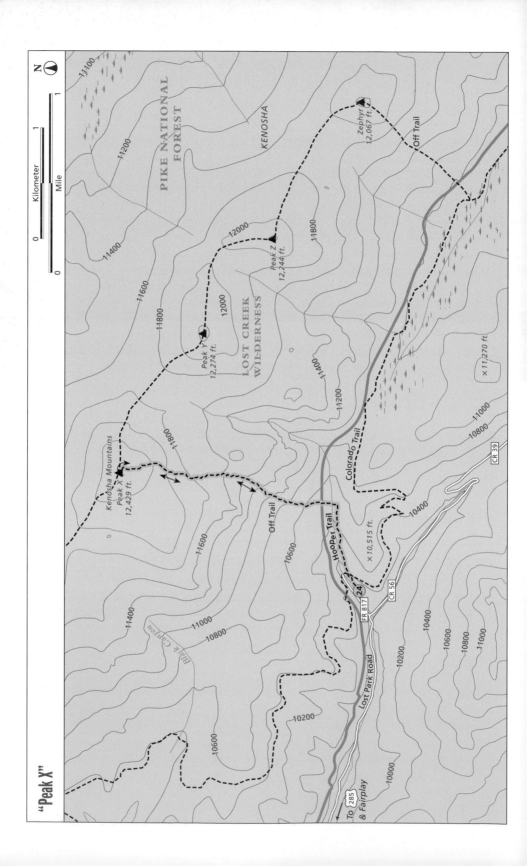

"Peak X"

Kenosha Mountains highpoint "Peak X" is the second-highest mountain in the Lost Creek Wilderness. PHOTO BY SUSAN JOY PAUL

2.9 miles, and from there you can drop southwest for less than a mile to rejoin the Colorado Trail and follow it west for about 3.6 miles back to the trailhead. The entire loop, sans "X Prime," is about 9.5 miles and will add elevation gain to your outing. You will be off-trail most of the day, so route-finding skills and a map and compass, plus a GPS, are a very good idea.

Miles and Directions

0.0 From the trailhead (10,078'), cross a north fork of Rock Creek on wooden planks, then turn left and hike east uphill on the Colorado Trail.

0.2 Leave the Colorado Trail and go right onto unsigned Hooper Trail. This is easy to miss, and if you come to another creek crossing on the Colorado Trail, you have gone too far (N39 20.906' / W105 36.993').

0.6 Depart Hooper Trail on left at about 10,500' and head north, following intermittent trail and bushwhacking steeply uphill and across a creek.

1.9 Reach treeline at about 12,100' and continue north up the south slopes of "Peak X," cross a flat area, and head uphill again, aiming for a small saddle southeast of the summit (N39 21.882' / W105 36.274').

2.1 Ascend north, then west, to the summit.

2.2 Arrive at ranked 12,434' "Peak X." Return the way you came (N39 22.085' / W105 36.312').

4.4 Arrive back at the trailhead (N39 20.844' / W105 37.140').

25 Tarryall Mountains Highpoint: Bison Peak

Elevation: 12,431' (NAVD88 12,436')

Distinctions: Tarryall Mountains Highpoint, Lost Creek Wilderness Highpoint, Prominence 100, P2K, Ranked 12er

Class: 2+; Class 1 to saddle at Bison Arm, Class 2 and 2+ to summit

Difficulty and skill level: Very Strenuous; Intermediate

Approximate moving time: 7 hours

Distance: 11.8 miles round-trip

Elevation trailhead to summit: 8,750' to 12,436' (+3,686'); about 3,900' round-trip

Terrain: Dirt trail, tundra, and boulders; minor creek crossing

Restrictions: Trail closed to bicycles and motor vehicles; dogs must be on leash; follow wilderness regulations

Amenities: Backcountry camping; seasonal campgrounds on CR 77; year-round camping at nearby Tarryall Reservoir; services in Fairplay and Lake George

Trailhead: Ute Creek Trailhead

Trails: Ute Creek Trail #629, Brookside-McCurdy Trail #607, off-trail South Slopes

Maps: DeLorme Page 49 C7, C6, D6; USGS McCurdy Mountain, Farnum Peak

County: Park

Land status: Pike National Forest, (719) 553-1400, www.fs.usda.gov/psicc; South Park Ranger District, (719) 836-2031; Lost Creek Wilderness, www.wilderness.net

Finding the trailhead: From Colorado Springs, take US 24 West and travel 38 miles to Lake George, then turn right onto CR 77 / Tarryall Road (towards Tarryall Reservoir). Drive 20.9 miles to the trailhead on the right side of the road. From Denver, take US 285 South towards Fairplay and travel 51.2 miles to Jefferson, then turn left onto CR 77. Continue 20.6 miles to the trailhead, on left (GPS: N39 11.887' / W105 33.212').

The Peak

Bison Peak is the highpoint of the Tarryall Mountains in the Lost Creek Wilderness. "Lost creek" refers to the creek that appears and disappears here, which has carved the largest granitic rock cave system in the United States, a convoluted, subterranean maze whose uneven terrain and swift waters have claimed the lives of hikers and cavers. The hike to Bison Peak is entirely aboveground, though, and it's the fantastical granite rock piles and towers along the final leg of the route that make this climb so unique. The Tarryall Mountains were named by miners who discovered gold in the area—enough, they believed, for everyone—and so they called the place "tarry-all" or "a place for all to tarry, or stay." Later arrivals believed the early miners may have tarried a bit too long and claimed too much of the land, and the gold. They disdainfully named the nearby town Fairplay. Bison Peak recalls the herds of American bison that once roamed the Lost Creek Wilderness area. Views from the top of the peak include the Mosquito Range to the west, the Kenosha Mountains and Platte River Mountains to the north, and the Front Range beyond. Closer in, ranked 12er McCurdy

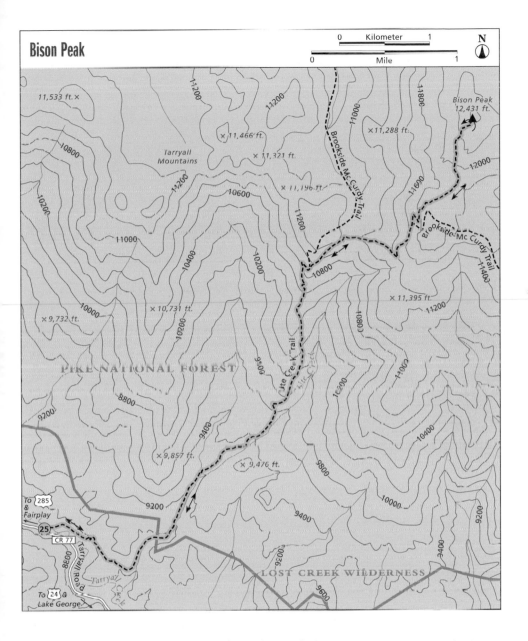

Kilometer

Mile

N

11,533 ft. ×

Bison Peak
12,431 ft.

× 11,288 ft.

Tarryall
Mountains

× 11,466 ft.

× 11,321 ft.

Brookside-McCurdy Trail

× 11,196 ft.

Brookside-McCurdy Trail

× 11,395 ft.

× 10,731 ft.

× 9,732 ft.

Ute Creek Trail

Ute Creek

PIKE NATIONAL FOREST

× 9,857 ft.

× 9,476 ft.

To 285 & Fairplay

25

CR 77

Tarryall Road

LOST CREEK WILDERNESS

Tarryall Creek

To 24 & Lake George

Mountain rises to the southeast with Pikes Peak directly beyond, and unranked 11er Farnum Peak is visible to the southwest.

The Climb

Easy access, miles of trail, and hundreds of rock formations make Lost Creek Wilderness a year-round favorite among hikers, backpackers, peakbaggers, rock climbers, and boulderers. Water sources are limited, though, so plan ahead for an enjoyable day,

Fantastical granite rock piles and towers line the final leg of the route to Bison Peak.
PHOTO BY SUSAN JOY PAUL

weekend, or extended stay in this sprawling, natural playground. As in any wilderness area, leave the place as you found it.

Miles and Directions

0.0   Begin at the trailhead (8,750'), cross the bridge over Tarryall Creek, and hike east through the forest along Ute Creek.

1.2   Enter Lost Creek Wilderness and hike northeast through the aspens.

1.7   Cross Ute Creek and climb switchbacks on the good trail.

4.0   At Bison Pass (11,200'), turn right onto the Brookside-McCurdy Trail. Climb east to timberline and up to the next saddle (N39 13.620' / W105 30.888').

5.0   The trail ends at Bison Arm (11,850'). Go northeast over a rise and around the right side of a large rock formation. Drop down the other side and hike up and through a narrow passage between more rocks. Ascend a steep slope, around boulders to the highest boulder pile, and scramble to the top (N39 13.781' / W105 30.293').

5.9   Arrive at ranked 12,436' Bison Peak. Return the way you came (N39 14.301' / W105 29.870').

11.8 Arrive back at the trailhead (N39 11.887' / W105 33.212').

26 Puma Hills Highpoint: "Puma Peak"

Elevation: 11,570' (NAVD88 11,575')
Distinctions: Puma Hills Highpoint, Promi-
nence 100, P2K, Ranked 11er
Class: 2; Class 1 to Puma-Little Puma saddle,
Class 2 to summit
Difficulty and skill level: Moderate;
Intermediate
Approximate moving time: 5 hours
Distance: 9.0 miles round-trip
Elevation trailhead to summit: 9,740' to
11,575' (+1,835')
Terrain: Dirt road, bushwhack
Restrictions: FR 144 is rough and narrow, and
a high-clearance 4WD vehicle may be required;
avoid the route if wet or muddy

Amenities: Seasonal campgrounds on CR 77;
year-round camping at nearby Tarryall Reser-
voir; backcountry camping; services in Fairplay
and Lake George
Trailhead: Packer Gulch Trailhead
Trail: FR 144 (Packer Gulch Road), off-trail
East Slope
Maps: Page 49 D6; USGS Farnum Peak
County: Park
Land status: Pike National Forest, (719)
553-1400, www.fs.usda.gov/psicc; South Park
Ranger District, (719) 836-2031

Finding the trailhead: From Colorado Springs, take US 24 West and travel 38 miles to
Lake George, then turn right onto CR 77 / Tarryall Road. Drive 24 miles and turn left (towards
Packer Gulch) onto unpaved Turner Gulch Road / CR 23. Or from Denver, take US 285 South
towards Fairplay and travel 51 miles to Jefferson, then turn left onto CR 77 / Tarryall Road
(towards Tarryall Reservoir). Drive 17.5 miles and turn right (towards Packer Gulch) onto
unpaved Turner Gulch Road / CR 23. At Turner Gulch Road, go 1.6 miles and turn left onto FR
144 (Packer Gulch Road). Pass several roads to the right, but stay left to remain on FR 144.
At 3 miles, bear right and continue another 1.2 miles. Park at a pullout on the left side of the
road (GPS: N39 10.619' / W105 35.318').

The Peak

Puma Hills is a 30-mile-long band of low peaks trending northwest to southeast on
either side of Wilkerson Pass, east of South Park. The hills and the peak are named for
the mountain lion, aka cougar, panther, or puma, a wild, carnivorous cat that inhabits
the Colorado backcountry. Attacks on humans are extremely rare, but with thousands
of them roaming the wilderness, it is wise to keep pets and children close at hand
when traveling in puma country. The hills here are all below 12,000' and scenic vistas
are scarce, but you will have some views from "Puma Peak," west across the flat lands
of South Park, over Reinecker Ridge and Red Hill, to the high peaks of the Mosquito Range west of Fairplay.

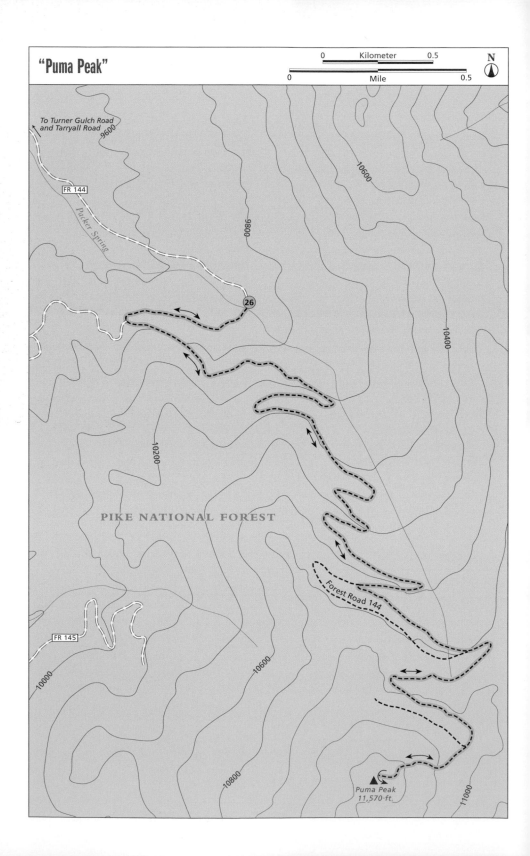

"Puma Peak"

0   Kilometer   0.5

0   Mile   0.5

N

To Turner Gulch Road
and Tarryall Road

9600

FR 144

Packer Spring

26

10600

9800

10400

10200

PIKE NATIONAL FOREST

FR 145

Forest Road 144

10000

10600

10800

11000

Puma Peak
11,570-ft.

Ranked 11er "Puma Peak" tops the Puma Hills flanked by "Little Puma" to the northeast (left) PHOTO BY SUSAN JOY PAUL

The Climb

"Puma Peak" is clearly visible ahead on your slow drive along FR 144—the best view of the peak you'll have all day. If you're a good route-finder and don't mind more bushwhacking, ranked 11ers "Little Puma" and "Burntop" and unranked 11er Farnum Peak may be added to your outing, and many more Puma Hills can be accessed from Wilkerson Pass and from forest roads northwest of the pass.

Miles and Directions

0.0 Begin at the unmarked trailhead at 9,740' and hike west on FR 144.

0.4 Pass the junction with FR 237 and bear left (southeast) to stay on FR 144.

0.5 Pass through the winter gate and continue on the road up many switchbacks.

4.2 At the Puma–Little Puma saddle (11,090'), turn right and bushwhack southwest up the steep slope (N39 9.517' / W105 34.578').

4.5 Arrive at ranked 11,575' "Puma Peak." The eastern summit is the highpoint, and a rock cairn marks the top. Return the way you came (N39 9.429' / W105 34.892').

9.0 Arrive back at the trailhead (N39 10.619' / W105 35.318').

27 Rampart Range Highpoint: Devils Head

Elevation: 9,748' (NAVD88 9,752')

Distinctions: Rampart Range Highpoint, Prominence 300, P1K, Ranked 9er; National Register of Historic Places (lookout tower)

Class: 1; note that trail to top of Devils Head is Class 1, but boulder highpoint, which is off-limits to the public, is Class 3

Difficulty and skill level: Easy; Beginner

Approximate moving time: 2 hours

Distance: 2.8 miles round-trip

Elevation trailhead to summit: 8,808' to 9,752' (+944')

Terrain: Hard-packed dirt, with metal stairs to summit area and Class 3 boulder highpoint

Restrictions: Rampart Range Road is closed Dec 1 to Apr 1 or later, depending on conditions; entrance to trailhead may be gated 0.5 mile back, adding 1 mile round-trip to your hike; trail closed to bicycles and motorized vehicles; dogs must be on leash; observe all Lookout Tower Visitor Rules posted at base of staircase; trail closed if lightning is observed or predicted

Amenities: Toilets near trailhead and near ranger's area; seasonal campgrounds and dispersed backcountry camping along Rampart Range Road; seasonal first-come, first-served camping at Devils Head Campground and Picnic Area; services in Sedalia

Trailhead: Devils Head Trailhead #611

Trail: Devils Head National Recreation Trail

Maps: DeLorme Page 50 C2; USGS Devils Head

County: Douglas

Land status: Pike National Forest, (719) 553-1400, www.fs.usda.gov/psicc; South Platte Ranger District, (303) 275-5610

Finding the trailhead: From I-25 in Castle Rock, about 28 miles south of Denver and 40 miles north of Colorado Springs, take exit 184 for Founders Parkway towards US-85N / CO-86E / Meadows Parkway. Go 0.3 mile and turn left onto US 85N / CO 86E / Meadows Parkway, then go 0.5 mile and turn right onto US 85N / Santa Fe Drive. Drive 5.3 miles and turn left onto CO 67S / Manhart Street, then go 9.9 miles and turn left onto unpaved Rampart Range Road. Continue for 9.3 miles on Rampart Range Road, following signs for Devils Head Campground. Drive past the campground and picnic area and turn right, then continue 0.2 mile to parking and the trailhead (GPS: N39 16.162' / W105 6.310').

The Peak

The Rampart Range trends south from Devils Head, along the west side of I-25 to Garden of the Gods, in Colorado Springs. The highpoint of the range, Devils Head, is a towering clump of Pikes Peak granite, accessed by a 143-step open metal staircase that leads to the Devils Head Fire Lookout Tower, one of the original Front Range lookout towers and the only one still in service. The tower was built in 1912, and a sign at the base of the stairs describes the area's history. The summit block of Devils Head is protected by a wooden fence, but from the lookout tower and wrap-around deck, you'll have views for more than a hundred miles in all directions. Most prominently featured is Pikes Peak to the south; the Platte River Mountains, Kenosha Mountains, and Tarryall Mountains to the west, with the Tenmile and Mosquito Ranges beyond; and the Front Range to the northwest.

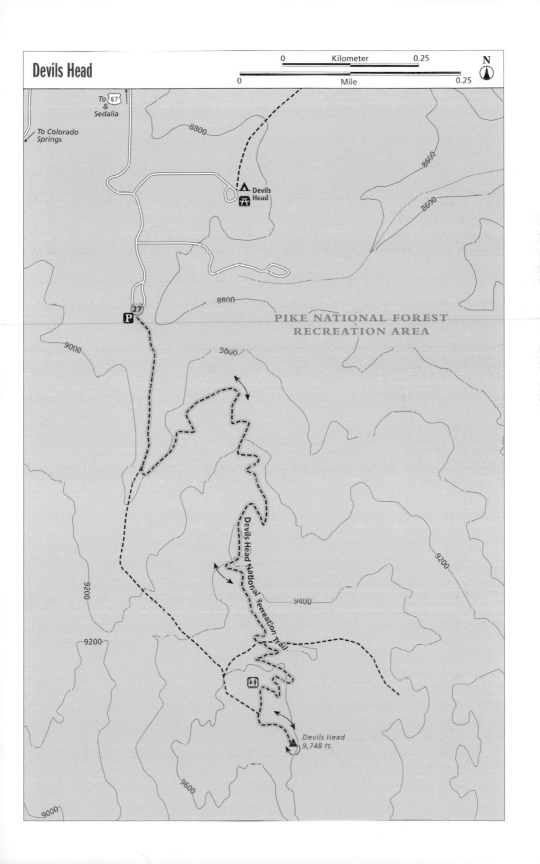

Devils Head

0   Kilometer   0.25

0   Mile   0.25

N

To 67
& Sedalia

To Colorado
Springs

8800

8600

8000

Devils
Head

8800

PIKE NATIONAL FOREST
RECREATION AREA

27

P

9000

9000

9200

Devils Head National Recreation Trail

9400

9200

9200

Devils Head
9,748 ft.

9600

9000

A fence protects the boulder summit of Rampart Range highpoint Devils Head in the Pike National Forest. PHOTO BY SUSAN JOY PAUL

The Climb

Rampart Range Road runs for about 60 miles from endpoint to endpoint and has just two turnoffs, one in Woodland Park and another behind the US Air Force Academy, near Monument. The Sedalia entrance is the most popular and quickest route to the trailhead, as the road from the south, in Colorado Springs, is much rougher. The unpaved road is laced with recreational trails open to dirt bikes and ATVs, so don't expect any peace, quiet, or solitude on this popular route. The Devils Head area is also popular with rock climbers, with access to more than 200 routes via a cutoff from the trail, past the Zinn Overlook on climber's trails.

Miles and Directions

0.0 Begin at the trailhead (8,808'), hike up the steps, and follow the trail as it gradually ascends south, through groves of aspen, fir, and spruce trees, and past piles of pink and gray granite.

1.2 Pass the Zinn Overlook to the left and continue straight, south-southeast, on the trail. Descend past the ranger's cabin on the left and toilet on the right, to the stairs ahead.

1.4 Climb the open staircase to the summit area of ranked 9,752' Devils Head. The summit boulder is on the other side of a wooden fence and off-limits. Return the way you came (N39 15.619' / W105 6.071').

2.8 Arrive back at the trailhead (N39 16.162' / W105 6.310').

28 Ute Pass Peak: Raspberry Mountain

Elevation: 10,605' (NAVD88 10,610')

Distinction: Ranked 10er

Class: 2+; Class 1 to summit area, Class 2+ to highpoint

Difficulty and skill level: Moderate; Beginner

Approximate moving time: 3 hours

Distance: 6.4 miles round-trip

Elevation trailhead to summit: 9,450' to 10,610' (11,160'); about 1,600' round-trip

Terrain: Dirt road and trail, boulders, exposure

Restrictions: Trail closed to motorized vehicles

Amenities: Backcountry camping; toilets at nearby Crags Trailhead; seasonal camping at nearby Crags Campground by permit, payable at self-serve kiosk; dispersed roadside camping along CR 62; services in Divide

Trailhead: Unofficial "Raspberry Mountain Trailhead"

Trail: Unofficial "Raspberry Mountain Trail"

Maps: DeLorme Page 62 A2, B2; USGS Divide

County: Teller

Land status: Pike National Forest, (719) 553-1400, www.fs.usda.gov/psicc; Pikes Peak Ranger District, (719) 636-1602

Finding the trailhead: From the stoplight at US 24 in Divide, go south on CO 67. Drive 4.3 miles, just past Mueller State Park, and turn left onto unpaved CR 62 / FR 383. Drive 1.1 miles and park in the pullout on the left side of the road. The unsigned trailhead is located on the left side of the road and marked by two upright posts (GPS: N38 53.435' / W105 8.678').

The Peak

Raspberry Mountain is located northwest of Pikes Peak and southeast of Ute Pass, and is visible from the town of Divide, on the south side of US 24. Ute Pass (9,165') was formed by an uplift of a section of the Pikes Peak batholith, forming the Ute Pass Fault and dividing the South Platte River drainage to the north and the Arkansas River drainage to the south. The pass's name is a shortening of the original Native American Utah, or Ute, for tribes that once made their home along the Front Range. There are five Ute Passes in Colorado, and while the one near Divide may not be the best known, its proximity to Colorado Springs gave that city its original name, El Paso, or "the pass." Raspberry Mountain likely got its name from the wild red raspberries that may be found along the trailside, tasty fruits that birds and other wildlife rely on for energy and nutrition in the fall. The signature blocks of the Pikes Peak batholith are evident near the summit of Raspberry Mountain, and from its bouldery summit you'll have unobstructed views of Pikes Peak to the southeast, North Catamount Reservoir to the east, the Rampart Range and Front Range to the north, the Sawatch Range to the west, and the Sangre de Cristo Range to the south.

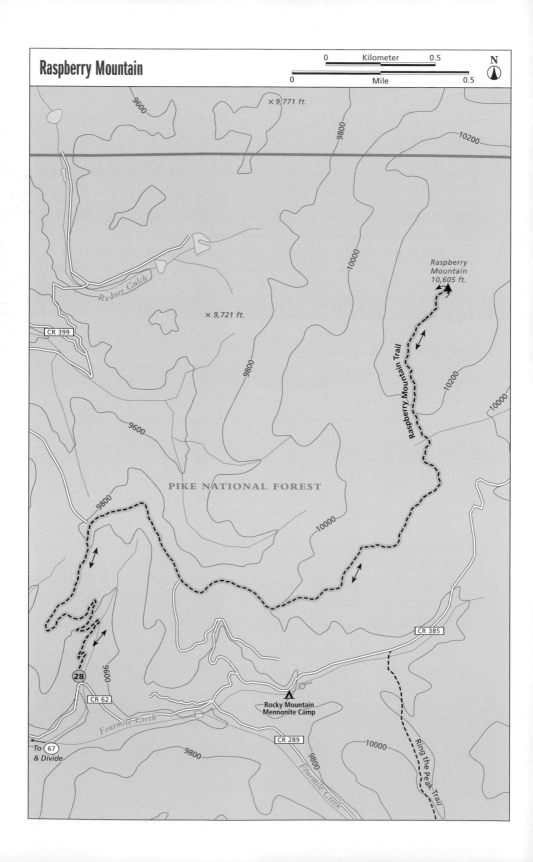

Raspberry Mountain

0 — Kilometer — 0.5
0 — Mile — 0.5

N

9600

× 9,771 ft.

9800

10200

10000

Redner Gulch

CR 399

× 9,721 ft.

9800

Raspberry
Mountain
10,605 ft.

Raspberry Mountain Trail

10200

10000

9600

PIKE NATIONAL FOREST

9800

10000

10000

CR 385

28

9600

Rocky Mountain
Mennonite Camp

CR 62

Fourmile Creek

CR 289

Ring the Peak Trail

To 67
& Divide

9800

9800

10000

Fourmile Creek

Ranked 10er Raspberry Mountain makes a fine warm-up for nearby Pikes Peak in the Pike National Forest. PHOTO BY STEWART M. GREEN

The Climb

Raspberry Mountain is a year-round favorite, with easy trailhead access and gentle slopes that make for a fine hike any time of year. You'll be in the shade for most of the hike, so wear microspikes or snowshoes and bring a trekking pole in snow, for traction and balance on the icy trail and rocks. There is exposure on the rocky summit area.

Miles and Directions

0.0 Begin at the trailhead (9,450') and hike north and west up the switchbacks on the dirt road.

0.6 At 9,700' the switchbacks end and the route trends north. Raspberry Mountain comes into view through the trees northeast of the trail, on the other side of Orchette Gulch. Your path skirts the gulch. To the right of the trail, the northwest slopes of Pikes Peak appear, with the pointed cone of soft-ranked 12,532' Sentinel Point standing guard to the south (N38 53.55' / W105 8.781').

2.6 The road narrows to a trail that continues north for 0.5 mile, then curves around to the north side of the peak. Hike through boulders and up a short, steep scramble to the summit area (N38 54.04' / W105 7.508').

3.2 Arrive at ranked 10,610' Raspberry Mountain, and hop up onto the boulder highpoint. Return the way you came (N38 54.421' / W105 7.448').

6.4 Arrive back at the trailhead (N38 53.435' / W105 8.678').

29 Colorado Springs Local Favorite: Pikes Peak

Elevation: 14,110' (NAVD88 14,115')

Distinctions: El Paso County Highpoint, Centennial, Prominence 100, Ultra-prominence Peak, Ranked 14er

Class: 2+; Class 1 for first 6.2 miles, Class 1, 2, and 2+ to summit

Difficulty and skill level: Very Strenuous; Advanced

Approximate moving time: 8 hours

Distance: 13.4 miles round-trip

Elevation trailhead to summit: 10,000' to 14,115' (+4,115')

Terrain: Dirt trail, talus, and boulders; creek crossings

Recommended extra gear: Crampons or microspikes and ice axe if snow exists; extra water if summit house is closed, cash or credit card if it's open and you want to eat there

Restrictions: CR 62 is not maintained past Mennonite Camp (1.2 miles from trailhead) in winter and may be impassable until May; trail closed to motorized vehicles; dogs must be on leash and are not allowed in summit house

Amenities: Trailhead toilets; backcountry camping 300' from the trail; seasonal camping at Crags Campground by permit, payable at self-serve kiosk; dispersed roadside camping on CR 62; summit house with restrooms, gift shop, and restaurant; services in Divide

Trailhead: Crags Trailhead

Trail: Devil's Playground Trail #753, off-trail Northwest Ridge

Maps: DeLorme Page 62 B2, B3; USGS Pikes Peak, Woodland Park

County: El Paso

Land status: Pike National Forest, (719) 553-1400, www.fs.usda.gov/psicc; Pikes Peak Ranger District, (719) 636-1602

Finding the trailhead: From the stoplight at US 24 in Divide, go south on CO 67 for 4.3 miles, past Mueller State Park, and turn left onto unpaved CR 62 / FR 383. Drive 2.8 miles and park in the large lot on the right. The trailhead is on the left side of the road (GPS: N38 52.420' / W105 7.420').

The Peak

Pikes Peak dominates the western skyline above Colorado Springs, rising 5,530' above the city and visible for more than a hundred miles in every direction. The mountain is the easternmost 14,000' peak in the country and the highpoint of the Pikes Peak batholith. Pikes Peak and Longs Peak are the only Colorado 14ers that do not lie along the Mineral Belt or the Rio Grande Rift, and the two peaks have more documented routes to their summits than any other 14er in the state. Pikes, Mount Elbert, and Blanca Peak are the only ultra–prominence peaks, or "ultras," in Colorado. The mountain is named for General Zebulon Montgomery Pike (1779–1813), who spotted the mountain on an 1806 expedition and made an attempt to its summit. Pike left his party and set out with three partners, expecting to reach the peak in a day. They fell short, in frigid November temperatures and snow, and likely settled for 11,499' Mount Rosa instead.

The Crags route rises from the forest near Divide and climbs the northwest ridge of Pikes Peak.
PHOTO BY STEWART M. GREEN

Pike had called the mountain "Grand Peak," and it was later changed to "James Peak," after botanist Dr. Edwin James, who made a successful ascent in 1820, but mapmaker Colonel Henry Dodge renamed it Pikes Peak in 1835.

Views from the western slopes of Pikes Peak are outstanding along the Crags route. As you break timberline, 180 degree views include La Garita highpoint San Luis Peak; South Park Hills highpoint Waugh Mountain; Mount Ouray at Marshall Pass; the Buffalo Peaks at Trout Creek Pass, and beyond, the 14ers of the Sawatch Range from Buena Vista to Leadville; and finally the peaks of the Mosquito Range and the Front Range at Mosquito, Hoosier, Boreas, and Loveland Passes. Farther up the trail, enjoy views of Sierra Blanca highpoint Mount Blanca, Crestone Mountains highpoint Crestone Peak, and Longs Peak at Rocky Mountain National Park.

The Climb

There are many ways to get to the summit of Pikes Peak. The Crags route is the easiest way to the top on foot, while still gaining more than 3,000' of elevation. The peak is climbed from this route year-round with consideration for avalanche danger that may exist above treeline on winter and spring climbs. The Devil's Playground Trail offers two unranked 13er peak options along the route. From the parking lot at Devil's Playground, it's a short detour to Teller County highpoint "Devils Playground Peak," and farther up the trail you'll pass by "Little Pikes Peak." Both are easy Class 2 hikes.

Pikes Peak is the only 14er in the country with a paved road all the way to the summit, and a restaurant and gift shop on top. There's a tourist train to the top, too—the Cog Railway—which you can access with reservations and a paid ticket in Manitou Springs. The road is limited to cars and bikes, and the railway is limited to the cog train, so stick to the trails and backcountry on your own ascent. Do not count on the summit house to be open year-round, as it closes occasionally, especially during winter storms when the road may be closed

Pikes Peak may also be accessed via the Barr Trailhead, along a 26-mile and 7,500' of elevation round-trip route that begins in Manitou Springs. This makes for a very long day, and some Barr Trail hikers overnight at Barr Camp midroute (go online to reserve a bunk or a camping spot, and meals, too), or settle for more primitive camping at the A-frame, an open-air structure located at treeline. For a much shorter climb, you can take the Pikes Peak Highway (off of US 24, west of Colorado Springs), pay the toll, and drive up the road to start at Devil's Playground. In consolidated snow, the Y Couloir, Railroad Couloir, and Little Italy (Couloir) are popular snow climbs that take you most of the way to the summit, and all are accessed via Glen Cove, on the Pikes Peak Highway. The Pikes Peak climb from the Crags is the author's favorite, but you are encouraged to explore the many various paths to the top of "America's Mountain."

Miles and Directions

0.0   Begin at the trailhead (10,000') behind the toilets across the road from the signed Crags Trailhead parking lot. Cross the footbridge over Fourmile Creek and hike southeast.

0.6   Pass a junction with a trail that switches back right and down to the Crags Campground. At the next junction, where the Crags Trail branches off to the left, bear right on the Devil's Playground Trail, also signed as section #664A on the "Ring the Peak Trail" system. Cross Fourmile Creek again, on a split log, and hike east-southeast (N38 52.297' / W105 7.039').

0.9   Cross a creek on rocks and branches.

1.6   Negotiate the final creek crossing on rocks and branches. Pass Banana Rock, north, and continue on gentle switchbacks. Climb a steep, loose path east to the ridge, gaining roughly 800' in less than 0.5 mile. This section, up and back, is the toughest part of the day.

Pikes Peak

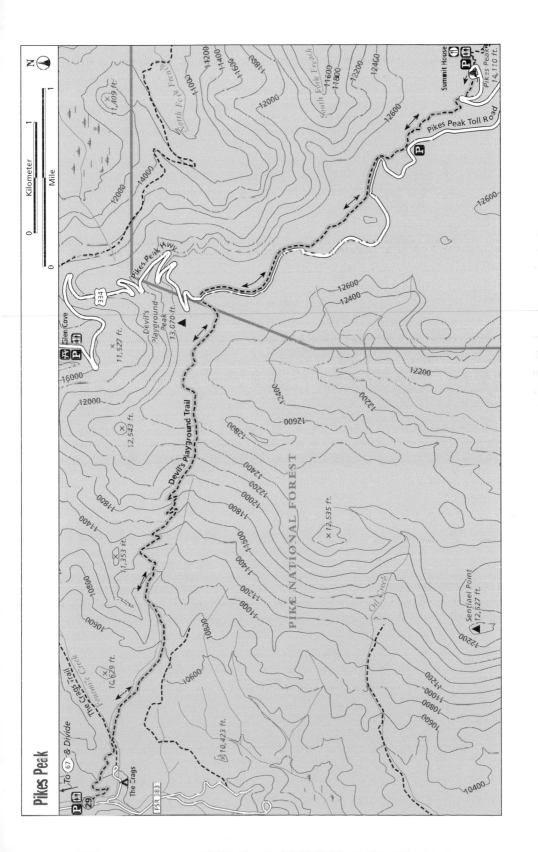

3.3 Top out on the ridge at 12,740' with Pikes Peak in view. Cairns mark the trail as it crosses the saddle northeast, then contours the mountainside southeast. Off-trail to the left, Rampart Range highpoint Devils Head and downtown Denver are in distant view north, and McReynolds Peak—known as the "toughest 12er in Colorado"—lies in the glacial valley below, to the south (N38 51.868' / W105 4.781').

3.9 Pass through the rocky Devil's Gate to Devil's Playground (12,860'). Cross the parking area and hike northeast up to the road (N38 51.774' / W105 4.290').

4.1 Cross the Pikes Peak Highway at the marked crossing and pick up the trail on the other side. Turn right to hike south on the trail that parallels the highway, past Crystal Reservoir and North Pit (N38 51.837' / W105 4.092').

4.7 The trail meets the road for a short section above a steep, exposed area (12,940') above the Bottomless Pit area. Walk on the road inside the barrier, rejoin the trail at the south end, and hike up the steep slope. Follow cairns south-southeast along the trail (N38 51.436' / W105 3.817').

6.2 Begin the Class 2/2+ section at 13,700'. Follow cairns south and east through talus and boulders up to the road. If you lose the path, just continue south and up, to the trail that leads to a road and the parking lot (N38 50.604' / W105 2.870').

6.5 Reach the road and hike east-southeast past the army building and toward a pile of rocks in the middle of the parking area (N38 50.497' / W105 2.778').

6.7 Arrive at ranked 14,115' Pikes Peak, marked by a geodetic survey marker. Return the way you came (N38 50.422' / W105 2.628').

13.4 Arrive back at the trailhead (N38 52.420' / W105 7.420').

30 South Park Hills Highpoint: Waugh Mountain

Elevation: 11,710' (NAVD88 11,716')
Distinctions: South Park Hills Highpoint, Prominence 100, P2K, Ranked 11er
Class: 2
Difficulty and skill level: Moderate; Intermediate
Approximate moving time: 3 hours
Distance: 4.2 miles round-trip
Elevation trailhead to summit: 10,720' to 11,716' (+996'); about 1,200' round-trip
Terrain: Bushwhack
Recommended extra gear: Protective clothing
Restrictions: CR 12 may be washed out and rutted; BLM Road 5760 is not maintained through winter, so you may need to park at bottom of road and hike up, adding 7.2 round-trip miles and 1,000' to your hike; avoid both roads if wet or muddy; camping is prohibited on state trust lands

Amenities: Limited services in Cotopaxi; full services in Salida and Cañon City
Trailhead: BLM Road 5760
Trail: Off-trail Northwest Ridge
Maps: DeLorme Page 61 D5; USGS Waugh Mountain
County: Fremont
Land status: Bureau of Land Management, Royal Gorge Field Office, (719) 269-8500, www.blm.gov/co/st/en/fo/rgfo.html; Badger Creek State Trust and Waugh Mountain State Trust Land Management Areas, State Land Board, South Central District, (719) 543-7403, www.trustlands.state.co.us/Districts/Pages/SouthCentral.aspx; Wildlife Management Areas, Colorado Division of Wildlife, (303) 297-1192, www.cpw.state.co.us

Finding the trailhead: From US 50 in Cotopaxi, about 24 miles east of Salida and 33 miles west of Cañon City, go north on CR 12. The road is unpaved at 8.6 miles. Continue another 1.5 miles and bear left towards Gribbles Park, then go 11.7 miles to BLM Road 5760. If it is passable, turn right onto the BLM road and drive 3.6 miles to a pullout on the right side of the road (GPS: N38 36.531' / W105 43.420').

The Peak

The South Park Hills, located north of the Arkansas River between Cañon City and Salida, lie below timberline in an area popular with ATVers, rafters, hunters, and anglers. The highpoint is in the trees, but a bit of summit roaming provides views north of Thirtynine Mile Mountain and the high peaks of the Front Range; south of the Sangre de Cristo Range; and west of the Continental Divide from the Sawatch Range to the San Juans at Marshall Pass.

The Climb

Waugh Mountain sees few visitors other than the occasional Fremont County or P2K peakbagger. Hunters frequent the BLM land here in the fall, so wear some blaze and keep a wide berth. Year-round access to the peak is restricted only by road conditions, but deep snow at this low altitude, and dense growth, can make this an

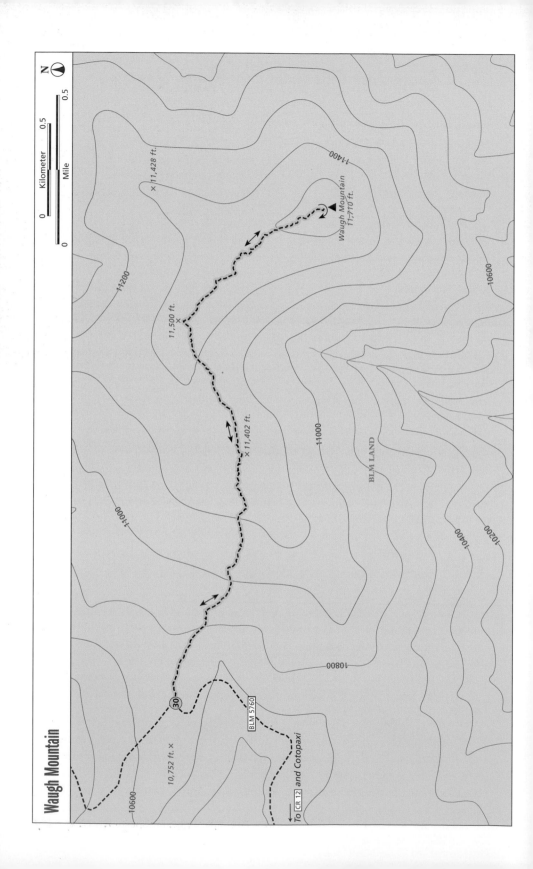

Waugh Mountain

Wander the summit of Waugh Mountain for views of surrounding mountain ranges.
PHOTO BY SUSAN JOY PAUL

unpleasant post-holing event. No special gear is required, but you'll want to keep your skin covered, and avoid wearing anything that might get hung up on the thick brush. If you can make it up to the pullout at 10,720' on BLM Road 5760 in your car, it's a short, steep hike and ridge walk through a dense pine forest. Otherwise, park at a pullout on the northeast corner of the intersection on CR 12 at 9,720' and hike up the BLM road. A longer, alternate route may be found from nearby ranked 11er Stoney Face Mountain, to the southeast, and a shorter, steeper route exists from 4WD roads to the east, but the extensive bushwhacking, additional miles, and steep climbing required make this route more appealing.

Miles and Directions

0.0 Begin at the pullout (10,720') and bushwhack east-southeast through Badger Creek State Trust land toward the highpoint on the ridge ahead.

0.9 From unranked Point 11402, head east-northeast on BLM land, crossing through Waugh Mountain Trust land and staying high on the ridge to avoid the densest areas of growth and deadfall (N38 36.361' / W105 42.612').

1.4 From unranked Point 11500, head south-southeast along the ridge crest. The trees open up along the route, and you'll have views to the south of the northern Sangre de Cristo Range (N38 36.513' / W105 42.123').

2.1 Arrive at ranked 11,716' Waugh Mountain. A 1938 marker sits at the highpoint. Return the way you came (N38 36.124' / W105 41.727').

4.2 Arrive back at the trailhead (N38 36.531' / W105 43.420').

31 Gorge Hills Highpoint: Fremont Peak

Elevation: 7,233'
Distinction: Gorge Hills Highpoint, Ranked 7er
Class: 2; Class 1 to saddle, Class 2 to summit
Difficulty and skill level: Easy; Beginner
Approximate moving time: 2 hours
Distance: 3.0 miles round-trip
Elevation trailhead to summit: 6,829' to 7,233' (+404'); about 500' round-trip
Terrain: Gravel road, dirt trail, and scree
Restrictions: CR 389B may not be passable all the way to gate in winter; no alcohol, firearms, trapping, or hunting in park; no vehicles on trail

Amenities: Toilets at nearby camping areas and picnic areas; camping at designated campsites in nearby East Ridge Campground; services in Cañon City
Trailhead: CR 389B
Trails: CR 389B and unofficial "Fremont Peak Trail," off-trail North Slope
Maps: DeLorme Page 72 A1; USGS Royal Gorge
County: Fremont
Land status: Royal Gorge Park, City of Cañon City Parks Division, (719) 269-9028, www.canoncity.org/Parks_Forestry_Cemetery/Parks/Parks_Division.htm

Finding the trailhead: From Cañon City, go west on US 50 for about 8 miles and turn left onto CR 3A toward the Royal Gorge Bridge. Drive 3.4 miles on CR 3A, past the picnic area, and turn left onto unsigned, gravel CR 389B. Go 0.7 mile, bearing left at the first fork to stay on the main road and right at the next fork to continue on CR 389B. Drive 0.1 mile and turn right at the T-intersection, then go another 0.1 mile and park at a pullout on the side of the road. Do not block the gate. The route begins on the service road on the other side of the gate (GPS: N38 27.777' / W105 17.666').

The Peak

Fremont Peak defines the Cañon City skyline, rising above ranked 6er YMCA Mountain and unranked 6er Nonans Peak. The mountain lies within the city-owned Royal Gorge Park, not to be confused with the nearby theme park, Royal Gorge Bridge and Park. West of the peak, the Arkansas River has carved out the Royal Gorge, a 10-mile-long, 1,000-feet-deep canyon popular with kayakers and river-rafters. The rock here is granite, common to the Front Range, but the lower altitude of the Gorge Hills presents a life zone more common to the foothills of western Colorado. Fremont Peak is named for John Charles Fremont, a military officer, professor of mathematics, and the first candidate of the Republican Party for the office of the president of the United States. The small summit of the peak offers views of Waugh Mountain to the northwest, Pikes Peak to the northeast, Cañon City and the Great Plains to the east, and Grand Canyon Hills highpoint YMCA Mountain across the Arkansas River drainage to the south. The Wet Mountains and Sangre de Cristo Range border the south and west horizon.

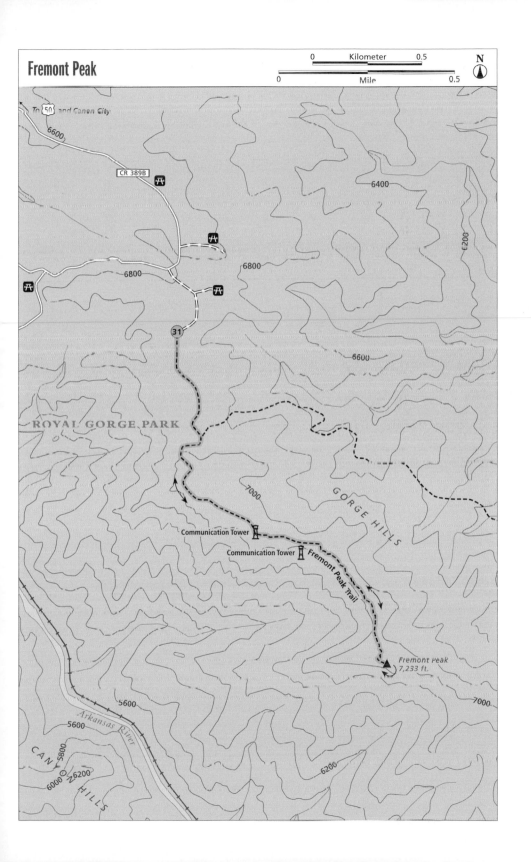

Fremont Peak

0 | Kilometer | 0.5
0 | Mile | 0.5

N

To 50 and Cañon City

6600

CR 389B

6400

6200

6800

6800

31

6600

ROYAL GORGE PARK

7600

GORGE HILLS

Communication Tower

Communication Tower

Fremont Peak Trail

Fremont Peak
7,233 ft.

7000

5600

Arkansas River

5600

CAÑON HILLS

6200

6000 6200

Fremont Peak rises up in the Gorge Hills north of Cañon City in southern Colorado.
PHOTO BY SUSAN JOY PAUL

The Climb

The trail to Fremont Peak is lined with piñon pine, juniper, mountain mahogany, Gambel oak, and yucca, and cholla, pincushion, and prickly pear cactus. Summertime heat can be extreme here, so bring plenty of water and sun protection. In winter, CR 389B may not be passable all the way to the gate, making for a longer hike.

Miles and Directions

0.0 Begin at the trailhead (6,829') and hike south up the road. Trailside views include Cañon City and Skyline Drive, the Royal Gorge Bridge and inner canyon, and the Sangre de Cristo Range and Crestones.

0.8 Hike past the first communication tower and continue east on the road.

1.0 Pass the second tower and follow the road as it curves to the right, and get on the unmarked "Fremont Peak Trail." Descend the trail south to a saddle, then ascend the steep, loose trail south and east toward a huge cairn.

1.5 Arrive at ranked 7,233' Fremont Peak. Return the way you came (N38 26.924' / E105 16.979').

3.0 Arrive back at the trailhead (N38 27.777' / W105 17.666').

32 Grand Canyon Hills Highpoint: YMCA Mountain

Elevation: 6,940'

Distinctions: Grand Canyon Hills Highpoint, Ranked 6er

Class: 2

Difficulty and skill level: Easy; Beginner

Approximate moving time: 1 hour

Distance: 2.0 miles round-trip

Elevation trailhead to summit: 6,790' to 6,940' (+150'); about 300' round-trip

Terrain: Light bushwhack on use trail

Restrictions: BLM Road 6100 may be closed at winter gate, adding 7.8 round-trip miles to your hike; Temple Canyon Road and BLM Road 6100 are rugged and may require a high-clearance 4WD vehicle, avoid if wet or muddy; visit the BLM website for complete list of current restrictions, including details on OPLA-PRP (Omnibus Public Lands Act–Paleontological Resources Preservation)

Amenities: Backcountry camping; primitive camping at nearby Temple Canyon Park; services in Cañon City

Trailhead: BLM Road 6100

Trail: Unofficial "YMCA Mountain Trail," off-trail West Ridge

Maps: DeLorme Page 71 A8; USGS Royal Gorge

County: Fremont

Land status: Bureau of Land Management, Royal Gorge Field Office, (719) 269-8500, www.blm.gov/co/st/en/fo/rgfo.html

Finding the trailhead: In Cañon City, go west on US 50 and turn left onto S. First Street. Go 1.1 miles and turn right onto CR 3 / Temple Canyon Road. After another 1.1 miles the paved road turns to dirt and becomes increasingly rugged, steep, and narrow. Drive 7 miles on the dirt road, through Temple Canyon Park, past Temple View Picnic and Camping Area, and over the bridge at Grape Creek. Turn right onto BLM 6100. The road is easy to miss and is located just prior to where Temple Canyon Road enters private property. Drive 3.9 miles on the BLM road. You will pass 6100C on the right and 6100E on the left, but remain on the main BLM road. Park at a large, flat pullout on the right side of the road (GPS: N38 25.731' / W105 18.053').

The Peak

The Grand Canyon Hills are a short string of peaks located on BLM land in Cañon City, south of the Arkansas River. Although a broad definition of the Front Range identifies the river as the southern terminus of the range, the peaks here are part of the same formation that defines the Gorge Hills to the north, rather than the Sangres to the south, and are part of the Front Range. From the summit, Cañon City lies to the east nearly 1,600' below, and peaks in view include Gorge Hills highpoint Fremont Peak and South Park Hills highpoint Waugh Mountain to the north, the Wet Mountains to the south, and the Sangre de Cristo Range to the west.

The Climb

This low-altitude Cañon City hike can be too hot in the summertime, and long and arduous in the winter due to a gate closure, so is best done in late spring or early

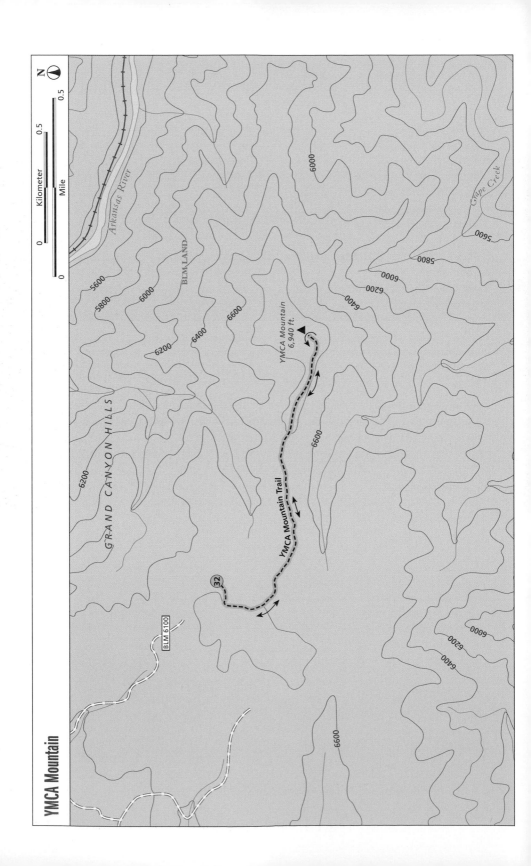

YMCA Mountain

YMCA Mountain looks down on Cañon City in the southern Front Range.
PHOTO BY SUSAN JOY PAUL

fall barring wet or muddy roads. The trail is loaded with cactus so wear appropriate footwear, watch where you step, and consider carrying tweezers to remove needles from your shoes and hands.

Miles and Directions

0.0   Begin at the parking area (6,790') and hike west to pick up an ATV trail that extends west and curves south (left) to a use trail, then heads east through the forest, marked for the entire route with pink surveyor's tape.

0.6   Gain the west ridge of the peak and continue east (N38 25.584' / W105 17.672').

1.0   Arrive at ranked 6,940' YMCA Mountain. The summit area is large and you may have to wander a bit to find the highpoint, marked by a small cairn. Return the way you came (N38 25.519' / W105 17.296').

2.0   Arrive back at the trailhead (N38 25.731' / W105 18.053').

33 McIntyre Hills Highpoint: Point 8543

Elevation: 8,543'
Distinctions: McIntyre Hills Highpoint, Ranked 8er
Class: 2, Class 1 for first 1.8 miles, Class 2 to summit
Difficulty and skill level: Moderate; Beginner
Approximate moving time: 3 hours
Distance: 4.4 miles round-trip
Elevation trailhead to summit: 7,210' to 8,543' (+1,333'); about 1,400' round-trip
Terrain: Dirt road and trail, brush
Restrictions: Stay off private property

Amenities: Dispersed backcountry camping on public lands; services in Cañon City
Trailhead: Mine Shaft Road
Trails: Mine Shaft Road (FR 6170), unofficial "Point 8543 Trail," off-trail North Ridge
Maps: DeLorme Page 71 A7; USGS McIntyre Hills
County: Fremont
Land status: Bureau of Land Management, Royal Gorge Field Office, (719) 269-8500, www.blm.gov/co/st/en/fo/rgfo.html

Finding the trailhead: From Cañon City, go west on US 50 for about 14 miles and turn left onto CR 3, which becomes CR 28 / Copper Gulch Road. Drive 10 miles to unmarked and unpaved Mine Shaft Road, on right. Park in the pullout (GPS: N38 23.346' / W105 27.287').

The Peak

The McIntyre Hills lie west of Cañon City and south of the Arkansas River Canyon. North of highpoint Point 8543, 16,650 acres comprise the McIntyre Hills Wilderness Study Area, but you will not enter this area on your hike. The rocky summit provides views of Waugh Mountain and Pikes Peak to the north and the northern Sangre de Cristo Range to the west, with the southern Sawatch beyond. The Wet Mountains and Crestones appear to the south.

The Climb

Point 8543 is best climbed in late spring or early fall, to avoid the extreme heat and thick brush of the summer and slippery, snow-covered boulders and talus near the summit in winter. You can drive most of this hike, but that would shorten it considerably and you would shortchange yourself a unique and beautiful hike.

Point 8543

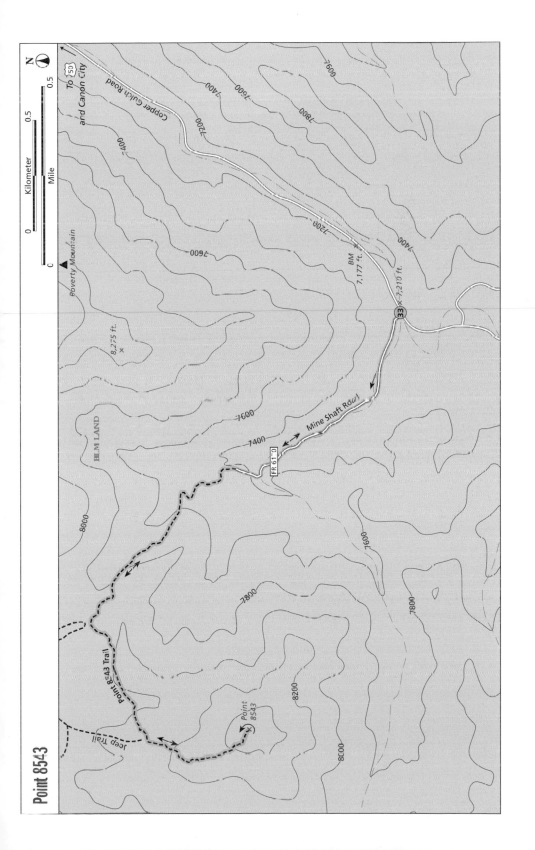

Point 8543, seen here from Point 8450, tops the McIntyre Hills in the Front Range.
PHOTO BY STEWART M. GREEN

Miles and Directions

0.0 Begin at the trailhead (7,210') and hike west-northwest on Mine Shaft Road. Straight ahead, an unranked bump along Point 8543's southeast ridge is in view, with Point 8543 peeking out from behind. The road enters public lands at 0.5 mile on FR 6170. Bear left at the fork where FR 6170A veers to the right.

1.4 Hike west-southwest, up an unmarked 4WD road on the left (N38 24.093' / W105 28.184').

1.6 At the highpoint of the road (8,000'), the peak and the rest of your route are in view. Drop southwest to the drainage below, and hike up the road to the ridge. If the road is holding snow, climb the hillside in the trees to avoid avalanche danger. From the ridge, locate a trail heading south-southwest and follow it until it disappears, then head southeast up the slope.

2.2 Arrive at ranked Point 8543. Return the way you came (N38 23.711' / W105 28.523').

4.4 Arrive back at the trailhead (N38 23.346' / W105 27.287').

The Sangre de Cristo Range

The Sangre de Cristo Range trends south from Poncha Pass to the New Mexico border in southern Colorado, splitting the Arkansas River Valley to the east and the San Luis Valley, west, and forming the eastern border of the Rocky Mountains in the southern part of the state. The range is the northern extension of the Sangre de Cristo Mountains, which trend south to Santa Fe, New Mexico. The Crestone Mountains and Sierra Blanca Range lie within the Sangre de Cristo Range in Colorado, and the Culebra Range is an extension of the range, while the Wet Mountains and Spanish Peaks are geologically and geographically distinct mountain ranges located adjacent to the Sangres but usually grouped with that range and included within this section. Wilderness areas within the ranges include the Sangre de Cristo, Greenhorn Mountain, and Spanish Peaks Wildernesses. La Veta Pass provides the only paved road through the Sangre de Cristo Range, but private property hinders access to peaks in that area. Trails and rough roads over Cordova, Music, Mosca, Hayden, and Hermit Passes cross the ranges and are popular entry points for climbing in the Sangres. There are 10 ranked 14,000' peaks in the Sangre de Cristo and surrounding ranges, including 5 in the Crestones, 4 in the Blanca group, and 1 in the Culebra Range. The mountains—especially the Crestones—provide some of the best climbing in the state, but are not as popular as peaks to the north and west due to their location in a less populated and more remote area that is also less accessible, due to its location along the Rio Grande Rift and not the Mineral Belt. At sunrise, alpenglow lights up the Sangre de Cristo, or "blood of Christ," mountains, and the rock, laced with sandstone and conglomerate strata, burns a fiery red, giving the peaks their colorful name.

Crestone Peak rises up in the Crestone Mountains of southern Colorado. PHOTO BY BILL MIDDLEBROOK

129

34 Wet Mountains Highpoint: Greenhorn Mountain

Elevation: 12,347' (NAVD88 12,352')
Distinctions: Wet Mountains Highpoint, Pueblo County Highpoint, Greenhorn Mountain Wilderness Highpoint, Prominence 100, P3K, Ranked 12er
Class: 2; Class 1 to Greenhorn–North Peak saddle, mixed Class 1 and 2 to summit
Difficulty and skill level: Moderate; Beginner
Approximate moving time: 3 hours
Distance: 5.2 miles round-trip
Elevation trailhead to summit: 11,444' to 12,352' (+908'); about 1,300' round-trip
Terrain: Dirt trail, talus, and tundra
Restrictions: Ophir Creek Road is closed seasonally; trail closed to bicycles and motorized vehicles; dogs must be on leash or under voice command; follow wilderness regulations
Amenities: Backcountry camping; seasonal camping at Ophir Creek Campground; services in Rye, Florence, and Colorado City
Trailhead: Upper Greenhorn Trailhead
Trail: Greenhorn Trail #1316, off-trail Northwest Ridge
Maps: DeLorme Page 82 B3, A3; USGS San Isabel
Counties: Pueblo, Huerfano
Land status: San Isabel National Forest, (719) 553-1400, www.fs.usda.gov/psicc; San Carlos Ranger District, (719) 269-8500; Greenhorn Mountain Wilderness, www.wilderness.net

Finding the trailhead: From CO 115 in Florence, about 38 miles south of Colorado Springs and 8 miles east of Cañon City, take CO 67 South for 11.1 miles and turn right at the T-intersection onto CO 96 West. Go 9.6 miles and turn left onto CO 165 South / Greenhorn Highway. Continue 11.8 miles to a hairpin curve and turn right onto unpaved FR 360 / Ophir Creek Road. From this point it's 24.3 miles on dirt roads to the trailhead. Drive 8.2 miles, past the Ophir Creek Trailhead to a signed junction, and turn left onto FR 369 / Greenhorn Mountain Road. The forest road jogs left at 15 miles, but continue on the main road instead, for 1.1 miles to the end of the road (GPS: N37 53.629' / W105 2.486').

The Peak

The Wet Mountains pick up where the Front Range ends, at the Cañon City Embayment south of the Arkansas River, near Cañon City. The Wet Mountains were formed by the San Isabel batholith and a faulted anticline, and the name "Wet" Mountains refers to the prevalent moisture found here, in a predominantly dry region of the state. The range parallels the Sangre de Cristo Range proper, located west, across the Wet Mountain Valley. Greenhorn Mountain is named for *Cuerno Verde*, or "Green Horn," the nickname of Comanche Chief Tabivo Naritgant, known for the green–tinted bison horn that adorned his battle helmet. From the top of Greenhorn Mountain, views include the Spanish Peaks, the Blanca Group, the Crestones, and many high peaks of the Sawatch Range, plus Pikes Peak. A herd of bighorn sheep makes its home on Greenhorn Mountain.

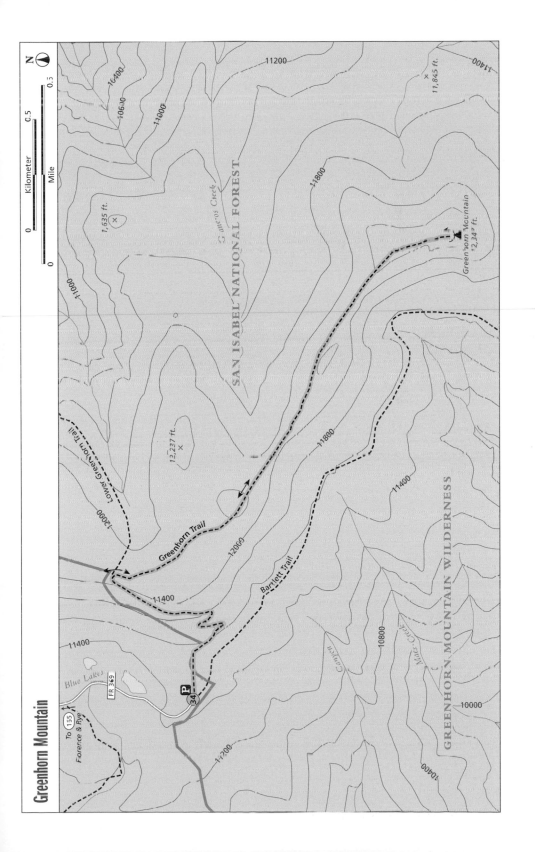

Greenhorn Mountain

N

0   0.5   Kilometer
0   0.5   Mile

Blue Lakes

To 155
Florence & Rye

FR 369

P 34

Lower Greenhorn Trail

Greenhorn Trail

Bartlett Trail

SAN ISABEL NATIONAL FOREST

11200

11000

11800

11400

11800

12060

11400

11400

11200

10800

10000

10400

11400

Canyon

Mace Creek

Gardeos Creek

1,635 ft.

12,237 ft.

11,845 ft.

Greenhorn Mountain
12,347 ft.

GREENHORN MOUNTAIN WILDERNESS

Talus litters the west slopes of Greenhorn Mountain in the Greenhorn Mountain Wilderness.
PHOTO BY STEWART M. GREEN

The Climb

The trail from the upper trailhead is a summer route, but you can do Greenhorn Mountain in winter from the Lower Greenhorn Trailhead or the Bartlett Trailhead in Rye. Both routes are much longer than the route described here. At the Upper Greenhorn Trailhead, be sure to get on the correct trail. Do not take the Bartlett Trail, a dirt road to the right of the wilderness sign near the trailhead. You are headed northeast, for the Greenhorn–North saddle. You can easily add unranked 12er North Peak (N37 54.083' / W105 1.940') to this hike, located 220' above the saddle.

Miles and Directions

0.0 Begin at the trailhead (11,444') and hike east into the Greenhorn Mountain Wilderness. The trail switches back up the hillside and turns to talus, with views of Blue Lakes and the Sangre de Cristos.

0.9 At the 12,000' Greenhorn–North Peak saddle, hike south-southeast up to the ridge, where the peak and the rest of your route are in view. Descend 200' to the next saddle and a trail that contours the northwest ridge and goes up to the ridge crest (N37 53.866' / W105 02.037').

2.6 Arrive at ranked 12,352' Greenhorn Mountain. Return the way you came (N37 52.888' / W105 00.804').

5.2 Arrive back at the trailhead (N37 53.629' / W105 2.486').

35 Crestone Mountains Highpoint: Crestone Peak

Elevation: 14,294' (NAVD88 14,300')

Distinctions: Crestone Mountains Highpoint, Saguache County Highpoint, Sangre de Cristo Wilderness Highpoint, Centennial, Prominence 100, P4K, Ranked 14er

Class: 3; Class 1 to South Colony Lakes, mixed Class 1, 2, and 3 to summit

Difficulty and skill level: Very Strenuous; Advanced

Approximate moving time: 10 hours

Distance: 13.0 miles round-trip

Elevation trailhead to summit: 9,900' to 14,300' (+4,400'); about 6,100' round-trip

Terrain: Dirt trail, scree, talus, ledges, and slabs; minor creek crossing; exposure, risk of rockfall

Recommended extra gear: Helmet; crampons or microspikes and ice axe if snow exists

Restrictions: Trailhead requires high-clearance 4WD and is impassable in snow, parking at lower 2WD trailhead at 8,768' will add 5.2 round-trip miles and about 1,150' to route; trail closed to bicycles and motor vehicles; dogs must be on leash or under voice command and due to rockfall danger are strongly discouraged on this peak; follow wilderness regulations

Amenities: Dispersed backcountry camping at trailhead and at South Colony Lakes, services in Westcliffe

Trailhead: South Colony Lakes Trailhead

Trail: South Colony Trail #1339, off-trail South Face / Red Gully

Maps: DeLorme Page 81 A6; USGS Crestone Peak

County: Saguache

Land status: San Isabel National Forest, (719) 553-1400, www.fs.usda.gov/psicc; San Carlos Ranger District, (719) 269-8500; Sangre de Cristo Wilderness, www.wilderness.net

Finding the trailhead: From Westcliffe, take CO 69 South for 4.5 miles and turn right onto CR 119 / Colfax Lane. Go 5.6 miles and turn right onto unpaved CR 120 / South Colony Road. The 2WD parking area is 1.5 miles up the road, but if you have a high-clearance 4WD vehicle, you can continue for another 2.6 miles to the trailhead (GPS: N37 58.581' / W105 30.357').

The Peak

The Crestones rise up at the eastern edge of the state's largest park, the San Luis Valley. The chunky coarse conglomerate of Crestone Peak and nearby 14er Crestone Needle make them favorites of Colorado mountaineers, with fun Class 3 climbing on tilted slabs of rock and handholds aplenty. "Crestone" is derived from the Spanish *creston*, or "cock's comb"; viewed from a distance, the high peaks rise and fall in a jagged row resembling the bright red crest of a proud rooster. Crestone Peak provides views west across the San Luis Valley to the San Juan Mountains, south across the Great Sand Dunes to the Sierra Blanca, and east to the Wet Mountains. Northwest, the Sangre de Cristo Range continues along the Rio Grande Rift to Poncha Pass.

A climber takes in views of Crestone Needle from the summit of Crestone Peak.
PHOTO BY BILL MIDDLEBROOK

The Climb

All of Colorado's 14,000' peaks have been climbed in every season, but winter conditions demand a special set of mountaineering skills, and a summer climb of Crestone Peak is highly recommended. The climb to Broken Hand Pass is especially avalanche-prone, so winter climbs are usually made from an alternate start at Cottonwood Creek. Even in the best conditions, the easy handholds and solid rock do not ensure an easy or inherently safe climb, and many people have lost their lives on these peaks. Crestone Peak is a serious step up from the standard trail-to-the-top walk-ups found on many of Colorado's 14ers, so ensure you are prepared with proper gear, skills, and route-finding abilities before attempting this peak. If this is your first Class 3 climb, go with an experienced mentor who knows the route. Consider camping at the trailhead, or packing in to South Colony Lakes for the night, to shorten your summit day. After you have summited Crestone Peak, you can scramble from the notch to the eastern summit and add in Custer County highpoint and unranked 14er "East Crestone." Likewise, from the top of Broken Hand Pass you can add ranked 13er Broken Hand Peak, to the southeast. Crestone Peak and Crestone Needle can

Crestone Peak

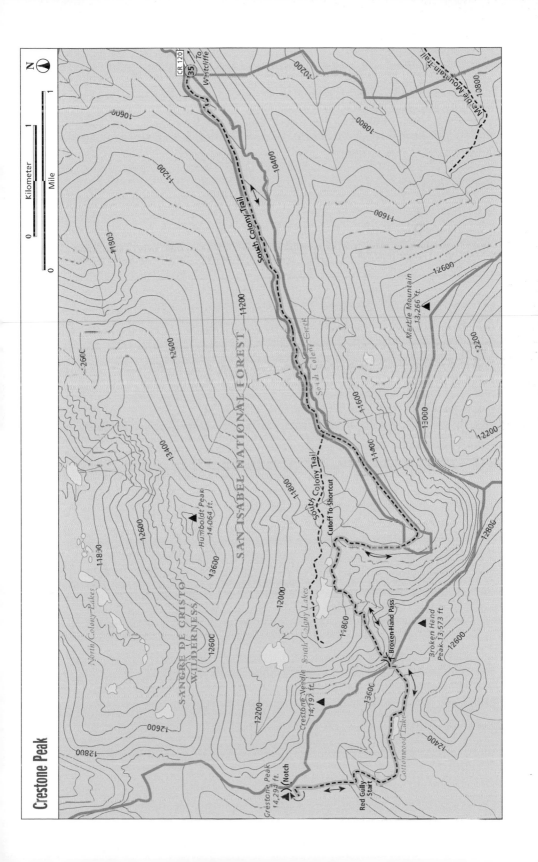

N

0   1   Kilometer
0   1   Mile

CR 120
35
To Westcliffe

South Colony Trail

South Colony Creek

South Colony Trail
Cutoff To Shortcut

10200
10600
11200
11803
12600
13400
13600
10400
11600
11400
11500
13000
12200
12800
12400
12600
12200
11800
12000
11800
13600
12600
12800
12600
12200

Marble Mountain Trail
13800

Marble Mountain
13,266 ft.

SAN ISABEL NATIONAL FOREST

SANGRE DE CRISTO WILDERNESS

Humboldt Peak
14,064 ft.

North Colony Lakes

South Colony Lakes

Crestone Needle
14,197 ft.

Crestone Peak
14,294 ft.

Notch

Red Gully Start

Cottonwood Lake

Broken Hand Pass

Broken Hand Peak 13,573 ft.

also be combined via an exposed Peak-to-Needle, Class 5 traverse between the two summits, which reduces the overall distance and elevation but increases the difficulty dramatically, and should not be attempted unless you are experienced with technical climbing at high altitudes. Finally, the seldom-climbed North Pillar on Crestone Peak is another option for summiting the peak, and is for very advanced, technical climbers only.

Miles and Directions

0.0 Begin at the trailhead (9,900'), cross a footbridge, and hike west-southwest up the dirt road, following signs for South Colony Lake and Crestone Needle.

2.5 Pass the cutoff, on right, to dispersed camping at South Colony Lakes. This is an optional "shortcut" that rejoins the main trail and takes about 0.75 mile off the distance each way, but it's hard to locate or follow in the predawn darkness. Instead, continue on the road and cross South Colony Creek and the old parking area and trailhead at 11,080' (N37 57.880' / W105 32.750').

2.7 Pass through a gate and continue southeast, then contour north at 11,400' and enter the Sangre de Cristo Wilderness. The road narrows to trail.

4.0 Pass the other end of the cutoff to dispersed camping at South Colony Lakes. The trail turns west and contours above the lakes (N37 57.827' / W105 33.457').

4.2 At the trail junction, bear left to go southwest, then climb the steep, loose, Class 2+ gully up to Broken Hand Pass (N37 57.832' / W105 33.634').

5.0 At the top of Broken Hand Pass (12,900'), descend the west side on a steep trail to Cottonwood Lake (N37 57.533' / W105 34.270').

5.4 Go around the north side of the lake (12,310') and hike north around the southwest ridge of Crestone Needle. The Red Gully on Crestone Peak appears to the north. Do not take a direct route to the gully. Instead, climb easier terrain right of the direct route, toward a point to the right of the gully, then traverse up and left to the bottom of the gully (N37 57.494' / W105 34.585').

6.1 From the base of the Red Gully at 12,800', climb mixed Class 2+ and 3 dirt, rocks, and ledges, following the easiest and most solid path to the obvious notch (N37 57.718' / W105 35.034').

6.4 At the notch (14,100'), "East Crestone" appears to the east and unranked Class 5 "Northeast Crestone" is northeast, and the northeast couloir of Crestone Peak drops below your feet. Turn left and go west, scrambling up steep and exposed ledges for about 200'. Note your exit point near the summit so you can locate it for the descent (N 37 58.025' / W105 35.071').

6.5 Arrive at ranked 14,300' Crestone Peak. Return the way you came (N37 58.002' / W105 35.118').

13.0 Arrive back at the trailhead (N37 58.581' / W105 30.357').

36 Music Pass Peak: Tijeras Peak

Elevation: 13,604' (NAVD88 13,610')

Distinctions: Great Sand Dunes National Preserve Highpoint, Bicentennial, Ranked 13er

Class: 3; Class 1 to Lower Sand Creek Lake, mixed Class 2 and 3 to summit

Difficulty and skill level: Very Strenuous; Advanced

Approximate moving time: 10 hours from Grape Creek Trailhead; 7 hours from 4WD parking

Distance: 14.0 miles round-trip from Grape Creek Trailhead; 8.8 miles round-trip from 4WD parking

Elevation trailhead to summit: 9,260' to 13,610' (+4,350'), about 5,700' round-trip from Grape Creek Trailhead; 10,560' to 13,610' (+3,050'), about 4,400' round trip from 4WD parking

Terrain: Dirt trail, grass, willows, scree, talus, boulders, ledges, and slabs; exposure, risk of rockfall

Recommended extra gear: Helmet; crampons or microspikes and ice axe if ice exists on ramp

Restrictions: Music Pass Road is not maintained in winter; trail closed to bicycles and motor vehicles; the crux ramp may hold snow and ice, so a late summer to early fall climb is recommended; follow wilderness and preserve regulations

Amenities: Toilet at Grape Creek Trailhead; backcountry camping; services in Westcliffe

Trailhead: Grape Creek Trailhead

Trails: Music Pass Trail #1337, Lower Sand Creek Lake Trail #877, off-trail East Slopes and Northwest Ridge

Maps: DeLorme Page 81 A6, A7; USGS Crestone Peak, Beck Mountain

County: Saguache

Land status: San Isabel National Forest, (719) 553 1400, www.fo.usda.gov/psicc; San Carlos Ranger District, (719) 269-8500; Great Sand Dunes National Preserve, (719) 378-6300, www.nps.gov/grsa/index.htm; Sangre de Cristo Wilderness, www.wilderness.net

Finding the trailhead: From Westcliffe, take CO 69 South for 4.5 miles and turn right onto CR 119 / Colfax Lane. Go 5.6 miles and turn left onto unpaved CR 120 / South Colony Road. Drive 0.7 mile to rejoin CR 119 / Music Pass Road, and continue for another 4.5 miles to ample 2WD parking at the Grape Creek Trailhead. You may choose to drive higher on the rough road for 2.3 miles to the Music Pass Trailhead, or another 0.3 mile to the 4WD parking area (GPS: N37 55.810' / W105 27.443').

The Peak

Tijeras Peak sits at the northern end of the Great Sand Dunes National Preserve, with the approach from the east, at Music Pass near Westcliffe. *Tijeras* is Spanish for "scissors," referencing the scissor-like summit of the peak, and Music Pass is named for the winds that spill through the surrounding valleys and whistle through the pass. Tijeras Peak looks out at ranked 13ers Music Mountain, Pico Aislado, and Milwaukee Peak to the north, with the Crestones looming beyond, the Wet Mountains to the east, the Great Sand Dunes and Sierra Blanca Massif to the south, and west across the San Luis Valley to the La Garitas.

Tijeras Peak rises at Lower Sand Creek Lake west of Music Pass. PHOTO BY KEVIN BAKER

The Climb

Tijeras is accessible from summertime to late fall, before snow covers the road. Consider backpacking to Lower Sand Creek Lake for some excellent camping, and enjoy an early morning ascent. West of the lake, you'll encounter the crux: a cliff band that protects the face and access to the northwest ridge. A boulder-filled ramp leads to the top of the cliff. Note that a second ramp exists about 0.1 mile to the left (southeast) of the one described here. This ramp may be easier to locate due to a well-worn climber's trail leading to its base, but it's steeper, narrower, and much more difficult. Both ramps can hold snow and ice late in the season. Many more 13ers can be accessed via Music Pass and added to your climb with some planning and route-finding.

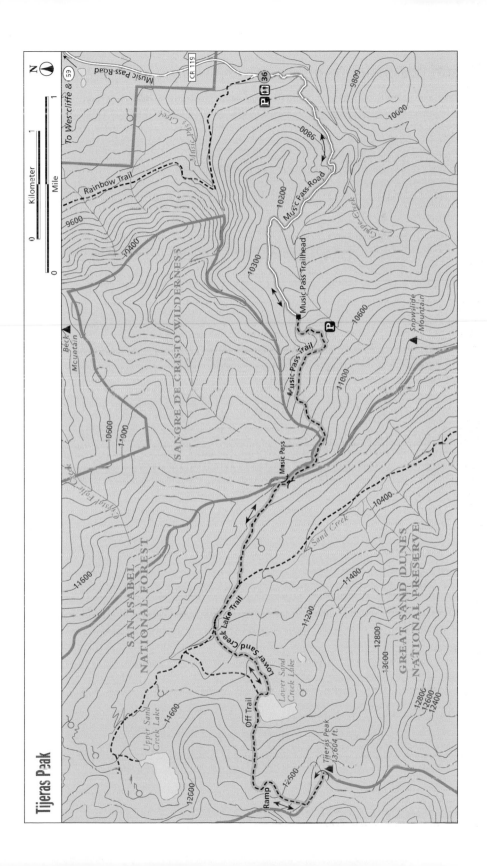

Tijeras Peak

To Westcliffe & 69

Music Pass Road

CR 119

Music Pass Road

Music Creek

Rainbow Trail

9600

10400

SANGRE DE CRISTO WILDERNESS

P 🚻 36

9800

10200

Music Pass Road

Grape Creek

Music Pass Trailhead

10300

10600

P

9800

Snowslide Mountain

11000

Music Pass Trail

Beck Mountain

10600

11400

Crestar Trail Creek

11600

Music Pass

Sand Creek

10400

GREAT SAND DUNES NATIONAL PRESERVE

SAN ISABEL NATIONAL FOREST

Sand Creek Lake Trail

Lower Sand Creek Lake

11400

11200

11600

Upper Sand Creek Lake

Off Trail

Lower Sand Creek Lake

12800

13600

12800
12600
12400

12600

12500

Ramp

Tijeras Peak
13,604 ft.

N

Kilometer
0   1
Mile
0   1

Miles and Directions

0.0 Begin at the Grape Creek Trailhead (9,260') and hike south on Music Pass Road.

2.3 At the Music Pass Trailhead (10,500'), continue west toward Music Pass (N37 55.641' / W105 29.126').

2.6 Pass the 4WD parking area (10,560') and continue west (N37 55.481' / W105 29.259').

3.9 At 11,446' Music Pass, go northwest on trail towards Lower Sand Creek Lake (N37 55.726' / W105 30.338').

4.7 Continue straight (northwest) at the 10,960' trail junction (N37 55.963' / W105 31.055').

5.0 Turn left onto Lower Sand Creek Lake Trail (11,020') and hike southwest through the forest. At the lake, turn right to skirt the north side of Lower Sand Creek Lake (N37 56.098' / W105 31.354').

5.9 Depart the trail at 11,480' and go west up grassy slopes, over talus and through willows, toward a large boulder and rocky ramp (N37 55.851' / W105 32.035').

6.4 At the base of the ramp (12,400'), climb southeast on loose talus and boulders (N37 55.832' / W105 32.526'). Exit the top of the ramp (N37 55.810' / W105 32.489') and climb south, up the steep slope to the top of the cliff band, where the terrain levels out at 12,600'. Set up a cairn at the top of the ramp, and the top of the cliff, so you can locate your exit on the descent. Hike south-southwest to a saddle left of unranked Point 13250.

6.8 At the 13,220' saddle, go southeast on the airy Class 3 ridge. Near the summit, bear left and approach the highpoint from the north side to avoid Class 4 moves (N37 55.571' / W105 32.640').

7.0 Arrive at ranked 13,610' Tijeras Peak. Return the way you came (N37 55.470' / W105 32.405').

14.0 Arrive back at the trailhead (N37 55.810' / W105 27.443').

37 Sangre de Cristo Range and Sierra Blanca Range Highpoint: Blanca Peak

Elevation: 14,345' (NAVD88 14,351')

Distinctions: Sangre de Cristo Mountains Highpoint, Sangre de Cristo Range Highpoint, Sierra Blanca Range Highpoint, Alamosa County Highpoint, Costilla County Highpoint, Huerfano County Highpoint, Centennial, Prominence 100, Ultra-prominence Peak, Ranked 14er

Class: 2+; Class 1 to Crater Lake, mixed Class 2 and 2+ to summit

Difficulty and skill level: Very Strenuous; Advanced

Approximate moving time: 12 hours

Distance: 20.0 miles round-trip

Elevation trailhead to summit: 7,600' to 14,351' (+6,751'); about 6,900' round-trip

Terrain: Rocky road, dirt trail, talus, ledges, and boulders; creek crossing; exposure, risk of rockfall

Recommended extra gear: Helmet; crampons or microspikes and ice axe if snow exists

Restrictions: Lake Como Road is extremely rough, the route described begins at 2WD trailhead; trail beyond Lake Como is closed to bicycles and motor vehicles; dogs must be on leash or under voice command

Amenities: Dispersed backcountry camping along FR 975 (Lake Como Road / Blanca Road) and between Lake Como and Crater Lake; limited services in Blanca; full services in Alamosa, Fort Garland, and Walsenburg

Trailhead: CO 150 and Lake Como Road

Trails: Lake Como Road, Blanca Peak Trail #886, off-trail Northwest Ridge

Maps: DeLorme Page 81 D7, E7; USGS Blanca Peak, Twin Peaks

Counties: Alamosa, Costilla

Land status: Rio Grande National Forest, (719) 852-5941, www.fs.usda.gov/riogrande; Saguache Ranger District, (719) 655-2547

Finding the trailhead: From Walsenburg, take US 160 West for 57.3 miles and turn right onto CO 150 North, or from Alamosa, take US 160 East for 14.4 miles and turn left onto CO 150 North. Drive 3.2 miles and turn right onto Lake Como Road, and park in a large open area on the side of the road (GPS: N37 31.317' / W105 36.083').

The Peak

Blanca Peak is one of just three ultra-prominence peaks, or "ultras," in the state and the highpoint of the Sierra Blanca Range, a massif that includes ranked 14ers Ellingwood Point, Little Bear Peak, and Mount Lindsey. The rock here is heavily faulted and fractured, and few solid routes exist on the peaks. The Sierra Blanca, or "white mountains," were likely named for snow that tips the highest reaches of the peaks, frosty beacons to Native Americans who once lived here and now to passersby on US 160. Blanca Peak is the easternmost of the four corners of the Navajo *Dinétah*, or native homeland, an area bounded to the west by the San Francisco Peaks of Arizona, to the south by Mount Taylor in New Mexico, and to the north by Hesperus Mountain. The summit offers views north across the Great Sand Dunes to the Crestones, and west across the San Luis Valley to the San Luis Hills and San Juan Mountains.

Blanca Peak is one of just three "ultras" in Colorado and the highpoint of three counties.
PHOTO BY BILL MIDDLEBROOK

The Climb

Blanca Peak is usually a two-day trip, hiking to Lake Como the first day and climbing the peak and hiking out on the next. You may be able to drive to a pullout about 1.6 miles up the road, or as high as 8,800'—an additional 1.7 miles—in a high-clearance SUV, but the road gets progressively rockier and eventually becomes unnavigable for street-legal vehicles. Look for pullouts and dispersed camping along the road, and park completely off the road so as not to block other vehicles. If you have the vehicle and the driving skills, consult off-road guidebooks for details on sketchy sections, known as Jaws 1, Jaws 2, Jaws 2.5, Jaws 3, and—beyond Lake Como—Jaws 4. The route described here begins at the 2WD parking area at the intersection of CO 150 and Lake Como Road. Blanca Peak is seldom climbed in the winter, due mainly to the very long approach. Three county highpoints converge near the summit, but only

Blanca Peak

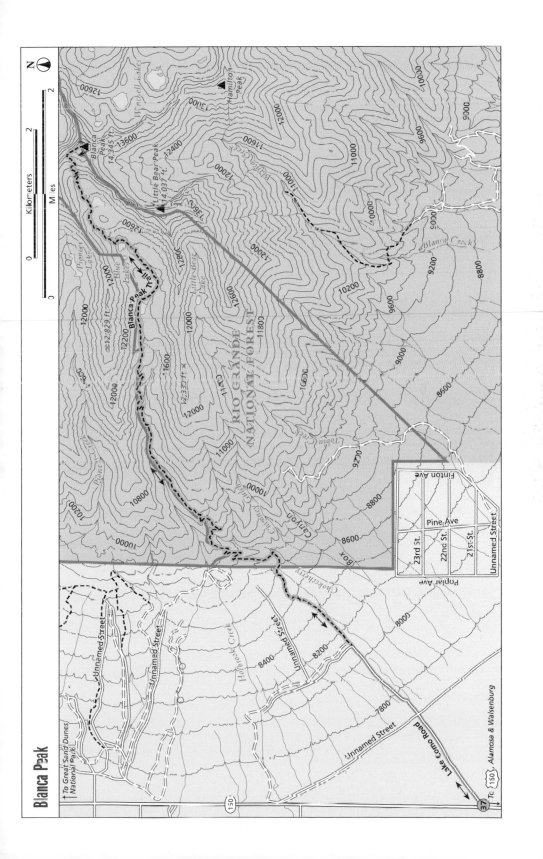

Rio Grande National Forest

To Great Sand Dunes National Park

Blanca Peak 14,345 ft.

Little Bear Peak 14,037 ft.

Hamilton Peak

Winchell Lakes

Pioneer Lakes

Blue Lakes

Blanca Peak Trail

Little Bear Lake

Big Bear Creek

Blanca Creek

Tobin Creek

Box Canyon

Choke cherry

Holbrook Creek

Lake Como Road

To 150, Alamosa & Walsenburg

Finton Ave

Pine Ave

Poplar Ave

23rd St.

22nd St.

21st St.

Unnamed Street

Unnamed Street

Unnamed Street

Unnamed Street

Unnamed Street

Kilometers

Miles

two of them, Alamosa and Costilla, are located at the highpoint. The third, "Huerfano County Highpoint," lies along Blanca's northeast ridge, near the summit. Blanca Peak can be combined with a trip to Ellingwood Point by returning to the Blanca-Ellingwood saddle and following cairns through talus, boulders, and ledges along the south face of the peak, up to the ridge and the summit. This is a loose route, and you may prefer Ellingwood Point's exciting and exposed, but more solid, Class 3 southwest ridge to get that peak. You can also access Blanca Peak from the north via the South Zapata Lake Trail, and from the south by climbing Little Bear Peak first—which is substantially more difficult—and then enjoy the very exposed, Class 5 Little Bear–Blanca traverse. Other technical routes on Blanca include Gash Ridge along the east ridge and Ormes Buttress on the northeast face. Whichever route you choose, do your homework, and be honest with yourself about your speed and skills. The Sierra Blanca offers a myriad of route options, but you will still have the long hike out.

Miles and Directions

0.0 Begin at the 2WD parking area at CO 150 and Lake Como Road (7,600') and hike northeast up the road, past Jaws 1 at 10,500'.

6.1 Cross Holbrook Creek on rocks (10,700'). Continue east up the road, past Jaws 2, 2.5, and 3 (N37 34.150' / W105 32.067').

7.3 Reach Lake Como (11,700') and continue east around the left side of the lake, where Lake Como Road becomes the official Blanca Peak Trail and Little Bear Peak is in view to the east. The trail bends south then north past Blue Lakes, passes below a waterfall, and climbs a steep, rocky slope above the fall. Continue past two small lakes (N37 34.211' / W105 30.902').

8.9 Reach Crater Lake (12,700') with Ellingwood Point and Blanca Peak straight ahead. Continue northeast to the Blanca face. The trail grows faint here, but cairns define the route through talus and boulders, and up and over ledges. Follow a faint trail east-northeast toward the ridge (N37 34.616' / E105 29.756').

9.7 Top out on the Blanca northwest ridge at about 13,800'. Turn right (southeast) and follow the ridge, at the crest or to the right (west) of the ridge, avoiding exposure on the east side (N37 34.813' / E105 29.231').

10.0 Arrive at ranked 14,351' Blanca Peak. Return the way you came (N37 34.650' / W105 29.142').

20.0 Arrive back at the trailhead (N37 31.317' / W105 36.083').

38 Spanish Peaks Highpoint: West Spanish Peak

Elevation: 13,626' (NAVD88 13,631')

Distinctions: Spanish Peaks Highpoint, Las Animas County Highpoint, Spanish Peaks Wilderness Highpoint, Bicentennial, Prominence 100, P3K, Ranked 13er; National Natural Landmark (Spanish Peaks)

Class: 2; Class 1 to timberline, mixed Class 1+ and 2 to summit

Difficulty and skill level: Moderate; Intermediate

Approximate moving time: 5 hours

Distance: 7.2 miles round-trip

Elevation trailhead to summit: 11,248' to 13,631' (+2,383')

Terrain: Dirt trail and talus

Restrictions: CR 46 to Cordova Pass is closed seasonally; trail closed to bicycles and motor vehicles; dogs must be on leash or under voice command; follow wilderness regulations

Amenities: Trailhead toilet; backcountry camping; seasonal camping along CR 46 and at Cordova Pass Picnic Area and Campground; services in La Veta and Aguilar

Trailhead: West Peak Trailhead

Trail: West Peak Trail #1390, off-trail Southwest Ridge

Maps: DeLorme Page 92 A3, B3; USGS Spanish Peaks, Herlick Canyon, Cucharas Pass

Counties: Huerfano, Las Animas

Land status: San Isabel National Forest, (719) 553-1400, www.fs.usda.gov/psicc; San Carlos Ranger District, (719) 269-8500, Spanish Peaks Wilderness, www.wilderness.net

Finding the trailhead: From US 160, about 11 miles west of Walsenburg and 30 miles east of Fort Garland, go south on CO 12 South (Highway of Legends). Drive 22 miles, through La Veta and Cuchara, following signs to stay on CO 12. Turn left onto unpaved CR 46, and drive 6 miles to the trailhead at Cordova Pass (GPS. N37 20.916' / W105 1.473').

The Peak

West Spanish Peak and its sister peak, ranked 12er East Spanish Peak, are known collectively as the Spanish Peaks. Each mountain is an individual igneous stock, an intrusion formed from molten lava that pushed up through rock, cooled and hardened, and became exposed as the surrounding rock eroded away. The west summit is the easternmost 4,000-meter peak in the United States and has the greatest prominence of any 13,000' peak in Colorado. The Spanish Peaks, or Huajatolla—pronounced "Wa-ha-toy-a" and meaning "breasts of the earth"—were landmarks for the Utes and are a National Natural Landmark. Hundreds of radial, igneous dikes surround West Spanish Peak, and you will have views of them—including the spectacular "Devils Staircase"—on your drive to the trailhead and from the summit. On a clear day you can see south into New Mexico from the top of West Spanish Peak and north to Pikes Peak. Closer in, East Spanish Peak lies east, with Fishers Peak southeast, the Culebra Range south, the Sierra Blanca northwest, and the Wet Mountains north.

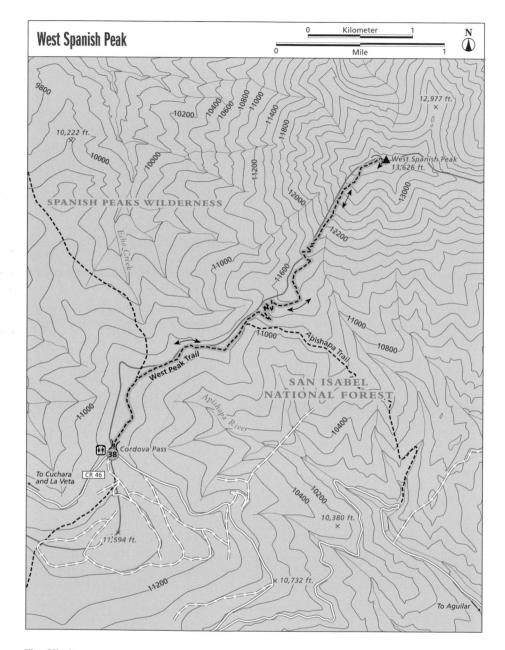

West Spanish Peak

0   Kilometer   1

0   Mile   1

N

9800

12,977 ft.

10,222 ft.

10,200

10,400

10,600

10,800

11,000

11,400

11,800

10,000

10,000

SPANISH PEAKS WILDERNESS

11,200

12,000

West Spanish Peak
13,626 ft.

13,000

Echo Creek

12,200

11,000

11,600

11,000

Apishapa Trail

10,800

West Peak Trail

11,000

SAN ISABEL
NATIONAL FOREST

Apishapa River

11,000

10,400

38 Cordova Pass

To Cuchara
and La Veta

CR 46

10,400

10,200

10,380 ft.

11,594 ft.

11,200

10,732 ft.

To Aguilar

The Climb

West Spanish Peak is isolated and covered with rock, with a southern approach, so it's
best climbed in the fall or spring to take advantage of cooler temperatures and when
lightning danger is less of a concern. East Spanish Peak is close by, but there is no
connecting ridge so they're climbed separately.

West Spanish Peak is the easternmost 4,000-meter peak in the United States and has the greatest prominence of any 13,000' peak in Colorado. PHOTO BY STEWART M. GREEN

Miles and Directions

0.0 From the trailhead (11,248'), hike northeast through the forest to a small meadow, with West Spanish Peak in view to the northeast.

0.3 Enter the Spanish Peaks Wilderness, pass the Salazar Trail to the left, and stay straight on West Peak Trail. Cross an open area with views of Fishers Peak Mesa, southeast.

0.5 Pass the Levy-Krier Trail to the left, and stay straight on West Peak Trail.

1.6 Make a hard switchback left to stay on the West Peak Trail at 11,300', and avoid getting onto the Apishapa Trail. Climb switchbacks northeast, to the southwest ridge of the peak (N37 21.655' / W105 0.390').

2.7 From the talus field at 11,950', the trail meanders northeast through talus and dirt, marked by dozens of cairns and yellow bull's-eyes (N37 22.077' / W105 0.109').

3.5 At the top of the ridge (13,500'), turn right and go northeast to the highpoint (N37 22.50' / W104 59.762').

3.6 Arrive at ranked 13,631' West Spanish Peak. The two summits east of the highpoint are lower. Return the way you came (N37 22.547' / W104 59.631').

7.2 Arrive back at the trailhead (N37 20.916' / W105 1.473').

39 Culebra Range Highpoint: Culebra Peak

Elevation: 14,047' (NAVD88 14,053')

Distinctions: Culebra Range Highpoint, Centennial, Prominence 100, P4K, Ranked 14er

Class: 2

Difficulty and skill level: Strenuous; Advanced

Approximate moving time: 5 hours

Distance: 5.4 miles round-trip

Elevation trailhead to summit: 11,630' to 14,053' (+2,423'); about 2,900' round-trip

Terrain: Dirt, grass, tundra, talus, and boulders

Recommended extra gear: Crampons or microspikes and ice axe if snow exists

Restrictions: Advance reservations waiver and fee required; climbers must check in at 6 a.m. and out by 6 p.m.; days open to climb and number of climbers allowed is limited; no bicycles or pets; no motor vehicles allowed beyond the 4WD parking area

Amenities: Primitive camping outside the gate, toilet inside the gate; services in San Luis and Fort Garland

Trailhead: 4WD start on Road K S

Trail: Off-trail Northwest Ridge

Maps: DeLorme Page 92 D1; USGS Culebra Peak, El Valle Creek

County: Costilla

Land status: Cielo Vista Ranch, www.cielovista ranchco.com

Finding the trailhead: From US 160 in Fort Garland, take CO 169 South for 15.5 miles to San Luis. At the Conoco gas station, turn left (east) on P.6 Road and drive 4 miles, then turn left onto L.7 Road. Drive 3.5 miles, cross a bridge, and turn right onto an unpaved Road 25.5. Go 0.5 mile, turn left onto M.5 Road, and continue 0.9 mile to the locked gate. You can camp here the night before your climb. A ranch representative will open the gates the next morning and escort you 2 miles to the ranch headquarters to check in. From there, drive 0.1 mile on the dirt road, bear right, and continue 3.4 miles to the lower "Four Way" trailhead. You can park here to ensure a 3,000' elevation gain, or continue another 1 mile on 4WD CR K S to the upper trailhead with parking on the right (GPS: N37 8.344' / W105 12.941').

The Peak

The Culebra Range trends north–south from La Veta Pass, Colorado, to Costilla Creek, New Mexico, and Culebra Peak is the only 14,000' peak in the range. Unlike the stiff climbs of the Crestones and loose climbs of the Sierra Blanca, the Culebras offer easy hikes along the sloping hills of their western flanks. Most of the range is on private property, and access to Culebra Peak is controlled by owners of the Cielo Vista Ranch. Make a reservation on their website well in advance. The Culebra Range and peak are named for nearby Culebra Creek, or *Rio de la Culebra*, "snake river." From Culebra Peak, the Sangre de Cristo Range continues south into the Taos Mountains of New Mexico and state highpoint Wheeler Peak, 40 miles away.

The Climb

Access to Culebra Peak is allowed on summer Fridays and Saturdays, and occasional days in the winter for an additional fee, so check the Cielo Vista Ranch website for

Culebra Peak

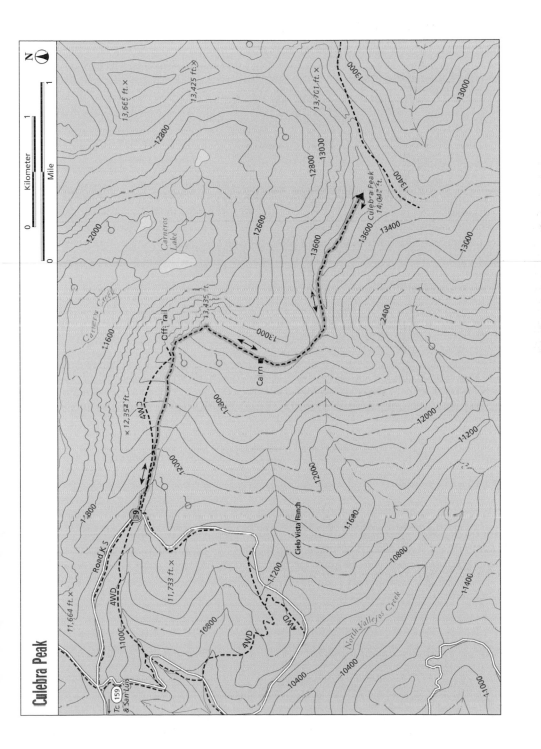

N

Kilometer
0   1

Mile
0   1

Tc 159
To San Luis

Road K.5

4WD
11,000

4WD

× 11,664 ft.

× 11,733 ft.

10800

4WD

4WD

10400

Cielo Vista Ranch

North Vallejos Creek

11,000

11400

11200

10800

11600

12000

12800

13,568 ft. ×

13,425 ft. ×

Carneros Lake

Carneros Creek

12000

11600

× 12,352 ft.

4WD

Cliff Trail

13,435 ft. ×

13200

12800

12600

13000

13000

13600

13,701 ft. ×

13600 Culebra Peak
14,047 ft.

13400

13400

13000

13000

Cam

12000

11200

12000

An enormous cairn marks the route on Culebra Peak in the Culebra Range.
PHOTO BY BILL MIDDLEBROOK

availability to plan your climb. You can start from the lower "Four Way" trailhead and hike up the road to gain 3,000' of elevation, a standard rule adopted by many Colorado 14er climbers to ensure they have made a worthy ascent of the peak, or you can not worry about the protocol and just start at the 4WD trailhead at the end of the road. Centennial peak Red Mountain is also located on Cielo Vista land, so if you want to do that peak, too, let the landowners know, pay the extra fee, and follow the ridge south from Culebra for less than a mile to the summit. Winter climbs/skis start lower, so expect a much bigger day!

Miles and Directions

0.0   Begin at the trailhead (11,630') and hike east on the left side of the drainage, contouring east-southeast to the ridge ahead. Stay above the boulder field to your right.

1.0   At the ridge (13,000'), turn right (south) and follow the crest over tundra, talus, and boulders (N37 8.173' / W105 11.969').

1.2   Climb over unranked Point 13435 and bear right (south-southwest) on the ridge (N37 8.037' / W105 11.882').

1.6   Pass a large cairn and go southeast on the ridge (N37 7.777' / W105 12.070').

2.0   Turn left and follow the ridge east. Pay attention to this turn on your descent, and do not take the other ridge that goes south. Hike over a false summit, with Red Mountain in view, and continue east-southeast over grass and tundra, then climb the final rocky pitch to the summit (N37 7.509' / W105 11.864').

2.7   Arrive at ranked 14,053' Culebra Peak. Return the way you came (N37 07.341' / W105 11.147').

5.4   Arrive back at the trailhead (N37 8.344' / W105 12.941').

Southern Sand Dunes, Hills, and Mesas

The Great Sand Dunes and Hills of the San Luis Valley and the Raton Mesas rise up in southern Colorado, west and east of the Sangre de Cristo Range, their formations presenting unique highpointing alternatives for the Colorado mountaineer. Great Sand Dunes National Park borders the Sangre de Cristo Range in the San Luis Valley, with the national preserve

The Great Sand Dunes border the Crestone Mountains of the Sangre de Cristo Range, with unique highpointing alternatives for the Colorado mountaineer. PHOTO BY STEWART M. GREEN

extending east into the mountain range. The park is home to the tallest and highest dunes in North America. Sandy dunes may seem out of place in a state known for Rocky Mountains, but geologists believe the 30-square-mile dune field was formed when a lake at the eastern edge of the San Luis Valley was breached and drained, leaving behind the upper crust, or "sand sheet," of the lake bed. Opposing winds funnel through the surrounding mountain passes—Mosca, Medano, and Music—driving the sand into high, spiraling "star dunes." The Great Sand Dunes Wilderness lies within the park.

The San Luis Valley extends west to the San Juan Mountains, north to the Sawatch Mountains at Poncha Pass, and south into New Mexico. The 8,000-square-mile valley is the largest of Colorado's four great parks and was formed by the Rio Grande Rift, the north-to-south-trending fault along which many of the state's 14,000' peaks are found. The highest peaks in Colorado exist where this fault intersects the Mineral Belt, near Leadville. In contrast, the low, scrubby peaks of the San Luis Hills dot the valley floor, miles away from the towering peaks that border the rift and valley.

On the other side of the Sangre de Cristo Range, the Raton Mesas comprise 20,000 square miles of tablelands above the Great Plains of southeastern Colorado, western Oklahoma, and northern Texas and New Mexico. The mesas are formed of soft shale and sandstone capped with a layer of hard basalt. The protective capstones maintain the flat tops of the mesas, while the exposed softer rock erodes at the edges, falling away into deep canyons and precipices. The Raton Mesas reach a highpoint in Colorado, and along with the sand dunes and hills west of the Sangres, introduce a new dimension of climbing possibilities in Colorado.

40 Great Sand Dunes Local Favorites: High Dune and Star Dune

Elevations: 8,694' (High Dune); 8,620' (Star Dune)

Distinctions: Ranked 8er (High Dune); Tallest sand dune from base to summit in North America, Unranked 8er (Star Dune)

Class: 2

Difficulty and skill level: Moderate; Beginner

Approximate moving time: 4 hours

Distance: 7.1-mile loop

Elevation trailhead to summit: 8,060' to 8,694' (+634'); about 800' round-trip

Terrain: Sand; creek crossing

Recommended extra gear: Protective gear against wind-driven sand including sunglasses, a snug-fitting hat, and a buff for your nose and mouth; GPS

Restrictions: Fee area; dogs must be on leash and are allowed in day-use area only, not on dunes; no bicycles or motor vehicles allowed on dunes; follow wilderness regulations

Amenities: Restrooms at visitor center; seasonal camping in park at Piñon Flats Campground; backcountry camping on dunes and overnight parking at trailhead limited to 6 per party, by free permit available at visitor center; picnic tables near Dunes Parking Lot and along dunes area; additional camping at campgrounds outside park; toilets at picnic areas; services in Blanca, Fort Garland, and Alamosa

Trailhead: Dunes Parking Lot

Trail: Off-trail East Slopes and South Ridge

Maps: DeLorme Page 81 C6, C7; USGS Liberty, Zapata Ranch

County: Alamosa

Land status: Great Sand Dunes National Park and Preserve, (719) 378-6300, www.nps.gov/grsa/index.htm; Great Sand Dunes Wilderness, www.wilderness.net

Finding the trailhead: From US 160, about 56 miles west of Walsenburg and 15 miles east of Alamosa, go north on CO 150. Drive 19.8 miles, into Great Sand Dunes National Park and Preserve and past the visitor center, and turn left towards the Dunes Picnic Area. Continue 0.7 mile to paved parking and the trailhead at the northwest edge of the lot (GPS: N37 44.370' / W105 31.047').

The Peak

Star Dune rises 750' from the sand valley floor, and High Dune rises 650' but is higher in elevation—height above sea level—than Star Dune. Together they make for a fine loop hike in the Great Sand Dunes Wilderness. Sand dunes develop in several ways; both Star Dune and High Dune are "star dunes," which tend to grow upwards rather than sideways, and are among the tallest in the world. From each summit, you will be treated to views of cream and tan dunes for miles around in freeform curves, domes, and spirals. The high peaks of the Sangre de Cristo Range provide a backdrop, with the Crestones guarding the northern skies and ranked 13er Mount Herard to the east. Although Herard's summit lies outside the park, "Herard Ridge," a point on its southern slopes, is the highest point within the park and a destination for national park highpointers, while ranked 13er Tijeras Peak is the highpoint of the entire park and preserve.

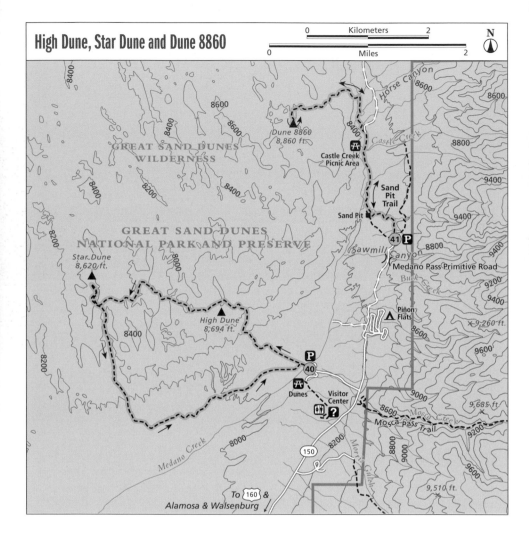

Kilometers

Miles

N

8400
8600
8600
Dune 8860
8,860 ft.
Castle Creek
GREAT SAND DUNES
WILDERNESS
8400
8200
8400
Castle Creek
Picnic Area
8800
9400
Horse Canyon
8600
8600
Castle Creek
8800

GREAT SAND DUNES
NATIONAL PARK AND PRESERVE
Star Dune
8,620 ft.
8000
8400
High Dune
8,694 ft.
8200
8400
8200
Sand
Pit
Trail
Sand Pit
41
P
Sawmill Canyon
8800
Medano Pass Primitive Road
Buck Creek
9400
9200
9400
9400
9400
9600

P
40
Dunes
Visitor
Center
Piñon
Flats
×–9,260 ft.
8600
9000
9,685 ft.
8600
Mosca Creek
Mosca Pass Trail
9200

Medano Creek
8000
150
8200
8800
9000
9600
9,510 ft.
×

To 160 &
Alamosa & Walsenburg

The Climb

Great Sand Dunes National Park and Preserve is open 24 hours a day, 365 days a year, so you can climb the dunes any time. The dunes area is treeless and exposed to the elements, so bring plenty of water and sun protection. In warmer months, the surface temperature of the sand can rise to 140°F; wear shoes or hiking boots and not sandals, and start early to avoid hiking in the midday sun and when storms may be moving in. Any time of year, check the weather report to avoid hiking on days where high winds are predicted or when there is a threat of lightning. Avoid steep slopes and seek out gentle ridgelines to follow on your ascent, and hike on or near the ridge crests on the windward—rather than leeward—side, where the sand is more compact. Avoid losing elevation and choose your route carefully—the most direct route may not be the best route. Uphill progress is slow on the sand dunes, but the descents are fast. With

Unranked 8er Star Dune is the tallest sand dune from base to tip in North America.
PHOTO BY STEWART M. GREEN

a little skill and good balance, standing and seated glissades are possible. Choose your endpoint before you begin, and don't slide into a sand crater.

Miles and Directions

0.0 Begin at the trailhead (8,060') and hike northwest on a short walkway to the day-use area. Cross Medano Creek, with High Dune straight ahead. Approach the summit on ridges to the left of center that switch back and forth to the top.

1.4 Arrive at ranked 8,694' High Dune. Locate Star Dune, in view to the west. Descend the western slopes of High Dune and hike west, using ridges to switch back and forth toward Star Dune. Do not take the final ridge that climbs directly to the summit, but head for the base of a gentler slope located to the left (south) of the ridge (N37 44.957' / W105 31.976').

3.1 Ascend the sand slope to the ridge crest, then turn right and follow the ridge north to the summit (N37 45.010' / W105 33.475').

3.4 Arrive at unranked 8,620' Star Dune. Retrace your steps to descend the ridgeline and the slope. Instead of climbing back over High Dune, head south (right), across a flat area and to the edge of the dunes, then curve left and descend to the creek bed (N37 45.098' / W105 33.481').

5.2 From the creek bed, go east, following Medano Creek back to the day-use area (N37 43.844' / W105 32.818').

7.1 Arrive back at the trailhead (N37 44.370' / W105 31.047').

41 Great Sand Dunes Highpoint: Dune 8860

See map on page 154.

Elevation: 8,860'

Distinctions: Highest sand dune in Great Sand Dunes National Park and Preserve, highest sand dune in North America, highest ranked summit in Great Sand Dunes Wilderness, Ranked 8er

Class: 2; Class 1 to dunes area, Class 2 to summit

Difficulty and skill level: Moderate; Intermediate

Approximate moving time: 4 hours

Distance: 5.6 miles round-trip

Elevation trailhead to summit: 8,360' to 8,860' (+500')

Terrain: Dirt and sand; creek crossing

Recommended extra gear: Protective clothing including sunglasses, a snug-fitting hat for your ears, and a buff for your nose and mouth; GPS

Restrictions: Fee area; dogs must be on leash and are allowed in day-use area only, not on dunes; no bicycles or motor vehicles allowed on trail or on dunes; follow wilderness regulations

Amenities: Visitor center open year-round; seasonal camping at Piñon Flats Campground; backcountry camping on dunes and overnight parking at trailhead limited to 6 per party, by free permit available at visitor center; primitive camping along 4WD sections of Medano Pass Road; additional camping at campgrounds out-side park; restrooms at visitor center; toilets at Sand Pit and Castle Creek Picnic Area; services in Blanca, Fort Garland, and Alamosa

Trailhead: Point of No Return Trailhead

Trail: Sand Ramp Trail, off-trail North Ridge

Maps: DeLorme Page 81 C6, C7; USGS Liberty

County: Saguache

Land status: Great Sand Dunes National Park and Preserve, (719) 378-6300, www.nps.gov/grsa/index.htm; Great Sand Dunes Wilderness, www.wilderness.net

Finding the trailhead: From US 160, about 56 miles west of Walsenburg and 15 miles east of Alamosa, go north on CO 150. Drive 18.7 miles to the entrance gate of Great Sand Dunes National Park and Preserve. Continue for 1.5 miles, past the visitor center, and turn left onto unpaved Medano Pass Primitive Road. Drive 1.2 miles to a small parking area on the right (GPS: N37 45.488' / W105 30.071').

The Peak

Dune 8860 rises higher in elevation above sea level than any other dune in Great Sand Dunes National Park and Preserve, the Great Sand Dunes Wilderness, and in all of North America. It sees few visitors, though, due to route-finding challenges that can be overcome with good directions and a GPS. Like the other dunes in the park, Dune 8860 offers fantastic views of miles of dunes and the Sangre de Cristo Range.

The Climb

The dunes can be climbed year-round, but avoid days of high winds, which can reach a fever pitch on springtime afternoons. Cover your eyes, nose, mouth, and ears to keep out wind-driven sand. A GPS comes in handy to locate the highpoint.

A GPS and a hand level come in handy to locate the unmarked summit of Dune 8860 in Great Sand Dunes National Park and Preserve. PHOTO BY SUSAN JOY PAUL

Miles and Directions

0.0 From the trailhead, cross the road to the Sand Pit Trail (8,360') and hike north along the east banks of Medano Creek. Alternatively, you can skip the trail and just hike the road to the Sand Pit, but you will add 0.2 mile to the route, and it is not as scenic.

0.4 Exit the trail at the Sand Pit and follow the 4WD dirt road north (N37 45.734' / W105 30.366').

1.1 Pass through a gate and hike north past the Castle Creek Picnic Area. Medano Creek and the sand dunes border your route to the west, while high peaks line the horizon ahead, including Mount Herard to the north and ranked 12er Mount Zwischen, east.

1.3 Depart the road to the left and follow a faint trail north (N37 46.484' / W105 30.408').

1.7 Cross Medano Creek and go west, up a steep embankment and onto the sand dunes.

1.8 Contour the sand bench north and then west, across the sandy flats. The dune summit lies southwest (N37 46.799' / W105 30.564').

2.2 Continue west to an east-to-west-lying ridge (N37 46.715' / W105 30.886').

2.3 Climb a short slope to gain the low point at the east end of the ridge, and follow it west (N37 46.715' / W105 30.971').

2.6 Gain the north ridge, and go south toward the summit.

2.8 Arrive at ranked 8,860' Dune 8860. Return the way you came (N37 46.543' / W105 31.21').

5.6 Arrive back at the trailhead (N37 45.488' / W105 30.071').

42 San Luis Hills Highpoint: "Piñon Hills"

Elevation: 9,476' (NAVD88 9,480')
Distinctions: San Luis Hills Highpoint, Piñon Hills Highpoint, Prominence 200, P1K, Ranked 9er
Class: 2
Difficulty and skill level: Easy; Intermediate
Approximate moving time: 2 hours
Distance: 2.6 miles round-trip
Elevation trailhead to summit: 8,025' to 9,480' (+1,455')
Terrain: Dirt and brush

Restrictions: None posted
Amenities: Limited services in Manassa; full services in San Luis and Fort Garland
Trailhead: BLM unsigned "Old Lantern Well"
Trail: Off-trail Northwest Ridge
Maps: DeLorme Page 90 D4; USGS Manassa NE
County: Conejos
Land status: Bureau of Land Management, San Luis Valley Field Office, (719) 655-2547, www.blm.gov/co/st/en/fo/slvfo.html

Finding the trailhead: From US 160 in Fort Garland, take CO 159 South / Miranda Avenue for 15.6 miles and turn right onto CO 142 West. Drive 28.5 miles and turn left onto unpaved CR 20. Follow CR 20 for 1.8 mile and turn left at the T-intersection onto Road M, then go 0.9 mile and follow the dirt road as it curves left. Continue for another 2.2 miles as the road passes through a gate, then bends to the right and dead-ends at the base of a drainage (GPS: N37 8.956' / W105 50.556').

The Peak

"Piñon Hills" is named for the pine nut of the piñon pine, and the San Luis Hills are named for nearby San Luis, the oldest town in Colorado. The peaks here attract folks desperate for a summit when the rest of the state is on high avalanche alert. From the top of "Piñon Hills" you'll have views east to the Culebra Range, west to the San Juan Mountains, and south into New Mexico. More San Luis Hills, including "South Piñon Hills," Flat Top, and "Brownie Hills," are also in view.

The Climb

This is a long drive to a short climb of a seldom-visited highpoint. Since you have come all this way, you may want to hit other summits in the area. Check the land status of each before you go, as access may be blocked by private property. Consider a stop in San Luis to visit the Stations of the Cross shrine, a short, scenic hike to a lovely chapel that makes for a good leg-stretcher on the way out or back.

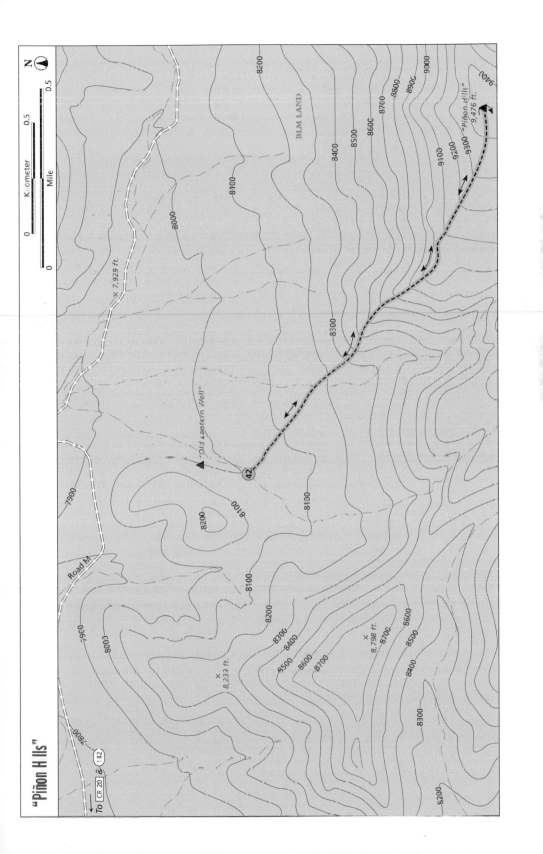

"Piñon Hills"

N

0   0.5
Kilometer

0   0.5
Mile

To CR 20 & 112

Road M

7900

8008

7900

× 8,233 ft.

7900

8000

8100

8200

8100

8100

"Old Lantern Well"

42

8200

8300

8400
8500
8600
8700

8600
8500

× 8,798 ft.

8700

8600

8500

8400

8300

8200

× 7,929 ft.

8000

8100

8300

8300

8400

8500

8600

8700
8800
8900

9100

9200

9300 "Piñon Hills"
9,476 ft.

9400

9000

8200

BLM LAND

Ranked 9er "Piñon Hills," one of the 200 most prominent peaks in the state, rises in the San Luis Hills of southern Colorado. PHOTO BY SUSAN JOY PAUL

Miles and Directions

0.0 Begin at the trailhead (8,025') and hike southeast on a use trail to the base of the northwest ridge. Do not follow the trail deep into the drainage, or you'll be forced onto very rough terrain on the western slopes of the peak.

0.8 Climb southeast on the ridge and east to the summit (N37 8.500' / W105 49.920').

1.3 Arrive at ranked 9,480' "Piñon Hills" and a rocky cairn at the highpoint. Return the way you came (N37 8.377' / W105 49.438').

2.6 Arrive back at the trailhead (N37 8.956' / W105 50.556').

43 Fishers Peak Mesa and Raton Mesa Highpoints: Fishers Peak Mesa and Fishers Peak

Elevations: 9,626' (NAVD88 9,630') Fishers Peak Mesa; 9,627' (NAVD88 9,631') Fishers Peak

Distinctions: Fishers Peak Mesa Highpoint, Ranked 9er (Fishers Peak Mesa); Raton Mesa Highpoint, Prominence 100, P1K, Ranked 9er (Fishers Peak)

Class: 3, Class 1 to top of mesa, mixed Class 1 and 2 to Fishers Peak Mesa, mixed Class 1, 2, and 3 to Fishers Peak

Difficulty and skill level: Very Strenuous; Advanced

Approximate moving time: 15 hours

Distance: 22.8 miles round-trip

Elevation trailhead to summit: 7,583' to 9,631' (+2,048'); about 5,000' round-trip

Terrain: Dirt trail, tundra, scree, brush, and boulders; exposure

Recommended extra gear: Protective clothing, GPS

Restrictions: Access to James M. John State Wildlife Area is prohibited Dec 1 through Apr 1; trail closed to bicycles and motor vehicles; dogs must be on leash; camping prohibited within 200 yards of Lake Dorothey; observe all state wildlife area regulations

Amenities: Seasonal camping, picnic areas, showers, visitor center, and restrooms at Sugarite Canyon State Park; toilet at trailhead; trailhead camping and backcountry camping; services in Raton

Trailhead: Lake Dorothey Trailhead

Trails: James M. John State Wildlife Area Access Trail, Pipeline Trail, off-trail South Ridge

Maps: DeLorme Page 93 E8, D8; USGS Yankee (NM), Barela, Fishers Peak (CO)

County: Las Animas

Land status: Lake Dorothey State Wildlife Area and James M. John State Wildlife Area, www.cpw.state.co.us; Colorado Parks & Wildlife, Southeast Office-Pueblo, (719) 561-5300

Finding the trailhead: From Trinidad, take I-25 South for 26 miles to Raton Pass. Continue into New Mexico for 7.5 miles and take exit 452 for NM 72 East towards Raton/Folsom. Go 0.2 mile and turn left onto NM 72 East / E. Cook Avenue and continue onto NM 526 East. Drive 10.1 miles, through Sugarite Canyon State Park and back into Colorado, then continue for 0.4 mile on unpaved CR 85.5 to a parking area on the left (GPS: N36 59.903' / W104 21.937').

The Peaks

Fishers Peak and Fishers Peak Mesa define the skyline at Trinidad, near Raton Pass. The peak, a tower at the northern tip of the mesa, is the highpoint of Raton Mesa, the highest of the Raton Mesas. Fishers Peak Mesa is the highpoint of the tableland that shares its name, Fishers Peak Mesa, a section of the larger Raton Mesa. Rising more than 3,000 feet above the plains, the peaks provide stunning views west and north. The Spanish Peaks, Culebra Range, Sangre de Cristo Range, and even Pikes Peak are in view from Fishers Peak.

The exposed south ridge of Fishers Peak looks out over Trinidad to the Spanish Peaks.
PHOTO BY SUSAN JOY PAUL

The Climb

Private property surrounds Fishers Peak in Colorado, but the summits of Fishers Peak and Fishers Peak Mesa lie within Colorado State Wildlife Area, with access from the south, in New Mexico. This is a very long day, and there are no trees on the mesa, and no shelter from wind, rain, or sun. Lightning is a danger, and water sources are few, muddied, and not to be trusted, so bring enough fresh water to last the entire route. The climb is best done in the spring and fall, and not in extreme heat or when there is lightning danger. A 900-feet-deep gorge separates the summits of Fishers Peak and Fishers Peak Mesa, and an exposed ridge guards the summit of the highest point, presenting the crux of the climb. On your descent, be sure to depart the Pipeline Trail in time to pick up the road off the mesa. The trail continues south into New Mexico, miles from the trailhead, and a canyon separates this trail from your required route. A GPS is useful here. There are many deep-cut canyons in the mesa, and if you accidentally hike along one in the wrong direction, you will be forced to hike the length of it back out to get on track. There are many dirt roads, too, so pay attention

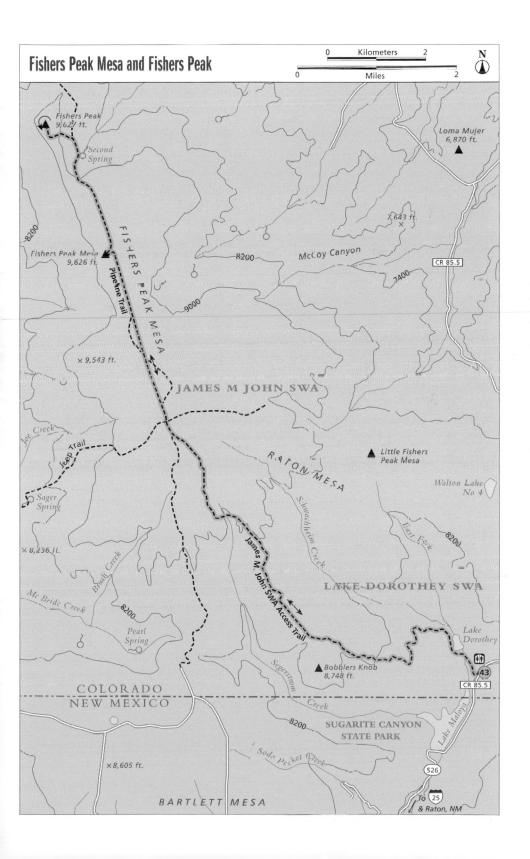

Fishers Peak Mesa and Fishers Peak

Kilometers
0   2

Miles
0   2

N

Fishers Peak
9,625 ft.

Second
Spring

Loma Mujer
6,870 ft.

8200

7,643 ft.
×

FISHERS PEAK MESA

Fishers Peak Mesa
9,626 ft.

McCoy Canyon

8200

7400

CR 85.5

Pipeline Trail

9000

× 9,543 ft.

JAMES M JOHN SWA

Joe Creek

Jeep Trail

RATON MESA

Little Fishers
Peak Mesa

Walton Lake
No 4

Sager
Spring

Schwachheim Creek

East Fork

8200

× 8,256 ft.

Brush Creek

James M. John SWA Access Trail

LAKE DOROTHEY SWA

Mc Bride Creek

8200

Pearl
Spring

Lake
Dorothey

43

CR 85.5

COLORADO
NEW MEXICO

Segerstrom Creek

Bobblers Knob
8,748 ft.

Lake Maloya

× 8,605 ft.

Creek

8200

SUGARITE CANYON
STATE PARK

Soda Pocket Creek

526

To 25
& Raton, NM

BARTLETT MESA

and don't get off on the wrong track. You can split the climb over two days and camp on the mesa, or at Sugarite Canyon State Park, then get an early start in the morning, descend the peak before dark, and take advantage of the hot showers at the park and a meal in Raton or Trinidad.

Miles and Directions

0.0 Begin at the trailhead (7,583') and hike south, then north and west up the road. Don't cut switchbacks. The terrain is thick with sharp, thorny locust and sticky burrs.

0.5 Continue north on the road around the west side of Lake Dorothey (7,626'), with ranked 8er Bobblers Knob to the left, and join the James M. John SWA Access Trail. Hike the road/trail northwest to the top of the mesa (N37 0.123' / W104 22.253').

5.5 Depart the road at 9,140' and go north-northwest on open terrain to pick up the Pipeline Trail (N37 1.586' / W104 25.500').

6.9 Go north-northwest on the Pipeline Trail, at about 9,520' (N37 2.589' / W104 26.143').

9.2 Arrive at ranked 9,630' Fishers Peak Mesa. The highpoint is on a small outcrop to the left of the trail, and there's a cairn with a register to the right of the trail. Tag both, to ensure your summit. Fishers Peak is visible to the north. Continue on the Pipeline Trail (N37 4.423' / W104 26.974').

10.1 Descend the steep, loose dirt and scree trail to the right of the pipeline (9,400'). Deep in the canyon, your views of Fishers Peak are obscured by the forest (N37 5.177' / W104 27.220').

10.8 Depart the trail on the left (8,720') and bushwhack west through trees and up a steep, thorny gully to a weakness in the cliffs on the south side of the peak (N37 5.681' / W104 27.423').

11.2 At the top of the gully (9,400'), clamber up rock slabs and a short Class 3 section to gain the ridge. The ridge crest is exposed, with a sharp drop-off to the west. Turn right (north) and cross a short catwalk, then follow the trail to the right and up another short Class 3 section through the cliffs and up to the mesa (N37 5.710' / W104 27.755').

11.3 On top of the mesa (9,560'), hike north-northwest to the highest point (N37 5.753' / W104 27.756').

11.4 Arrive at ranked 9,631' Fishers Peak, marked by a small cairn and Forest Service marker. Return the way you came (N37 5.847' / W104 27.808').

22.8 Arrive back at the trailhead (N36 59.903' / W104 21.937').

The Park Ranges

The Park Ranges begin at the Wyoming border northwest of Steamboat Springs and trend south through central Colorado to Trout Creek Pass near Buena Vista. The ranges lie west of the Front Range and east of the Sawatch Range, and border the western edges of North, Middle, and South Parks. The Sierra Madre, Sawtooth, Park, Elkhead, Rabbit Ears, Gore, Tenmile, and Mosquito Ranges comprise the Park Ranges of Colorado and are home to the Mount Zirkel, Sarvis Creek, Eagles Nest, and Buffalo Peaks Wilderness Areas. The Continental Divide enters Colorado from the north in the Park Ranges' Sierra Madre Range. The Great Divide runs south through the Park Range and east through the Rabbit Ears Range, and joins the Front Range in the Never Summer Mountains. The Divide follows the Front Range south to Hoosier Pass, where it rejoins the Park Ranges at the Mosquitos, and turns west toward the southern Gores at Fremont Pass. The five ranked 14ers of the Park Ranges are clustered in the Tenmile-Mosquito Range. Roads and trails at Rabbit Ears Pass, Vail Pass, Hoosier Pass, Mosquito Pass, Weston Pass, and Trout Creek Pass provide easy access to many peaks in Colorado's Park Ranges.

Quandary Peak is one of five ranked 14ers in Colorado's Tenmile-Mosquito Range, a subrange of the Park Ranges. PHOTO BY BILL MIDDLEBROOK

44 Elkhead Range Highpoint: Black Mountain

Elevation: 10,860'
Distinctions: Elkhead Range Highpoint, Moffat County Highpoint, Prominence 100, P2K, Ranked 10er
Class: 1+; Class 1 to summit area, Class 1+ to highpoint
Difficulty and skill level: Easy; Beginner
Approximate moving time: 2.5 hours
Distance: 5.4 miles round-trip
Elevation trailhead to summit: 9,895' to 10,860' (+965')
Terrain: Dirt trail and duff
Recommended extra gear: GPS

Restrictions: CR 27 closed seasonally; no camping at trailhead; trail closed to motorized vehicles
Amenities: Backcountry camping; campsites at nearby Sawmill Creek Campground; services in Craig
Trailhead: Black Mountain Trailhead
Trail: Black Mountain Trail #1185
Maps: Page 15 C7; USGS Buck Point
County: Moffat
Land status: Routt National Forest, (307) 745-2300, www.fs.usda.gov/mbr; Hahns Peak/Bears Ears Ranger District, (970) 870-2299

Finding the trailhead: From US 40 in Craig, take CO 13 North for 12.9 miles and turn right onto unpaved CR 27. Drive 14 miles and park at the pullout on the right side of the road. The trailhead is on the left (north) side of the road (GPS: N40 45.546' / W107 20.674').

The Peak

Black Mountain is the highpoint of the Elkhead Range, an 18-mile-long, east-to-west-trending spur of the Park Range located northeast of the town of Craig. "Elkhead" and "Black" are common terms in Colorado geography, referring to the elk that roam the higher elevations and to the dark-colored wooded areas, lowlands, and canyons of the state. Elk are common in the mountains here, and you will likely see more hunters than hikers on your visit to the Elkheads. Black Mountain—a long, low plateau, never rising above timberline—appears as a dark, forested oblong when viewed from a distance, and your best views of the peak are had by walking along the road west of the trailhead. Summit views from Black Mountain's highpoint are limited, but a short detour affords a scenic overlook. As you top out on the east end of the mesa at the "Black Mountain East Summit" sign, leave the trail and cross an open area to the exposed northeast edge of the plateau. Take in views to the east, where the Continental Divide stretches north through the Mount Zirkel Wilderness and Sierra Madres, into Wyoming.

The Climb

The Black Mountain summit is located on a large flat area in the woods, so a GPS and a hand level come in handy to ensure you hit the highpoint.

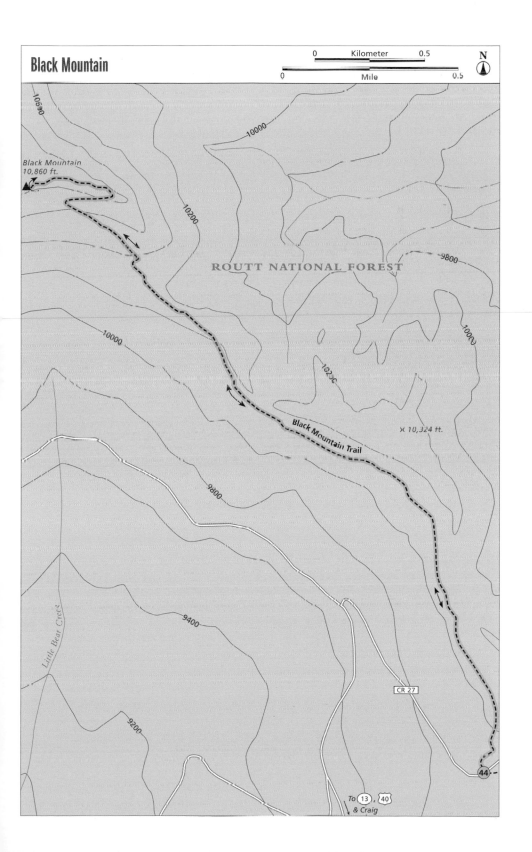

Black Mountain

0   Kilometer   0.5

0   Mile   0.5

N

10600

10000

Black Mountain
10,860 ft.

10200

ROUTT NATIONAL FOREST

9800

10000

10000

10200

Black Mountain Trail

✕ 10,324 ft.

9800

9400

Little Bear Creek

9200

CR 27

44

To 13 , 40
& Craig

Elkhead Range highpoint Black Mountain lies below timberline but is visible from CR 27 west of the trailhead. PHOTO BY SUSAN JOY PAUL

Miles and Directions

0.0 Begin at the trailhead (9,895') on the north side of the road and hike into the forest. The trail contours the hillside, and there are a few breaks in the trees to the west with distant views of the Uinta Mountains at Dinosaur National Monument.

1.7 Gain the southeast ridge at 10,265' with the east end of Black Mountain in view, ahead, as the trail begins to climb.

2.2 Switchback right and contour the hillside through a talus field.

2.4 Switchback left and hike straight up to the summit area. Continue past the "Black Mountain East Summit" sign, or enjoy the detour to the overlook, then hike west on the trail and across the flat summit area.

2.7 Depart the trail on the right, and walk to the highest point of ranked 10,860' Black Mountain. Return the way you came (N40 46.998' / W107 22.140').

5.4 Arrive back at the trailhead (N40 45.546' / W107 20.674').

45 Steamboat Springs Local Favorite: Hahns Peak

Elevation: 10,839' (NAVD88 10,844')
Distinction: Prominence 200, P1K, Ranked 10er
Class: 2; Class 1 to saddle, Class 2 to summit
Difficulty and skill level: Easy from 4WD trailhead and 2WD trailhead, Moderate from CR 129; Beginner
Approximate moving time: 2 hours from 4WD trailhead and 2WD trailhead; 3.5 hours from CR 129
Distance: 2.8 miles round-trip from 4WD trailhead; 3.2 miles round trip from 2WD trailhead; 6.0 miles round-trip from CR 129
Elevation trailhead to summit: 9,400' to 10,844' (+1,444') from 4WD trailhead; 9,280' to 10,844' (+1,564') from 2WD trailhead; 8,680' to 10,844' (+2,164') from CR 129

Terrain: Dirt road and trail, talus
Restrictions: CR R1 / FR 490 passes through private property, so stay on the road
Amenities: Camping at nearby Hahns Peak Lake Campground; limited services in Columbine, Clark, and Hahns Peak; full services in Steamboat Springs
Trailhead: Hahns Peak Trailhead
Trail: Hahns Peak Trail #1158
Maps: DeLorme Page 16 B3, B2; USGS Hahns Peak
County: Routt
Land status: Routt National Forest, (307) 745-2300, www.fs.usda.gov/mbr; Hahns Peak / Bears Ears Ranger District, (970) 870-2299

Finding the trailhead: From US 40 in Steamboat Springs, go north on CR 129 / Elk River Road. Drive 30.8 miles on CR 129, through Clark and Hahns Peak, and turn right onto unpaved CR R1 / FR 490, at Columbine. If road conditions prevent safe passage, you may request parking availability at the General Store in Columbine and return the favor with a purchase. If you can continue, go 1 mile on FR 490 and bear left, then go another 0.4 mile to the 2WD trailhead, and bear left again for another 0.2 mile to the 4WD trailhead (GPS: N40 50.608' / W106 56.678').

The Peak

More than 1,600' of prominence make Hahns Peak a 10er to remember, with a trail nearly all the way to the summit and an old fire lookout on top. The mountain was formed as a laccolith, an igneous intrusion covered in sedimentary rock and since eroded to its conical core. The peak is named for Joseph Hahn, a miner who discovered gold here in the 1860s and lived in a camp near the base of the peak with his mining partner, Doyle. When provisions ran low in the winter of 1867, the two set out across the Gore Range, headed for Empire, but a storm caught them by surprise and Hahn perished in the snow. From the peak, you'll have views north into Wyoming and west for more than 100 miles into Utah. The Continental Divide rises east, where you can pick out Park Range highpoint Mount Zirkel, Sawtooth Range highpoint Big Agnes, and Buck Mountain South, the highpoint of the Sierra Madres.

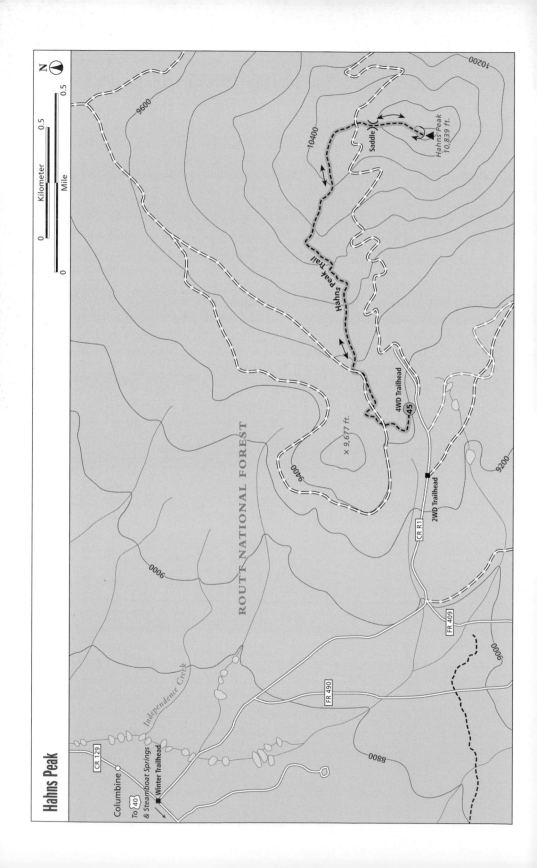

Hahns Peak

ROUTT NATIONAL FOREST

Columbine

To 40

CR 129

& Steamboat Springs

Winter Trailhead

Independence Creek

FR 490

FR 409

CR R1

2WD Trailhead

4WD Trailhead

45

Hahns Peak Trail

Saddle

Hahns Peak
10,839 ft.

× 9,677 ft.

10200

10400

9600

9400

9200

9000

8800

9000

N

Kilometer

Mile

0   0.5

0   0.5

Hahns Peak is climbed year-round with regard for cornices to the east, avalanche-prone slopes west, and a steep north-facing finish. PHOTO BY SUSAN JOY PAUL

The Climb

Hahns Peak is climbed year-round on boot, ski, or snowshoe, depending on conditions. Summer hikes should begin and end early, to avoid lightning strikes at the rocky summit. The official trailhead begins in the Routt National Forest, but if your vehicle can't make it that far, you may have to park as far back as the highway. The peak may also be accessed via a longer, summer route from Hahns Peak Lake, west of CR 129. Lakeside campsites are available by reservation, so if you're driving a long way to do this peak, an overnight stay may be a good option. You can start your hike from the lake, or drive to the Hahns Peak Trailhead in the morning.

Miles and Directions

0.0 Begin at the 4WD trailhead (9,400') and hike on the road and trail that curves west, north, and east, up to a saddle located north of the summit.

1.2 Arrive at the saddle (10,500') and hike south, up the slope. In snow, you will want microspikes and an ice axe on this section (N40 50.698' / W106 55.732').

1.4 Arrive at ranked 10,844' Hahns Peak. Return the way you came (N40 50.566' / W106 55.780').

2.8 Arrive back at the trailhead (N40 50.608' / W106 56.678').

46 Sierra Madre Range Highpoint: Buck Mountain South

Elevation: 11,396' (NAVD88 11,401')

Distinctions: Sierra Madre Range Highpoint, Prominence 200, P1K, Ranked 11er

Class: 2; Class 1 to Encampment Meadows, Class 2 and 2+ to summit

Difficulty and skill level: Very Strenuous; Intermediate

Approximate moving time: 10 hours

Distance: 17.4 miles round-trip

Elevation trailhead to summit: 8,600' to 11,401' (+2,801'); about 3,400' round-trip

Terrain: Dirt trail, grass, scree, and talus; creek crossings

Recommended extra gear: GPS

Restrictions: Trailhead access is seasonal June 1 to Dec 1, conditions permitting; high-clearance 4WD vehicle is recommended for FR 433 and required for FR 44; no bicycles or motorized vehicles; dogs must be on leash; follow wilderness regulations

Amenities: Backcountry camping; seasonal campgrounds and dispersed camping at designated areas on Seedhouse Road; limited services in Clark; full services in Steamboat Springs

Trailhead: Diamond Park Trailhead

Trail: Main Fork Trail #1152, off-trail Southeast Ridge

Maps: DeLorme Page 16 B4; USGS Mount Zirkel

County: Routt

Land status: Routt National Forest, (307) 745-2300, www.fs.usda.gov/mbr; Hahns Peak / Bears Ears Ranger District, (970) 870-2299; Mount Zirkel Wilderness, www.wilderness.net

Finding the trailhead: From US 40 in Steamboat Springs, go north on CR 129 / Elk River Road. Drive 17.6 miles, through Clark, and turn right onto CR 64 / Seedhouse Road, toward Slavonia. The road becomes unpaved FR 400 / Seedhouse Road at 5.8 miles and passes through two winter gates. Go 9.2 miles total on Seedhouse Road and turn left onto FR 433, then go 3.9 miles and turn left onto FR 44. Descend switchbacks for 2.3 miles, across the bridge, and bear right to drive uphill 0.9 mile to the trailhead (GPS: N40 49.856' / W106 46.959').

The Peak

The Sierra Madre Range, or "mother mountain range," crosses the Wyoming border into Colorado in the Routt National Forest and trends southeast to its highest point, Buck Mountain South. The summit of the peak lies about a quarter mile south of the Continental Divide. From the top, views of the Sawtooth Range might take your breath away, but you'll want to save some for the long hike out.

Sierra Madre highpoint Buck Mountain South provides views southeast to Little Agnes Mountain and the Sawtooth Range. PHOTO BY SUSAN JOY PAUL

The Climb

This is a long adventure with an easy start, and most of the elevation gained in the final 3 miles. Although this can be done as a day hike, you may want to backpack it and camp to the north of the cutoff to Lake Diana, at Encampment Meadows, then take in the summit the next day, and add ranked 11er Buck Mountain North, located 1.75 miles to the north, on the Continental Divide.

Buck Mountain South

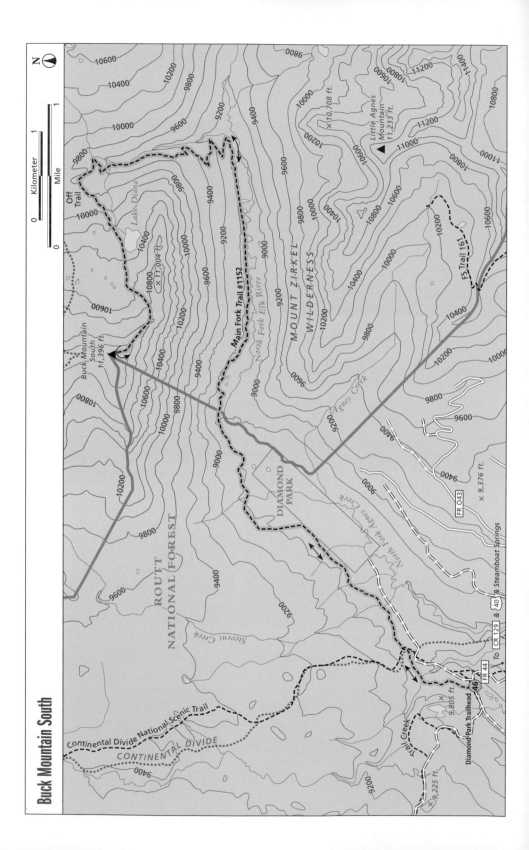

Miles and Directions

0.0 At the Diamond Park Trailhead, get on the signed multiuse trail located to the left of the gated road (8,600') and hike north on the trail.

0.4 Cross Trail Creek on a footbridge and go northeast on trail.

0.6 Depart the defined trail where Wyoming Trail #1101 (part of the Continental Divide Trail) continues north, and go northeast on the overgrown Main Fork Trail #1152. Cross a meadow and hike through a short stand of aspens (N40 50.258' / W106 46.702').

1.0 Step across Stevens Creek, emerge from trees, and take note of your exit point so you can locate it on your return. If you get off-trail in the trees, you will be wading chest-deep in corn lilies and deadfall. Locate the first of thirteen 5' wooden posts, to the northeast. The posts mark the next mile of trail, keeping you on route and above the private property, below.

1.2 First post. Continue northeast, following trail and posts (N40 50.522' / W106 46.227').

1.3 Second post (N40 50.584' / W106 46.181').

1.4 Fourth post (N40 50.626' / W106 46.086').

1.6 Sixth post (N40 50.658' / W106 46.007').

1.8 Seventh post (N40 50.771' / W106 45.877').

1.9 Eighth post (N40 50.834' / W106 45.765').

2.0 Tenth post (N40 50.898' / W106 45.685').

2.1 Eleventh post (N40 50.925' / W106 45.682').

2.3 Thirteenth post (N40 51.179' / W106 45.706').

2.6 Enter the aspens and follow the trail east-northeast.

3.2 Enter the Mount Zirkel Wilderness (8,840'). The next couple of miles are an easy stroll along the north banks of the North Fork of the Elk River (N40 51.420' / W106 44.795').

5.3 At 9,000' the trail leaves the river and follows a drainage north, switching back and forth toward the Continental Divide and Encampment Meadows (N40 51.376' / W106 42.591').

6.7 Cross the creek on rocks.

7.1 Leave the trail at about 9,800', at an unmarked cutoff located just below an open, flat area. Bushwhack southwest, across marshes and up a steep slope. Cross the creek twice on rocks (N40 52.269' / W106 42.933').

7.6 Cross the creek again and continue southwest to Lake Diana. Hike west, past the lake at 10,268' and through the trees to the bottom of a talus slope west of the lake (N40 52.060' / W106 43.322').

8.0 Hike upslope, on an ascending traverse below talus, southwest toward the saddle (N40 51.977' / W106 43.751').

8.3 Follow the ridge northwest to the summit. The faint trail contours to the right (east), then to the left of the ridgeline (west), to avoid cliffs and boulders. Scramble up rocks to the highpoint (N40 51.840' / W106 44.076').

8.7 Arrive at ranked 11,401' Buck Mountain South. Return the way you came (N40 52.061' / W106 44.322').

17.4 Arrive back at the trailhead (N40 49.856' / W106 46.959').

47 Sawtooth Range Highpoint: Big Agnes Mountain

Elevation: 12,060'

Distinctions: Sawtooth Range Highpoint, P1K, Ranked 12er

Class: 2+; Class 1 to Mica Basin, Class 2 and 2+ to summit

Difficulty and skill level: Very Strenuous; Advanced

Approximate moving time: 8 hours

Distance: 11.2 miles round-trip

Elevation trailhead to summit: 8,400' to 12,060' (+3,660')

Terrain: Dirt trail, talus, scree, and tundra; creek crossings; exposure, risk of rockfall

Recommended extra gear: Helmet for rockfall; crampons or microspikes and ice axe if snow exists

Restrictions: Trailhead access is seasonal June 1 to Dec 1, conditions permitting; no camping at trailhead; trail closed to bicycles and motorized vehicles; dogs must be on leash; follow wilderness regulations

Amenities: Trailhead toilet; backcountry camping; seasonal campgrounds and dispersed camping at designated areas on Seedhouse Road; limited services in Clark; full services in Steamboat Springs

Trailhead: Slavonia

Trails: Gilpin Lake Trail #1161, Mica Basin Trail #1162, off-trail South Slopes and Southeast Ridge

Maps: DeLorme Page 17 B5, C5, Page 16 4C; USGS Mount Zirkel

County: Routt

Land status: Routt National Forest, (307) 745-2300, www.fs.usda.gov/mbr; Hahns Peak / Bears Ears Ranger District, (970) 870-2299; Mount Zirkel Wilderness, www.wilderness.net

Finding the trailhead: From US 40 in Steamboat Springs, go north on CR 129 / Elk River Road, toward Clark and Hahns Peak. Drive 17.6 miles on CR 129, through Clark, and turn right onto CR 64 / Seedhouse Road, toward Slavonia. Drive 5.8 miles, onto unpaved FR 400 / Seedhouse Road, and another 6 miles to the Slavonia Trailhead (GPS: N40 46.991' / W106 43.370').

The Peak

Big Agnes Mountain and little sister peak, 11er Little Agnes Mountain, are the only ranked peaks in the Sawtooth Range. Big Agnes was named by gold prospector Robert McIntosh, who owned a small mine in King Solomon Creek in the 1870s, but the origin of the name, and who Big Agnes might have been, has been lost over the years. Unranked, rotten, rock "teeth" comprise the rest of the Sawtooth summits. "The Spike" rises along the connecting ridge between the ranked summits, and the broken line of "Baby Teeth," "Grand Central Tooth," "Big Agnes Tower," "Molar Tooth," "Diamond Tooth," "Capped Tooth," and "The Castle" line up from west to east, north of the Agneses. Finally, "Exclamation Point Peak" dots the range at the southeast corner. From Big Agnes Mountain, you will have unparalleled views of the Sawtooths, as well as Park Range highpoint Mount Zirkel to the east and Hahns Peak to the west.

Sawtooth Range highpoint Big Agnes Mountain provides stunning views east to Park Range highpoint Mount Zirkel. PHOTO BY SUSAN JOY PAUL

The Climb

Big Agnes Mountain shares a trailhead with Routt County highpoint Mount Zirkel, so if you're driving a long way, consider staying a few days and taking in the Park Range, county, and wilderness area highpoint, too. You can also add Buck Mountain South to your trip, with a detour to the nearby Diamond Park Trailhead. To help with your planning, consider that Mount Zirkel is the longest and has the most elevation gain, Big Agnes Mountain is the most technically difficult, and Buck Mountain South is seldom visited and may require a bit more route-finding. A trek to all three mountain range highpoints offers more than 46 miles of hiking and over 10,000' of elevation, for a long, exhausting, gorgeous weekend of Colorado mountaineering in the Mount Zirkel Wilderness.

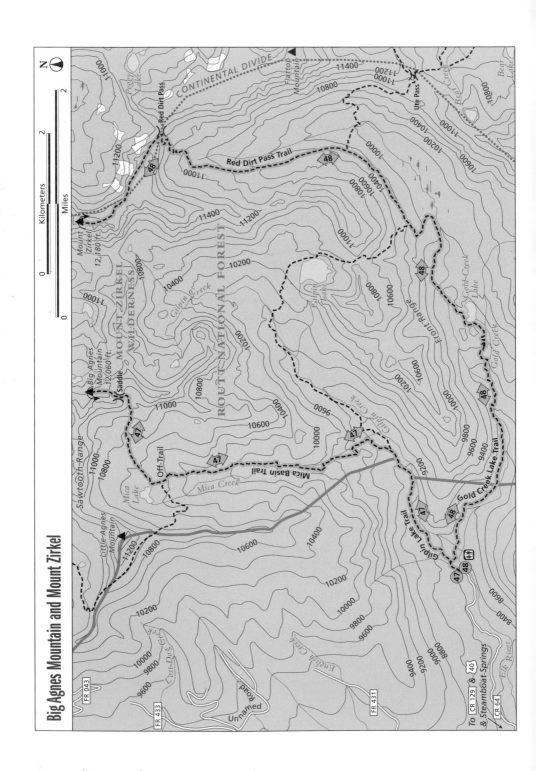

Big Agnes Mountain and Mount Zirkel

N

Kilometers
0   2   2

Miles
0   2

CONTINENTAL DIVIDE

Peggy Lake

Red Dirt Pass

Flattop Mountain
11400

Ute Pass

Bear Lake

Mount Zirkel
12,180 ft.

MOUNT ZIRKEL WILDERNESS

Red Dirt Pass Trail

48

48

Gilpin Creek

Gilpin Lake

ROUTT NATIONAL FOREST

Front Range

48

Gold Creek Lake

Big Agnes Mountain
12,060 ft.

Saddle

47

Off-Trail

Sawtooth Range

Mica Lake

Mica Creek

47

Mica Basin Trail

9600

Gilpin Creek

Gold Creek

48

47

Gilpin Lake Trail

Gold Creek Lake Trail

Little Agnes Mountain

Lost Dog Cr.

FR 043

FR 433

Unnamed Road

English Creek

47

48

47

48

FR 431

To CR 129 & 40
& Steamboat Springs

CR 64

Elk River

Miles and Directions

0.0   Begin at the trailhead (8,400') and hike north.

0.1   At the wilderness register, go left to stay on the Gilpin Lake Trail. Cross Gilpin Creek a couple of times on rocks and logs, and enter the Mount Zirkel Wilderness (N40 47.062' / W106 43.287').

1.5   Turn left to leave the Gilpin Lake Trail and get onto Mica Basin Trail (9,100'). Hike north, through the forest and across open areas, following Mica Creek past several trailside cascades and a waterfall, and switchback higher into the basin (N40 47.538' / W106 42.116').

2.7   Cross Mica Creek on rocks and logs, or wade across. Continue across a flat area and then switchback uphill, continuing north, with views of Little Agnes Mountain to the northwest and the broad, south slope of Big Agnes Mountain to the northeast (N40 48.181' / W106 42.316').

4.2   At Mica Lake (10,400') depart the trail and hike east upslope toward the Agnes-Exclamation Point saddle, staying high on grassy slopes south of and above the marshes (N40 49.358' / W106 42.479').

5.1   Cross the talus at the base of Big Agnes Mountain's south slopes (11,240'), and climb north on steep scree, talus, and tundra (N40 49.535' / W106 41.584').

5.5   Locate a small weakness in the jagged ridge at 12,000', and cross to the east side. The crossing is somewhat exposed, with the east slopes falling away steeply to a basin 600' below. Drop down about 30' on loose scree, cross left on talus rubble, and get back up on the ridge, where the summit is in view. Go over a false summit, continue northwest on the ridge, and hike up the final, rocky pitch to the top (N40 49.781' / W106 41.542').

5.6   Arrive at ranked 12,060' Big Agnes Mountain. Return the way you came (N40 49.822' / W106 41.559').

11.2   Arrive back at the trailhead (N40 46.991' / W106 43.370').

48 Park Range Highpoint: Mount Zirkel

See map on page 178.

Elevation: 12,180' (NAVD88 12,185')

Distinctions: Park Range Highpoint, Routt County Highpoint, Mount Zirkel Wilderness Highpoint, Prominence 100, P3K, Ranked 12er

Class: Class 2+; Class 1 to Red Dirt Pass, Class 2 to South Ridge, Class 2+ to summit

Difficulty and skill level: Very Strenuous; Intermediate

Approximate moving time: 12 hours

Distance: 18.2 miles round-trip

Elevation trailhead to summit: 8,400' to 12,185' (+3,785')

Terrain: Dirt, scree, grass, tundra, talus, and boulders; creek crossings

Restrictions: Trailhead access is seasonal June 1 to Dec 1, conditions permitting; no camping at trailhead; backcountry camping restricted to more than 0.25 mile from Gilpin, Gold, and Three Mile Lakes; trail closed to bicycles and motorized vehicles; dogs must be on leash; follow wilderness regulations

Amenities: Trailhead toilet; backcountry camping; seasonal campgrounds and dispersed camping at designated areas on Seedhouse Road; limited services in Clark; full services in Steamboat Springs

Trailhead: Slavonia

Trails: Gilpin Lake Trail #1161, Gold Creek Lake Trail #1150, Red Dirt Pass Trail #1142, off-trail South Ridge

Maps: Page 17 B5, C5, Page 16 C4; USGS Mount Zirkel

County: Routt

Land status: Routt National Forest, (307) 745-2300, www.fs.usda.gov/mbr; Hahns Peak / Bears Ears Ranger District, (970) 870-2299; Mount Zirkel Wilderness, www.wilderness.net

Finding the trailhead: From CO 40 in Steamboat Springs, go north on CR 129, toward Clark and Hahns Peak. Drive 17.6 miles on CR 129, through Clark, and turn right onto CR 64 / Seedhouse Road, toward Slavonia. The road becomes unpaved FR 400 / Seedhouse Road at 5.8 miles and passes through two winter gates. Drive a total of 11.8 miles on Seedhouse Road to the Slavonia Trailhead (GPS: N40 46.995' / W106 43.377').

The Peak

Mount Zirkel is the northernmost Colorado 12er and the highpoint of the Park Range, a subrange of Colorado's Park Ranges. The peak is named for German geologist and petrologist Ferdinand Zirkel (1838–1912), who is credited with introducing microscopic petrography—the detailed study of rocks, often cut into thin slices for microscopic viewing—to the United States. From the summit, the Sawtooth Range and Sierra Madre Range are in view west of the peak, while south and southeast the Continental Divide continues into the Rabbit Ears Range and the Never Summer Range. The Rawahs appear to the east.

The Climb

Mount Zirkel lies in a beautiful wilderness area and is well suited for a backpack. There are good sites for setting up a tent at Gold Creek Lake—ensuring you maintain

Mount Zirkel's irregular and exposed south ridge takes you to the top of the Park Range on the Continental Divide. PHOTO BY JOHN KIRK

the required quarter-mile perimeter—and below Red Dirt Pass. The trail is well-defined all the way to the pass, but pay attention to trail signs to make the transitions from Gilpin Lake Trail, to Gold Creek Lake Trail, to Red Dirt Pass Trail. If you are combining Mount Zirkel and Big Agnes Mountain in one trip, you can shave some miles from the combined peaks and avoid retreating back to the trailhead by taking the cutoff to Gilpin Lake, located 4.7 miles from the trailhead on Gold Creek Lake Trail, and approach Agnes from the southeast by following Gilpin Creek (off-trail) north to a small lake and climbing northwest over the Agnes–Exclamation Point saddle. Alternatively, you can take the cutoff and then just stay on the Gilpin Lake Trail past Gilpin Lake to the cutoff to Mica Basin Trail, and then follow the standard approach to Mica Basin.

Miles and Directions

0.0 Begin at the trailhead (8,400') and hike north on the Gilpin Lake Trail.

0.1 Go right at the wilderness register onto Gold Creek Lake Trail. Hike east along the creek.

1.9 Cross Gold Creek on a log and turn right on the other side to continue on the trail, then cross the creek again, on logs or rocks. The first crossing of Gold Creek is the most difficult, with a sturdy log connecting the banks. Alternatively, wade through shallower water upstream, or cross the rocks downstream.

3.0 Hike north around Gold Creek Lake (9,555'), past the junction with the Wyoming Trail, and northeast to a flat area, with ranked 12er Flattop Mountain rising to the northeast (N40 46.881' / W106 40.836').

3.4 At the next trail junction, continue straight (left) on Gold Creek Lake Trail, then cross the creek again on rocks and logs (N40 47.064' / W106 40.614').

4.7 Bear right at another trail junction to remain on Gold Creek Lake Trail (N40 47.389' / W106 39.792').

5.6 At the trail junction, leave Gold Creek Lake Trail and bear left onto Red Dirt Pass Trail (10,240'). Red Dirt Pass appears to the north, and there are cabin ruins left of the trail (N40 47.856' / W106 39.060').

7.1 Begin the steep ascent up switchbacks (10,880') north-northeast to Red Dirt Pass.

7.9 At Red Dirt Pass (11,560'), turn left and leave the trail to hike northwest up the grass slope, where Mount Zirkel appears. Cross a flat section toward the ridge (N40 49.316' / W106 38.946').

8.6 Gain the ridge for views west. Continue northwest across slopes, staying clear of the exposed west face and gullies (N40 49.552' / W106 39.568').

9.0 Climb the south ridge on Class 2+ talus and boulders. Go over or around two minor (false) summits and continue north to the summit.

9.1 Arrive at ranked 12,185' Mount Zirkel. Return the way you came. Alternatively, once you are off the summit area, you can descend the east slope and omit the ridge (N40 49.883' / W106 39.789').

18.2 Arrive back at the trailhead (N40 46.995' / W106 43.377').

49 Rabbit Ears Pass Peak: Rabbit Ears Peak

Elevation: 10,654' (NAVD88 10,659')

Distinction: Unranked 10er

Class: 4; Class 1 to base of block, mixed Class 3 and 4 to summit

Difficulty and skill level: Moderate; Beginner to base and Advanced to summit

Approximate moving time: 4 hours

Distance: 5.2 miles round-trip

Elevation trailhead to summit: 9,590' to 10,659' (+1,069')

Terrain: Dirt road, scree, and rock to base; soft rock to summit; exposure, risk of rockfall

Restrictions: None posted

Recommended extra gear: Backpack large enough to carry gear, food, and water; rock-climbing shoes, helmet, harness, personal anchor system (PAS) with locking carabiner,

belay device (ATC) with locking carabiner, 165' (50 m) rope, cams to 2", 20' of webbing for belay anchor, and slings

Amenities: Backcountry camping; seasonal camping and toilets at nearby Dumont Lake Campground; services in Steamboat Springs and Kremmling

Trailhead: "Rabbit Ears Peak Trailhead" (FR 311 and FR 291)

Trail: FR 291 / Rabbit Ears Peak Road, off-trail West Chimney

Maps: DeLorme Page 27 A5, B5; USGS Rabbit Ears Peak

County: Jackson

Land status: Routt National Forest, (307) 745-2300, www.fs.usda.gov/mbr; Hahns Peak / Bears Ears Ranger District, (970) 870-2299

Finding the trailhead: From US 40, 20 miles east of Steamboat Springs and 30 miles west of Kremmling, turn north at the sign for Dumont Lake onto FR 315. Continue 1.5 miles and turn left at the stone monument onto unpaved FR 311. Proceed for 0.3 mile to the unmarked trailhead at the junction of FR 311 and FR 291 / Rabbit Ears Peak Road. If the road is washed out, park 0.1 mile past the monument, near the porta-potty, and walk the final 0.2 mile to the trailhead (GPS: N40 24.229' / W106 37.147').

The Peak

Rabbit Ears Peak sits north of Rabbit Ears Pass in the Park Range. The pass crosses the Continental Divide on US 40 at 9,426' as a dip rather than a rise on the road, with signed "highpoints" east and west of the pass. The Rabbit Ears Peak formation is clearly visible from the road, twin blocks of volcanic rock comprising the "body" and twin "ears" of the "rabbit." The west "body" block is unranked Rabbit Ears Peak, and the east "ears" block is ranked 10er "Rabbit Ears." A jeep road leads to the base of the summit blocks. This is a popular hike, and experienced climbers can enjoy summit views, too, south to the Gores; north to the Park Range; east to the Rawahs, Never Summer, and Rabbit Ears ranges; and west to Steamboat Springs.

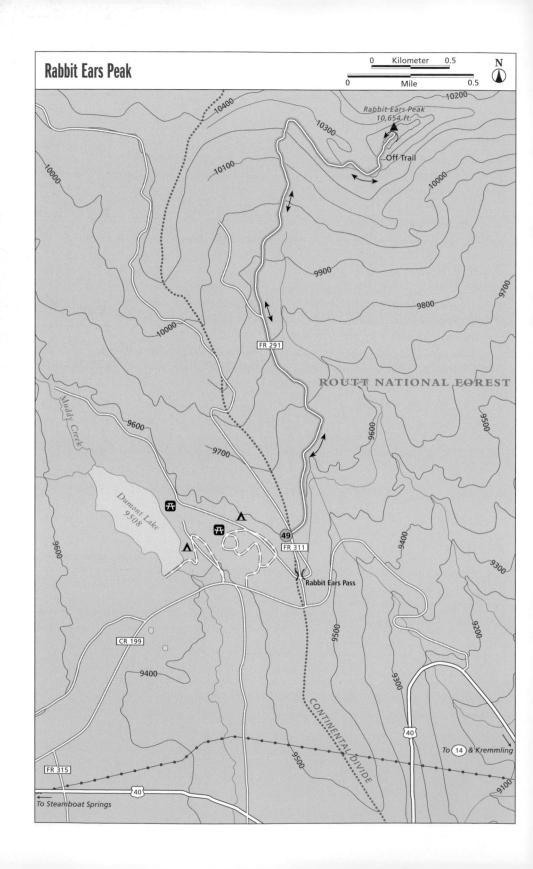

Rabbit Ears Peak

0 — Kilometer — 0.5
0 — Mile — 0.5

N

Rabbit Ears Peak
10,654 ft.

Off Trail

10400
10300
10200
10100
10000
9900
9800
9700
9600

ROUTT NATIONAL FOREST

FR 291

Muddy Creek

9600
9700
9600
9500
9400
9300
9200

Dumont Lake
9508

49
FR 311

Rabbit Ears Pass

CR 199

9400

9500

9500

CONTINENTAL DIVIDE

40

To 14 & Kremmling

9300
9100

FR 315

40

To Steamboat Springs

The Climb

Rabbit Ears Peak is usually enjoyed as a hike, sans climb, forfeiting the summits. A climber's trail leads to the bases of the summit blocks, wrapping around the south side of Rabbit Ears Peak and heading east to encircle "Rabbit Ears." If you have the skills and the gear, you can make your way to the top of the lower, west summit, described below. The climbing is not difficult, but the volcanic rock is soft and crumbly, so a rope is highly recommended. The eastern tower of the east block, "Rabbit Ears," is the actual highpoint of the formation. A climb of the ranked summit via a crack on the northeast face, with a 5.5 C2 technical rating, requires difficult gear placement on rotten rock and is not recommended for most climbers.

Climber David Goldstein leads up an awkward crack on "Rabbit Ears" in the Park Range. PHOTO BY TERESA GERGEN

Miles and Directions

0.0 At the FR 311 / 291 junction (9,590'), hike east on FR 291. The road bends north and climbs to 10,200', then contours east, and finally climbs steeply north on a climber's trail to the base of the summit blocks.

2.5 Arrive at the base (10,575') of Rabbit Ears Peak. Two wide cracks lead to the top, and the crack on the right is the easier route. Begin Class 4 climbing (N40 25.606' / W106 36.674').

> **Pitch 1:** Scramble up onto the rock at the base of the crack and climb 30' through a wide, chunky chimney to a ledge, protecting the climb with cams and slings as needed, and set up a belay for your climbing party.

> **Pitch 2:** Climb 50' of Class 3 rock to the summit.

2.6 Arrive at unranked 10,659' Rabbit Ears Peak. Downclimb the Class 3 section, and lower the final 30' to the base. Rejoin the trail and return the way you came (N40 25.620' / W106 36.672').

5.2 Arrive back at the trailhead (N40 24.229' / W106 37.147').

50 Rabbit Ears Range Highpoint: Parkview Mountain

Elevation: 12,296' (NAVD88 12,301')

Distinctions: Rabbit Ears Range Highpoint, Prominence 100, P2K, Ranked 12er

Class: 2; Class 1 to end of road, Class 2 to summit

Difficulty and skill level: Moderate; Intermediate

Approximate moving time: 5 hours

Distance: 8.4 miles round-trip

Elevation trailhead to summit: 9,570' to 12,301' (+2,731')

Terrain: Dirt road, grass, scree, talus, and tundra

Restrictions: Summer route

Amenities: Backcountry camping; campgrounds located along CO 125; services in Granby

Trailhead: Arapaho National Forest Road 266-1H

Trails: FR 266-1H, FR 266, FR 751, unnamed road, off-trail East Slopes and Southeast Ridge

Maps: DeLorme Page 28 B1, B2; USGS Parkview Mountain, Radial Mountain

Counties: Grand, Jackson

Land status: Arapaho National Forest, (970) 295-6600, www.fs.usda.gov/arp; Sulphur Ranger District, (970) 887-4100

Finding the trailhead: From I-70, about 29 miles west of Denver and 26 miles east of Silverthorne, take exit 232 to US 40 for Empire/Granby. Drive 49 miles and turn right onto CO 125 North, then continue 21.3 miles, past mile marker 21, and turn left to an unmarked pullout at FR 266-1H (GPS: N40 20.941' / W106 5.748').

The Peak

The Rabbit Ears Range trends east–west along the Continental Divide between North Park and Middle Park, from Radial Mountain to Rabbit Ears Pass. The range is named for Park Range summit Rabbit Ears Peak, and a fire lookout—the second highest in Colorado—stands at the summit of the range highpoint, Parkview Mountain. The structure was built in 1916 and is no longer in use. Parkview Mountain offers views northeast to southeast of the Rawah Range, Never Summer Mountains, and Indian Peaks; and northwest to southwest of the Park Range, the Flat Tops, the Gore Range, and the Williams Fork Mountains.

The Climb

This is a summer route only, as it crosses an avalanche path. There is no water available for the entire route. An alternative route to the peak is a drive up 4WD CR 125-A, which starts just north of Mile Marker 24 on CR 125, 2 miles south of Willow Creek Pass, and goes to the base of the peak. The road is gated at 1.25 miles in the winter and closed periodically for logging activity in the summer. Winter access to the peak may be gained from the northeast and west ridges.

Parkview Mountain

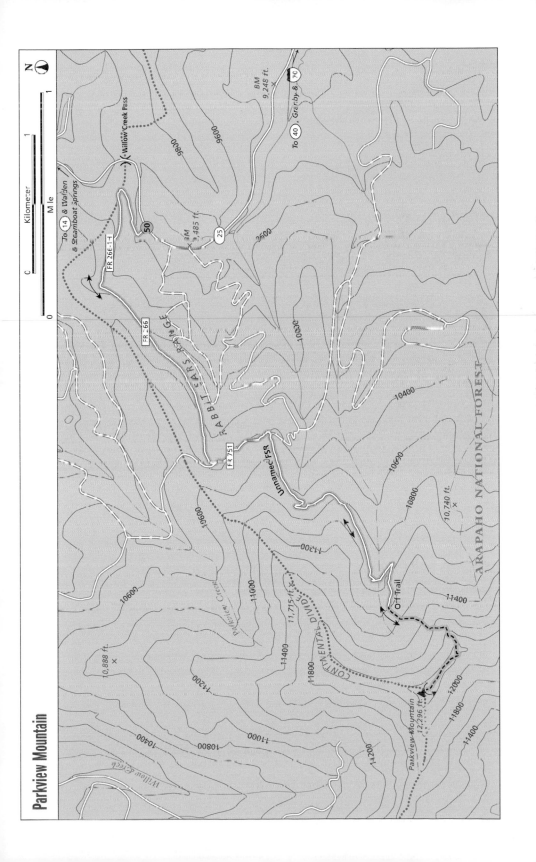

An old fire lookout stands at Parkview Mountain, the highpoint of the Rabbit Ears Range.
PHOTO BY SUSAN JOY PAUL

Miles and Directions

0.0 Begin at the trailhead (9,570') and hike north, then east and west on FR 266-1H.

0.7 Bear left at cabin ruins (9,950') to go southwest onto FR 266 (N40 21.137' / W106 6.037').

1.8 Turn left onto FR 751 (N40 20.646' / W106 6.967').

2.1 Turn right onto an unnamed road and follow switchbacks north and south below an avalanche chute. Parkview Mountain comes in and out of view, eventually showing its broad, talus-lined eastern slopes straight ahead (N40 20.427' / W106 6.834').

3.1 Bear left on the road as it drops down and then curves up the mountainside (N40 20.044' / W106 7.547').

3.3 Cross a 4WD parking area and hike west through a rockslide over the road (N40 19.962' / W106 7.598').

3.4 Depart the road and climb the steep slope south-southwest, left of the talus field, to the southeast ridge. The terrain here is grass, tundra, and scree marked by occasional cairns, and talus at the top.

3.9 Top out on the ridge and go right, northwest toward the summit (N40 19.683' / W106 7.965').

4.2 Arrive at ranked 12,301' Parkview Mountain. There's a summit marker embedded in the northwest corner of the concrete base of the summit shelter. Return the way you came (N40 19.813' / W106 8.176').

8.4 Arrive back at the trailhead (N40 20.941' / W106 5.748').

51 Gore Range Highpoint: Mount Powell

Elevation: 13,580'

Distinctions: Gore Range Highpoint, Eagles Nest Wilderness Highpoint, Bicentennial, Prominence 100, P3K, Ranked 13er

Class: 2+; Class 1 to Kneeknocker Pass, mixed Class 2 and 2+ to summit

Difficulty and skill level: Very Strenuous; Advanced

Approximate moving time: 8 hours

Distance: 10.2 miles round-trip

Elevation trailhead to summit: 9,360' to 13,580' (+4,220'); about 4,900' round-trip

Terrain: Dirt trail, grass, scree, talus, and boulders; creek crossings; exposure, risk of rockfall

Recommended extra gear: Helmet for rockfall; crampons or microspikes and ice axe if snow exists; GPS

Restrictions: FR 700 is closed in winter and opens around Memorial Day weekend, and access to trailhead may require 4WD year-round, depending on snow and road conditions; trail closed to bicycles and motor vehicles; dogs must be on leash; follow wilderness regulations

Amenities: Dispersed camping along FR 701; backcountry camping; services in Vail

Trailhead: Piney Lake Trailhead

Trails: Upper Piney Trail #1885, Kneeknocker Pass Trail, off-trail South Slopes and West Ridge

Maps: DeLorme Page 37 C8, C7; USGS Mount Powell, Vail East, Vail West

County: Summit

Land status: White River National Forest, (970) 945-2521, www.fs.usda.gov/whiteriver; Eagle–Holy Cross Ranger District, (970) 827-5715; Eagles Nest Wilderness, www.wilderness.net

Finding the trailhead: From I-70, about 30 miles west of Dillon, take exit 176 for Vail and drive 1.2 miles, bearing right to take the second exit at the traffic circle onto N. Frontage Road West, then turn right onto Red Sandstone Road. Go 0.7 mile and turn left onto unpaved Piney Lake Road / FR 700. Drive 2.6 miles and bear left to stay on FR 700, then go 4 more miles and turn right onto Piney River Road / FR 701. Continue 3.8 miles to a parking area on the right, before the entrance to Piney River Ranch. Do not block the gate with your vehicle. The trailhead is across the road from the lot (GPS: N39 43.225' / W106 24.301').

The Peak

The Gore Range runs south–southeast from Rabbit Ears Pass, over Gore and Vail Passes, then trends south—flanked by the Sawatch Range to the west and Tenmile Range to the east—to Fremont Pass. The central Gores near Vail are coveted by local climbers for ridge traverses that top out on unnamed summits, identified north to south by the letters A through Z. Mount Powell, "Peak B," is one of the few officially named peaks of the central Gore Range. The range was named for Sir St. George Gore, who came to the United States from England with dozens of servants and hundreds of dogs, which he used to hunt and slaughter thousands of buffalo, elk, deer, and bear throughout nearby Grand County in the 1850s. Mount Powell was named for John Wesley Powell, who led the 1868 ascent of 14er Longs Peak. From the top

South-facing slopes and a rocky ridge lead to the eastern summit and highpoint of ranked 13er Mount Powell. PHOTO BY JOHN KIRK

of Mount Powell, you'll have Front Range views from northeast to southeast. Closer in, from south clockwise, other Gore Range summits in view include ranked 13er "Peak C," with ridge traverse "Ripsaw Ridge" continuing to the south; ranked 12ers "East Corner," "Corner Peak," "Northwest Corner," and Meridian Peak to the west; ranked 13er Eagles Nest to the north; and ranked 12er "Dwarf Pyramid" to the east.

The Climb

Mount Powell is usually climbed in the summer due to the crux of the route, a snowfield located on the east side of Kneeknocker Pass. The exposed slope holds snow and can be corniced or full of steep snow and ice, and an ice axe and crampons or microspikes may be required, if the route is safely passable at all. Whenever you climb it, you'll have to come over 12,300' Kneeknocker Pass each way and will need a long day of good weather for your climb and your descent.

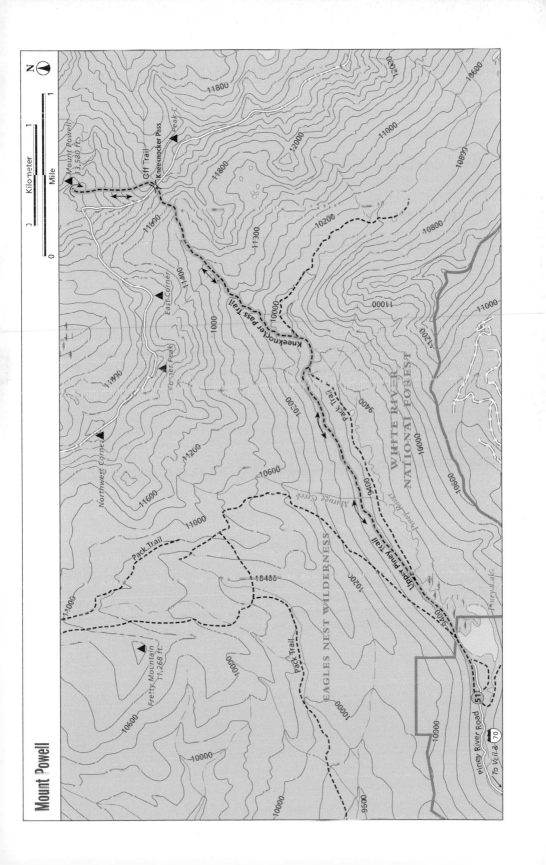

Miles and Directions

0.0 Begin at the trailhead (9,360') and hike east-northeast on Upper Piney Trail, past Piney Lake. Stay off the road leading to the ranch, which is private property.

0.6 Stay left at the first trail junction, just past the lake, and continue northeast paralleling Piney River.

0.7 Pass the junction with the Marugg Creek Trail on the left, and continue straight on the Upper Piney Trail (N39 43.494' / W106 23.591').

1.2 Enter the forest and cross Marugg Creek and an unnamed creek.

2.8 Depart the Upper Piney Trail on left at about 9,680' and get on the unsigned Kneeknocker Pass Trail. Look for a cairn and a trail heading north. Hike through trees, alongside a rivulet that drains from the pass (N39 44.227' / W106 21.637').

3.8 Emerge from the trees (11,040') and cross some marshes and a meadow in the basin below the pass, with "Peak C" to the east.

4.2 Start the steep climb on a trail to the left of the talus gully (11,400') and up to the pass (N39 44.999' / W106 20.646').

4.5 Top out on Kneeknocker Pass (12,300') with Mount Powell in view to the north. The right (east) summit is the higher one. Descend the steep slope to the east side of the pass on dirt and scree, dropping 50 to 200', depending on conditions. If snow exists, you can scramble down a Class 3 rib, or use your ice axe for a secure descent (N39 45.133' / W106 20.429').

4.6 Head north up the steep, grassy slopes of Mount Powell, picking the best path as the route turns to scree, loose talus, and boulders. Aim for the saddle between the twin summits, and from the ridge, turn right and go east to the highpoint (N39 45.159' / W106 20.404').

5.1 Arrive at ranked 13,580' Mount Powell. Return the way you came (N39 45.601' / W106 20.449').

10.2 Arrive back at the trailhead (N39 43.225' / W106 24.301').

52 Vail Pass Peak: Uneva Peak

Elevation: 12,522' (NAVD88 12,528')
Distinction: P1K, Ranked 12er
Class: 2; Class 1 to basin, Class 2 to summit
Difficulty and skill level: Moderate; Beginner
Approximate moving time: 3 hours
Distance: 6.0 miles round-trip
Elevation trailhead to summit: 10,600' to 12,528' (+1,928')
Terrain: Dirt trail, talus, and tundra; minor creek crossing
Restrictions: Trail closed to bicycles and motor vehicles; dogs must be on leash or under voice command; follow wilderness regulations

Amenities: Services in Frisco and Vail
Trailhead: Vail Pass
Trail: Unofficial "Uneva Peak Trail," off-trail South Ridge
Maps: DeLorme Page 38 E1; USGS Vail Pass
Counties: Eagle, Summit
Land status: White River National Forest, (970) 945-2521, www.fs.usda.gov/whiteriver; Dillon Ranger District, (970) 468-5400; Eagles Nest Wilderness, www.wilderness.net

Finding the trailhead: From Frisco, drive about 10 miles on I-70 West, take exit 190 to Shrine Pass Road, and continue for 0.3 mile to pullout parking on the east (right) side of the road. Or from Vail, drive about 14 miles on I-70 East and take exit 190, then go 0.2 mile, turn left onto Shrine Pass Road, and drive 500'; turn left at the T-intersection, and park on the right (east) side of the road. The trail starts on the east side of the pullout. If the pullout is full, you can get back on the highway and drive up to the large rest area on top of Vail Pass, then walk east across the overpass on Shrine Pass Road (GPS: N39 31.802' / W106 12.921').

The Peak

Uneva Peak lies in the Gore Range north of I-70 at Vail Pass. In a mountain range known for difficult access to its summits—with limited trails to its northern peaks; rocky, technical traverses defining its central peaks; and ski resorts and mining claims prohibiting access to many of its southern peaks—Uneva Peak is a readily accessible, nontechnical Gore summit. Vail Pass, at 10,662' above sea level, was originally called Black Gore Pass but renamed for Charles Vail, chief engineer on the highway project when a route over the pass was paved in 1939. The pass is well known for the bike path that crosses it, paralleling the highway from Copper Mountain Ski Area to the town of Vail. Uneva Peak is named for the Ute *yunávi*, or "mountainous country." Views along the south ridge to Officer's Gulch, 1,000' below, are dramatic, and from the summit you will have views of the Gore Range, including highpoint Mount Powell to the north and ranked 13er Jacque Peak to the south. Across Officer's Gulch to the south and east, the high peaks of the Mosquito and Front Ranges line up with 14ers Grays Peak and Torreys Peak in view.

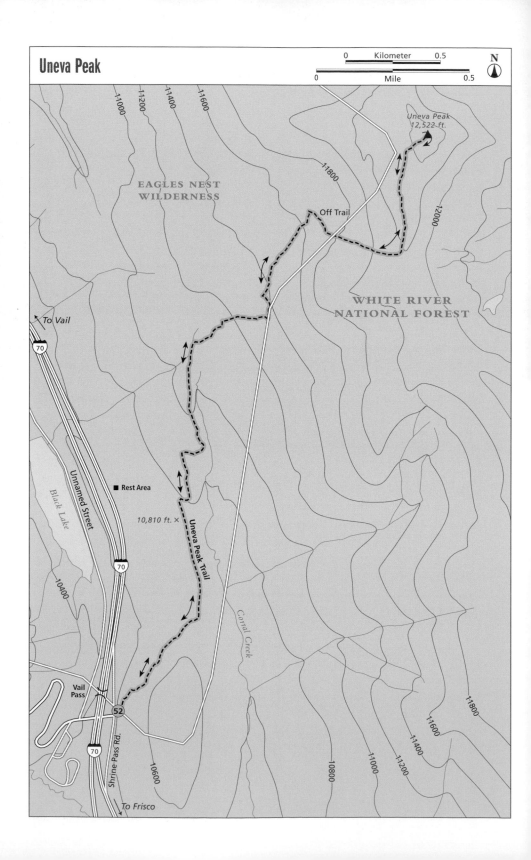

Uneva Peak

From the false summit at 12,390', the true summit of the Gore Range's Uneva Peak appears to the north. PHOTO BY SUSAN JOY PAUL

The Climb

Uneva Peak is climbed year-round, but the bowl south of the peak should be avoided from winter to early spring if snow has not consolidated and may be prone to avalanche.

Miles and Directions

0.0 Begin at the pullout (10,600') and hike north-northeast, through the forest on the unmarked dirt trail.

0.5 The trail joins an old logging road and goes north along Corral Creek, then weaves in and out of trees and turns back to trail.

1.9 Enter the Eagles Nest Wilderness. As views open up, you'll see the flanks of Uneva Peak to the northeast, but the summit is not in view. Continue north, cross the creek, and hike past a cascade to your right and up onto a large flat basin (N39 33.008' / W106 12.353').

2.2 Turn right and go east as the trail runs out, then climb the steep slope toward the saddle.

2.6 From the saddle, turn left to head north over tundra and talus to a false bump (N39 33.098' / W106 11.861').

2.7 Hike past the bump at 12,390', where Uneva Peak is finally in view. Descend to the next saddle and veer to the left to approach the peak from the gentler southwest slope.

3.0 Arrive at ranked 12,528' Uneva Peak. Return the way you came (N39 33.423' / W106 11.767').

6.0 Arrive back at the trailhead (N39 31.802' / W106 12.921').

53 Frisco Local Favorite: Royal Mountain

Elevation: 10,502' (NAVD88 10,508')
Distinction: Unranked 10er
Class: 2; Class 1 most of the way, with a short Class 2 finish
Difficulty and skill level: Easy; Beginner
Approximate moving time: 2.5 hours
Distance: 3.2 miles round-trip
Elevation trailhead to summit: 9,122' to 10,508' (+1,386')
Terrain: Dirt and rocky trail
Restrictions: Access year-round, but avoid in snow as avalanche danger exists on east side of peak; multiuse trail; trail closed to motor vehicles; dogs must be on leash or under voice command; do not disturb historical structures or artifacts
Amenities: Services in Frisco
Trailhead: Mount Royal Trailhead
Trail: Mount Royal / Masontown Trail #1
Maps: DeLorme Page 38 E2; USGS Frisco
County: Summit
Land status: White River National Forest, (970) 945-2521, www.fs.usda.gov/whiteriver; Dillon Ranger District, (970) 468-5400

Finding the trailhead: From I-70, about 4 miles west of Silverthorne and 25 miles east of Vail, take exit 201 for Frisco and turn east onto Main Street. Drive 0.7 mile and turn right onto Second Avenue, then continue 0.5 mile to parking at the trailhead (GPS: N39 34.143' / W106 5.990').

The Peak

Royal Mountain anchors the north end of the Tenmile Range, southeast of I-70 at Frisco. It's the first peak summited in the "Tenmile Traverse," a climb of 12 peaks in the Tenmile Range, from Royal Mountain south to Peak 10, at Breckenridge. It's also the site of the old mining town Masontown, which was destroyed in a 1926 avalanche. The summit views are outstanding, with Dillon Reservoir below to the north and the Tenmile Range south. Uneva Peak rises at Vail Pass to the west, with the Gores extending northwest to Mount Powell, the Williams Fork Mountains stretching north, and the Front Range lining the eastern sky.

The Climb

This hike crams a lot of elevation into a short distance, so don't underestimate it. At Masontown, leave everything as you found it, and keep in mind that removing historical artifacts is not only unethical, it is also illegal. On your return, you may opt to take the cutoff down to Rainbow Lake, and then return to the trailhead on the Peaks Trail #45, located at the north side of the lake.

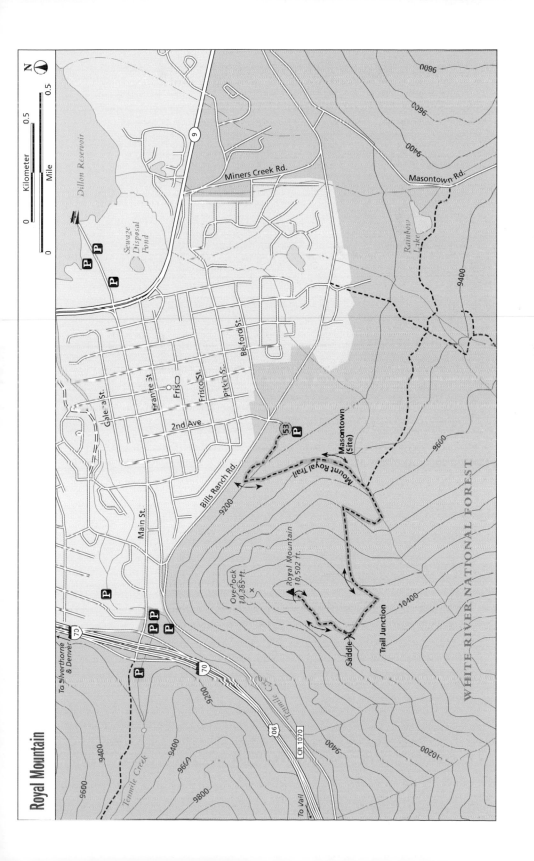

Royal Mountain

Royal Mountain rises above I-70 at Frisco, at the north end of the Tenmile Range.
PHOTO BY JOHN KIRK

Miles and Directions

0.0 Begin at the trailhead (9,122') at the northwest side of the parking lot and hike up the path. Bear left to get off the bike path and onto the hiking trail.

0.2 Switchback left (south) on the trail.

0.6 Pass the Masontown ruins and continue southwest, then go straight past the next trail fork, which goes southeast to Rainbow Lake. The Mount Royal Trail contours north and then climbs steeply west (N39 33.960' / W106 6.128').

1.2 Go right at the fork, heading northwest. The other trail goes southwest, to Peak 1 and the "Tenmile Traverse" route (N39 33.883' / W106 6.587').

1.4 Reach the saddle at 10,400' and continue north, as the trail gets rougher.

1.6 Arrive at the unranked 10,508' summit of Royal Mountain. There's a nice overlook beyond the highpoint at 10,391', so take a few minutes to head that way for views of the reservoir and surrounding peaks. This will add about 200 round-trip feet of elevation to your hike. Return the way you came (N39 34.113' / W106 6.571').

3.2 Arrive back at the trailhead (N39 34.143' / W106 5.990').

54 Tenmile Range Highpoint: Quandary Peak

Elevation: 14,265' (NAVD88 14,272')
Distinctions: Tenmile Range Highpoint, Centennial, P1K, Ranked 14er
Class: 2; Class 1 for most of route, mixed Class 1 and 2 to summit
Difficulty and skill level: Strenuous; Advanced
Approximate moving time: 6 hours
Distance: 7.0 miles round-trip
Elevation trailhead to summit: 10,820' to 14,272' (+3,452')
Terrain: Dirt trail and road, talus
Recommended extra gear: Crampons or microspikes and ice axe if snow exists

Restrictions: Trail closed to motor vehicles; dogs must be on leash or under voice command
Amenities: Porta-potty at trailhead; backcountry camping; services in Alma and Breckenridge
Trailhead: Quandary Peak Trailhead (lower parking lot)
Trail: Quandary Peak Trail #47, East Ridge
Maps: DeLorme Page 48 B2; USGS Breckenridge
County: Summit
Land status: White River National Forest, (970) 945-2521, www.fs.usda.gov/whiteriver; Dillon Ranger District, (970) 468-5400

Finding the trailhead: From Breckenridge, take CO 9 South for 9 miles and turn right onto CR 850 / Blue Lakes Road, or from Fairplay, take CO 9 North for 14 miles and turn left onto Blue Lakes Road. Continue 0.1 mile and park in the lower lot on the right side of the road. There is an upper lot farther up on McCullough Gulch Road / CR 851, but it is usually full. Do not park along the road (GPS: N39 22.962' / W106 3.780').

The Peak

Quandary Peak is the only 14,000' mountain in the Tenmile Range, a 12-mile-long rib of peaks between Tenmile Canyon, near Frisco, and Hoosier and Fremont Passes, south of Breckenridge. The Tenmile Range and adjoining Mosquito Range are geographically one mountain range, with the Tenmiles lying west of the Continental Divide and the Mosquitos on the east side. Quandary was named for the confusion caused when silver outcroppings were unexpectedly found in the area in the mid-1800s, a discovery that led to mining activity. The summit offers views south to Mosquito Range peaks North Star Mountain and Mounts Democrat and Lincoln; east to the Front Range peaks at Hoosier and Boreas Passes; west to 13,000' Tenmile peaks including Atlantic Peak, Fletcher Mountain, and Wheeler Mountain; and north across McCullough Gulch to the rest of the Tenmile Range.

The Climb

Quandary Peak is a popular destination, climbed year-round, with easy trailhead access, a good trail below treeline, and a straightforward ridge route to the top. Avalanche danger may exist in winter and spring as you contour below the east ridge of the peak above treeline, so give that area a wide berth in snow. You will likely encounter many people along the trail, and on summer weekends you'll have to get

Quandary Peak and North Star Mountain

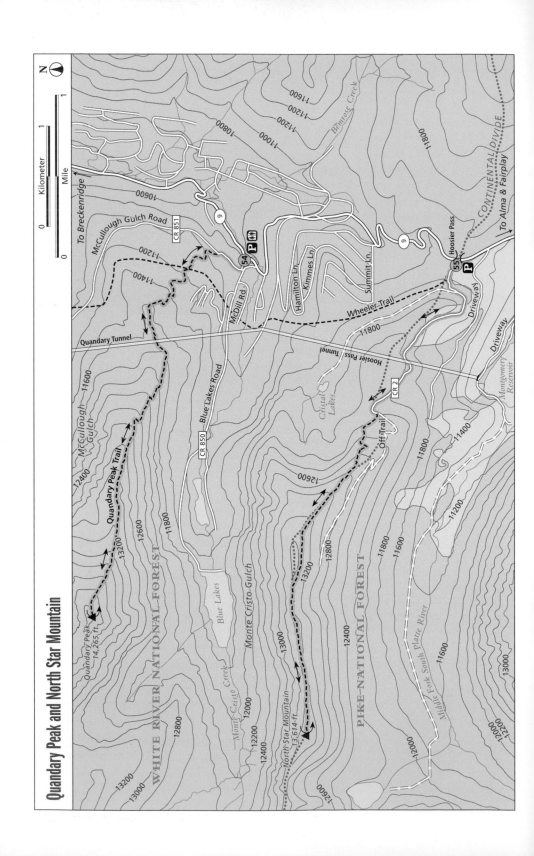

Mountain goats take in views of the human parade on Quandary Peak's east ridge.
PHOTO BY BILL MIDDLEBROOK

there very early for a parking spot. Do not confuse "busy trail" with "safe trail." The number of people on a trail does not lessen the inherent dangers of climbing any 14,000' peak, so be prepared with proper clothing, gear, food, water, and skills. This is the standard route on Quandary, and there are more demanding routes to the summit from the north (Quandary Couloir) and south (Cristo Couloir) in consolidated snow, and from the Class 3 West Ridge and, finally, the Class 5 Inwood Arête.

Miles and Directions

0.0 Begin at the trailhead (10,820') in the northwest corner of the lower parking lot and hike west on trail for about 300', then turn right and hike northeast up Blue Lakes Road.

0.3 Pass the upper parking lot and get on the trail on the left side of the road. Hike north, then west, on switchbacks up Quandary Peak Trail (N39 23.129' / W106 3.716').

0.4 Bear right around a large rock (11,050') and hike northwest on trail. This is easy to miss, especially under snow. As you emerge from the trees, North Star Mountain comes into view to the south and the trail contours below the east ridge of Quandary Peak, ahead (N39 23.184' / W106 3.742').

1.7 Start the east ridge ascent. At about 12,000', the dirt trail turns to mixed talus and dirt (N39 23.452' / W106 4.404').

2.5 The trail levels out and goes due west. Look for mountain goats here (N39 23.691' / W106 5.387').

2.9 Start the final ascent at 13,300' on loose talus and trail (N39 23.706' / W106 5.809').

3.5 Arrive at ranked 14,272' Quandary Peak. Return the way you came (N39 23.838' / W106 6.383').

7.0 Arrive back at the trailhead (N39 22.962' / W106 3.780').

55 Hoosier Pass West Peak: North Star Mountain

See map on page 200.
Elevation: 13,614' (NAVD88 13,621')
Distinctions: Bicentennial, Ranked 13er
Class: 2+; Class 1 to gate, Class 2 to ridge, mixed Class 2 and 2+ to summit
Difficulty and skill level: Moderate; Intermediate
Approximate moving time: 5 hours
Distance: 7.8 miles round-trip
Elevation trailhead to summit: 11,542' to 13,621' (+2,079'); about 2,400' round-trip
Terrain: Dirt road, tundra, scree, and talus; exposure

Restrictions: Trail closed to bicycles and motor vehicles; dogs must be on leash or under voice command
Amenities: Dispersed camping west of trailhead; services in Alma and Breckenridge
Trailhead: Hoosier Pass
Trail: CR 2 / FR 2, off-trail East Ridge
Maps: DeLorme Page 48 B2; USGS Breckenridge, Alma
Counties: Park, Summit
Land status: White River National Forest, (970) 945-2521, www.fs.usda.gov/whiteriver; Dillon Ranger District, (970) 468-5400

Finding the trailhead: From Breckenridge, take CO 9 South for 11 miles, or from Fairplay, take CO 9 North for 12 miles, to the top of Hoosier Pass. Park in the large lot on the west side of the road (GPS: N39 21.711' / W106 3.792').

The Peak

North Star Mountain sits on the Continental Divide in the Mosquito Range west of Hoosier Pass. "North Star" (Polaris) refers to a bright star in the northern sky, used by navigators to locate due north. The long, east ridge of North Star Mountain may have once guided Ute hunters and, later, miners over Hoosier Pass. The peak lies between Tenmile Range highpoint Quandary Peak to the north and Mosquito Range highpoint Mount Lincoln to the south, and offers views east to the Front Range, with the nearby "Wheeler Group" of 13ers to the west, from north to south: ranked Wheeler Mountain and Clinton Peak, and unranked McNamee Peak and Traver Peak.

The Climb

North Star Mountain is climbed year-round. There is a short section that crosses below an avalanche slope on the road, which can be avoided. Under snow, the narrow east ridge demands your attention and winter gear, including spikes or snowshoes for your boots and an ice axe, but there are no especially steep sections along the route. In the summertime, be wary of storms, as you are on top of a ridge for a long time, with no escape route.

The long east ridge of North Star Mountain provides an airy and exciting adventure west of Hoosier Pass. PHOTO BY SUSAN JOY PAUL

Miles and Directions

0.0 From the northwest corner of the lot (11,542'), hike northwest through the forest on CR 2 / FR 2.

0.2 At the road junction, go left and follow signs to stay on FR 2. The trail contours the mountainside above the Middle Fork of the South Platte River, and Lincoln Falls lies along the lower flanks of nearby Mount Lincoln. At about 0.75 mile, there is a trail to the right that takes you above the avalanche-prone slope, ahead, but if the route is snow-free, continue on the road.

1.4 Stay left at the junction, and go past the "Dead End" sign.

1.5 At the Magnolia Mine gate (12,180'), leave the road and do not enter private property. Hike northwest, off-trail and upslope, on grass, talus, and occasional use trails that switchback up the hillside. Avoid mining sites (N39 22.185' / W106 4.891').

1.7 Continue northwest on talus, aiming for the ridge ahead (N39 22.285' / W106 05.163').

2.5 At about 13,200', the summit you see is not the highpoint, even though it's labeled as North Star Mountain on older maps. Contour west on a talus trail below the false summit and ascend to ridgeline (N39 22.623' / W106 05.797').

2.9 Gain the ridge and continue west, staying atop the crest where the rock is more solid, or going around the left (south) side of bumps. Watch for loose rocks and cornices (N39 22.679' / W106 06.180').

3.9 Arrive at ranked 13,621' North Star Mountain. Return the way you came (N39 22.598' / W106 07.265').

7.8 Arrive back at the trailhead (N39 21.711' / W106 03.792').

56 Park Ranges and Mosquito Range Highpoint: Mount Lincoln

Elevations: 14,286' (NAVD88 14,293') Mount Lincoln; 14,238' (NAVD88 14,245') Mount Cameron
Distinctions: Park Ranges Highpoint, Mosquito Range Highpoint, Park County Highpoint, Centennial, Prominence 100, P3K, Ranked 14er (Mount Lincoln); Unranked 14er (Mount Cameron)
Class: 2; Class 1 for most of route, Class 2 to summit areas of each peak
Difficulty and skill level: Strenuous; Advanced
Approximate moving time: 4 hours
Distance: 5.8 miles round-trip
Elevation trailhead to summit: 12,013' to 14,293' (+2,280'); about 2,600' round-trip
Terrain: Dirt trail, talus, and scree
Recommended extra gear: Crampons or microspikes and ice axe if snow exists
Restrictions: Fee-area parking, payable by cash or check at self-serve kiosk; Buckskin Gulch Road may require high-clearance 4WD; in winter the road is not plowed for last 3 miles, adding 6 miles round-trip to your climb; dogs must be on leash; trail closed to motor vehicles
Amenities: Trailhead toilets; pullout parking and primitive camping spots located along road; seasonal camping at Kite Lake Campground by permit, payable at self-serve kiosk; services in Alma
Trailhead: Kite Lake Trailhead
Trail: Lincoln-Democrat Loop Trail
Maps: DeLorme Page 48 B2, B1; USGS Alma, Climax
County: Park
Land status: Pike National Forest, (719) 553-1400, www.fs.usda.gov/psicc; South Park Ranger District, (719) 836-2031

Finding the trailhead: From CO 9 / Main Street in Alma, turn west onto unpaved CR 8 / Buckskin Gulch Road, towards Kite Lake. Drive 5.6 miles to parking at the trailhead (GPS: N39 19.678' / W106 7.765').

The Peak

The Mosquito Range trends north–south from Hoosier Pass to Trout Creek Pass. The range was named—the story goes—for a dead mosquito on a legal document, and Mount Lincoln, one of four ranked 14ers in the range, was named by historian Wilbur F. Stone for President Abraham Lincoln. Mount Cameron is named for General Robert A. Cameron, founder of Fort Collins. Mount Lincoln is located near ranked 14ers Mount Democrat and Mount Bross and unranked 14ers Mount Cameron and "South Bross," and all five peaks are sometimes climbed together, in a loop. Much of the land in the area is private property, owned by mining companies and leased by the town of Alma, allowing recreational use. As of 2015 there is no legal access to Mount Bross and "South Bross."

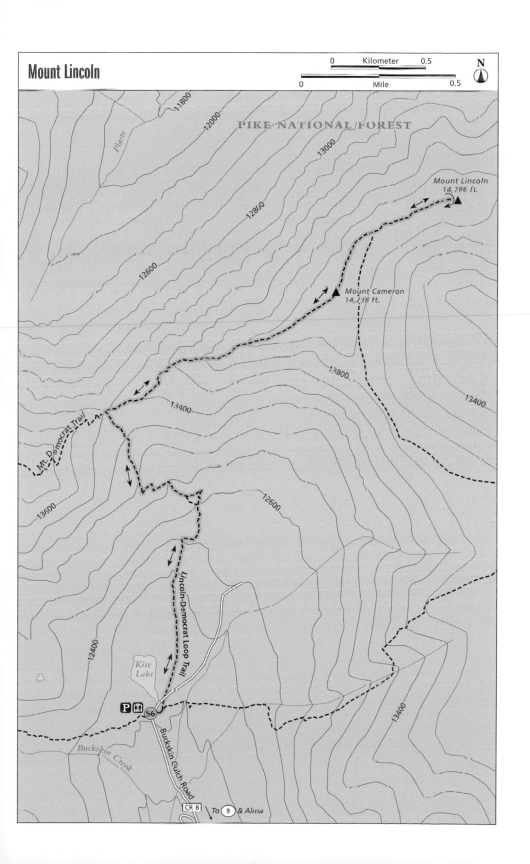

Mount Lincoln

0 Kilometer 0.5

0 Mile 0.5

N

PIKE NATIONAL FOREST

11800

12000

13000

12800

12600

Platte

Mount Lincoln
14,286 ft.

Mount Cameron
14,238 ft.

13800

13400

Mt. Democrat Trail

13400

13600

13400

12600

12400

Lincoln-Democrat Loop Trail

Kite
Lake

P 56

13400

Buckskin Creek

Buckskin Gulch Road

CR 8 To 9 & Alma

Mosquito Range highpoint Mount Lincoln offers spectacular views from an airy summit.
PHOTO BY BILL MIDDLEBROOK

The Climb

The 14ers at Kite Lake are climbed year-round, with proper gear, clothing, skill, and respect for the weather. Stay on the trail while hiking in this area and avoid potentially dangerous mine shafts hidden off-trail. In snow, bear right of the Democrat-Cameron saddle if avalanche danger exists west of the trail. Winter and spring snow and ice can make the stretch from the Lincoln-Cameron saddle to Mount Lincoln tricky, and the Mount Lincoln summit is small, so you may have to wait for others to come down before you can go to the top. Despite the hazards and restrictions, this is one of the easiest 14ers in Colorado. You'll tag Mount Cameron en route, and you can pick up Mount Democrat with a short detour at the Democrat-Cameron saddle, increasing your round-trip distance by 1.2 miles and 750' of elevation.

Miles and Directions

0.0 At the 12,013' trailhead, hike east and north up the gravel road with Kite Lake to your left.

0.6 Pass mine shack ruins and follow the trail as it jogs right (east) and heads north up switchbacks with Mount Democrat to your left (N39 20.158' / W106 7.660').

1.4 Reach the Democrat-Cameron saddle at 13,400' and turn right (east-northeast) towards Mount Cameron. The trail follows the south side of the ridge, then gains the crest and climbs over several false summits (N39 20.502' / W106 7.938').

2.3 Arrive at unranked 14,245' Mount Cameron, to the right of the trail. Descend the north side of the peak, cross the Lincoln-Cameron saddle, and hike up the gravel road on Mount Lincoln. The road turns to trail and follows the narrow, exposed west ridge crest. Follow the ridge and the steep trail east-northeast to the summit (N39 20.829' / W106 7.119').

2.9 Arrive at ranked 14,293' Mount Lincoln. Return the way you came (N39 21.086' / W106 6.695').

5.8 Arrive back at the trailhead (N39 19.678' / W106 7.765').

57 Mosquito Pass Peaks: Kuss Peak ("Repeater Peak") and Mosquito Peak

Elevations: 13,548' (NAVD 88 13,555') Kuss Peak; 13,781' (NAVD88 13,788') Mosquito Peak

Distinctions: Unranked 13er (Kuss Peak); Bicentennial, Ranked 13er (Mosquito Peak)

Class: 2; Class 1 for most of route, Class 2 to Mosquito Peak summit area

Difficulty and skill level: Moderate; Intermediate

Approximate moving time: 5 hours

Distance: 9.6 miles round-trip

Elevation trailhead to summit: 11,580' to 13,788' (12,208'); about 2,000' round-trip

Terrain: Dirt road, talus, scree, and tundra

Restrictions: CR 12 may require high-clearance 4WD and is not maintained beyond Park City in winter, adding 5 miles round-trip; avoid private property, mining sites, equipment, and historical artifacts; do not filter water for drinking in this area, due to mining activity

Amenities: Backcountry camping, services in Alma

Trailhead: CR 12

Trail: CR 12, unnamed mining road, off-trail Southeast Ridge

Maps: DeLorme Page 48 C1; USGS Climax

Counties: Lake, Park

Land status: Pike National Forest, (719) 553-1400, www.fs.usda.gov/pslcc; South Park Ranger District, (719) 836-2031; Bureau of Land Management, Royal Gorge Field Office, (719) 269-8500, www.blm.gov/co/st/en/fo/rgfo.html

Finding the trailhead: From US 285 in Fairplay, take CO 9 North for 4.8 miles, or from Breckenridge, take CO 9 South for 17 miles, and turn west onto unpaved CR 12. The trailhead is 7 miles from this point, as follows: bear right at 4.5 miles, and bear left at 6.9 miles. Cross the creek and drive 0.1 mile to a pullout (GPS: N39 17.950' / W106 9.317').

The Peak

Mosquito Pass rises to 13,185' in the Mosquito Range between Alma and Leadville. The road over the pass is traversed by high-clearance 4WDs, dirt bikes, and ATVs, and only in the summer. Mosquito Gulch has a long mining history, and you'll pass historic remains of the London Mine on your hike. At the top of the pass, a marker honors Reverend John "Father" Dyer, who came to Colorado in 1861 to see Pikes Peak and stayed to preach. Dyer's autobiography, *The Snow-Shoe Itinerant*, details his adventures, and he was posthumously inducted into the Colorado Ski and Snowboard Hall of Fame. Three Mosquito Range peaks—Dyer Mountain, Father Dyer Peak, and West Dyer Mountain—are named for him. From Mosquito Peak, you'll have views of the surrounding 13ers, clockwise from the north: unranked Treasurevault Mountain and ranked Mounts Arkansas, Tweto, and Buckskin; to the east, unranked Loveland Mountain; and south, ranked London and Pennsylvania Mountains and Mount Evans B.

Kuss Peak ("Repeater Peak") and Mosquito Peak

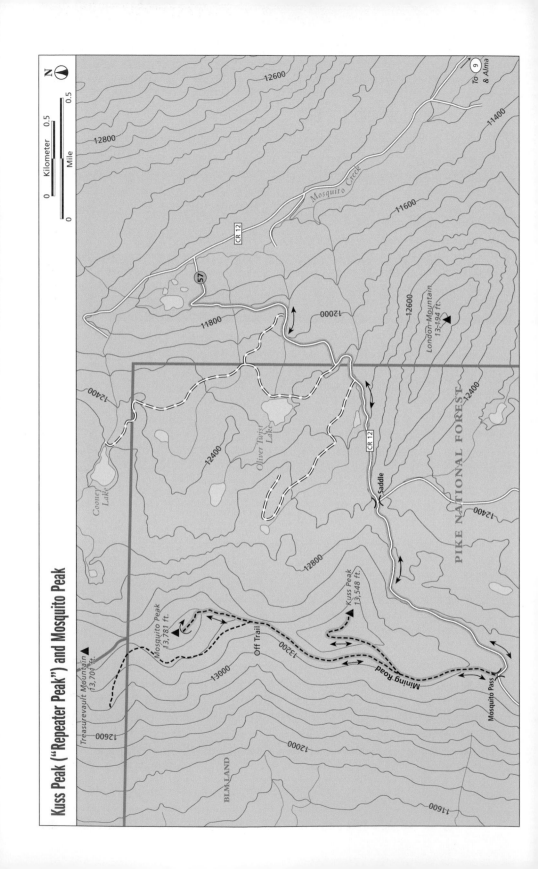

N

0 Kilometer 0.5

0 Mile 0.5

12600

12800

12400

Cooney Lake

12400

Oliver Twist Lake

11800

57

CR 12

12000

Mosquito Creek

11600

To 9 & Alma

11400

12600

London Mountain 13,194 ft.

12400

PIKE NATIONAL FOREST

12400

Saddle

CR 12

12800

Treasurevault Mountain 13,701 ft.

Mosquito Peak 13,781 ft.

13000

Off Trail

13200

Kuss Peak 13,548 ft.

Mining Road

Mosquito Pass

12600

BLM LAND

12000

11600

Kuss ("Repeater") Peak lies north of Mosquito Pass in the Mosquito Range near Fairplay.
PHOTO BY SUSAN JOY PAUL

The Climb

The Mosquito Gulch peaks are climbed year-round, with consideration for road access, avalanche danger, and mining activity. The route contours below London Mountain, and you can add that peak from the Kuss–London saddle via a use trail that climbs the west ridge. The road below London should be avoided if unconsolidated snow exists, as avalanches are possible.

Miles and Directions

0.0 Hike southwest on CR 12 (11,580'), up switchbacks toward the saddle west (right) of London Mountain.

1.0 Bear left at the first fork to remain on CR 12 (N39 17.458' / W106 9.707').

1.2 Pass the London Mine and take the left fork to continue west toward the saddle (N39 17.389' / W106 9.781').

1.7 At the Kuss-London saddle (12,640'), continue west on the road, then south toward Mosquito Pass (N39 17.312' / W106 10.323').

2.8 At 13,185' Mosquito Pass, go north on the dirt road (N39 16.867' / W106 11.161').

3.2 Turn right at the gate and go up the road toward Kuss Peak (N39 17.206' / W106 11.158').

3.7 Arrive at unranked 13,555' Kuss Peak. Return to the gate, then continue north toward Mosquito Peak (N39 17.405' / W106 10.887').

4.9 Depart the road on the right and head north and northwest along the ridge to the summit (N39 17.748' / W106 10.915').

5.3 Arrive at ranked 13,788' Mosquito Peak. Return the way you came, bypassing Kuss Peak (N39 18.016' / W106 10.962').

9.6 Arrive back at the trailhead (N39 17.950' / W106 9.317').

58 Weston Pass Peak: Weston Peak

Elevation: 13,572' (NAVD88 13,578')
Distinction: Unranked 13er
Class: 2
Difficulty and skill level: Moderate; Beginner
Approximate moving time: 3 hours
Distance: 2.6 miles round-trip
Elevation trailhead to summit: 11,921' to 13,578' (+1,657'); about 1,800' round-trip
Terrain: Grass, tundra, and talus; exposure
Restrictions: Weston Pass is closed seasonally and reopened when snow allows; road from the east is rugged but passable in a car, from the west is 4WD
Amenities: Campgrounds located on CR 22; services in Fairplay
Trailhead: Weston Pass
Trail: Off-trail West Ridge
Maps: DeLorme Page 48 D1; USGS Mount Sherman
Counties: Park, Lake
Land status: San Isabel and Pike National Forests, (719) 553-1400, www.fs.usda.gov/psicc; South Park Ranger District, (719) 836-2031

Finding the trailhead: From CO 9 in Fairplay, drive 4.4 miles south on US 285 and turn right onto CR 5. The road becomes unpaved at about 1.8 miles, and turns into CR 22 at about 7.1 miles. Bear right and continue for another 8.8 miles to the top of the pass (GPS: N39 7.887' / W106 10.932').

The Peak

Weston Peak lies northeast of Weston Pass in the Mosquito Range. Just two roads cross the mountain range—Mosquito Pass and Weston Pass—and at 11,921', Weston Pass, the lower of the two, is the only one that can be reached in a passenger car, from the east side. The road west from Leadville is 4WD. Weston Peak offers views north to the Mosquito Range's higher peaks, including 13ers Ptarmigan Peak, Horseshoe Mountain, Peerless Mountain, and Mount Sheridan, and ranked 14er Mount Sherman. The Sawatch Range lies to the south and west, and South Park sprawls east, bordered by the Front Range.

The Climb

The route up the south slopes is off-trail and very steep, so take your time and spread out if you are in a group, to minimize impact. To add unranked 13er Ptarmigan Peak, return to the spot where you first topped the ridge, then go north for less than a mile along the ridge. Other peaks accessible from Weston Pass include ranked 12er South Peak and a number of unnamed 12ers, all located south of the pass.

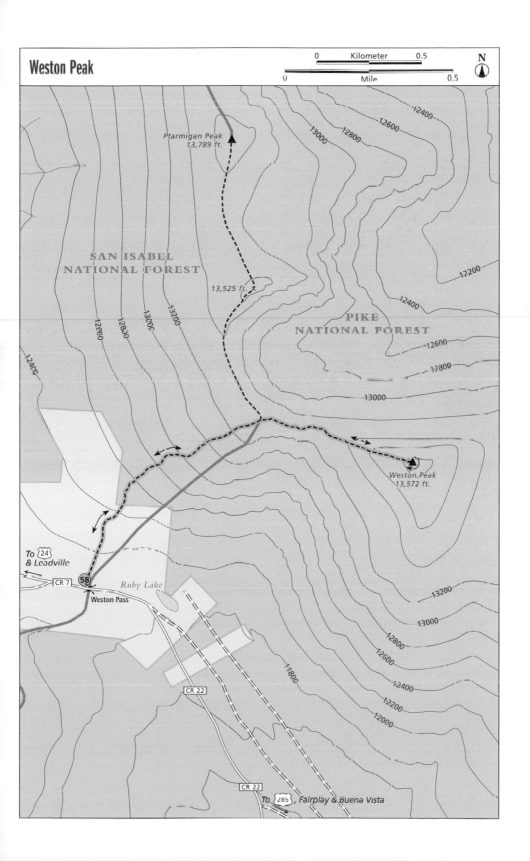

Weston Peak

0   Kilometer   0.5
0   Mile   0.5

N

Ptarmigan Peak
13,789 ft.

12400
12600
12800
13000
13200

SAN ISABEL
NATIONAL FOREST

13,525 ft.

12200

12400

PIKE
NATIONAL FOREST

12600

12800

13000

12600
12800
13000
13200
12400

Weston Peak
13,572 ft.

To 24
& Leadville

CR 7   58

Ruby Lake

Weston Pass

13200

13000

12800

12600

12400

12200

12000

11800

CR 22

CR 22

To 285, Fairplay & Buena Vista

Summiters are treated to views of a bevy of Mosquito peaks north of Weston Peak.
PHOTO BY SUSAN JOY PAUL

Miles and Directions

0.0 Begin at the pullout on the north side of the top of the pass (11,921') and hike northeast, up the grass slope, staying left of the talus field and cornices.

0.8 At the top, turn right to go east on the narrow ridge (N39 8.304' / W106 10.335').

1.0 Cross the low point and head upslope on tundra and talus, over a couple of false bumps, and up the final talus slope (N39 8.270' / W106 10.141').

1.3 Arrive at unranked 13,578' Weston Peak. Return the way you came (N39 8.192' / W106 9.855').

2.6 Arrive back at the trailhead (N39 7.887' / W106 10.932').

59 Trout Creek Pass Peak: West Buffalo Peak

Elevation: 13,326' (NAVD88 13,332')

Distinctions: Buffalo Peaks Wilderness Highpoint, Prominence 100, P1K, Ranked 13er

Class: 2; Class 1 for first 0.8 mile, Class 2 to summit

Difficulty and skill level: Strenuous; Intermediate

Approximate moving time: 5 hours

Distance: 6.4 miles round-trip

Elevation trailhead to summit: 9,960' to 13,332' (+3,372'); about 3,500' round-trip

Terrain: Dirt trail, duff, bushwhack, grass, tundra, scree, and talus; creek crossing

Restrictions: CR 377 and CR 375 are not maintained in winter; CR 375-3 is closed and gated Dec 1 to Apr 15 and designated as a 4WD road, but may be navigable in a passenger car, starting at the bottom adds 3 round-trip miles and 800' of elevation; trail closed to bicycles and motorized vehicles; dogs must be on leash; groups of 10 or more must obtain a special use permit through South Park District Ranger Office; follow wilderness regulations

Amenities: Camping at nearby campgrounds; backcountry camping; services in Buena Vista

Trailhead: Four Mile Trailhead

Trail: Rough and Tumbling Creek Trail ("Tumble Creek Trail"), off-trail Northwest Ridge

Maps: DeLorme Page 60 A1; USGS Marmot Peak

Counties: Chaffee, Park

Land status: San Isabel National Forest, (719) 553-1400, www.fs.usda.gov/psicc; Salida Ranger District, (719) 539-3591; Buffalo Peaks Wilderness, www.wilderness.net

Finding the trailhead: From US 24 in Buena Vista, go east on E. Main Street for 0.1 mile and turn left on N. Colorado Avenue / CR 371. Drive 2.5 miles and turn right just before the tunnel, onto unpaved CR 375. Go 5.2 miles and turn right (downhill) to remain on CR 375 and go 1 mile, past a pullout, then continue onto 4WD CR 375-3 for 1.5 miles, to a pullout above the trailhead (GPS: N38 57.685' / W106 8.477').

The Peak

West Buffalo Peak and East Buffalo Peak, the "Buffalo Peaks," rise at the south end of the Mosquito Range, near Trout Creek Pass. The 9,487' pass—located south of the US 285 and US 24 junction—divides South Park to the east and the Arkansas River Valley, west. The Buffalo Peaks are located northwest of Trout Creek Pass in the Buffalo Peaks Wilderness, the smallest wilderness area in the state and home to the largest herd of bighorn sheep. From the top of the Buffaloes, the Sawatch Range rises to the west, the Mosquitos lie to the north, and the Front Range lines the eastern horizon, beyond South Park.

The Climb

West Buffalo Peak is often climbed from the east, after the lower, ranked 13er East Buffalo Peak, but the route described here takes you directly to the western summit. To add the east peak, continue southeast off the west summit, drop to a saddle, and then climb

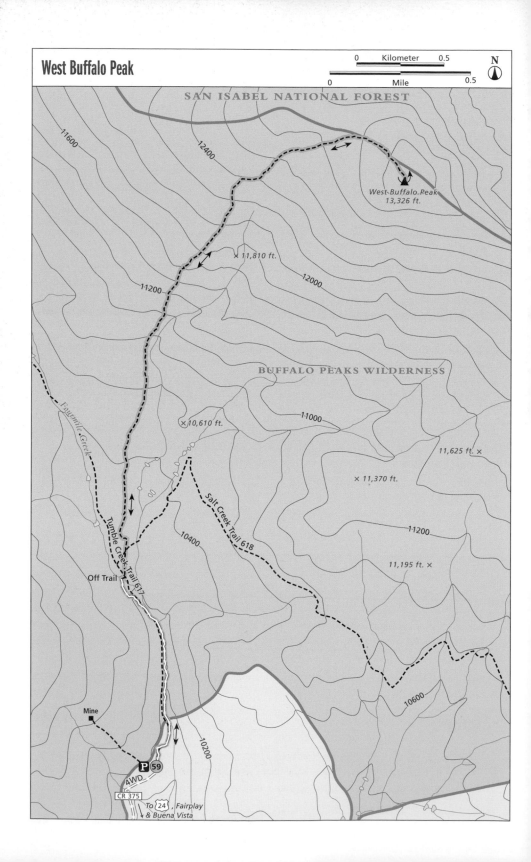

West Buffalo Peak

SAN ISABEL NATIONAL FOREST

11600

12400

West Buffalo Peak
13,326 ft.

× 11,810 ft.

11200

12000

BUFFALO PEAKS WILDERNESS

11000

× 10,610 ft.

11,625 ft. ×

× 11,370 ft.

Fourmile Creek

Salt Creek Trail 618

11,195 ft. ×

11200

10400

Off Trail

Tumble Creek Trail 617

10600

Mine

10200

P 59

AWD

CR 375

To 24 , Fairplay
& Buena Vista

0   Kilometer   0.5

0   Mile   0.5

N

An ancient bristlecone twists in the wind on the west slopes of West Buffalo Peak.
PHOTO BY SUSAN JOY PAUL

to the east summit, adding about 2 miles and 1,000' of elevation to your round-trip climb. The forest south of West Buffalo Peak is remarkably flat, with lots of places to set up a tent, but stay clear of the ponds, which are designated as a sensitive species habitat.

Miles and Directions

0.0 Begin at the 9,960' trailhead and hike north, with Fourmile Creek to your right and West Buffalo Peak in view ahead. Enter the wilderness area and go through a gate, then pass a creek crossing (to Salt Creek Trail) and continue on Tumble Creek Trail.

0.8 Cross the creek and continue past the ponds, then go off-trail, north, through the forest (N38 58.273' / W106 8.622').

1.9 Bushwhack steeply upslope, gaining 400' in 0.1 mile. A GPS or compass comes in handy here.

2.0 Reach timberline at 11,580'. West Buffalo Peak is in sight to the northeast. Hike on grass, tundra, and talus toward the saddle left (west) of the summit (N38 59.227' / W106 8.391').

2.9 Gain the northwest ridge and hike over tundra, scree, and talus toward the summit.

3.2 Arrive at ranked 13,332' West Buffalo Peak. A marker for Marmot Peak is embedded at the summit area. Return the way you came (N38 59.502' / W106 7.495').

6.4 Arrive back at the trailhead (N38 57.685' / W106 8.477').

The Sawatch Range

The Sawatch Range trends northwest-southeast through central Colorado west of the Park Ranges, from the Eagle River at Vail Valley to Marshall Pass near Sargents. Unlike Colorado's other major mountain ranges, the Sawatch Range does not contain many subranges, but it does hold 8 of the 20 highest peaks of the Rocky Mountains and 15 ranked 14ers, more than any other range in Colorado. The Collegiate Peaks lie within the Sawatch proper, while the Williams Mountains are a spur of the range. Most of the high peaks of the Sawatch Range—including state highpoint Mount Elbert—lie along Colorado's Mineral Belt, and the Continental Divide follows the south end of the range from Leadville to Marshall Pass. Paved roads cross the Sawatch at Tennessee Pass, Independence Pass, and Monarch Pass, and dirt roads cross the range at Cottonwood Pass and Marshall Pass, providing short approaches to many high peaks. Wilderness areas within the Sawatch Range include the Holy Cross, Hunter-Fryingpan, Mount Massive, Collegiate Peaks, and Fossil Ridge Wildernesses. "Sawatch" is a variation of Saguache, from the Ute sagwáchi, or "blue-green," referring to the jewel tones of the open sky and forested earth of Colorado's prominent Sawatch Range, in the heart of the Rockies.

A mountaineer scrambles through blocks on the north ridge of Williams Mountain in the Williams Mountains of the Sawatch Range. PHOTO BY DOUG HATFIELD

60 Tennessee Pass Peak: Galena Mountain B

Elevation: 12,893'

Distinction: Ranked 12er

Class: 2+; Class 1 for first 2 miles, Class 2 and 2+ to summit

Difficulty and skill level: Strenuous; Intermediate

Approximate moving time: 5 hours

Distance: 7.0 miles round-trip

Elevation trailhead to summit: 10,040' to 12,893' (+2,853'); about 3,000' round-trip

Terrain: Dirt trail, grass, tundra, talus, and boulders

Restrictions: Organized hiking groups must obtain pass from Leadville Ranger District Office; trail closed to bicycles and motorized vehicles; dogs must be on leash; follow wilderness regulations

Amenities: Seasonal toilets, picnic areas, and camping at nearby lakeside campgrounds; backcountry camping; services in Leadville

Trailhead: Timberline Lake Trailhead

Trails: Timberline Lake Trail, Colorado Trail, off-trail South Slopes

Maps: DeLorme Page 47 B7, C7; USGS Homestake Reservoir

County: Lake

Land status: San Isabel National Forest, (719) 553-1400, www.fs.usda.gov/psicc; Leadville Ranger District, (719) 486-0749; Holy Cross Wilderness, www.wilderness.net

Finding the trailhead: From US 24 in Leadville, go north on CR 4 / McWethy Drive, toward Turquoise Lake. Drive 2.6 miles and bear right to stay on CR 4, then continue for 4.3 miles and bear right onto CR 9 / Turquoise Lake Road. Drive 2 miles and turn left onto FR 104E and continue 0.1 mile to the Timberline Lake Trailhead. If the road is closed at Turquoise Lake, due to unsafe snow conditions, the trailhead may be approached from the north side of the lake by taking CR 4 to CR 9C to CR 9 to FR 104E (GPS: N39 17.101' / W106 26.806').

The Peak

Galena Mountain rises southwest of Tennessee Pass near the town of Leadville. The peak is named for the mineral galena, the primary ore of lead and a source of silver, and Leadville—at 10,152', the highest incorporated city in the United States—was one of the world's largest silver mining camps in the late 1800s. Tennessee Pass was named by Southern gold miners who came to the area during the Pikes Peak Gold Rush. A ski area is located at the top of the pass, and a memorial honors the Camp Hale 10th Mountain Division, which trained here during World War II. Views from Galena Mountain are expansive, with Colorado's highest peaks, Mount Elbert and Mount Massive, rising south of the peak; Mount of the Holy Cross to the north with the Gore Range beyond; the Mosquito Range to the east; and the Elk Range, west.

The Climb

Galena Mountain's sheer east face greets road travelers along US 24, but your route follows the gentle south slopes, from a recreational area near Turquoise Lake. The

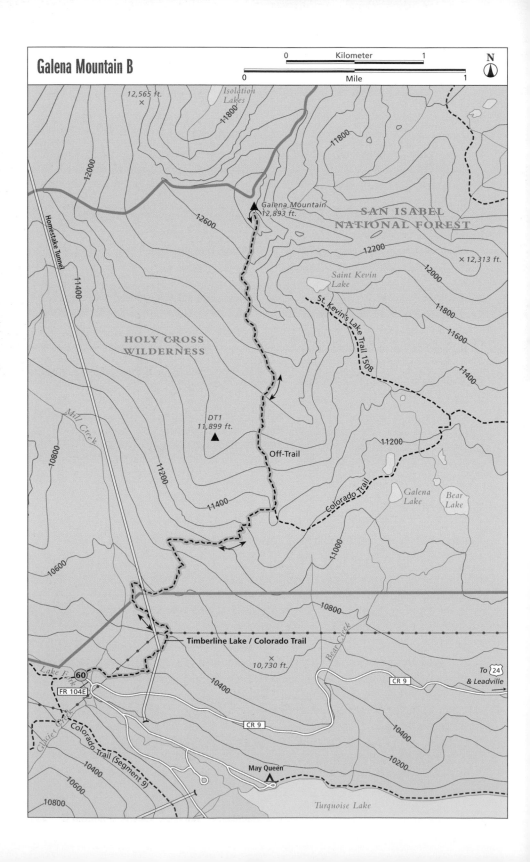

Kilometer

Mile

N

12,565 ft.

Isolation
Lakes

11800

11800

12600

Galena Mountain
12,893 ft.

SAN ISABEL
NATIONAL FOREST

12200

× 12,313 ft.

Saint Kevin
Lake

12000

Homestake Tunnel

11400

11800

St. Kevin's Lake Trail 1508

11600

HOLY CROSS
WILDERNESS

11400

Mill Creek

11200

DT1
11,899 ft.

11200

Off-Trail

Colorado Trail

10800

11400

Galena
Lake

Bear
Lake

11000

10600

10800

Bear Creek

Timberline Lake / Colorado Trail

×
10,730 ft.

To 24
& Leadville

Lake Fork

60

FR 104E

CR 9

CR 9

10400

Colorado Trail (Segment 9)

10400

10200

Glacier Creek

10400

May Queen

10600

Turquoise Lake

10800

Galena Mountain's sheer east face greets road travelers along US 24.
PHOTO BY STEWART M. GREEN

first 2 miles are on the Colorado Trail, and the final 1.5 miles run directly north, with route-finding limited to working your way around light patches of willows and boulders, to the summit.

Miles and Directions

0.0 Begin at the trailhead (10,040') on the north side of the lot and hike northeast. Cross a footbridge over Mill Creek and pass by a wilderness kiosk, where campers should complete a permit. The trail swings east and north through a lodgepole pine forest, entering the Holy Cross Wilderness at just over 0.5 mile, and breaks out of the trees at about 1.5 miles, where Mount Massive appears to the south. Continue east, then north, where switchbacks ease the climb to the top of the ridge.

2.0 Turn left and leave the trail at the top of the ridge, at 11,400'. The Mosquito Range is visible to the east, and a small cairn marks the turnoff. Head upslope north, on tundra and through scattered fields of willows and talus. Climb through a tumble of boulders to the rocky summit area (N39 17.751' / W106 25.828').

3.5 Arrive at ranked 12,893' Galena Mountain. Return the way you came (N39 18.908' / W106 25.929').

7.0 Arrive back at the trailhead (N39 17.101' / W106 26.806').

61 Sawatch Range Highpoint: Mount Elbert

Elevation: 14,433' (NAVD88 14,440')
Distinctions: Sawatch Range Highpoint, State Highpoint, Lake County Highpoint, Centennial, Prominence 100, Ultra-prominence Peak, Ranked 14er
Class: 1
Difficulty and skill level: Very Strenuous; Advanced
Approximate moving time: 8 hours
Distance: 9.0 miles round-trip
Elevation trailhead to summit: 10,070' to 14,440' (+4,370'); about 4,700' round-trip
Terrain: Dirt and talus trail
Recommended extra gear: Crampons or microspikes and ice axe if snow exists
Restrictions: Summer route; CR 11 closed in winter about 5 miles from trailhead; organized hiking groups must obtain pass from Leadville Ranger District Office; trail closed to bicycles and motor vehicles; dogs must be on leash or under voice command
Amenities: Trailhead toilets; backcountry camping; seasonal camping at nearby Halfmoon Creek and Elbert Creek Campgrounds; services in Leadville
Trailhead: Mount Elbert Trailhead
Trail: North Elbert Trail, off-trail Northeast Ridge
Maps: DeLorme Page 47 D7; USGS Mount Elbert
County: Lake
Land status: San Isabel National Forest, (719) 553-1400, www.fs.usda.gov/psicc; Leadville Ranger District, (719) 486-0749

Finding the trailhead: From Leadville, take US 24 South for about 3 miles and turn right onto CO 300 West. Drive 0.8 mile and take the second left onto CR 11 / Halfmoon Road, then go 1.3 miles and turn right to remain on Halfmoon Road. Continue another 5 miles, on unpaved 2WD CR 11, to the parking area on the left (GPS: N39 9.102' / W106 24.739').

The Peak

Mount Elbert is the highest peak in Colorado and the second-highest peak in the contiguous United States, topping the Sawatch Range at 14,440'—just 12' higher than the second-highest peak in the state, nearby Sawatch peak 14,428' Mount Massive. Good trails lead all the way to the summit and make it a popular introduction to the state's long list of 14,000' peaks. Situated east of Independence Pass near Leadville, Mount Elbert is named for Samuel Hitt Elbert, who served as the sixth governor of the Colorado Territory in the 1870s, and the peak was climbed in 1874 by H. W. Stuckle of the Hayden Survey. From the top of Mount Elbert, you'll have views of surrounding 14,000' Sawatch peaks, including Mount Massive to the north and La Plata Peak, Huron Peak, Missouri Mountain, Mount Belford, and Mount Oxford to the south.

The Climb

Mount Elbert is climbed year-round, but the northeast ridge route described here is a summer route and the shortest way to the top of the peak. In winter, Mount Elbert

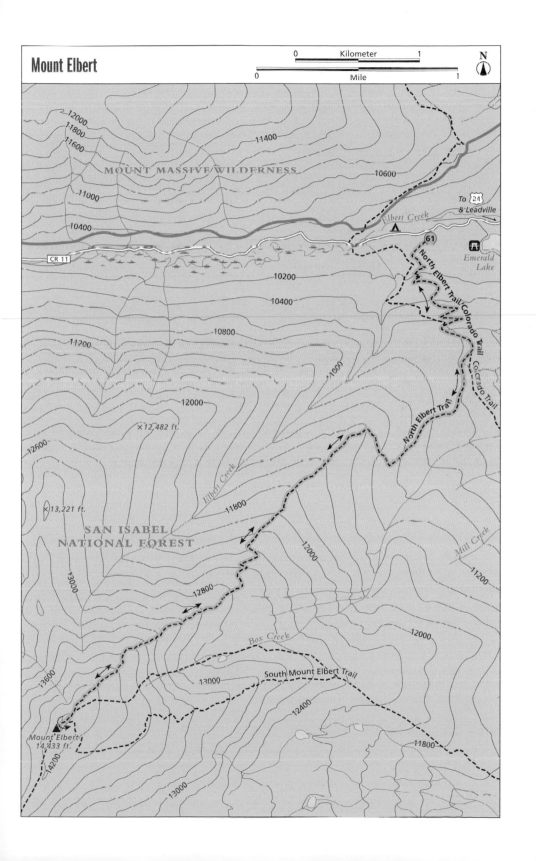

Mount Elbert

0 — Kilometer — 1

0 — Mile — 1

N

MOUNT MASSIVE WILDERNESS

12000
11800
11600
11400
11000
10600
10400
Elbert Creek
To 24 & Leadville
61
Emerald Lake
CR 11
10200
10400
North Elbert Trail/Colorado Trail
10800
11200
1000
Colorado Trail
12000
North Elbert Trail
×12,482 ft.
12600
Elbert Creek
11800
Mill Creek
×13,221 ft.
SAN ISABEL NATIONAL FOREST
11200
12000
13000
12800
12000
13600
Box Creek
South Mount Elbert Trail
13000
12400
11800
Mount Elbert 14,433 ft.
14200
13000
11800

A well-worn trail rises along the northeast ridge of Mount Elbert. PHOTO BY BILL MIDDLEBROOK

may be approached along the east ridge from the South Elbert Trailhead, or along the southeast ridge from the Black Cloud Trailhead. In good spring snow, it is also accessed via the west face and by the Box Creek Couloirs on the east face.

Miles and Directions

0.0 Begin at the trailhead in the southwest corner of the lot (10,070') and hike south through the forest. Bear left at the junction with the Colorado Trail and continue south on the North Elbert Trail.

1.2 Switchback up and over the lowest flanks of the northeast ridge to a trail junction. Bear right to leave the Colorado Trail and remain on the North Elbert Trail. The trail bends southwest, climbs north, and goes southwest again, through the forest (N39 8.646' / W106 24.484').

2.7 Break treeline at 11,900' and continue southwest with the north slopes of the peak in view, ahead (N39 7.977' / W106 25.515').

3.3 Gain the ridge crest, where the steep walls of Box Creek Canyon appear against the false summit ahead. Continue southwest, as the dirt trail turns to talus and climbs steeply along the right (northwest) side of the ridge crest (N39 7.655' / W106 25.733').

4.1 Regain the ridge at about 13,900' and go southwest. The trail rises, then flattens, and the summit is in view (N39 7.334' / W106 26.380').

4.5 Arrive at ranked 14,440' Mount Elbert. Return the way you came (N39 7.066' / W106 26.719').

9.0 Arrive back at the trailhead (N39 9.102' / W106 24.739').

62 Independence Pass Peaks: Point 13500 and Twining Peak

Elevations: 13,500' Point 13500; 13,711' (NAVD88 13,718') Twining Peak

Distinctions: Tricentennial, Ranked 13er (Point 13500); Bicentennial, Prominence 300, P1K, Ranked 13er (Twining Peak)

Class: 2 ; Class 2 most of route, Class 2+ to Twining Peak highpoint

Difficulty and skill level: Moderate; Intermediate

Approximate moving time: 3 hours

Distance: 4.6 miles round trip

Elevation trailhead to summit: 12,095' to 13,718' (+1,623'); about 2,200' round trip

Terrain: Dirt, rocks, marshes, talus, and tundra

Restrictions: Independence Pass is closed seasonally from about Nov 7 to the Thurs prior to Memorial Day weekend, depending on snow conditions; CO 82 is closed to all vehicles more than 35' in length; terrain closed to bicycles and motor vehicles; dogs must be on leash; follow wilderness regulations

Amenities: Trailhead toilets; camping at nearby campgrounds along CO 82; limited services in Twin Lakes; full services in Aspen, Buena Vista, and Leadville

Trailhead: Independence Pass

Trail: Use trail, off-trail South Ridge

Maps: DeLorme Page 47 D6; USGS Independence Pass, Mount Champion

Counties: Pitkin, Lake

Land status: San Isabel National Forest, (719) 553-1400, www.fs.usda.gov/psicc; Leadville Ranger District, (719) 486-0749; Mount Massive Wilderness, Hunter-Fryingpan Wilderness, www.wilderness.net

Finding the trailhead: From Buena Vista, take US 24 West for about 19 miles, or from Leadville, take US 24 East for about 15 miles. Turn west onto CO 82 West and travel 23.5 miles to the top of Independence Pass. Park on the left (south) side of the road, and cross the highway to begin your climb on the north side (GPS: N39 6.504' / W106 33.839').

The Peaks

Point 13500 and Twining Peak ride the Continental Divide north of Independence Pass. The pass is named for the town of Independence, located west of the pass and founded on Independence Day in 1879. At 12,095', Independence Pass is the highest paved mountain pass in Colorado and the highest paved crossing of the Continental Divide in North America. It's also the summer route into Aspen, with twists, turns, lots of exposure, and even more tourists, parked at the pass and enjoying the paved trail and scenic overlook, south. The Point 13500 and Twining Peak summits provide fantastic views, with the Williams Mountains and Elk Mountains to the west and the Sawatch Range sprawling all around, most notably 13ers Deer Mountain and Mount Champion to the east and ranked 13er Grizzly Peak—the highest 13er in the state—to the south.

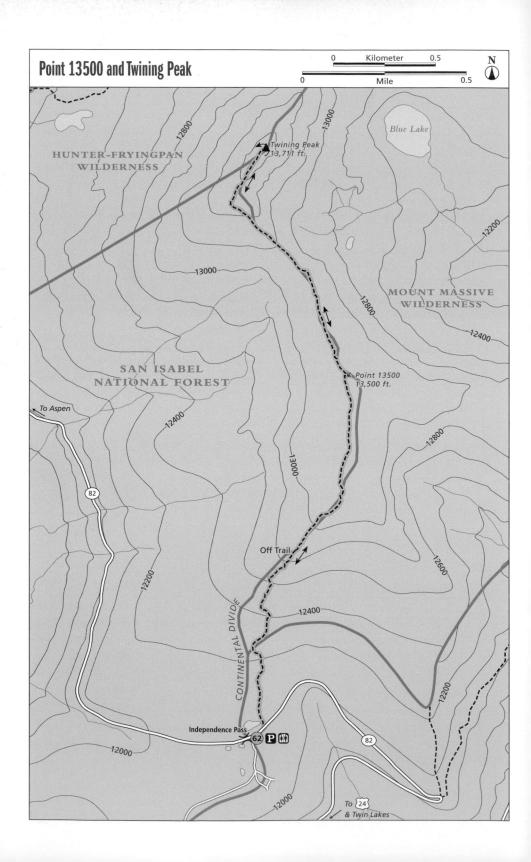

Point 13500 and Twining Peak

0   Kilometer   0.5

0   Mile   0.5

N

HUNTER-FRYINGPAN
WILDERNESS

Blue Lake

12800

13000

Twining Peak
13,711 ft.

12200

MOUNT MASSIVE
WILDERNESS

13000

12800

12400

SAN ISABEL
NATIONAL FOREST

Point 13500
13,500 ft.

12400

12800

To Aspen

13000

82

Off Trail

12600

12200

CONTINENTAL DIVIDE

12400

12200

12000

Independence Pass

62 P

82

12000

To 24
& Twin Lakes

A scenic ridge walk leads to the summit of bicentennial Twining Peak. PHOTO BY SUSAN JOY PAUL

The Climb

This is a short climb to two ranked 13ers with easy route-finding and an exciting finish. The route is above timberline for the entire distance, exposed to full sun and wind. The Mount Massive Wilderness lies east of the peaks and the Hunter-Fryingpan Wilderness lies to the north, so wilderness rules apply if you travel beyond the peaks.

Miles and Directions

0.0   From the top of 12,095' Independence Pass, hike north, around a small lake, and head up to the left (west) side of the first peak. Follow a use trail to a point north of the summit that avoids the steep crags and boulders on the south slopes, then turn right to the highpoint.

1.4   Arrive at ranked Point 13500, marked by an enormous rock. Depart north and follow the ridge down to the Twining-13500 saddle (N39 7.476' / W106 33.509').

1.8   From the saddle at 13,200', head north and upslope toward Twining Peak. East of the ridge, the mountain falls away 1,000' to the basin below and Blue Lake. Follow the west side of the ridge as it bends northeast, over a false summit and down to a small saddle, and up to the true summit. If the final pitch is corniced on the trail, to the right, scramble up through rocks on the left side of the ridge (N39 7.764' / W106 33.692').

2.3   Arrive at ranked 13,718' Twining Peak. Return the way you came, bypassing the Point 13500 summit (N39 8.079' / W106 33.797').

4.6   Arrive back at the trailhead (N39 6.504' / W106 33.839').

63 Williams Mountains Highpoint: Point 13382 "Williams Mountain"

Elevation: 13,382' (NAVD88 13,389')

Distinctions: Williams Mountains Highpoint, Prominence 200, P1K, Ranked 13er

Class: 3+; Class 1 to South Fork Pass, mixed Class 2, 3, and 3+ to summit

Difficulty and skill level: Very Strenuous; Advanced

Approximate moving time: 10 hours

Distance: 12.4 miles round-trip

Elevation trailhead to summit: 10,500' to 13,389' (+2,889'); about 4,500' round-trip

Terrain: Dirt trail, grass, scree, talus, boulders, slabs, and ledges; creek crossings; exposure, risk of rockfall

Recommended extra gear: Helmet

Restrictions: Independence Pass is closed seasonally from about Nov 7 to the Thurs prior to Memorial Day weekend, depending on snow conditions; CO 82 is closed to all vehicles more than 35' in length; terrain closed to bicycles and motor vehicles; dogs must be on leash; follow wilderness regulations

Amenities: Seasonal toilets and camping at Lost Man Campground; backcountry camping; limited services in Twin Lakes; full services in Aspen, Buena Vista, and Leadville

Trailhead: Lost Man Trailhead

Trail: Lost Man Trail #1996, off-trail North Ridge

Maps: DeLorme Page 47 D5, D6; USGS Mount Champion, Independence Pass

County: Pitkin

Land status: White River National Forest, (970) 945-2521, www.fs.usda.gov/whiteriver; Aspen-Sopris Ranger District, (970) 925-3445; Hunter-Fryingpan Wilderness, www.wilderness.net

Finding the trailhead: From Buena Vista, take US 24 West for about 19 miles, or from Leadville, take US 24 East for about 15 miles. Turn west onto CO 82 West and travel 29.2 miles, and park at the trailhead on the right (north) side of the road. The parking lot and trailhead are located 5.7 miles past Independence Pass, and 14 miles east of Aspen, across the road from Lost Man Campground (GPS: N39 7.303' / W106 37.463').

The Peak

The Williams Mountains are a spur of the Sawatch Range, trending north–south from Foster Gulch to the Roaring Fork River in the Hunter-Fryingpan Wilderness. Unlike the surrounding wilderness areas—Holy Cross, Collegiate Peaks, Mount Massive, and Maroon Bells–Snowmass—the Hunter-Fryingpan holds no ranked 14ers, but rather a handful of very challenging low 13ers. From the top of Williams Mountain, you'll have views north to more Williams peaks, northeast to 14er Mount of the Holy Cross, east to the Continental Divide and 14er Mount Massive, southeast to the twin summits of Geissler Mountain, south to 13er Grizzly Peak, southwest to the Elks, and west across the Hunter Creek Valley to Aspen.

Climbers navigate through jumbled boulders and exposed ledges on Williams Mountain's north ridge. PHOTO BY DOUG HATFIELD

The Climb

The Williams Mountains are not like the steep, solid climbs found among the Sawatch peaks at Buena Vista and Leadville, but rather a tumble of rocky summits strung together with broken, airy ridges, jagged rock, and loose gullies. Patience, solid route-finding and scrambling skills, and a helmet will be your best friends on this climb. There is no easy way to the top of Williams Mountain, but the north ridge presents the most solid route. You can add ranked Point 13108 by returning to the Williams-13108 saddle and going north on Class 2 terrain—bypassing rocky gendarmes along the ridge—for less than a mile to the summit, and then reversing your route back to the trailhead.

This route to Williams Mountain starts at the Lost Man Trailhead, but South Fork Pass, and the peak, may also be accessed from a trailhead west of Independence Pass, at the final switchback. From South Fork Pass, alternate routes to Williams Mountain include the east ridge and the southwest ridge. The east ridge is shorter but more technically difficult than the route described here, and the southwest ridge is much more difficult, due to gaps in the ridge that will force you onto Class 4 rock or to descend the west side, across steep talus and scree slopes, and then ascend back up to the ridge. The

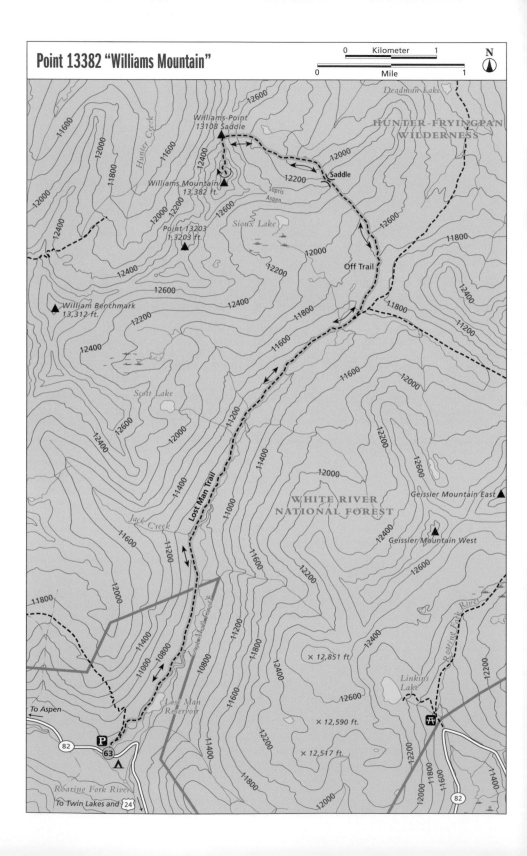

Point 13382 "Williams Mountain"

0 Kilometer 1

0 Mile 1

N

Deadman Lake

HUNTER-FRYINGPAN WILDERNESS

Hunter Creek

Williams-Point 13108 Saddle

Saddle

Williams Mountain 13,382 ft.

Sopris Aspen

Sioux Lake

Point 13203 13203 ft.

Off Trail

William Benchmark 13,312 ft.

Scott Lake

Lost Man Trail

Jack Creek

WHITE RIVER NATIONAL FOREST

Geissler Mountain East

Geissler Mountain West

Lower Lost Man Creek

× 12,851 ft.

Roaring Fork River

Linkins Lake

To Aspen

× 12,590 ft.

Lost Man Reservoir

82

P

63

× 12,517 ft.

Roaring Fork River

To Twin Lakes and 24

82

southwest ridge route is used by mountaineers completing the "Williams Traverse," a series of five ranked 13ers starting at Point 13033 and continuing north to Point 13108.

Miles and Directions

0.0 Begin at the trailhead to the left of the information board (10,500'), and cross the footbridge over the Roaring Fork River. Hike north past a trail junction to Midway Pass, and bear right toward Lost Man Reservoir.

0.5 Hike past the reservoir on Lost Man Trail, and continue north along Lost Man Creek and through the forest towards South Fork Pass (N39 7.587' / W106 37.249').

1.9 Leave the forest and cross Jack Creek, where the southernmost peaks of the "Williams Traverse" border the trail to the west and Geissler Mountain rises to the east. Hike in and out of the forest and cross three more creeks, as the eastern slopes of Williams Mountain and its southwest and east ridges appear above Sioux Lake (N39 8.715' / W106 36.839').

3.9 Reach the junction where the trail goes south to Lost Man Lake, and continue north (straight) toward South Fork Pass (N39 10.043' / W106 35.552').

4.3 Near South Fork Pass, at 11,700', depart the trail on the left and head northwest on steep terrain to a saddle on the ridge, located to the right (northeast) of unranked Point 12683 (N39 10.312' / W106 35.406').

5.0 Gain the saddle at 12,400'. The rest of your route is in view, across the basin and up to a saddle between Williams Mountain and Point 13108. Descend/traverse the slope to the bottom of the gully on the other side of the basin. Pick your best route across the basin, minimizing elevation loss, while avoiding loose terrain and tedious boulders. Climb the scree and talus gully, which gets very steep near the top, to the Williams-13108 saddle (N39 10.791' / W106 35.793').

5.9 Gain the saddle at 12,700' and turn left to the north ridge. There is no defined route from this point, and the ridge is spiked with ledges, blocks, and towers that you will climb over or sidestep, over loose rock, exposure, and mixed climbing to Class 3+. Take note of your exit point at the summit area so you can locate it on the descent (N39 11.072' / W106 36.623').

6.2 Arrive at 13,389' Williams Mountain. Return the way you came (N39 10.836' / W106 36.618').

12.4 Arrive back at the trailhead (N39 7.303' / W106 37.463').

64 Collegiate Peaks Highpoint: Mount Harvard

Elevation: 14,420' (NAVD88 14,427')

Distinction: Collegiate Peaks Highpoint, Chaffee County Highpoint, Collegiate Peaks Wilderness Highpoint, Centennial, Prominence 100, P2K, Ranked 14er

Class: 2; Class 1 for most of route, Class 2 to summit

Difficulty and skill level: Very Strenuous; Advanced

Approximate moving time: 8 hours

Distance: 12.6 miles round-trip

Elevation trailhead to summit: 9,900' to 14,427' (+4,527')

Terrain: Dirt trail, tundra, talus, and boulders; creek crossing

Recommended extra gear: Crampons or microspikes and ice axe if snow exists

Restrictions: Access to trail is seasonal; 2WD road to trailhead may require 4WD during heavy precipitation or spring melt; no camping at trailhead; trail closed to bicycles and motorized vehicles; follow wilderness regulations

Amenities: Dispersed camping along CR 365; backcountry camping; services in Buena Vista

Trailhead: North Cottonwood Creek Trailhead

Trail: North Cottonwood Trail, Horn Fork Basin Trail #1449, off-trail South Slopes

Maps: DeLorme Page 59 A8, B8; USGS Mount Harvard, Mount Yale

County: Chaffee

Land status: San Isabel National Forest, (719) 553-1400, www.fs.usda.gov/psicc; Salida Ranger District, (719) 539-3591; Collegiate Peaks Wilderness, www.wilderness.net

Finding the trailhead: From US 24 in Buena Vista, north of the stoplight, turn left onto CR 350 / Crossman Avenue and drive 2.1 miles, then turn right onto CR 361. Drive 0.9 mile and turn left onto unpaved CR 365. Continue for 5.1 miles and turn right into the parking area, and the trailhead at the west end of the lot (GPS: N38 52.247' / W106 15.972').

The Peak

The Collegiate Peaks of the Sawatch Range trend southeast from Independence Pass to Cottonwood Pass, in central Colorado. Eight ranked 14ers—La Plata Peak, Mount Oxford, Mount Belford, Missouri Mountain, Huron Peak, Mount Harvard, Mount Columbia, and Mount Yale—are located within the range, east of the Continental Divide and within the Collegiate Peaks Wilderness Area. The trend of naming 14ers in this area after Ivy League universities began when Professor Josiah D. Whitney, the head of the mining and geology school at Harvard University, led his students in a survey of the area in 1869. Summit views include the many 14ers of the area, as well as the "Three Apostles"—ranked 13ers West Apostle, North Apostle, and Ice Mountain—to the west, on the Divide.

The Climb

An excellent trail leads nearly all the way to the top of Mount Harvard, thanks to the handiwork of the Colorado 14ers Initiative (www.14ers.org). The nonprofit

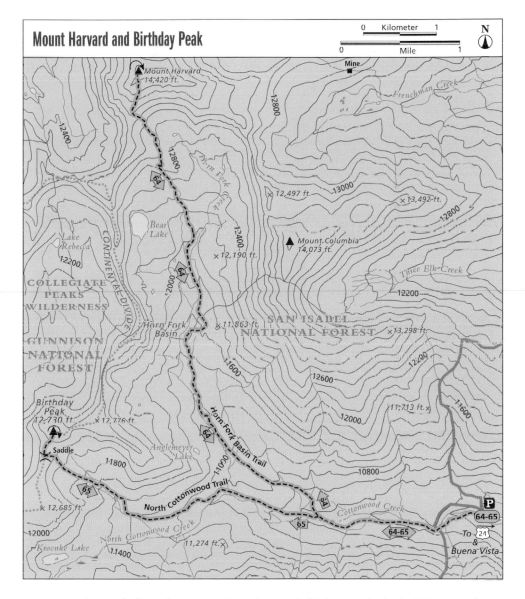

Mine

Mount Harvard
14,420 ft.

Frenchman Creek

12800

x 12,497 ft.

x 13,492 ft.

13000

12800

12400

64

Horn Fork Creek

64

Bear Lake

Mount Columbia
14,073 ft.

Three Elk Creek

12200

Lake Rebecca

12200

x 12,190 ft.

x 11,863 ft.

x 13,298 ft.

COLLEGIATE PEAKS WILDERNESS

CONTINENTAL DIVIDE

64

2000

Horn Fork Basin

SAN ISABEL NATIONAL FOREST

GUNNISON NATIONAL FOREST

11600

12600

12200

Birthday Peak
12,730 ft.

x 12,776 ft.

11,713 ft. x

64

Horn Fork Basin Trail

12000

Saddle

Anglemeyer Lake

11000

10800

11800

65

North Cottonwood Trail

64

Cottonwood Creek

P

64-65

x 12,685 ft.

65

64-65

12000

North Cottonwood Creek

11,274 ft. x

64-65

To 24 &
Buena Vista

Kroenke Lake

11400

organization is dedicated to protecting the state's highest peaks by building sustainable trails, while educating the public about Leave No Trace (www.lnt.org) principles, to ensure environmentally friendly and free access. If climbing 14ers becomes a hobby, you can pay it forward by volunteering for trail work, or making a donation to the organization. The peak is climbed year-round with regard for limited trailhead access and avalanche danger, and may also be accessed from the north, at Frenchman Creek. Ranked 14er Mount Columbia may be added via a very loose ridge traverse known as The Rabbits that requires route-finding and a short 5.7 pitch, or just return to Horn Fork Basin from Mount Harvard and pick up the cutoff south of the basin, and take the steep and talusy west slopes to gain the south ridge of the peak. You can do both peaks with a very early start from the trailhead, with an overnight stay in Buena Vista, or backpack into Horn Fork Basin the night prior.

Miles and Directions

0.0 Begin at the trailhead (9,900') on the west side of the parking area, cross a bridge to the south side of North Cottonwood Creek, and hike west along the creek.

1.4 Cross a footbridge (10,320') to the north side of the creek, and hike northwest to the Kroenke Lake / Horn Fork Basin Trail junction.

1.5 At the trail junction, bear right onto Horn Fork Basin Trail (10,360') and go northwest (N38 52.260' / W106 17.579').

Mount Harvard tops the Collegiate Peaks in the Sawatch Range. PHOTO BY DOUG HATFIELD

3.7 Pass the cutoff to Mount Columbia, come out of the trees and into Horn Fork Basin at 11,580', and go east then north, contouring below Mount Columbia. Mount Harvard is in view, north (N38 53.603' / W106 18.690').

4.1 Cross Horn Fork Creek at about 11,720' (N38 53.877' / W106 18.663').

5.0 At the Bear Lake Trail junction (12,360'), bear right to stay on Horn Fork Basin Trail and continue to the north end of the basin. Mount Harvard's south ridge is ahead, but you need to climb over a shoulder first, an east-trending spur of the ridge from unranked Point 13598. Climb switchbacks, through talus, to the top of the shoulder (N38 54.539' / W106 18.859').

5.4 From the shoulder at about 12,940', go north-northwest on cairned trail, across a flat area and then up to Mount Harvard's south ridge, aiming for a point on the ridge midway between Point 13598 and Harvard (N38 54.833' / W106 19.036').

6.0 Gain the south ridge of Mount Harvard (13,670') and go north, contouring east of the ridge toward the summit. The final 50 vertical feet are not marked and climb steeply through boulders, so choose the best route to the top and note your exit point for the descent (N38 55.210' / W106 19.309').

6.3 Arrive at ranked 14,427' Mount Harvard (N38 55.468' / W106 19.246'). Return the way you came.

12.6 Arrive back at the trailhead (N38 52.247' / W106 15.972').

65 Buena Vista Local Favorite: Birthday Peak

See map on page 231.
Elevation: 12,730'
Distinction: Ranked 12er
Class: 2; Class 1 for first 3.2 miles, Class 2 to summit
Difficulty and skill level: Strenuous; Intermediate
Approximate moving time: 5 hours
Distance: 8.8 miles round-trip
Elevation trailhead to summit: 9,900' to 12,730' (+2,830')
Terrain: Dirt trail, off-trail grass, tundra, and talus
Restrictions: Access to trail is seasonal; 2WD road to trailhead may require 4WD during heavy precipitation or spring melt; no camping at trailhead; trail closed to bicycles and motorized vehicles; follow wilderness regulations
Amenities: Dispersed camping along CR 365; backcountry camping; services in Buena Vista
Trailhead: North Cottonwood Creek Trailhead
Trail: North Cottonwood Trail, off-trail East Slopes and South Ridge
Maps: DeLorme Page 59 B8; USGS Mount Harvard, Mount Yale
Counties: Chaffee, Gunnison
Land status: San Isabel National Forest, (719) 553-1400, www.fs.usda.gov/psicc; Salida Ranger District, (719) 539-3591; Collegiate Peaks Wilderness, www.wilderness.net

Finding the trailhead: From US 24 in Buena Vista, north of the stoplight, turn left onto CR 350 / Crossman Avenue and drive 2.1 miles, then turn right onto CR 361. Drive 0.9 mile and turn left onto unpaved CR 365. Continue for 5.1 miles and turn right into the parking area, and the trailhead at the west end of the lot (GPS: N38 52.247' / W106 15.972').

The Peak

Birthday Peak sits on the Continental Divide north of Browns Pass and Kroenke Lake, surrounded by 14,000' peaks of the Collegiate Wilderness. From the top, you have views east into Horn Fork Basin, with Harvard and Columbia rising to the north-northeast, along with other 14ers including Mounts Oxford and Belford and Missouri Mountain. Huron Peak and the "Three Apostles" lie to the northwest, and Mount Yale sits to the south. Consider packing in a birthday cupcake for a summit snack, while you sit up there and try to name all the peaks.

The Climb

The trail to Birthday Peak will look familiar to you if you've done 14ers Mount Harvard or Mount Columbia. You'll start at the same trailhead, but instead of taking the junction north to Horn Fork Basin, continue west on the North Cottonwood Trail, along the north side of the creek, toward Kroenke Lake. If you have time, you can enjoy some other ranked 12ers on the ridge, including ranked Point 12776 to the east and Points 12685 and 12955, about 0.75 mile and 2.5 miles south and southeast, respectively.

Birthday Peak sits on the Continental Divide above Kroenke Lake in the Sawatch Range.
PHOTO BY JOHN KIRK

Miles and Directions

0.0 Begin at the trailhead (9,900') on the west side of the parking area, cross a bridge to the south side of North Cottonwood Creek, and hike west along the creek.

1.4 Cross a footbridge (10,320') to the north side of the creek, and hike northwest to the Kroenke Lake / Horn Fork Basin trail junction.

1.5 At the junction (10,360'), continue straight on North Cottonwood Trail, going west toward Kroenke Lake (N38 52.260' / W106 17.579').

3.2 Depart the trail before the next creek crossing (11,240'), and hike northwest to a saddle south of the peak. Be sure to aim for the lower of the two peaks to the northwest, the one on the left (N38 52.287' / W106 19.370').

4.1 Reach the 12,360' saddle and go north on the ridge (N38 52.710' / W106 20.134').

4.4 Arrive at ranked 12,730' Birthday Peak. Return the way you came (N38 52.884' / W106 20.034').

8.8 Arrive back at the trailhead (N38 52.247' / W106 15.972').

66 Cottonwood Pass Peaks: Point 12580, Point 12792, and "Chalk Rock Mountain"

Elevations: 12,580' (Point 12580), 12,792' (Point 12792), and 13,055' ("Chalk Rock Mountain")

Distinctions: Ranked 12ers (Point 12580 and Point 12792); Ranked 13er ("Chalk Rock Mountain")

Class: 2; Class 1 for first 1.6 miles, mixed Class 1 and 2 for rest of route

Difficulty and skill level: Strenuous; Intermediate

Approximate moving time: 6 hours

Distance: 9.0 miles round-trip

Elevation trailhead to summit: 12,126' to 13,055' (+929'); about 2,000' round-trip

Terrain: Dirt trail, off-trail grass, tundra, and talus

Restrictions: Cottonwood Pass is closed seasonally Nov through May; route closed to bicycles and motorized vehicles

Amenities: Camping at nearby Cottonwood Lake Campground; services in Buena Vista

Trailhead: Cottonwood Pass

Trail: Continental Divide National Scenic Trail, off-trail North Ridge

Maps: DeLorme Page 59 B7; USGS Tincup

Counties: Chaffee, Gunnison

Land status: San Isabel National Forest, (719) 553-1400, www.fs.usda.gov/psicc; Salida Ranger District, (719) 539-3591

Finding the trailhead: From US 24 in Buena Vista, go west on W. Main Street, which becomes CR 306 / Cottonwood Pass Road. Drive 19.3 miles to the top of the pass and park at the pullout on the left (south) side of the road (GPS: N38 49.669' / W106 24.577').

The Peak

Cottonwood Pass is one of just three mountain passes through the Sawatch Range that can be traversed by car, and the road from Buena Vista to the top of the 12,126' pass is the highest paved route to a mountain pass in the state. The west side of the pass is a gravel road leading down to Taylor Park Reservoir, and then paved to Almont and Gunnison. A good collection of Sawatch Range 12ers and 13ers line the Continental Divide north and south of Cottonwood Pass, and "Chalk Rock Mountain" and Points 12580 and 12792 provide three ranked peaks with easy route-finding, plus opportunities to add more peaks. Cottonwood Pass receives many visitors, but few venture beyond the first 12er south, so you can expect a peaceful trek above treeline. Views are endless, with the Sawatch stretching north, east, and south, and the West Elks and Elk Mountains to the west.

The Climb

Route-finding for the three peaks presented here is straightforward, as your path follows the Continental Divide south from Cottonwood Pass. Stay clear of the exposed east face, choose the path of least resistance, and only lose elevation when necessary

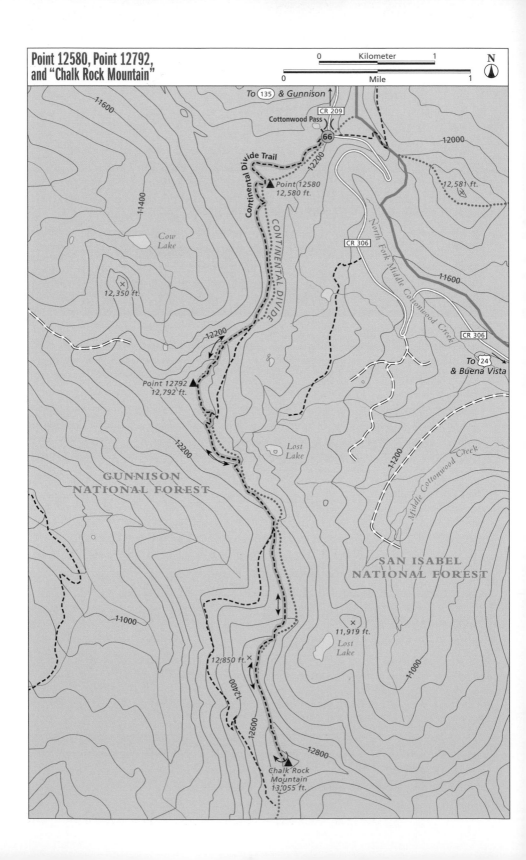

Point 12580, Point 12792, and "Chalk Rock Mountain"

0   Kilometer   1

0   Mile   1

N

To 135 & Gunnison

CR 209

Cottonwood Pass

66

12000

Continental Divide Trail

▲ Point 12580
12,580 ft.

12200

12,581 ft.

CONTINENTAL DIVIDE

Cow
Lake

CR 306

North Fork Middle Cottonwood Creek

×
12,350 ft.

12200

11600

CR 306

12200

To 24
& Buena Vista

Point 12792
12,792 ft. ▲

Lost
Lake

11200

12200

GUNNISON
NATIONAL FOREST

Middle Cottonwood Creek

SAN ISABEL
NATIONAL FOREST

11000

×
11,919 ft.

Lost
Lake

12,850 ft. ×

11000

12400

12600

12800

▲
Chalk Rock
Mountain
13,055 ft.

"Chalk Rock Mountain" is one of a slew of ranked peaks accessible from Cottonwood Pass.
PHOTO BY SUSAN JOY PAUL

and you will be on route. Although not included in this route description, ranked 13ers Mount Kreutzer and Emma Burr Mountain may be reached by continuing south on the Divide over increasingly more difficult terrain, 1.7 and 3.5 miles farther, respectively, beyond "Chalk Rock Mountain."

Miles and Directions

0.0   Begin at the 12,126' trailhead on the south side of the pass and hike southwest up the trail.

0.2   Pass the winter cutoff, on the left, and continue right on the trail. If snow exists, take the winter cutoff instead and go directly up the slope.

0.6   Arrive at ranked Point 12580. Continue south on the trail (N38 49.461' / W106 24.954').

1.6   Depart the trail before it descends below the west slopes of the next peak, and ascend the slope to the southwest.

2.0   Arrive at ranked Point 12792. Descend the south slopes and rejoin the trail west of ridgeline (N38 48.520' / W106 25.360').

3.6   Depart the trail again and continue south, contouring the western slope and topping out on the next highpoint.

3.9   Arrive at unranked Point 12850. Descend south and follow the ridgeline to the next highpoint (N38 47.257' / W106 24.995').

4.5   Arrive at ranked 13,055' "Chalk Rock Mountain." Return the way you came. You may skirt the highpoints on your return to the trailhead, to slightly reduce the total distance and elevation gain (N38 46.756' / W106 24.828').

9.0   Arrive back at the trailhead (N38 49.669' / W106 24.577').

67 Monarch Pass Peak: Mount Peck

Elevation: 12,208'

Distinction: Ranked 12er

Class: 2; Class 1 for first 1.8 miles, Class 2 to summit

Difficulty and skill level: Moderate; Beginner

Approximate moving time: 2.5 hours

Distance: 4.6 miles round-trip

Elevation trailhead to summit: 11,312' to 12,208' (+896')

Terrain: Dirt road and trail, grass, and tundra

Restrictions: Trail closed to motor vehicles; off-trail slopes closed to bicycles and motor vehicles

Amenities: Gift shop with restaurant and restrooms open seasonally Apr to Nov; backcountry camping; limited services in Poncha Springs and Sargents; full services in Salida and Gunnison

Trailhead: Monarch Pass Trailhead

Trails: CR 906, Continental Divide National Scenic Trail (section known locally as the "Crest Trail" at "Monarch Crest"), off-trail North Ridge

Maps: DeLorme Page 69 A8, Page 59 E8; USGS Pahlone Peak

Counties: Chaffee, Gunnison

Land status: San Isabel National Forest, (719) 553-1400, www.fs.usda.gov/psicc; Salida Ranger District, (719) 539-3591

Finding the trailhead: From Salida, take US 50 West for about 22 miles to Monarch Pass, or from Gunnison, take US 50 East for about 42 miles to Monarch Pass, and park on the south side of the road at Monarch Crest. The trailhead is located on CR 906, near the base of the chairlift, at the southeast corner of the parking lot (GPS: N38 29.779' / W106 19.514').

The Peak

Monarch Pass crosses the Continental Divide at 11,312' on US 50 between Gunnison and Salida, and is the highpoint of the 3,000-plus–mile-long highway that stretches from Maryland to California. Monarch Mountain Ski Resort and the Monarch Crest Scenic Tram are located at the top of the pass, along with a seasonal restaurant and gift shop. The tram operates through the summer, and for a fee, you can ride it to the top and get off near ranked 11er Monarch Ridge South. Mount Peck is located southeast of Monarch Pass, atop the Great Divide. The summit offers views north of the southernmost Sawatch 14ers, including Mounts Shavano, Tabeguache, and Antero and 13ers Mounts Taylor and Aetna. East of the peak, across the South Fooses drainage, ranked 12er Pahlone Peak rises, and to the south, the Divide continues over Peel Point, Point 12195, and Chipeta Mountain and towards Mount Ouray and Antora Peak, at Marshall Pass.

The Climb

This is a short hike with minimal elevation to a ranked 12er, and a great leg-stretcher if you are driving US 50 and need a break, or if you are planning on climbing area

Mount Peck

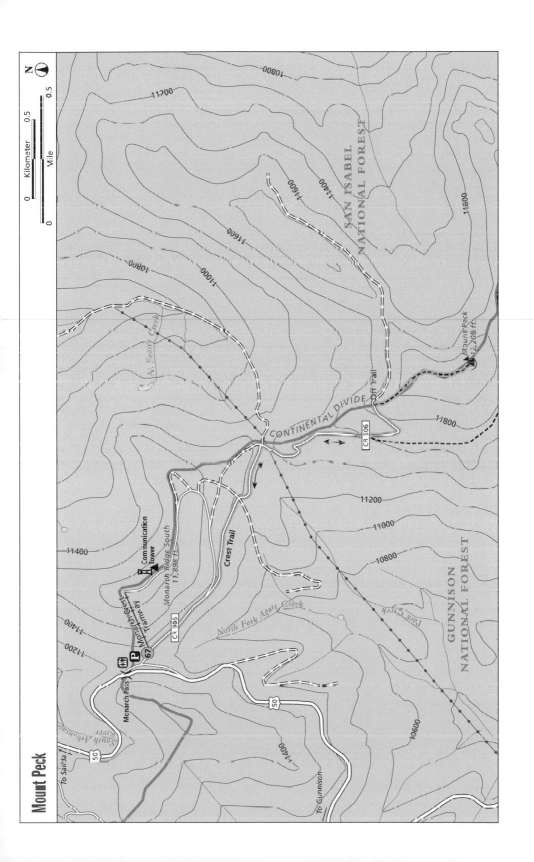

Gentle slopes lead to Mount Peck above the Crest Trail on the Continental Divide at Monarch Pass. PHOTO BY STEWART M. GREEN

14ers and need some acclimatization. The route along the Continental Divide Trail is a popular hiking and biking path in the summer, as it continues south to Marshall Pass, and may be snowshoed or skied in snow.

Miles and Directions

0.0 Head southeast from the 11,312' parking lot at Monarch Crest, toward the chairlift, and hike up CR 906.

0.3 Depart the road on the right to get on the Continental Divide National Scenic Trail. Mount Peck quickly comes into view, with the highpoint tucked beyond the broad, flat summit area (N38 29.598' / W106 19.265').

1.0 At the 11,400' saddle, the trail joins the road and continues south and uphill right (N38 29.374' / W106 18.567').

1.5 Bear left to remain south on CR 906 (N38 28.997' / W106 18.527').

1.6 Bear left to depart the Continental Divide Trail and switchback northeast up CR 906.

1.8 Depart the road at 11,840' and hike south off-trail and upslope (N38 28.986' / W106 18.387').

2.1 Hike over a false bump and continue south-southeast across the flat summit area to the highpoint.

2.3 Arrive at ranked 12,208' Mount Peck. Return the way you came (N38 28.632' / W106 18.210').

4.6 Arrive back at the trailhead (N38 29.779' / W106 19.514').

68 Marshall Pass Peak: Mount Ouray

Elevation: 13,971' (NAVD88 13,977')

Distinctions: Centennial, Prominence 100, P2K, Ranked 13er

Class: 2; Class 1 for first 0.25 mile, Class 2 for rest of route

Difficulty and skill level: Strenuous; Intermediate

Approximate moving time: 5 hours

Distance: 6.2 miles round-trip

Elevation trailhead to summit: 10,830' to 13,977' (+3,147'); about 3,400' round-trip

Terrain: Dirt road, grass, talus, and tundra

Restrictions: Marshall Pass is closed seasonally about 12 miles from trailhead at winter gate; trail closed to bicycles and motor vehicles; dogs must be on leash or under voice command

Amenities: Trailhead toilet; backcountry camping; limited services in Sargents and Poncha Springs; full services in Gunnison and Salida

Trailhead: Marshall Pass Trailhead

Trails: Marshall Pass Road, FR 200C, Continental Divide National Scenic Trail, off-trail West Ridge

Maps: DeLorme Page 70 A1, Page 69 A8; USGS Mount Ouray

Counties: Chaffee, Saguache

Land status: San Isabel National Forest, (719) 553-1400, www.fs.usda.gov/psicc; Salida Ranger District, (719) 539 3591

Finding the trailhead: From US 50 at Sargents, about 10 miles southwest of Monarch Pass and 32 miles east of Gunnison, go south on unpaved CR XX-32 / Marshall Pass Road. Drive 5.4 miles and bear right onto signed FR 243 / Marshall Pass Road, and continue through the winter gate. Go 11.5 miles, over Marshall Pass, to the trailhead on the right. Additional parking is available 0.3 mile west of the trailhead, at a pullout on Marshall Pass. The trailhead may also be accessed from the east, via US 285 south of Poncha Springs, on FR 202 / Marshall Pass Road, but the route is much rougher and not recommended for low-clearance or 2WD vehicles (GPS: N38 23.694' / W106 14.849').

The Peak

Mount Ouray stands above Marshall Pass at the southern tip of the Sawatch Range, due south of Monarch Pass. Mount Ouray is named for Native American Ute Chief Ouray, and nearby unranked 12er Chipeta Mountain is named for his wife. Marshall Pass straddles the Continental Divide, with the Gunnison River and Pacific Ocean watersheds to the west, and the Arkansas River and Atlantic Ocean watersheds to the east. The pass was named by Lieutenant William L. Marshall of the Wheeler Survey, in 1873. Today, Marshall Pass is well known as the intersection of the Continental Divide National Scenic Trail (CDT) and the Colorado Trail. Views abound on Mount Ouray, with the Sawatch stretching north over ranked 14ers Mounts Tabeguache and Shavano and south to ranked 13er Antora Peak. The San Juan Mountains lie southwest, and the Sangre de Cristos trend from east to southeast. The Front Range is also in view, northeast across South Park to the South Park Hills and Pikes Peak, beyond.

Ranked 13er Mount Ouray rises at the southern tip of the Sawatch Range near Marshall Pass.
PHOTO BY SUSAN JOY PAUL

The Climb

Marshall Pass is accessible from spring to late fall, when the winter gates are open and the road is passable. Much of the route lies above 12,000', exposed to the elements and afternoon lightning, so keep an eye on the sky and descend if necessary. To add Chipeta Mountain, return to Point 12685 and go north on the Divide, adding 3 round-trip miles to your climb. Mount Ouray may also be reached from the east, via the Grays Creek Trailhead and Devils Armchair cirque. The route is longer and Class 1 the whole way, and has its own beauty, but you will forfeit the long ridge run that makes the route from Marshall Pass so memorable.

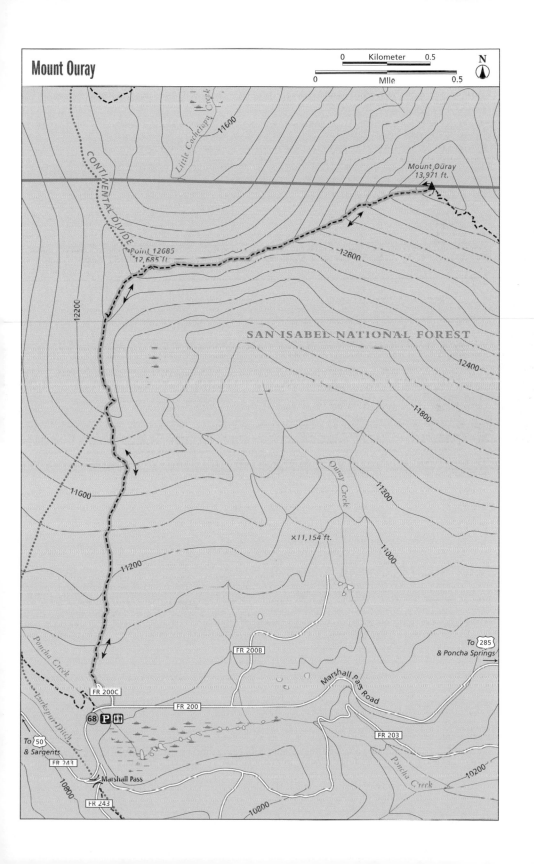

Mount Ouray

Kilometer
0   0.5

MIle
0   0.5

N

Little Cochetopa Creek

11600

CONTINENTAL DIVIDE

Mount Ouray
13,971 ft.

Point 12685
12,685 ft.

12800

12200

SAN ISABEL NATIONAL FOREST

12400

11800

Ouray Creek

11200

11600

×11,154 ft.

11000

11200

To 285
& Poncha Springs

FR 200B

Marshall Pass Road

Poncha Creek

FR 200C

FR 200

68 P ⫟

FR 203

Larkspur Ditch

To 50
& Sargents

FR 243

Poncha Creek

10200

Marshall Pass

10800

10800

FR 243

Miles and Directions

0.0 Begin at the trailhead (10,830') and hike northeast on FR 200, past the cutoff for the Colorado Trail, on your left.

0.1 Turn left onto FR 200C and hike north, through free range.

0.2 Hike past the Hutchinson & Burnett cabin on your left and continue as the road curves right and ends near an outhouse, below the forest. Hike north up a steep grass slope. There is no trail, so pick your best route around or through the trees, and head north to the ridge on the Continental Divide, above the Ouray Creek drainage. Do not descend into the drainage or aim for the south slopes of the peak's west ridge, which are loose, steep, and prone to erosion. This is a ridge climb.

1.1 Pass by some obvious white rocks on the slope at 11,820', a good marker for your descent back out (N38 24.510' / W106 14.740').

1.4 Gain the ridge at about 12,250', and continue north on a faint trail left of the crest.

2.0 Contour below and to the right of unranked Point 12685, and turn right to depart the Continental Divide and get on Mount Ouray's west ridge. This is an important junction, and if you miss it and continue north on the Divide, you'll end up on Chipeta Mountain. Head east, over several bumps along the ridge. The terrain steepens considerably near the summit, with the ridge crest rising and falling over slabs of quartz and granite, but a use trail on the north (left) side avoids the Class 3 and 4 rock. Hike through steep talus for the last half-mile to the summit. The use trail is faint, but the route is obvious, with slopes falling away to the Ouray Creek drainage to the south and the Little Cochetopa Creek drainage, north (N38 25.114' / W106 14.617').

3.1 Arrive at ranked 13,977' Mount Ouray, marked with a large cairn. Return the way you came (N38 25.364' / W106 13.486').

6.2 Arrive back at the trailhead (N38 23.694' / W106 14.849').

The Elk Range

The Elk Range lies west of the Sawatch and east of the Grand Mesa on Colorado's western slope, bound by the Crystal River, north, and the Gunnison River, south. The Elk Mountains, Raggeds Range, Ruby Range, West Elk Mountains, and Anthracite Range are all part of the Elk Range, covering an area north to south for 60 miles and east to west for 57 miles. The Maroon Bells–Snowmass, Raggeds, and West Elk Wilderness Areas lie within the mountain range. The Elks were so named when Lieutenant E. G. Beckwith of the Gunnison Survey visited them in 1853, noting "numerous elk horns . . . scattered whitening on the hills." Kebler Pass crosses the range between the Rubies and the West Elk Mountains, and Ohio Pass divides the Anthracites, but roads over each pass are mostly gravel and only open seasonally. Five ranked 14ers grace the Elk Range and are among the most challenging of the high peaks in the state. Many other scenic summit options rise in the Elks, and are much easier to climb.

The Elk Range is home to five ranked 14ers including Castle Peak in the Elk Mountains.
PHOTO BY BILL MIDDLEBROOK

69 Carbondale Local Favorite: Mount Sopris

Elevation: 12,953' (NAVD88 12,958')
Distinctions: Prominence 200, P1K, Ranked 12er
Class: 2; Class 1 for first 5 miles, Class 1 and 2 to summit
Difficulty and skill level: Very Strenuous; Intermediate
Approximate moving time: 8 hours
Distance: 13.4 miles round-trip
Elevation trailhead to summit: 8,500' to 12,958' (+4,458'); about 4,500' round-trip
Terrain: Dirt trail, talus, scree, and boulders; creek crossings; exposure
Restrictions: Camping is prohibited within 0.25 mile of Thomas Lakes; bear canisters required; trail closed to bicycles and motor vehicles; dogs must be on leash; follow wilderness regulations

Amenities: Trailhead toilet; dispersed camping at designated and numbered campsites at Thomas Lakes and backcountry camping with self-registration form, available at the trailhead; services in Carbondale
Trailhead: Thomas Lakes Trailhead
Trails: Thomas Lakes Trail #1958, Mount Sopris Trail
Maps: DeLorme Page 46 C1; USGS Mount Sopris, Basalt
County: Pitkin
Land status: White River National Forest, (970) 945-2521, www.fs.usda.gov/whiteriver; Aspen Ranger District, (970) 925-3445; Maroon Bells-Snowmass Wilderness, www.wilderness.net

Finding the trailhead: From CO 82, about 10 miles south of Glenwood Springs and 30 miles north of Aspen, take CO 133 South for 2.7 miles, through Carbondale, and turn left onto CR 111 / Prince Creek Road. Go 6.3 miles and turn right onto CR 6A / Dinkle Lake Road, and continue for 2 miles to parking on the left side of the road and the trailhead on the right (GPS: N39 18.236' / W107 7.478').

The Peak

Mount Sopris lies at the north end of the Elk Range, south of Glenwood Springs in the Maroon Bells–Snowmass Wilderness. There are two summits on the peak with equal elevation, but the eastern highpoint is the ranked one, and most hikers turn around after reaching this point. The peak is named for Richard Sopris, who led an exploratory trip in the area in 1860, during which he and his party discovered the hot springs at Glenwood Springs. From the summit, you'll have views north into the Roaring Fork Valley and across the White River Plateau and Flattops; the Sawatch lie to the east; and Capitol Peak is in view south, with the Maroon Bells, Snowmass Mountain, West Elks, Ruby Range, and the Raggeds beyond.

The Climb

Easy trailhead access, a gentle approach through aspen forest and flowered meadows, dispersed camping at wilderness lakes, and a rocky ridge climb to a lofty summit make this a very popular peak from late spring through the fall. In good spring snow,

A trail with views of the exposed north face makes for an exciting climb on Mount Sopris in the Maroon Bells–Snowmass Wilderness. PHOTO BY JOHN KIRK

it's snow-climbed via the Thomas Lakes Bowl above Thomas Lakes. Mount Sopris offers the alpine feel of a remote, high peak, with the luxury of a trail to the top. The distance and elevation gain required make for a very long day, though, so you may want to camp at Thomas Lakes and make an early ascent. On the east ridge, you'll make slow progress through talus, earning the peak a Class 2 rating despite the faint trail. The exposed north face and rock glaciers will get your attention. From the top of the peak, the unranked west summit, West Sopris Benchmark (N39 15.789' / W107 10.547'), is another 0.7 mile west, and unranked "Northwest Sopris" (N39 15.979' / W107 10.523') is 0.2 mile north of the west summit.

Miles and Directions

0.0 Begin at the Thomas Lakes Trailhead (8,500') and hike south.

1.7 Bear right at the trail junction (9,350') and go west to remain on the Thomas Lakes Trail. Mount Sopris is in view above the trees, to the southwest, as you head into the forest (N39 17.426' / W107 7.355').

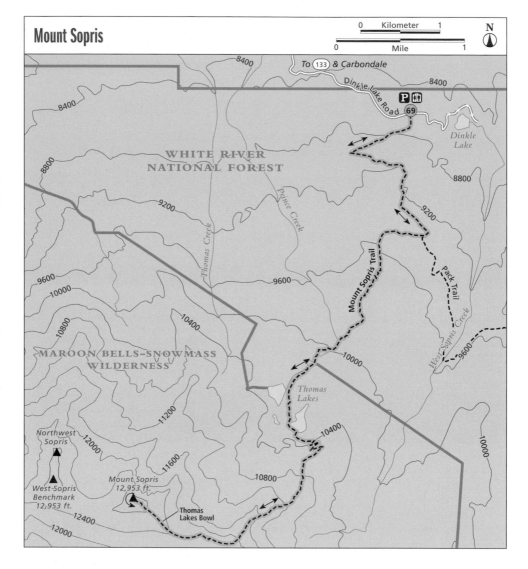

Mount Sopris

0   Kilometer   1

0   Mile   1

N

To ⑬ & Carbondale

Dinkle Lake Road   ⑥⑨

Dinkle Lake

8400

8400

8800

8800

WHITE RIVER
NATIONAL FOREST

9200

9200

Prince Creek

Thomas Creek

9600

9600

Mount Sopris Trail

Pack Trail

West Sopris Creek

9600

10000

10000

10000

10400

MAROON BELLS–SNOWMASS
WILDERNESS

10400

Thomas
Lakes

10800

11200

Northwest
Sopris

12000

11600

Mount Sopris
12,953 ft.

10800

10400

West-Sopris
Benchmark
12,953 ft.

12400

Thomas
Lakes Bowl

12000

3.2   Cross Prince Creek (10,000') twice and continue southwest through the forest. Enter the Maroon Bells–Snowmass Wilderness, pass lower and upper Thomas Lakes, and continue southeast on Mount Sopris Trail toward the slope ahead (N39 16.663' / W107 8.162').

4.3   Start up the switchbacks (10,400') toward the east ridge of the peak. At the end of the switchbacks, the trail goes southwest on the ridge, emerges from the trees at about 10,900', and climbs steeply through talus and a narrow, exposed section (N39 16.051' / W107 8.315').

5.8   Continue on the trail (12,300') as it turns west-northwest and climbs over two false summits along the ridge (N39 15.363' / W107 9.059').

6.7   Arrive at ranked 12,958' Mount Sopris. If you are not continuing to the west summit, return the way you came (N39 15.672' / W107 9.876').

13.4   Arrive back at the trailhead (N39 18.236' / W107 7.478').

70 Elk Range and Elk Mountains Highpoint: Castle Peak

Elevation: 14,265' (NAVD88 14,272')

Distinctions: Elk Range Highpoint, Elk Mountains Highpoint, Gunnison County Highpoint, Pitkin County Highpoint, Maroon Bells–Snowmass Wilderness Highpoint, Centennial, Prominence 100, P2K, Ranked 14er

Class: 2+; Class 1 to upper parking area, Class 2 and 2+ to summit

Difficulty and skill level: Very Strenuous; Advanced

Approximate moving time: 8 hours

Distance: 12.4 miles round-trip from trailhead; 6.2 miles round-trip from Montezuma / Pearl Pass Road junction; 2.0 miles round-trip from upper parking area

Elevation trailhead to summit: 9,728' to 14,272' (+4,544') from trailhead; about 3,150' from Montezuma / Pearl Pass Road junction; about 1,500' from upper parking area

Terrain: Dirt road and trail, scree, snow, boulders, and talus; exposure, risk of rockfall

Recommended extra gear: Helmet; crampons or microspikes and ice axe if snow exists

Restrictions: Summer route, susceptible to avalanche danger in snow; FR 102 / Montezuma Basin Road is not maintained through winter and may not be passable at creek crossings during periods of heavy melt; self registered permit required for overnight camping; bear canisters required; trail beyond upper parking area closed to bicycles and motor vehicles; dogs must be on leash; follow wilderness regulations

Amenities: Dispersed camping along Montezuma Basin Road; backcountry camping; services in Aspen

Trailhead: Castle Creek Trailhead

Trails: Montezuma Basin Road, unofficial Castle Creek Trail, off-trail Northeast Ridge

Maps: DeLorme Page 46 E3, E4; USGS Hayden Peak

Counties: Gunnison, Pitkin

Land status: White River National Forest, (970) 945-2521, www.fs.usda.gov/whiteriver; Aspen Ranger District, (970) 925-3445; Maroon Bells Snowmass Wilderness, www.wilderness.net

Finding the trailhead: From Aspen, take CO 82 West for 0.5 mile, enter the roundabout, and bear right at the third exit onto Castle Creek Road. Drive 6.4 miles, through Ashcroft, and turn right onto Montezuma Basin Road / Pearl Pass Road / FR 102. Park in the lot on the right (GPS: N39 1.753' / W106 48.473'). You may be able to drive another mile up the road in a sturdy, good-clearance passenger car to a pullout and dispersed camping, or if you have a high-clearance 4WD vehicle and the road is clear, you may drive 5.2 miles up the road to the upper parking area (GPS: N39 1.156' / W106 51.287').

The Peak

Castle Peak is the highpoint of the Elk Mountains west of Aspen, a range that's home to some more famous—and much more difficult—14ers, including the Maroon Bells, Snowmass Mountain, and Capitol Peak. Castle Peak was named by the Hayden Survey, likely for its rocky "towers" that line the ridges. The summit offers turret-worthy 360 degree views of the surrounding Elk Mountains, including unranked 14er North Maroon Peak and ranked 14ers Maroon Peak and Pyramid Peak northwest, and many 13,000' peaks around Montezuma Basin to the east and Conundrum Basin, west.

A climber makes his way up the talus slopes of Castle Peak in the Elk Range.
PHOTO BY BILL MIDDLEBROOK

The Climb

This is the easiest route on the mellowest ranked 14er in the Elk Range, but it should not be taken lightly. While there are no roaring creeks, rotten ledges, or exposed knife-edges to negotiate, Castle Peak is essentially a big pile of rock with a trail to the top, and its own unique challenges. The path beyond Montezuma Basin Road goes through talus and boulders, and you will want to pay attention to where you are going to avoid getting off-route. Snow lingers in the basin through the summer, and boot traction and an ice axe come in handy year-round. If you are driving to the upper parking area, be advised that the road is rugged and there is a creek crossing that may thwart even high-clearance vehicles, so be prepared to park at a lower pullout and hike up the road. You can park at the Pearl Pass junction, to ensure that

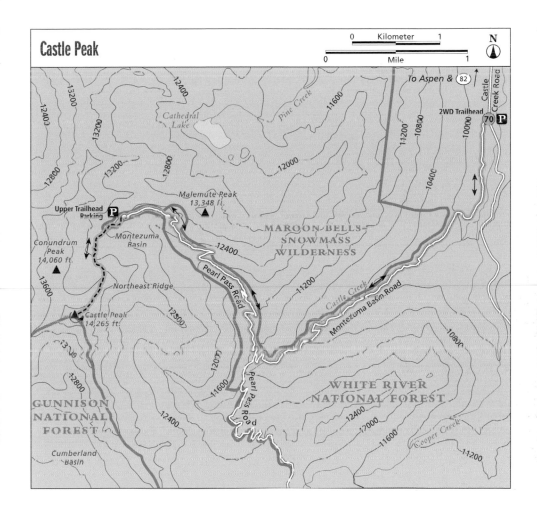

Castle Peak

To Aspen & (82)

2WD Trailhead

Castle Creek Road

70 P

Cathedral Lake

Pine Creek

Pine Creek

Malemute Peak
13,348 ft.

Upper Trailhead
Parking P

Conundrum
Peak
14,060 ft.

Montezuma
Basin

MAROON-BELLS-
SNOWMASS
WILDERNESS

Northeast Ridge

Pearl Pass Road

Castle Creek

Montezuma Basin Road

Castle Peak
14,265 ft.

Pearl Pass Road

WHITE RIVER
NATIONAL FOREST

GUNNISON
NATIONAL
FOREST

Cumberland
Basin

Cooper Creek

you gain at least 3,000' of elevation on the climb, or bear right on Montezuma Basin Road and continue past the Montezuma Mine to the upper parking area.

You can add unranked 14er Conundrum Peak by continuing north from the summit and dropping down to the Castle-Conundrum saddle, then ascending the ridge to Conundrum Peak. If you add Conundrum, rather than descending over Castle Peak, return to the saddle and descend the very steep slope east, down to the basin. Be advised that the scree slope from the saddle holds snow through most of the year and an ice axe is highly recommended. Also, a small ice-rimmed "lake" often forms in the middle of Montezuma Basin, and you will want to avoid getting sucked into it and drowned. The approach to Castle Peak from any direction presents the potential for high avalanche danger in snow, so the peak is usually climbed in summer. There are many other routes on Castle and Conundrum, each with its own thrills and challenges, including the loose West Ridge from Conundrum Hot Springs and the snow route Castle Couloir (also known as North Face Couloir).

Miles and Directions

0.0   Begin at the trailhead (9,728') and hike south up Montezuma Basin Road.

1.3   Cross a bridge over Castle Creek (10,200') and continue southwest.

3.1   Bear right at the junction where Pearl Pass Road goes south (11,120'), and head north on Montezuma Basin Road.

5.2   Reach the upper parking area (12,750') and the end of the road. Head southwest up the steep talus or snow slope to the saddle. Follow the cairned trail southwest to Montezuma Basin (N39 1.156' / W106 51.287').

5.7   At the basin (13,400'), go south and follow a talus trail, left and up toward a saddle on the northeast ridge (N39 0.875' / W106 51.522').

5.9   Start the northeast ridge (13,700'), following a loose, cairned route southwest along the ridge through talus and boulders (N39 0.727' / W106 51.491').

6.2   Arrive at ranked 14,272' Castle Peak. Return the way you came (N39 0.579' / W106 51.686').

12.4 Arrive back at the trailhead (N39 1.753' / W106 48.473').

71 Raggeds Range Highpoint: Treasure Mountain

Elevation: 13,528' (NAVD88 13,535')

Distinctions: Raggeds Range Highpoint, Raggeds Wilderness Highpoint, Tricentennial, Prominence 100, P2K, Ranked 13er

Class: 2; Class 1 to Yule Pass, Class 2 to summit

Difficulty and skill level: Very Strenuous; Advanced

Approximate moving time: 7 hours

Distance: 10.2 miles round-trip

Elevation trailhead to summit: 11,320' to 13,535' (+2,215'); about 3,100' round-trip

Terrain: Dirt trail, grass, talus, and scree

Recommended extra gear: Helmet; crampons or microspikes and ice axe if snow exists

Restrictions: Access to trailhead is seasonal and may require high-clearance 4WD year-round; trail closed to bicycles and motor vehicles; dogs must be on leash or under voice command; follow wilderness regulations

Amenities: Backcountry camping, dispersed camping along CR 734; services in Crested Butte

Trailhead: Yule Pass Trailhead

Trail: Yule Pass Trail #576, off-trail Southeast Ridge

Maps: DeLorme Page 46 E1, Page 58 A1; USGS Snowmass Mountain, Oh-Be-Joyful

County: Gunnison

Land status: White River National Forest, (970) 945-2521, www.fs.usda.gov/whiteriver; Aspen Ranger District, (970) 925-3445; Gunnison National Forest, (970) 874-6600, www.fs.usda.gov/gmug; Paonia Ranger District, (970) 527-4131; Raggeds Wilderness, www.wilderness.net; www.wilderness.net

Finding the trailhead: From Crested Butte, take CR 317 / Gothic Road north for 7.7 miles, through Mount Crested Butte and onto the unpaved road, to Gothic. Continue past Gothic for another 5.6 miles on CR 317 over Schofield Pass and turn left onto CR 734 / Paradise Divide Road, then go 4.5 miles, bearing left at 0.6 mile and right at 1.6 miles, to a large flat area at Paradise Divide. Make a hard right onto CR 734.4 and drive 0.2 mile to the trailhead (GPS: N38 59.481' / W107 4.001').

The Peak

The Raggeds Range is a subrange of the Elk Range, situated southwest of the Elk Mountains and north of the Ruby Range, in the Raggeds Wilderness. The Treasure Mountain / Treasury Mountain massif is enormous, with the peaks' combined ridgelines trending nearly 4 miles northwest from Yule Pass. The highpoint of the Raggeds, Treasure Mountain, is believed to be one of three sites of buried gold. Prospector William Yule came into possession of one of two maps of the locations of the hidden gold, and while others searched the San Juans—location of two other "Treasure Mountains"—Yule focused his search in the Elk Range. Treasure Mountain is the source of pristine Yule Marble, mined from its depths and on display in sculpted, man-made massifs including the Lincoln Memorial in Washington, DC, and the Tomb of the Unknown Soldier at Arlington Cemetery, Virginia. From the top of the peak, you'll have pristine views of the surrounding Elk Range peaks, including Mount

Treasure Mountain, seen here from Treasury Mountain, tops the Raggeds Range west of Scho-field Pass. PHOTO BY JOHN KIRK

Sopris to the north and Capitol Peak, Snowmass Mountain, and the Maroon Bells to the northeast. Mount Owen and the Ruby Range lie to the south, with the West Elk Mountains visible southwest and the Grand Mesa westward. Closer in, you are surrounded by the Raggeds, including Whitehouse Mountain to the north; Treasury Mountain, south; and Chair Mountain, west.

The Climb

There are many routes up Treasure Mountain, but the southeast ridge from Yule Pass starts high and entails the least overall elevation gain. Be sure to stay in the national forest and wilderness area, and away from private, active mining operations. If you like, you can add ranked 12er Cinnamon Mountain and ranked 13er Treasury Mountain to your day. From the trailhead, climb Cinnamon's southeast slopes to the summit, descend northwest, then climb up the southeast ridge of Treasury Mountain. Alternatively, you can skip Cinnamon and get on the southeast ridge of Treasury at the saddle between the two peaks, accessed at a cutoff on the north side of the Yule Pass Trail. The route reaches a plateau near the summit of Treasury, then narrows dramatically, with exciting exposure to the north, looking down the Wine Bottle Couloirs

Treasure Mountain

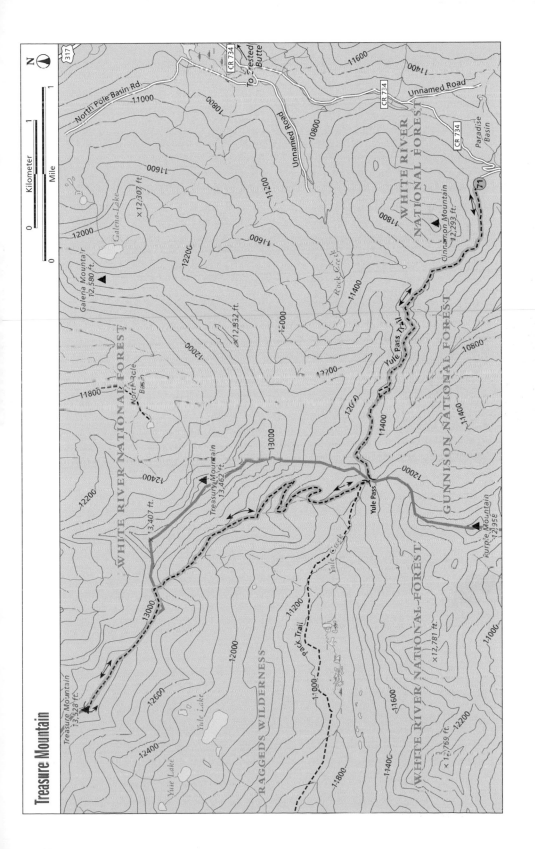

into North Pole Basin. Note that the ridge between Treasury Mountain and Treasure Mountain cliffs out west of Point 13407, so don't expect a nice ridge walk between the peaks. If you want to combine the two summits, descend more than 1,000' from Treasury Mountain to get below the cliffs, and contour the west slopes to regain the ridge, in order to avoid the Class 5 section, and continue to Treasure Mountain.

Miles and Directions

0.0 Begin at Yule Pass Trailhead (11,320') and hike west on mining road Yule Pass Trail.

2.1 Cross 11,700' Yule Pass and enter the Raggeds Wilderness. The trail continues west along Yule Creek toward Yule Lakes, but you will turn right and head north on an old mining road. The trail forks again, with the left fork heading west. Take the right fork north, and stay on it as it switches east and west up the southwest face of Treasury Mountain (N39 0.026' / W107 5.876').

2.5 The trail switches back to the southeast.

2.6 The trail switches back to the northwest.

2.9 The trail switches back southeast again at 12,040'.

3.1 The trail switches back northwest again.

3.3 Come to the end of the trail, 1,100' directly below the summit of Treasury Mountain. Continue northwest (N39 0.555' / W107 6.022').

3.4 Descend a gully to get below the cliffs, and traverse the steep grass and talus slopes, aiming for the ridge to the northwest (N39 0.597' / W107 6.121').

4.0 Start up a steep talus gully at 12,400', and climb north-northwest up to the ridge (N39 0.961' / W107 6.462').

4.2 Top out on the 13,000' ridge between unranked Points 13211 and 13407. Enjoy the ridge walk northwest to the summit (N39 1.112' / W107 6.582').

5.1 Arrive at ranked 13,535' Treasure Mountain. Return the way you came. Alternatively, you can descend the gully that you climbed to the ridge, and rather than contour the slopes, descend to the basin below, then hike out southeast, on the trail (N39 1.452' / W107 7.368').

10.2 Arrive back at the trailhead (N38 59.481' / W107 4.001').

72 Ruby Range Highpoint: Mount Owen B

Elevation: 13,058' (NAVD88 13,065')

Distinctions: Ruby Range Highpoint, Prominence 200, P1K, Ranked 13er

Class: 2; Class 1 road to below Owen-Ruby saddle, mixed Class 1 and 2 to summit

Difficulty and skill level: Strenuous; Intermediate

Approximate moving time: 5 hours

Distance: 9.2 miles round-trip

Elevation trailhead to summit: 10,330' to 13,065' (+2,735')

Terrain: Dirt road, scree, talus, and tundra; moderate exposure

Restrictions: Kebler Pass Road is closed to motor vehicles seasonally mid-Nov to mid-May;

dogs must be on leash or under voice command; follow wilderness regulations

Amenities: Trailhead toilet; camping at nearby Lake Irwin Campground; backcountry camping; services in Crested Butte

Trailhead: Lake Irwin

Trail: CR 826, off-trail South Ridge

Maps: DeLorme Page 58 A1, B1; USGS Oh-Be-Joyful, Marcellina Mountain

County: Gunnison

Land status: Gunnison National Forest, (970) 874-6600, www.fs.usda.gov/gmug; Paonia Ranger District, (970) 527-4131; Raggeds Wilderness, www.wilderness.net

Finding the trailhead: From CO 135 in Crested Butte, go west on Whiterock Avenue, which becomes CR 12 / Kebler Pass Road. Drive 6.8 miles and turn right onto CR 826, then go 2 miles to Lake Irwin and park on the west side of the lake. The directions here describe the route from the lake to the peak, but if road conditions allow, you can continue north on CR 826 and park at a pullout along the road, for a shorter hike (GPS: N38 52.726' / W107 6.368').

The Peak

The Ruby Range trends north–south from Yule Pass to Kebler Pass, west of Crested Butte. Mount Owen lies near the midpoint of the range, with unranked 12er Purple Peak to the north and ranked 12er Ruby Peak, south, and its western slopes in the Raggeds Wilderness. The Ruby Range may be named for the colorfully striated sediments that define the peaks, which drew miners to the area in the late 1800s, or for "ruby silver," which was mined nearby. Views from Mount Owen are nothing short of spectacular: The Ruby Range stretches from north to south, bordered by the Raggeds Range to the north and the Anthracite Range, south. The Continental Divide and Sawatch Range line the eastern horizon, and the Grand Mesa lies west. Notable peaks in view beyond the Rubies include East and West Beckwith Mountains in the Anthracites, south; Treasure Mountain in the Raggeds, north; and Pyramid Peak and Castle Peak in the Elk Mountains, to the northeast.

The Climb

The route to Mount Owen follows a dirt road north from Lake Irwin to Green Lake, a short, steep ascent to the saddle between Mount Owen and Ruby Peak, and

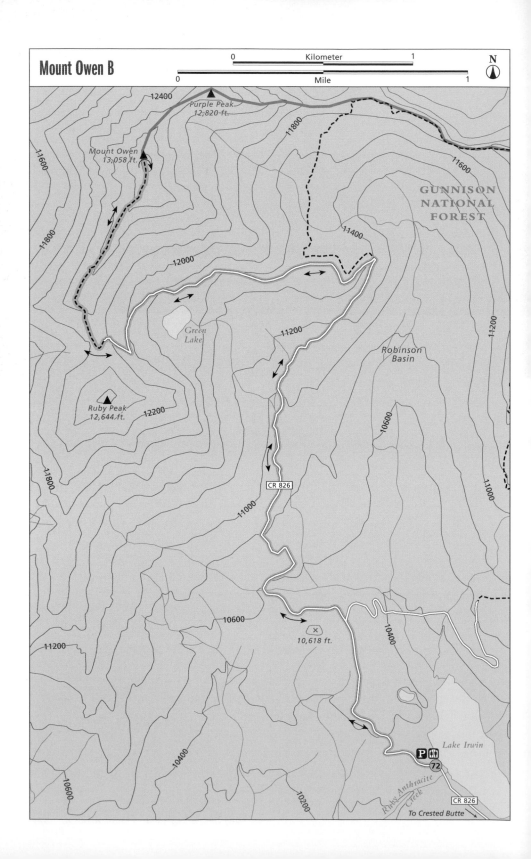

Mount Owen B

0 Kilometer 1
0 Mile 1

N

Purple Peak
12,820 ft.

12400

Mount Owen
13,058 ft.

11800

11600

GUNNISON
NATIONAL
FOREST

11600

12000

11600

11800

11400

11200

Green
Lake

11200

Robinson
Basin

11200

Ruby Peak
12,644 ft.

12200

10600

11800

11000

CR 826

10600

11200

10600

×
10,618 ft.

10400

11200

10400

10400

Lake Irwin

10400

P 🚻

72

10600

10200

Ruby Anthracite Creek

CR 826

To Crested Butte

Mount Owen tops the Ruby Range in the Elks north of Kebler Pass. PHOTO BY JOHN KIRK

a glorious ridge climb to the summit. Mount Owen is the only 13er in the Ruby Range, but there are many 12ers you can add to your day with a little planning.

Miles and Directions

0.0 Begin at the parking area at Lake Irwin (10,330) and hike northwest up the dirt road. "The Dyke" forms the long ridge west of the road.

0.1 Bear left at the fork (N38 52.750' / W107 6.447').

0.4 Bear right at the fork (N38 52.892' / W107 6.689').

0.7 Bear left at the fork (N38 53.167' / W107 6.714').

1.1 Pass the junction with the Dyke Trail on left (10,600'), and continue north on the road, with Scarp Ridge to the east. The road climbs past waterfalls fed by Green Lake, and as you ascend above Robinson Basin to the east, the lake comes into view to the west, below Ruby Peak (N38 53.275' / W107 7.030').

2.6 CR 826 continues north (11,360'), but you will turn left and switchback west-southwest on the trail over Green Lake (N38 54.253' / W107 6.599').

3.7 At the end of the good trail (12,000'), climb the faint, loose trail through scree and talus west up to the Owen-Ruby saddle (N38 53.968' / W107 7.547').

3.8 From the saddle at 12,240', turn right and climb the ridge north on an intermittent trail (N38 53.982' / W107 7.674').

4.6 Arrive at ranked 13,065' Mount Owen. Return the way you came (N38 54.55' / W107 7.503').

9.2 Arrive back at the trailhead (N38 52.726' / W107 6.368').

73 Crested Butte Local Favorite: Crested Butte

Elevation: 12,162' (NAVD88 12,168')

Distinctions: Prominence 100, P2K, Ranked 12er

Class: 2; Class 1 for most of route, Class 2 the final 200' to summit

Difficulty and skill level: Moderate from base area, Easy from top of chairlift; Intermediate

Approximate moving time: 5 hours hike from base area to summit to base area; 3 hours hike from top of Silver Queen Chairlift to summit and hike down to base area; 1.5 hours hike from chairlift to summit to chairlift

Distance: 10.0 miles round-trip base area to summit to base area; 6.4 miles round-trip top of chairlift to summit to base area; 1.4 miles round-trip chairlift to summit to chairlift

Elevation trailhead to summit: 9,475' to 12,168' (+2,693') and about 2,800' round-trip from base area to summit; 11,400' to 12,168' (+768') and about 900' round-trip from top of Silver Queen Chairlift to summit

Terrain: Dirt road and trail most of the route, with talus and boulders the last 200'

Recommended extra gear: Microspikes for a snowfield that lingers below the summit area

Restrictions: Summer route only; stay off mountain bike–only trails; fee for use of chairlifts

Amenities: Restaurants, toilets, bank with ATM, and other services located near trailhead; porta-potty at top of chairlift; services in Mount Crested Butte and Crested Butte

Trailheads: Up and Away Trailhead, Silver Queen Road, or Lower West Side Trailhead

Trails: Up and Away Trail, Silver Queen Road, Westside Trail, Crested Butte Mountain Summer Trail #605 (Summit Trail)

Maps: DeLorme Page 58 B2, B3; USGS Gothic

County: Gunnison

Land status: Gunnison National Forest, (970) 874-6600, www.fs.usda.gov/gmug; Gunnison Ranger District, (970) 641-0471; Crested Butte Mountain Resort, (877) 547-5143, www.skicb.com; Emergency contact on the peak (970) 349-2347

Finding the trailhead: From Crested Butte, go north on CR 317 / Gothic Road for about 2.6 miles to the town of Mount Crested Butte, and turn right onto Treasury Road. There is public parking available on the right, and overflow parking on CR 317 just past the turn onto Treasury Road. From parking it is a 0.3- to 0.4-mile walk down to the base area and the trailhead (GPS: N38 53.94' / W106 57.929').

The Peak

Crested Butte's steep slopes are home to Crested Butte Mountain Resort and down-hill skiing in the winter months, but in the summertime a network of trails and two chairlifts provide lots of hiking and biking, and a lofty summit for the less experienced mountaineer-in-training. The peak rises nearly 3,000' above the mountain town, sandwiched between the higher peaks of the Elk Mountains at Aspen to the north and the West Elk Mountains to the west, and surrounded by condominiums, restaurants, shops, and the usual ski town accoutrements. Despite the development, the area is stunning in every way, and the peak is a relatively easy P2K peak and a good excuse to visit the town. From the top, you'll have views of Elk Mountains highpoint Castle

Crested Butte is a popular summer destination for visitors to the town of Crested Butte.
PHOTO BY SUSAN JOY PAUL

Peak to the north-northwest, and continuing counterclockwise, the Maroon Bells north, Ruby Range highpoint Mount Owen west, the Anthracite Range Highpoint west-southwest, and West Elk Range highpoint West Elk Peak to the southwest. The Sawatch Mountains lie 30 miles to the east.

The Climb

This is a summer route, with the trail open and mostly dry from about mid-June through September. Microspikes are helpful for a small snowfield on the east slopes of the summit area, and you can leave them on for the scree ahead. If you plan on taking either of the chairlifts partway up the mountain, you will need to purchase a pass at the Adventure Center located in Mountaineer Square, a small shopping center between parking and the trailhead. The Silver Queen Express stops running at 2:30 p.m. each day, and the Red Lady Express runs later, but will not take you as far, so if you opt for these routes, grab a map and get the latest days and times at the Adventure

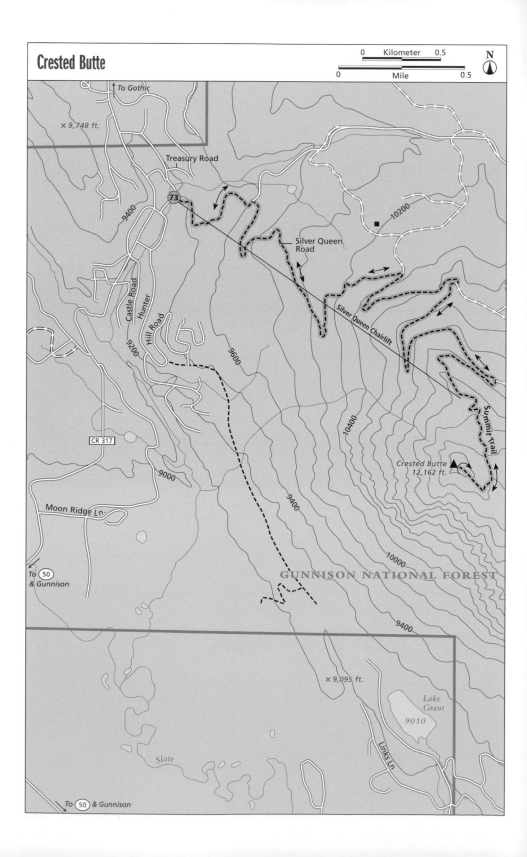

Crested Butte

0   Kilometer   0.5
0   Mile   0.5

N

↑ To Gothic

× 9,748 ft.

Treasury Road

9400

73

Castle Road

Hunter Hill Road

9200

CR 317

9000

Moon Ridge Ln

To 50 & Gunnison

Silver Queen Road

10200

Silver Queen Chairlift

9600

10400

9400

Summit Trail

Crested Butte
12,162 ft.

10000

GUNNISON NATIONAL FOREST

9400

× 9,095 ft.

Lake Grant
9010

Links Ln

Slate

To 50 & Gunnison

Center. Ten miles is a long hike, even on a good trail, and so taking a chairlift up or down can be a pleasant way to begin or end the hike. From the parking area, follow the road and a paved walkway to the base area and take the chairlift, or start up Silver Queen Road or the Lower Westside Trail to the right of the lift, or the Up and Away Trail to the left of the lift. Each route goes southeast, up the peak, and they intersect in several places, but if you just go up and zigzag your way under the ski lift, you will be going in the right direction. Do not cut switchbacks, and stay off the mountain bike trails.

Miles and Directions

0.0 Begin at the trailhead near the bottom of the Silver Queen Chairlift, and hike southeast up the switchbacked roads and trails beneath the lift.

4.3 At the top of the Silver Queen Chairlift, join the Summit Trail and continue south-southeast up and over a ridge on the east side of the peak. Descend about 70' and switchback northwest on the steep, rocky trail. The last part of the route climbs through boulders and is unmarked, but the summit is just ahead. Stay away from the exposed east edge of the ridge (N38 53.245' / W106 56.622').

5.0 Arrive at ranked 12,168' Crested Butte. Return the way you came (N38 52.994' / W106 56.616').

10.0 Arrive back at the trailhead (N38 53.940' / W106 57.929').

74 Kebler Pass Peak: East Beckwith Mountain

Elevation: 12,432' (NAVD88 12,438')

Distinctions: Prominence 100, P2K, Ranked 12er

Class: 2+; Class 1 to Lost Lake, mixed Class 2 and 2+ to summit

Difficulty and skill level: Strenuous; Intermediate

Approximate moving time: 5 hours

Distance: 4.4 miles round-trip

Elevation trailhead to summit: 9,630' to 12,438' (+2,808')

Terrain: Dirt trail, grass, slabs, and talus; creek crossings; exposure

Restrictions: Kebler Pass Road is closed to motor vehicles seasonally, usually mid-Nov to mid-May; trail closed to bicycles and motor vehicles; dogs must be on leash or under voice command; follow wilderness regulations

Amenities: Backcountry camping; toilets and campsites at nearby Lost Lake Campground; services in Paonia, Gunnison, and Crested Butte

Trailhead: Lost Lake Slough

Trail: Three Lakes Trail #843, off-trail Northeast Ridge

Maps: DeLorme Pages 57 B8; USGS Anthracite Range

County: Gunnison

Land status: Gunnison National Forest, (970) 874-6600, www.fs.usda.gov/gmug; Paonia Ranger District, (970) 527-4131; West Elk Wilderness, www.wilderness.net

Finding the trailhead: From Crested Butte, take unpaved CR 12 / Kebler Pass Road west for 15.9 miles and turn left onto FR 706, or from Paonia, take CO 133 North for 14.7 miles and turn right onto unpaved CR 12 / Kebler Pass Road, then go 15 miles and turn right onto FR 706. Go 2.4 miles to a parking area and trailhead on the right side of the road (GPS: N38 52.160' / W107 12.537').

The Peak

Kebler Pass lies along the West Elk Loop Scenic Byway, one of the most beautiful drives in the state. East Beckwith Mountain rises west of the pass, at the northern edge of the West Elk Mountains near Paonia. The steep south slopes of the peak rest in the West Elk Wilderness, while the gentler north slopes that face the scenic road form five distinct cirques in the national forest. The pass is named for John Kebler, owner of the Colorado Fuel and Iron company and some coal mines in the area, and the peak, along with nearby West Beckwith Peak, is named for Lieutenant E. G. Beckwith, of the 1853 Gunnison expedition to discover a railroad route through the mountains. From the top of the peak, you'll have surrounding views of the largest stand of aspen trees in Colorado. The West Elk Mountains complete the picture, with West Elk Peak rising in the south, the Anthracite Range rimming the southeast sky, the Ruby Range to the northeast, and the Raggeds to the north.

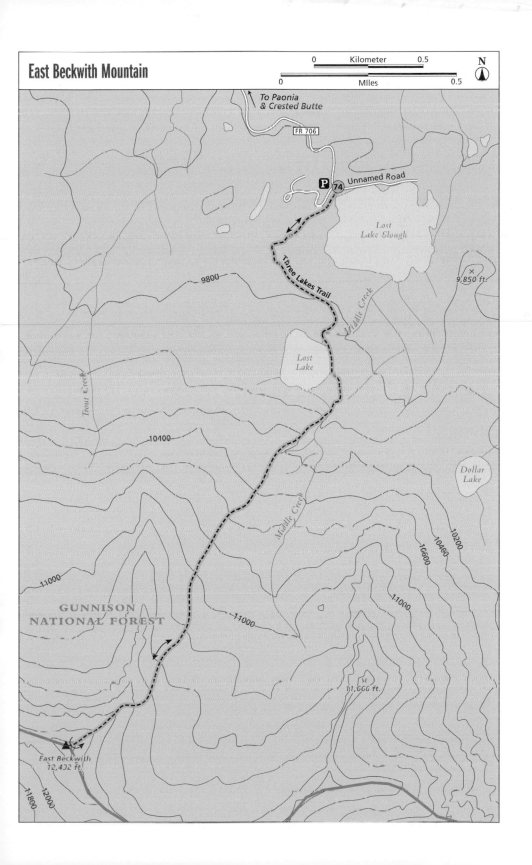

East Beckwith Mountain

0   Kilometer   0.5
0   Miles   0.5

N

To Paonia
& Crested Butte

FR 706

P 74   Unnamed Road

Lost
Lake Slough

Three Lakes Trail

Middle Creek

9800

× 9,850 ft.

Lost
Lake

Trout Creek

10100

Dollar
Lake

Middle Creek

10200

10400

10600

11000

11000

GUNNISON
NATIONAL FOREST

11000

H
11,666 ft.

East Beckwith
12,432 ft.

11800

12000

Glacial cirques formed the north slopes of East Beckwith Mountain on the West Elk Loop Scenic Byway. PHOTO BY STEWART M. GREEN

The Climb

Access to Kebler Pass is seasonal by car, and an autumn climb—when the leaves are turning—is best to take in the stunning views of the area aspens. Experienced climbers with a lot of time can extend their climb west of the summit on intermittent Class 3 terrain, over ranked 12er Point 12244 and on to ranked 12er West Beckwith Peak, about 3 miles away.

Miles and Directions

0.0 Begin at the trailhead (9,630') and hike southwest around Lost Lake Slough on Three Lakes Trail.

0.6 At the north end of Lost Lake, cross to the east side of Middle Creek and hike around the east side of the lake (N38 51.792' / W107 12.584').

0.9 Depart the trail and cross to the west side of Middle Creek at a waterfall. Hike southwest and away from the creek, and up into the basin (N38 51.625' / W107 12.556').

1.3 Ascend the rocky slabs and talus below the ridge, heading south-southwest toward the peak. Climb west up to the ridge at about 11,600'.

2.0 Gain the ridge at 11,960' and follow the steep, loose talus crest to the summit (N38 50.881' / W107 13.226').

2.2 Arrive at ranked 12,438' East Beckwith Mountain. Return the way you came (N38 50.784' / W107 13.404').

4.4 Arrive back at the trailhead (N38 52.160' / W107 12.537').

75 Anthracite Range Highpoint: Anthracite Range Highpoint

Elevations: 12,385' (NAVD88 12,391')
Anthracite Range Highpoint; 12,300' Point
12300; 12,271' (NAVD88 12,277') Ohio
Peak; 11,555' Point 11555
Distinctions: Anthracite Range Highpoint,
Prominence 100, P2K, Ranked 12er (Anthra-
cite Range Highpoint); Ranked 12er (Point
12300); Soft-ranked 12er (Ohio Peak);
Ranked 11er (Point 11555)
Class: 2
Difficulty and skill level: Very Strenuous;
Intermediate
Approximate moving time: 7 hours
Distance: 8.2 miles round-trip
Elevation trailhead to summit: 10,080' to
12,391' (+2,311'); about 4,200' round-trip
Terrain: Off-trail dirt, talus, and tundra

Recommended extra gear: GPS
Restrictions: Ohio Pass is closed to vehicles
seasonally, usually mid-Nov to mid-May, and
the area is popular with winter recreationists
during that time
Amenities: Services in Gunnison and
Crested Butte
Trailhead: Ohio Pass
Trail: Off-trail East Ridge
Maps: DeLorme Page 58 B1; USGS Anthracite
Range, Mount Axtell
County: Gunnison
Land status: Gunnison National Forest, (970)
874-6600, www.fs.usda.gov/gmug; Gunnison
Ranger District, (970) 641-0471; West Elk
Wilderness, www.wilderness.net

Finding the trailhead: From Crested Butte, take CR 12 / Kebler Pass Road west for 7 miles, then turn left onto CR 730 and go 1.3 miles to the pullout and unsigned trailhead, or from Paonia, take CO 133 North for 23.9 miles, then turn right onto CR 12 / Kebler Pass Road and go 1.3 miles to the pullout (GPS: N38 50.124' / W107 5.540').

The Peak

The Anthracite Range trends west from Ohio Pass to Beckwith Pass, in the West Elk Mountains south of Kebler Pass. Ohio Peak is the soft-ranked summit on the east end of the range, and ranked Anthracite Range Highpoint rises 114' higher at the west end. "Anthracite" refers to the black coal once mined in nearby Crested Butte, and Ohio Pass and Ohio Peak are named for the state and river of the same name, derived from the Seneca *ohiiyo'*, which translates to "good river." From the top of the peak, take in views of the Ruby Range across Kebler Pass to the north, East and West Beckwith Mountains to the northwest, the West Elks south, and the high peaks of the Sawatch Range at Cottonwood Pass to the east.

Mountaineer Dominic Meiser heads for the Anthracite Range Highpoint in the Elk Range.
PHOTO BY SARAH MEISER

The Climb

Anthracite Range access is limited by private property to the north and steep slopes in the West Elk Wilderness to the south. The highpoint may be legally accessed on trails from the northwest, via Beckwith Pass, or the southwest, via Swampy Pass, with an off-trail climb of the west ridge. A shorter and more scenic option lies along the eastern ridge with a traverse from Ohio Pass, over Point 11555, Ohio Peak, and Point 12300. Although most of the hike is a ridge walk with limited route-finding challenges, a GPS comes in handy to ensure proper turns from ridge to ridge, hitting all the summits, and below treeline where the route is less apparent.

Anthracite Range Highpoint

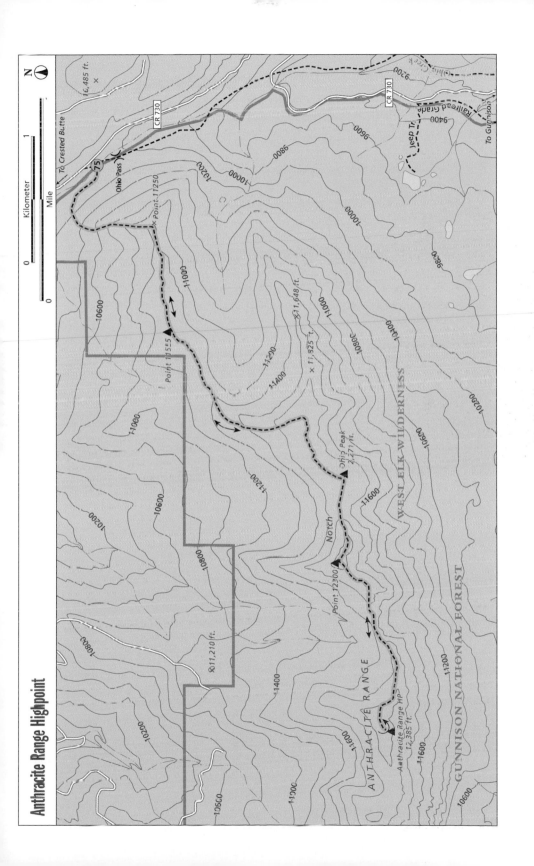

Miles and Directions

0.0 Begin at the unmarked trailhead (10,080') north of the pass, and hike northwest then south, to contour around to the north end of the ridge.

0.4 At about 10,600', climb south on loose talus to get onto the ridge (N38 50.131' / W107 5.885').

0.7 At unranked Point 11250, turn right to go west on the ridge and climb out of the trees and up to the next highpoint (N38 49.884' / W107 5.870').

1.3 Arrive at ranked Point 11555 and descend southwest to a small saddle (N38 49.800' / W107 6.450').

1.5 From the saddle (11,200'), climb southwest to gain the east ridge of the traverse (N38 49.685' / W107 6.652').

2.2 Top out on the ridge at about 12,000' and turn right to go southwest (N38 49.225' / W107 6.921').

2.7 Arrive at soft-ranked 12,277' Ohio Peak and go right to descend the west ridge of the peak (N38 49.056' / W107 7.278').

2.9 Descend to a notch at 12,000' and climb west back up to the ridge. This is the crux of the climb, as you will lose and have to regain a lot of elevation, both out and back (N38 49.070' / W107 7.472').

3.1 Arrive at ranked Point 12300 and go southwest on the ridge, dropping slightly north of ridgeline on easier slopes, then climb back up to the ridge and continue west-southwest to the next summit (N38 49.078' / W107 7.719').

4.1 Arrive at ranked 12,391' Anthracite Range Highpoint. Return the way you came (N38 48.870' / W107 8.664').

8.2 Arrive back at the trailhead (N38 50.124' / W107 5.540').

76 West Elk Mountains Highpoint: West Elk Peak

Elevation: 13,035' (NAVD88 13,042')

Distinctions: West Elk Mountains Highpoint, West Elk Wilderness Highpoint, Prominence 100, P3K, Ranked 13er

Class: 1

Difficulty and skill level: Very Strenuous; Intermediate

Approximate moving time: 10 hours

Distance: 17.6 miles round-trip

Elevation trailhead to summit: 8,991' to 13,042' (+4,051'); about 4,900' round-trip

Terrain: Dirt trail; creek crossing

Restrictions: Summer route, avalanche danger may exist; CR 727 is closed seasonally; trail closed to bicycles and motor vehicles; dogs must be on leash or under voice command; follow wilderness regulations

Amenities: Trailhead toilet and dispersed camping; backcountry camping; services in Gunnison and Crested Butte

Trailhead: Mill Creek Trailhead

Trails: Mill Castle Trail #450, unofficial West Elk Peak Trail and Southeast Ridge

Maps: DeLorme Page 57 C8, Page 58 C1; USGS West Elk Peak, Squirrel Creek

County: Gunnison

Land status: Gunnison National Forest, (970) 874-6600, www.fs.usda.gov/gmug; Gunnison Ranger District, (970) 641-0471; West Elk Wilderness, www.wilderness.net

Finding the trailhead: From Gunnison, take CO 135 North for 0.3 miles, or from Crested Butte, take CO 135 South for about 24 miles. Turn west onto CR 730, drive 8.9 miles, and bear left onto unpaved CR 727 / Mill Creek Road. Continue 4.4 miles to the trailhead (GPS: N38 41.693' / W107 4.319').

The Peak

The West Elk Mountains lie west of CO 135 between Crested Butte and Gunnison, south of Kebler Pass. The highpoint, West Elk Peak, sits in a wilderness area rife with waterfalls, hoodoos, wildlife, and rocky spires, remnants of volcanic activity that has eroded away over the millennia, leaving behind a series of pinnacles known as "The Castles" along the east ridge of the peak. Enjoy them all on your hike to Storm Pass and along the final ridge to the summit.

The Climb

This is a very long hike, best done in the summertime with an early start to avoid storms. The ridge around Storm Pass can be corniced into early summer, so take precautions as you head up to the pass.

West Elk Peak

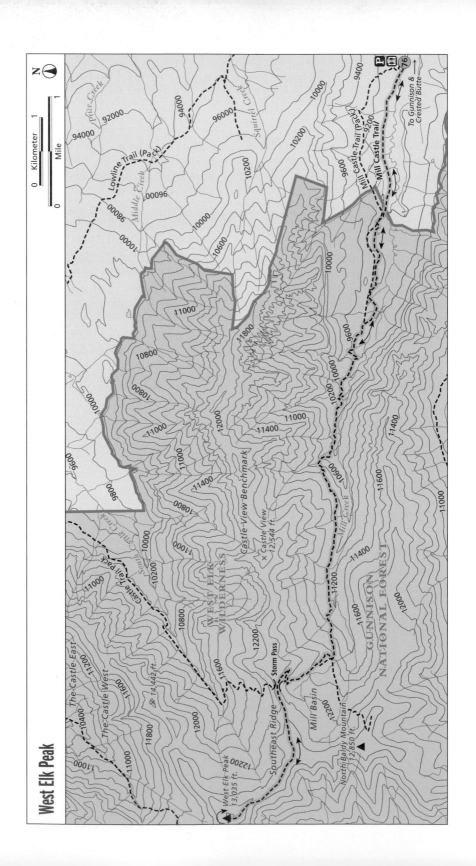

Ranked 13er West Elk Peak tops the West Elk Mountains, a subrange of the Elk Range near Gunnison. PHOTO BY JOHN KIRK

Miles and Directions

0.0 Begin at the trailhead (8,991'), cross Mill Creek, and hike west on Mill Castle Trail. The route follows an easy trail along the north bank of Mill Creek, through aspen and meadows, where you'll pass a number of cascades tumbling from the mountainside.

6.3 At the trail junction (11,840'), turn right to go north, above Mill Basin and toward Storm Pass. The trail west leads to unranked 12er North Baldy Mountain (N38 42.269' / W107 10.330').

6.8 Start switchbacks at 12,180' and climb up to the pass (N38 42.623' / W107 10.585').

7.3 Top out on Storm Pass at about 12,460'. West Elk Peak is in view to the west, and the Castles rise to the north, across the South Castle Creek drainage. The Mill Castle Trail continues down the other side of the pass to the drainage, but you will go west on the unofficial West Elk Peak Trail above West Elk Basin, following the southeast ridge to the peak (N38 42.712' / W107 10.626').

8.8 Arrive at ranked 13,042' West Elk Peak. Return the way you came (N38 43.075' / W107 11.968').

17.6 Arrive back at the trailhead (N38 41.693' / W107 4.319').

Western Mesas and Plateaus

The Flat Tops and White River Plateau define the northwestern edge of the Rocky Mountains in Colorado, while the Roan Plateau, Grand Mesa, Uncompahgre Plateau, and Uintah Mountains rise up from the Colorado Plateau, a geographic province that stretches west into Utah and southwest into Arizona and New Mexico. The highest points of the Flat Tops, White River Plateau, Roan Plateau, and Grand Mesa are accessible in Colorado, but the highpoint of the Uncompahgre Plateau sits on private property in the state, and the highpoints of the Colorado Plateau and the Uintah Mountains lie outside Colorado's borders, in Utah. Wildernesses within the western mesas and plateaus include the Flat Tops, Gunnison Gorge, Black Canyon of the Gunnison, Dominguez Canyon, Black Ridge Canyons, and Mesa Verde Wilderness Areas.

The Flat Tops rose about 30 million years ago as volcanoes along the northeast edge of the White River Plateau in northern Colorado. The eroded end result is a collection of gently sloped domes and flat-topped peaks, surrounded by more than a hundred lakes and dramatic cliff faces, dividing the jagged Gore Range to the east and Colorado's western plateaus. South and west of the Flat Tops, the White River Plateau rises north of Glenwood Springs, stretching north–south for 40 miles and east–west for 66 miles, and bound by the Roan Plateau to the west. The Roan Plateau rises nearly 4,000' above the town of Rifle in the Piceance Basin—a large natural gas resource and the subject of much political wrangling—located north of the Grand (River) Valley. The plateau extends west through the Book Cliffs near Grand Junction and into Utah. South of the Grand Valley (Grand River is the historical name for the Colorado River), the plateau of Grand Mesa rises as the largest flat-topped

Mount Garfield is a year-round favorite near Grand Junction in western Colorado.
PHOTO BY SUSAN JOY PAUL

mountain on the planet, covering an area of about 500 square miles. A hard layer of basalt protects the Grand Mesa from the fate suffered by surrounding sedimentary rock, which has been heavily eroded by the Colorado River to the north and the Gunnison River to the south. Colorado's western mesas and plateaus are like another planet in the state, far from the well-known summits of the Rocky Mountains and offering alternative adventures for the Colorado mountaineer.

77 The Flat Tops Highpoint: Flat Top Mountain

Elevation: 12,354' (NAVD88 12,360')
Distinctions: The Flat Tops Highpoint, Garfield County Highpoint, Flat Tops Wilderness Highpoint, Prominence 100, P4K, Ranked 12er
Class: 2; Class 1 to Flat Top–Derby saddle, Class 2 to summit
Difficulty and skill level: Moderate; Intermediate
Approximate moving time: 5 hours
Distance: 8.6 miles round-trip
Elevation trailhead to summit: 10,290' to 12,360' (+2,070'); about 2,400' round-trip
Terrain: Dirt trail, tundra, and talus
Restrictions: FR 900 is closed seasonally; trail closed to bicycles and motor vehicles; dogs must be on leash or under voice command; follow wilderness regulations
Amenities: Toilet at trailhead; backcountry camping; seasonal campgrounds at Stillwater Reservoir and along FR 900; services in Yampa, Meeker, Kremmling, and Steamboat Springs
Trailhead: Stillwater Trailhead
Trail: North Derby Trail #1122, off-trail West Ridge
Maps: DeLorme Page 36 A1, Page 26 E1; USGS Orno Peak, Devils Causeway
County: Garfield
Land status: Medicine Bow–Routt National Forest, (307) 745-2300, www.fs.usda.gov/mbr; Yampa Ranger District, (970) 638-4516; Flat Tops Wilderness, www.wilderness.net

Finding the trailhead: From I-70 at Silverthorne, take CO 9 North for 37.1 miles and turn left onto US 40 West. Drive 6.3 miles and turn left onto CO 134 West, then drive 26.9 miles and get onto CO 131 North for an additional 9 miles, to Yampa. Turn left onto CR 7 / Moffat Avenue. Drive 16.5 miles, through town and onto unpaved FR 900, to Stillwater Reservoir and parking at the trailhead (GPS: N40 1.646' / W107 7.409').

The Peak

Flat Top Mountain is the highpoint of the Flat Tops Range and the Flat Tops Wilderness, and attracts county peakbaggers as the Garfield County Highpoint. From the trailhead, your route is in sight. At the rocky summit, enjoy views east to the Gore Range, north to the Elkhead Range, south to the northern tip of the Sawatch and Elk mountain ranges and the Grand Mesa, and west to the White River Plateau.

The Climb

Flat Top Mountain provides an easy route-finding adventure in a wonderfully scenic part of the state. If you have an extra day to spare in the Flat Tops, add a trip to soft-ranked 11er Devils Causeway along the Chinese Wall, an airy and exciting ridge walk with some exposure. From the Stillwater Trailhead, take the East Fork Trail west (instead of turning left onto the North Derby Trail to Flat Top Mountain) to get to that peak. If you're working on the Colorado county highpoints, add a trip to Rio Blanco County highpoint and unranked 12er "Northwest Orno," located along the ridge on nearby ranked 12er Orno Peak and accessed via the Mandall Lakes Trail to

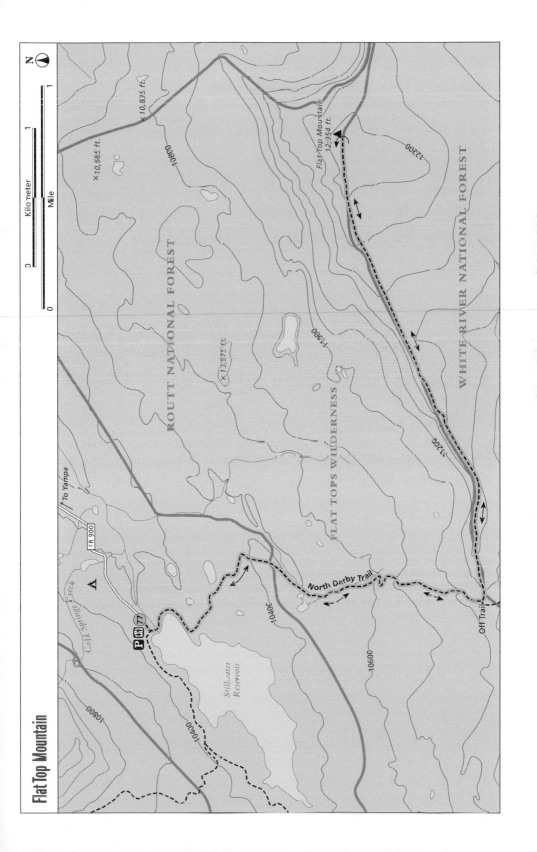

Flat Top Mountain

N

0 1 Kilometer

0 1 Mile

ROUTT NATIONAL FOREST

WHITE RIVER NATIONAL FOREST

FLAT TOPS WILDERNESS

To Yampa

FR 900

Cold Springs Creek

P 🏕 77

Stillwater Reservoir

North Derby Trail

Off Trail

Flat-Top Mountain 12,354 ft.

×10,835 ft.

×10,685 ft.

×11,575 ft.

10800

10500

12200

12200

12200

10400

10600

10000

10800

Flat Top Mountain tops the Flat Tops Wilderness of northern Colorado. PHOTO BY SUSAN JOY PAUL

Mandall Pass, where you can also get ranked Point 12008. The trailhead for those peaks begins across from the Bear Lake Campground, on the north side of FR 900, which you will pass on your way to the trailhead for Flat Top Mountain.

Miles and Directions

0.0 Begin at the trailhead (10,290') at the southwest end of the parking area and hike southwest toward the reservoir.

0.1 Take the left fork to get on the North Derby Trail. Cross the dam and hike around the reservoir and into the forest.

1.0 Enter the Flat Tops Wilderness and continue south up switchbacks to the Flat Top–Derby saddle.

2.1 At the saddle, with ranked 12er Derby Peak to the southwest and Flat Top Mountain east, bear left to leave the North Derby Trail, which continues south to Hooper Lake. Hike east on a use trail with dramatic exposure to the north, and spread out to lessen your impact as the trail disappears (N40 0.325' / W107 7.313').

3.2 Go over a false summit at 11,685' and continue east-northeast. The summit area is a large talus field, and cairns mark the route to the tallest cairn, and the highpoint (N40 0.583' / W107 6.166').

4.3 Arrive at ranked 12,360' Flat Top Mountain. Return the way you came (N40 0.876' / W107 4.998').

8.6 Arrive back at the trailhead (N40 1.646' / W107 7.409').

78 White River Plateau Highpoint: Blair Mountain

Elevation: 11,460'
Distinctions: White River Plateau Highpoint, Prominence 200, P1K, Ranked 11er
Class: 1
Difficulty and skill level: Easy; Beginner
Approximate moving time: None
Distance: Drive-up
Elevation trailhead to summit: None
Terrain: Dirt road
Restrictions: FR 651 and 601 are closed Nov 23 to May 20 and may close earlier and open later, based on snow and condition of terrain;

all roads on plateau require high-clearance 4WD vehicle year-round
Amenities: Toilet at nearby Blair Lake Trailhead; services in New Castle and Glenwood Springs
Trailhead: None
Trail: None
Maps: DeLorme Page 35 C6; USGS Blair Mountain
County: Garfield
Land status: White River National Forest, (970) 945-2521, www.fs.usda.gov/whiteriver; Rifle Ranger District, (970) 625-2371

Finding the trailhead: From I-70, about 14 miles east of Rifle and 11 miles west of Glenwood Springs, take exit 105 and turn right onto Castle Valley Boulevard. Go 1.4 miles, straight at the traffic circle, and continue another 0.8 mile. Turn right onto CR 245 / Buford Road and go 4.2 miles. Turn right onto New Castle–Buford Road, go 4.0 miles, and turn left onto CR 245, then go 1.1 miles and turn left onto Main Elk Creek Road. Go 16.8 miles and turn right onto FR 651, then go 8.4 miles, bearing right at the first two road junctions and left at the third one to remain on FR 651. Join FR 601 and drive 2.2 miles to the top of the plateau and the highpoint, to the right of the road. Blair Mountain may also be approached from Glenwood Springs, by taking Coffee Pot Road / FR 600 to a point northeast of Heart Lake, then taking FR 630, 601, 142, and finally FR 601 to the summit (GPS: N39 47.664' / W107 25.050').

The Peak

Blair Mountain trends north–south for about 3 miles and is the highest point of the White River Plateau. The area is popular with recreationists, and a jeep road will take you to the top. From the summit, you'll have views of the many lakes scattered across the plateau, with distant views of the Grand Hogback and Roan Cliffs west, the Flat Tops north and east, and the Elks and Grand Mesa south.

The Climb

The trip to Blair Mountain is a long, slow drive on rough roads, so pack a lunch and make a day of it. Once you've tagged the top, consider taking a nice hike along the lakes below the cliffs to the east. To reach the Blair Lake Trailhead, leave the summit and drive south, back down FR 601, but instead of rejoining CR 651, turn left at 2.2 miles to stay on FR 601, then go east for 0.6 mile and park at Elk Lakes and the Patterson Creek Portal. The rolling Blair Lake Trail goes north along the base of the

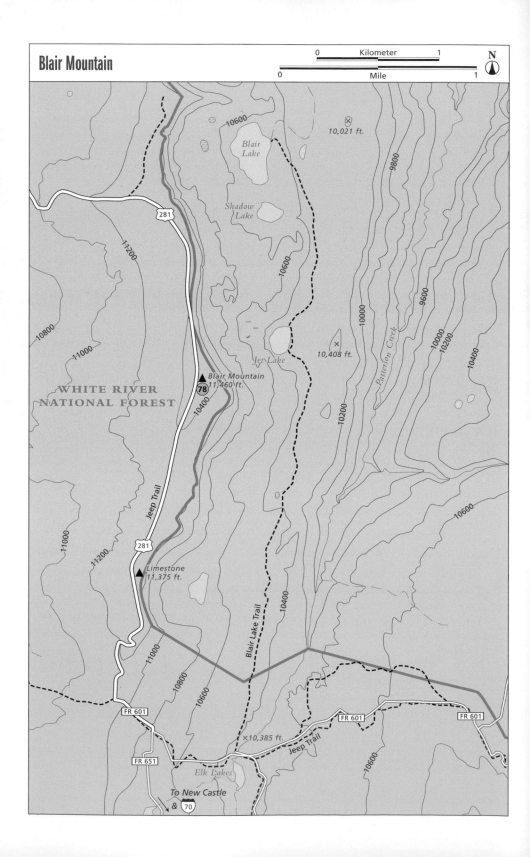

Blair Mountain

0   Kilometer   1

0   Mile   1

N

10,021 ft.

Blair Lake

Shadow Lake

281

11200

10800

11000

WHITE RIVER
NATIONAL FOREST

9800

9600

10000

10200

10400

Patterson Creek

10600

10000

Jet Lake

10,408 ft.

▲ Blair Mountain
11,460 ft.
78

10200

10400

Jeep Trail

11000

281

11200

▲ Limestone
11,375 ft.

Blair Lake Trail

10400

10600

11000

10800

10600

FR 601

FR 601

FR 601

FR 651

×10,385 ft.

Jeep Trail

10600

Elk Lakes

To New Castle
& 70

A rough road leads to the top of Blair Mountain on the White River Plateau
PHOTO BY ERIK PACKARD

cliffs, past 10,335' Jet Lake and 10,456' Shadow Lake, and finally meets 10,466' Blair Lake 3.4 miles from the trailhead, with the east face of Blair Mountain rising 1,000' above you.

Miles and Directions

0.0 Follow directions to the trailhead and walk east a few feet to the highpoint. Arrive at ranked 11,460' Blair Mountain. Drive back the same way you came in, or continue north over the peak and follow FR 601, 125, and 245 to New Castle-Buford Road, back to New Castle (N39 47.664' / W107 25.050').

79 Glenwood Springs Local Favorite: Storm King Mountain B

Elevation: 8,793'
Distinction: Ranked 8er
Class: 2; Class 1 for first 1.8 miles, Class 2 to summit
Difficulty and skill level: Very strenuous; Intermediate
Approximate moving time: 5 hours
Distance: 4.2 miles round-trip to memorials only; 5.8 miles round-trip to summit only; 6.4 miles round-trip to visit memorials and summit
Elevation trailhead to summit: 5,650' to 8,793' (+3,143'); about 1,700' round-trip to memorials only; about 3,500' round-trip to summit only; about 3,700' round-trip to memorials and summit

Terrain: Dirt trail and bushwhack
Restrictions: None posted
Amenities: Trailhead porta-potty and picnic benches; services in Glenwood Springs
Trailhead: Storm King Mountain Memorial Trailhead
Trail: Storm King Mountain Memorial Trail, off-trail Southwest Ridge
Maps: DeLorme Page 35 E7, E6; USGS Storm King Mountain
County: Garfield
Land status: Bureau of Land Management, Colorado River Valley Field Office, (970) 876-9000, www.blm.gov/co/st/en/fo/crvfo.html

Finding the trailhead: From Glenwood Springs, take I-70 West for about 6 miles and turn right at exit 109 for Canyon Creek. Bear right to follow the Frontage Road for a mile to the trailhead (GPS: N39 34.428' / W107 26.068').

The Peak

Storm King Mountain rises more than 3,000' above I-70 west of Glenwood Springs. The peak was the site of the tragic South Canyon fire that took the lives of 14 firefighters in 1994. A memorial trail honors the men and women who lost their lives here, and the route continues off-trail to the summit, with views south of the Grand Mesa, Mount Sopris, and the Elk Mountains.

The Climb

The trail to Storm King Mountain climbs steeply up the southern slopes of the peak, so bring your sunscreen, sunglasses, a hat, and plenty of water. An observation point overlooks where flames overtook the firefighters, and there are two cutoffs along the trail that you should take to visit the memorials, where plaques, interpretive signs, and memorabilia pay tribute to those who perished in the blaze. This is a worthwhile hike even if you don't reach the summit.

Storm King Mountain B

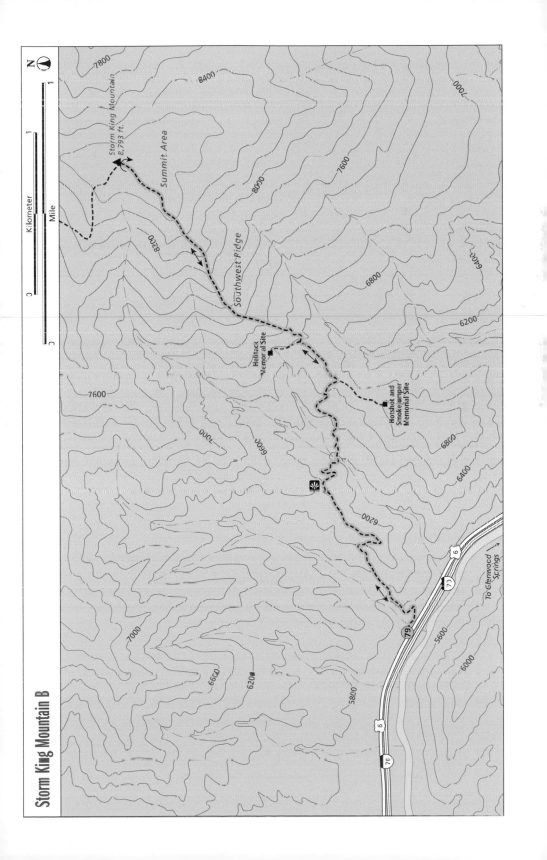

Storm King Mountain
8,793 ft.

Summit Area

Southwest Ridge

Helirack
Memorial Site

Hotshot and
Smokejumper
Memorial Site

To Glenwood
Springs

N

Kilometer

Mile

7800

8400

8000

7600

7000

6800

6200

7600

6800

6400

6200

7000

6600

6200

5800

5600

6000

6000

6
70
9
77
70

Storm King Mountain rises north of I-70 near Glenwood Springs. PHOTO BY STEWART M. GREEN

Miles and Directions

0.0 Begin at the parking area at 5,650' and hike north up the trail, pausing to enjoy the Observation Point at about 0.25 mile.

1.0 At the observation point (6,360'), follow the trail to the left that drops sharply into the gully below, then climb east to a ridge (N39 34.677' / W107 25.384').

1.6 Turn right off the main trail for a 0.4-mile round-trip to the Hotshot and Smokejumper Memorial Site. Alternatively, you can continue past the memorial for another 0.2 mile to the summit of ranked Point 7020. Then return to the main trail.

2.2 Pass by a large cairn on the right side of the trail, which is the cut-off to the southwest ridge. Continue on trail 0.1 mile to the Helitack Memorial Site, marked by a tree on the mountainside, and memorials in a deep gulch to the north. Return to this point and head off-trail north on rugged terrain (N39 34.788' / W107 24.813').

2.8 Gain the southwest ridge at about 7,640 and head northeast (N39 35.036' / W107 24.662').

3.2 The terrain levels out at the summit area. Continue northeast to the highpoint.

3.5 Arrive at ranked 8,793' Storm King Mountain. Return the way you came, bypassing the memorial cutoffs on your descent (N39 35.380' / W107 24.039').

6.4 Arrive back at the trailhead (N39 34.428' / W107 26.068').

80 Roan Plateau Highpoint: Gardner Benchmark

Elevation: 9,286' (NAVD88 9,290')
Distinctions: Roan Plateau Highpoint, Prominence 200, P1K, Ranked 9er
Class: 1
Difficulty and skill level: Easy; Beginner
Approximate moving time: 1 hour
Distance: 2.4 miles round-trip
Elevation trailhead to summit: 9,000' to 9,290' (+290')
Terrain: Dirt road and trail
Recommended extra gear: GPS
Restrictions: Cow Creek Road and Roan Cliffs Road may not be passable if wet, muddy, or rutted; 4WD vehicle recommended under any conditions; observe BLM regulations and recommendations; for camping, pack in water and pack out all trash, including human waste
Amenities: Backcountry camping permitted on public lands with 7-day limit Apr 1 to Aug 31, 14-day limit Sept 1 to Mar 31; services in Rifle
Trailhead: Unofficial "Gardner Benchmark Trailhead"
Trail: Unofficial "Gardner Benchmark Trail"
Maps: DeLorme Page 34 E2; USGS Anvil Points
County: Garfield
Land status: Bureau of Land Management, Colorado River Valley Field Office, (970) 876-9000, www.blm.gov/co/st/en/fo/crvfo.html

Finding the trailhead: From I-70 at Rifle, take CO 13 North (towards Meeker) for 19.2 miles and turn left onto Piceance Creek Road / CR 5. Drive 3.4 miles and turn left onto unpaved Cow Creek Road. Continue 7.7 miles onto Roan Cliffs Road (toward JQS Road), then go 12.3 miles and bear right to stay on Roan Cliffs Road. Drive 1.5 more miles to a pullout on the right side of the road (GPS: N39 34.643' / W107 53.719').

The Peak

The Roan Plateau is known for its biological diversity, providing safe haven to one of the most genetically pure strains of native trout in the country and rare plants like the Parachute penstemon. The area is also home to one of the largest mule deer herds in the state and one of the tallest waterfalls, 200' East Fork Falls, located in East Fork Canyon, or "Little Yosemite." Driving to the top of the plateau is an adventure in itself, and if you have a high-clearance 4WD vehicle—and the driving skills—you may opt for the alternative, rough and rugged JQS Road from CO 13 in Rifle for your ascent or descent, and make a scenic loop of it. From either route, the unobstructed views south across the valley to the Grand Mesa make this easy highpoint a worthy trip.

The Climb

This is more of a drive than a climb, and the route may be lengthened or shortened depending on your vehicle and how far you want to walk. The lands atop the Roan Cliffs are crisscrossed with a network of unmarked 2WD and 4WD roads, so spend some time driving about and taking in views along the way.

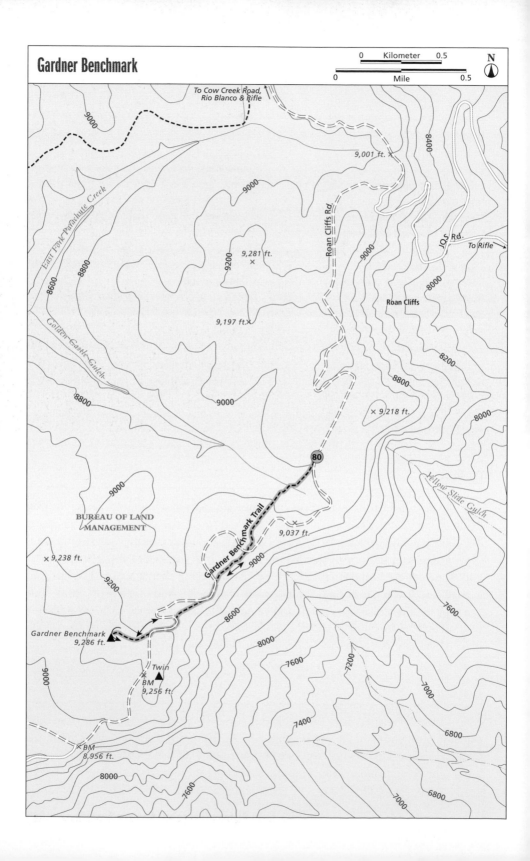

Gardner Benchmark

0   Kilometer   0.5

0   Mile   0.5

N

To Cow Creek Road,
Rio Blanco & Rifle

9000

9000

9,001 ft. ×

8400

East Fork Parachute Creek

9000

Roan Cliffs Rd.

8000

J.Q.S. Rd.

To Rifle

9200

9,281 ft. ×

9000

8800

Roan Cliffs

8600

8800

9,197 ft.×

8800

8200

Golden Gastle Gulch

8800

9000

8800

× 9,218 ft.

8000

80

Yellow Slide Gulch

9000

BUREAU OF LAND
MANAGEMENT

9,037 ft.

Gardner Benchmark Trail

9000

× 9,238 ft.

9200

8600

7600

8000

Gardner Benchmark
9,286 ft.

9000

Twin
×
BM
9,256 ft.

7600

7200

7000

6800

× BM
8,956 ft.

7400

7600

6800

8000

7600

7000

Gardner Benchmark tops the Roan Plateau in the Roan Cliffs north of Rifle.
PHOTO BY SUSAN JOY PAUL

Miles and Directions

0.0 From the pullout at 9,000', hike southwest on the trail and through the aspens. Cross the road and continue on the trail, then pick up the road again and continue southwest. Turn left at the first fork, then right up BLM Road 8015. Look for a post to the left of the road, marking the summit.

1.2 Arrive at ranked 9,290' Gardner Benchmark. Return the way you came. Alternatively, follow the rim of the cliff northeast back to the trailhead (N39 34.043' / W107 54.600').

2.4 Arrive back at the trailhead (N39 34.643' / W107 53.719').

81 Grand Mesa Highpoint: Crater Peak

Elevation: 11,327' (NAVD88 11,333')
Distinctions: Grand Mesa Highpoint, Prominence 100, P2K, Ranked 11er
Class: 2; Class 1 for first 3 miles, Class 2 to summit
Difficulty and skill level: Moderate; Intermediate
Approximate moving time: 5 hours
Distance: 9.0 miles round-trip
Elevation trailhead to summit: 9,560' to 11,333' (+1,773')
Terrain: Dirt trail and bushwhack through forest, marsh, and talus; creek crossing

Restrictions: FR 128 is closed and gated seasonally, and opens around Memorial Day; dam crossing is closed to motor vehicles
Amenities: Backcountry camping; services in Hotchkiss and Delta
Trailhead: "Goodenough Reservoir Trailhead"
Trail: FR 128 1C, off-trail Southwest Slope
Maps: DeLorme Page 44 E4;
USGS Chalk Mountain
County: Delta
Land status: Grand Mesa National Forest, (970) 874-6600, www.fs.usda.gov/gmug; Grand Valley Ranger District, (970) 242-8211

Finding the trailhead: From CO 92, 17 miles east of Delta and 3.8 miles west of Hotchkiss, go north on 3100 Road / CR 31. The paved road ends at 5 miles and meets the Grand Mesa National Forest at 12.9 miles. From the forest boundary, take FR 128 for 5.5 miles, just past the sign for Goodenough Reservoir and the trailhead at FR 128 1C, to a pullout on the left side of the road (GPS: N39 0.705' / W107 42.456').

The Peak

The Leroux Creek area attracts few mountain climbers, but Crater Peak is a worthy summit, with a unique craterlike face and excellent views of the Elk Mountains, Raggeds Range, Ruby Range, and West Elk Mountains to the east and the San Juan Mountains to the south.

The Climb

Crater Peak is best climbed from summer to fall, when the dirt road allows access to the Goodenough Reservoir Trailhead, and to avoid post-holing through snow in the forest. After climbing the peak, you can return the way you came, or descend to the open area below the peak and go around the north end of the reservoir, rather than the south. This will shorten the hike out by 0.25 mile, but the route may be extremely muddy, and you will not recross the dam. Crater Peak is often climbed with ranked 11er Mount Hatten and unranked 11er Mount Darline, as all three summits lie along a 2-mile section of ridge. The route demands a good bit of ups and downs, over scrub, talus, and scree, so plan on a slow traverse and a bushwhack back to the reservoir.

Crater Peak

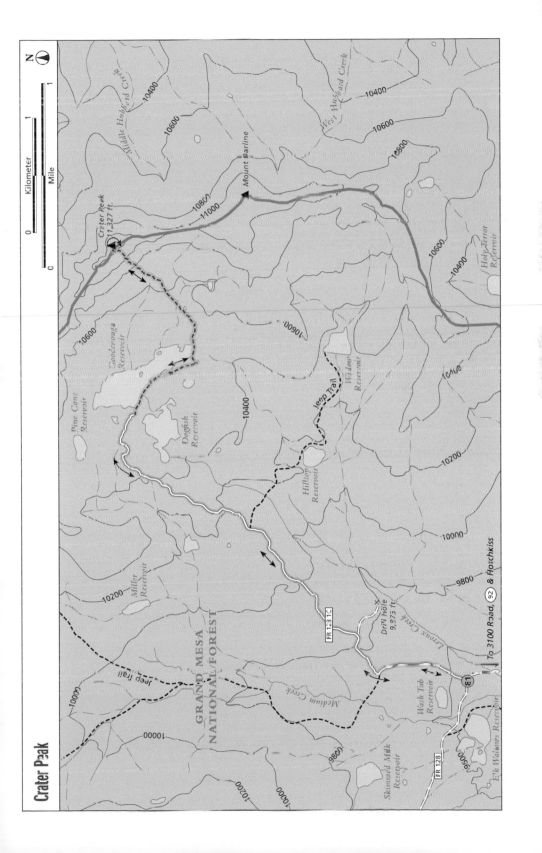

Goodenough and Dogfish Reservoirs shimmer in the sunshine below Crater Peak.
PHOTO BY SUSAN JOY PAUL

Miles and Directions

0.0 Begin at the trailhead (9,560') with Crater Peak in view, and hike north up the ATV road, signed FR 128 1C. Cross a meadow and continue through an aspen grove and past a stock pen and cabin.

0.5 Pass the junction with East Leon Trail #730 on the left (west), and turn right (northeast) to continue on FR 128 1C toward Goodenough Reservoir. Northwest of the trail, ranked 10er Priest Mountain rises gently from the forest. Hike past bogs and meadows and around the north end of Dogfish Reservoir, where the high, rounded mound of ranked 11er Mount Hatten appears to the north (N39 1.129' / W107 42.418').

2.9 At the clearing west of Goodenough Reservoir, take the trail across the dam (10,500'). Follow a use trail southwest through the forest along the west bank of the reservoir (N39 2.279' / W107 40.818').

3.5 Descend to the south end of the reservoir, then go northeast, climbing steeply through a boulder field, over a creek, past a pond, across a willowy marsh, and through some trees to a clearing below the southwest face of the peak (N39 2.004' / W107 40.459').

4.2 At the clearing (10,740'), begin the steep climb to the summit. Head for the saddle to the left (west) of the highpoint, then turn right and go up the ridge to the top of the peak (N39 2.246' / W107 39.935').

4.5 Arrive at ranked 11,333' Crater Peak and a geodetic marker at the summit. Return the way you came (N39 2.388' / W107 39.780').

9.0 Arrive back at the trailhead (N39 0.705' / W107 42.456').

82 Grand Junction Local Favorite: Mount Garfield C

Elevation: 6,765' (NAVD88 6,768')
Distinction: Ranked 6er
Class: 2+; Class 1 first 1.25 miles, mixed Class 1, 2, and 2+ to summit
Difficulty and skill level: Moderate; Beginner
Approximate moving time: 3 hours
Distance: 3.6 miles round-trip
Elevation trailhead to summit: 4,865' to 6,768' (+1,903')
Terrain: Dirt trail for most of route, with some Class 2 and 2+ rock sections

Restrictions: Water under tunnel may restrict access to trailhead; do not attempt if route is wet or storms threaten
Amenities: Services in Palisade and Grand Junction
Trailhead: Mount Garfield Trailhead
Trail: Mount Garfield Trail
Maps: DeLorme Page 43 D6; USGS Clifton
County: Mesa
Land status: Bureau of Land Management, Grand Junction Field Office, (970) 244-3000, www.blm.gov/co/st/en/fo/gjfo.html

Finding the trailhead: From I-70 at Palisade, about 5 miles east of Grand Junction, take exit 42 to 37 3/10 Road. Drive south 0.1 mile and turn right onto G 7/10 Road, then go 1.5 miles (to the end of the road) and curve right onto unpaved 35 8/10 Road. Drive under the tunnel and follow the road as it curves left to a parking area (GPS: N39 7.144' / W108 23.312').

The Peak

Mount Garfield lies on the Colorado Plateau in the Book Cliffs east of Grand Junction, at Palisade. The Book Cliffs begin at De Beque Canyon and trend west for nearly 200 miles to Price Canyon, Utah, and are the remains of an uplifted and eroded seabed, remnants of the ancient Mancos Sea. Rippled cliffs, or palisades, of Mancos shale capped with Mesa Verde sandstone rise more than 2,000' above the town of Palisade, forming the south face of Mount Garfield. The peak sits within the Little Book Cliffs Wild Horse Area, where more than 36,000 acres provide a safe haven for over 100 mustangs. You may spot some of these wild horses on the flat areas of your ascent along the south-facing butte. Named for President James Garfield, Mount Garfield is also the site of the abandoned Gearhart Mine. Tons of coal were extracted from the area during the 1930s–60s, and the historic remains of the mine and the diggings should be avoided for your safety. This lowly 6er's prominence and position provide the lucky summiter with dizzying views of Grand Junction, west, and the Grand Mesa and Uncompahgre Plateau, south.

The Climb

The route here is short, steep, and rugged, with slippery shale giving way to loose, rocky terrain and occasional swaths of easy trail that cut through dusty flats of sagebrush dotted with stray boulders that have tumbled from the cliffs. Shale becomes

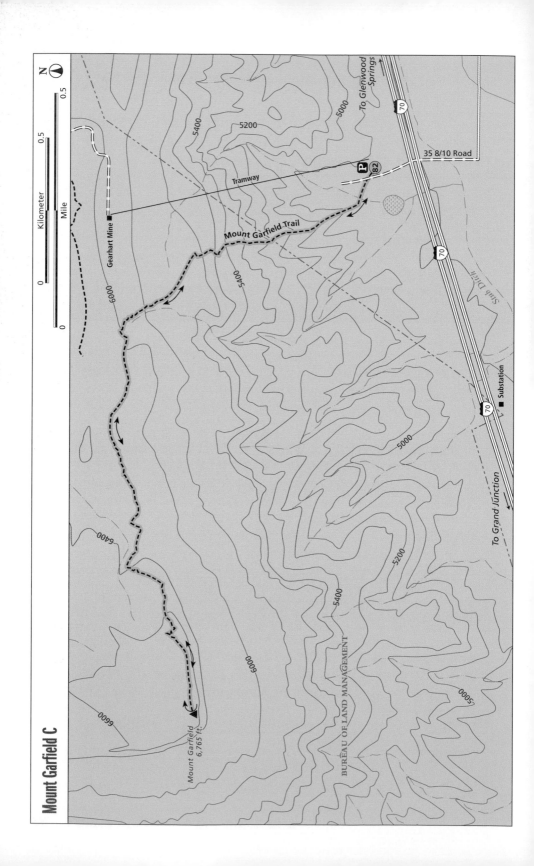

Mount Garfield C

N

Kilometer
0   0.5

Mile
0   0.5

To Glenwood Springs

70

35 8/10 Road

P 82

Tramway

Gearhart Mine

Mount Garfield Trail

5000

5200

5400

5400

5400

6000

6400

6600

6600

6000

6000

5400

5200

5200

5000

5000

Mount Garfield
6,765 ft.

BUREAU OF LAND MANAGEMENT

Stub Ditch

70

70

Substation

To Grand Junction

The Mount Garfield Trail climbs steeply through rough terrain. PHOTO BY SUSAN JOY PAUL

extremely slick when wet, so the hike should be avoided if the ground is moist or if precipitation is a threat. Trekking poles will help to maintain balance and keep you on your feet for the descent. Mount Garfield may also be climbed via the Gearhart Mine Trail, which is slightly longer, less steep, less defined, and begins at the same trailhead and heads east.

Miles and Directions

0.0 Begin at the trailhead (4,865') at the north side of the lot. Pass through the gate and hike the trail northwest, toward the first large pile of shale.

0.1 Follow the trail north, up the steep shale ridge. This is the most difficult part of the climb.

0.5 Reach the half-mile marker and the top of the first steep section (5,840'). Continue northwest on the trail, cross a flat area, and ascend the steep, rocky section of trail on the other side (N39 7.479' / W108 23.514').

0.7 Reach the mile marker and the top of the second steep section. Go west across another flat area, and start up the steep trail on the other side. The route flattens, then contours a narrow shelf along the mountainside, and ascends through another rocky area (N39 7.602' / W108 23.670').

1.6 Reach the top of the third steep section. Hike west toward the summit (N39 7.521' / W108 24.427').

1.8 Arrive at ranked 6,768' Mount Garfield. Return the way you came (N39 7.476' / W108 24.618').

3.6 Arrive back at the trailhead (N39 7.144' / W108 23.312').

The San Juan Mountains

The San Juan Mountains contain many subranges covering an area north to south for 189 miles and east to west for 178 miles in southwest Colorado, bordered by the Uncompahgre Plateau to the west and the San Luis Valley to the east. The Cochetopa Hills, La Garita Mountains, South San Juan Mountains, Cimarron Range, Sneffels Range, San Miguel Mountains, West Needle Mountains, Rico Mountains, Grenadier Range, Needle Mountains, and La Plata Mountains all lie within the San Juan Mountains, and wilderness areas of the range include the La Garita, South San Juan, Powderhorn, Uncompahgre, Mount Sneffels, Lizard Head, Hermosa Creek, and Weminuche Wildernesses. The Continental Divide follows the range southwest from Marshall Pass through the Cochetopa Hills and into the La Garita Mountains, bends west over Spring Creek Pass, continues west and then south through the Grenadiers, then trends back east and over Wolf Creek Pass. The Divide completes its Colorado journey in the South San Juans at Cumbres Pass. The San Juan Mountains were named for the San Juan River, which was named for Saint John—from the Bible, John the Apostle—by the Dominguez-Escalante Expedition of 1776. A number of peaks in the range may be reached with short approaches via paved roads at Spring Creek, Wolf Creek, Lizard Head, Red Mountain, Molas, and Coal Bank Passes, and a dirt road over Ophir Pass, while a dozen San Juan ranked 14ers require longer approaches and are generally climbed over long weekends.

Mount Wilson tops the San Miguels of the San Juan Mountains near Telluride.
PHOTO BY BILL MIDDLEBROOK

83 Cochetopa Hills Highpoint: Long Branch Baldy

Elevation: 11,974'
Distinctions: Cochetopa Hills Highpoint, Prominence 200, P1K, Ranked 11er
Class: 2; Class 1 for first 5 miles, Class 2 to summit area
Difficulty and skill level: Strenuous; Intermediate
Approximate moving time: 6 hours
Distance: 11.4 miles round-trip
Elevation trailhead to summit: 8,800' to 11,974' (+3,174')
Terrain: Dirt trail, talus, and tundra; creek crossings

Restrictions: Long Branch Road closed seasonally; trail closed to motorized vehicles; access may require high-clearance 4WD
Amenities: Backcountry camping; limited services in Sargents and Poncha Springs; full services in Gunnison and Salida
Trailhead: Long Branch Trailhead
Trail: Baldy Lake Trail #491, off-trail North Ridge
Maps: DeLorme Page 69 B6, B7; USGS Sargents Mesa
County: Saguache
Land status: Gunnison National Forest, (970) 874-6600, www.fs.usda.gov/gmug; Gunnison Ranger District, (970) 641-0471

Finding the trailhead: From US 50, about 30 miles east of Gunnison and 30 miles west of US 285 (0.9 mile west of the town of Sargents), take unpaved Long Branch Road / FR 780 South. Drive 0.2 mile on Long Branch Road / FR 780 and turn right on FR 780 / CR 31XX. Continue 2.6 miles, into the Gunnison National Forest, and to the winter gate at the abandoned Long Branch Guard Station. The road beyond the gate is rutted and may require a high-clearance 4WD vehicle. Continue through the gate on Road FR 780, bearing right at the fork, for 1.2 miles to the trailhead (GPS: N38 21.259' / W106 24.910').

The Peak

Long Branch Baldy enjoys a unique position on the Continental Divide in the Cochetopa Hills south of the Sawatch Range at the northeast tip of the San Juan Mountains. The Cochetopa Hills begin at the shared corners of Gunnison, Chaffee, and Saguache Counties and roll south over Marshall Pass, North Pass, and Cochetopa Pass, to the La Garitas near Creede. The peaks may be accessed at Sargents, described here, and from CO 114 at North Pass. "Cochetopa" is derived from the Ute word *kuchu-pupan*, or "pass of the buffalo," and the roads and trails that cross the Divide here were defined by American natives and buffalo traveling between the east and west watersheds of the Great Divide. Long Branch Baldy offers spectacular views of the Sawatch Range to the north, the San Juan Mountains to the southwest, and the Sangre de Cristo Range to the east. On a clear day, mountain range highpoints visible from the summit include San Luis Peak, Crestone Peak, and Blanca Peak.

Mixed talus and tundra top Long Branch Baldy on the Continental Divide in Gunnison National Forest. PHOTO BY SUSAN JOY PAUL

The Climb

Two trails at the Long Branch Trailhead lead to Summit Trail #486 on the Continental Divide. The Long Branch Trail goes directly south, while the Baldy Lake Trail goes west, then curves south to Baldy Lake below Long Branch Baldy. Be sure to get on the correct trail, Baldy Lake Trail #491, to the right (west) at the trailhead. Peak baggers can add ranked Point 10153 with a 1-mile detour and bushwhack north from the trail junction at 2.8 miles, adding 2 miles to the hike. For a longer outing, descend back to the trail from the summit of Long Branch Baldy and continue to Baldy Lake. Hike past the lake on the Baldy Lake Trail to the Continental Divide, then go east on the Summit Trail to connect with the Long Branch Trail, and take that north back to the trailhead.

Miles and Directions

0.0 Begin at the trailhead (8,800') and go west on Baldy Lake Trail. Cross Long Branch Creek and the West Fork of Long Branch Creek. Hike through a talus field and catch your first glimpse of Long Branch Baldy to the south. Emerge from aspens to full views of the peak (southwest) and the high peaks at Marshall Pass (northeast).

2.8 At the trail junction, go left (south) to stay on Baldy Lake Trail #491. The junction lies on a ridge between the Hicks Creek and West Fork of Long Branch Creek drainages. The Hicks Gulch Trail drops west to Hicks Creek and Dutchman Creek, but you'll stay on the Baldy Lake Trail. Pass through a wooden gate and into the forest, and contour the slope on a good trail above Long Branch Creek (N38 21.236' / W106 27.790').

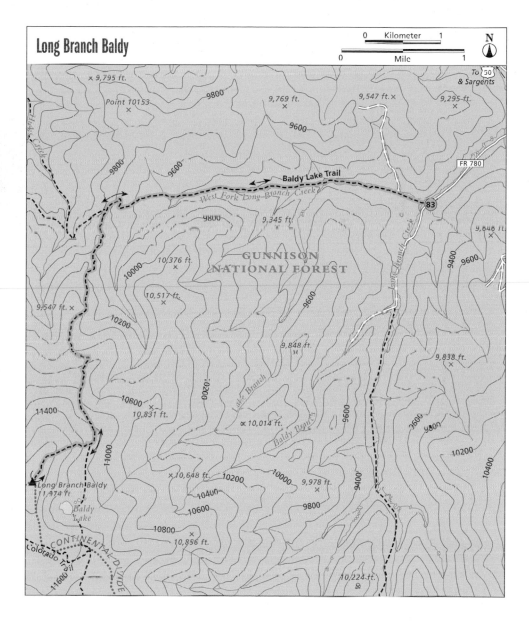

Long Branch Baldy

x 9,795 ft.

To 50
& Sargents

Point 10153
×

9800

9,769 ft.
×

9,547 ft. ×

9,295 ft.
×

9600

9800

9600

FR 780

Hot Creek

Baldy Lake Trail

West Fork Long Branch Creek

Long Branch Creek

83

9800

9,345 ft.

9,648 ft.
×

GUNNISON
NATIONAL FOREST

10,376 ft.
×

9400

9600

10000

10,517 ft.
×

9,547 ft. ×

10200

9600

9,848 ft.
×

9,838 ft.
×

11400

10800
×
10,831 ft.

Lake Branch

× 10,014 ft.

Baldy Branch

9600

9800

10200

10400

11000

Long Branch Baldy
11,974 ft.

× 10,648 ft.

10200

10000

9,978 ft.
×

9400

9800

Baldy
Lake

10400

10600

10800

CONTINENTAL DIVIDE

Colorado Trail

10,856 ft.
×

11600

10,224 ft.
×

5.0   As the trail descends at 11,270', go off-trail west, through the forest. Climb the steep volcanic talus slope, aiming for the ridge to the right (north) of the summit (N38 19.572' / W106 27.924').

5.5   Gain the ridge at 11,880' and head south-southwest to the summit area (N38 19.478' / W106 28.334').

5.7   Arrive at ranked 11,974' Long Branch Baldy. Return the way you came (N38 19.329' / W106 28.439').

11.4   Arrive back at the trailhead (N38 21.259' / W106 24.916').

84 La Garita Mountains Highpoint: San Luis Peak

Elevation: 14,014' (NAVD88 14,021')
Distinctions: La Garita Mountains Highpoint, La Garita Wilderness Highpoint, Centennial, Prominence 100, P3K, Ranked 14er
Class: 1
Difficulty and skill level: Very Strenuous; Advanced
Approximate moving time: 8 hours
Distance: 12.8 miles round-trip
Elevation trailhead to summit: 10,470' to 14,021' (+3,551')
Terrain: Dirt and talus trail; creek crossings
Recommended extra gear: Crampons or microspikes and ice axe if snow exists
Restrictions: Road to trailhead is closed seasonally; trail closed to bicycles and motor vehicles; dogs must be on leash; follow wilderness regulations
Amenities: Toilet at nearby Eddiesville Trailhead; trailhead and backcountry camping; services in Gunnison
Trailhead: Stewart Creek Trailhead
Trail: Stewart Creek Trail #470
Maps: DeLorme Page 68 E3; USGS San Luis Peak, Stewart Peak, Elk Park
County: Saguache
Land status: Gunnison National Forest, (970) 874-6600, www.fs.usda.gov/gmug; Gunnison Ranger District, (970) 641-0471; La Garita Wilderness, www.wilderness.net

Finding the trailhead: From CO 50, about 8 miles east of Gunnison, take CO 114 East for 20.2 miles and turn right onto unpaved CR NN-14. Go 7 miles and turn right onto CR 15-GG / FR 794, then go 4.2 miles to an intersection and continue straight onto CR 14 / FR 794. Continue 16.4 miles to the trailhead (GPS: N38 1.488' / W106 50.464').

The Peak

The La Garita Mountains rise along the Continental Divide between the Cochetopa Hills and Spring Creek Pass. Most of the peaks of the range lie within the La Garita Wilderness, and the Colorado Trail and Continental Divide National Scenic Trail follow the range, along the Divide. *La Garita* means "The Lookout" in Spanish, and peaks here were used as lookouts in past centuries. Native Americans communicated with friends across the upper Rio Grande Valley and San Luis Valley by sending smoke signals from La Garita summits that could be seen from as far away as the Sangre de Cristo Range. *San Luis* is Spanish for "Saint Louis," the King of France from 1226 to 1270. King Louis was known as the Peace King, and you will have a lot of peace on San Luis Peak. Due to the long drive to the trailhead and long hike to the summit, San Luis Peak is one of the least popular 14,000' mountains in Colorado. Your journey will pay off with stunning summit views of nearby La Garita peaks, including, north to east, Organ Mountain, Baldy Alto, and Stewart Peak, with the Rio Grande and San Luis Valleys stretching for many miles east to the Sangre de Cristo Range. The San Juan Mountains line the sky to the west.

San Luis Peak

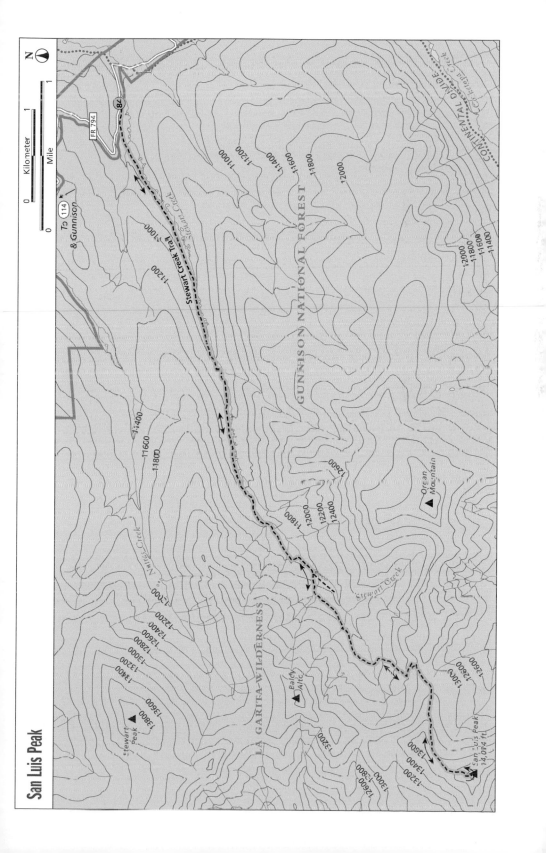

San Luis Peak is a remote 14er in the La Garita Mountains near Gunnison.
PHOTO BY BILL MIDDLEBROOK

The Climb

Access to Stewart Creek Trail is seasonal, so if you choose to climb San Luis Peak in the winter months, you will have a very long walk, ski, or snowshoe to the trailhead. This 14er makes for a good late summer hike, when the weather is settled, and you may wish to camp near the trailhead and climb some 13ers in the area, too. San Luis Peak may also be accessed via the West Willow Creek Trailhead, near Creede, and approached on the south ridge of the peak. The route is slightly shorter, with more elevation gain, and is popular in the spring for snow-climb access to the Yawner Gullies on the west face of the peak.

Miles and Directions

0.0 Begin at the trailhead (10,470') and hike west-southwest on the trail along the north banks of Stewart Creek. Enter the forest and continue on the trail.

3.1 Cross Stewart Creek to the south side, and soon after, cross back to the north side of the creek (N38 0.677' / W106 53.602').

3.3 Emerge from the trees at 11,420' and continue southwest. The trail cuts through willows as it approaches the saddle between ranked 13ers Baldy Alto to the north and Organ Mountain to the south (N38 0.617' / W106 53.769').

3.9 Leave the creek and go southwest, climbing steep terrain to the San Luis–Organ saddle (N38 0.245' / W106 54.224').

5.5 Gain the saddle at 13,100' and head west to the northeast ridge, contouring along the left (south) side of the ridge (N37 59.500' / W106 55.135').

6.1 Climb to a false summit at about 13,600', then go south-southwest toward the highpoint over mixed dirt and talus trail, from the right (east) side of the ridge up to the ridge crest (N37 59.443' / W106 55.728').

6.4 Arrive at ranked 14,021' San Luis Peak. Return the way you came (N37 59.213' / W106 55.880').

12.8 Arrive back at the trailhead (N38 1.488' / W106 50.464').

85 Spring Creek Pass Peaks: "Baldy no es Cinco," Baldy Cinco, Point 13162, and Point 13510

Elevations: 13,313' (NAVD88 13,320') "Baldy no es Cinco"; 13,383' (NAVD88 13,390') Baldy Cinco; 13,162' Point 13162; and 13,510' Point 13510

Distinctions: Tricentennial, Prominence 200, P1K (Point 13510); Ranked 13ers (all 4 peaks)

Class: 2; Class 2 for all 4 summits, Class 1 and 2 back to trailhead

Difficulty and skill level: Strenuous; Intermediate

Approximate moving time: 8 hours

Distance: 13.7-mile loop

Elevation trailhead to summits: 10,889' to 13,510' (+2,621'); about 4,500' round-trip

Terrain: Dirt trail, grass, tundra, and talus; creek crossing

Restrictions: Trail closed to bicycles and motor vehicles; dogs must be on leash; follow wilderness regulations

Amenities: Trailhead toilet; seasonal camping at nearby Spring Creek Pass Campground and other campgrounds along CO 149; backcountry camping; services in Lake City and Creede

Trailhead: Spring Creek Pass

Trails: Colorado Trail, off-trail West Ridge

Maps: DeLorme Page 78 A1; USGS Baldy Cinco, Slumgullion Pass

Counties: Hinsdale, Mineral

Land status: Gunnison National Forest, (970) 874-6600, www.fs.usda.gov/gmug; Gunnison Ranger District–Lake City Office, (970) 641-0471, Rio Grande National Forest, (719) 852-5941, www.fs.usda.gov/riogrande; Divide Ranger District Creede Office, (719) 658-2556, La Garita Wilderness, www.wilderness.net

Finding the trailhead: From Creede, take CO 149 North for 33 miles, or from Lake City, take CO 149 South for 17 miles, to Spring Creek Pass, and park at the pullout on the east side of the road (GPS: N37 56.395' / W107 9.518').

The Peaks

Four ranked 13ers make for a long, high ridge run east of the Silver Thread Scenic Byway at Spring Creek Pass. The route follows the Continental Divide and descends on the Colorado Trail to the expansive plateau of Snow Mesa. *Baldy no es Cinco* translates literally to "Baldy it's not Five," while *Baldy Cinco* means "Baldy Five." With 51 variations of "Baldy Mountain" in the state, you will have just 49 left to complete them all, after this trip. The summits offer views west to San Juan Mountains highpoint Uncompahgre Peak and other 14ers at Lake City, with the Sneffels range beyond; east to La Garita Range highpoint San Luis Peak; and southwest to the Grenadiers and Needles.

The Climb

These peaks may be climbed year-round, but if you do it as a snow climb, carry snowshoes, crampons or microspikes, and an ice axe, and stay clear of deep cornices

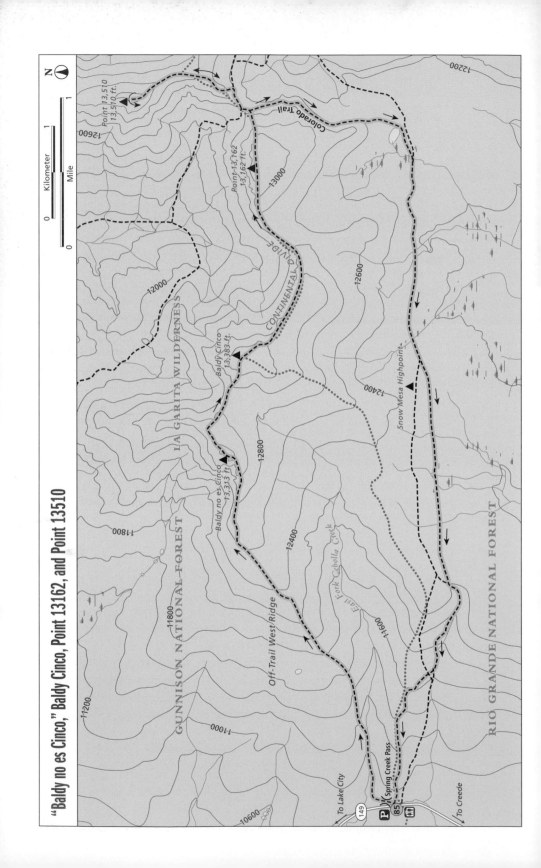

"Baldy no es Cinco," Baldy Cinco, Point 13162, and Point 13510

N

0   Kilometer   1

0   Mile   1

Point 13,510
13,510 ft.

12600

12200

Point 13,162
13,162 ft.

13000

CONTINENTAL DIVIDE

Colorado Trail

12000

LA GARITA WILDERNESS

Baldy Cinco
13,383 ft.

12600

12400

Snow Mesa Highpoint

Baldy no es Cinco
13,313 ft.

12800

GUNNISON NATIONAL FOREST

11800

11800

Off-Trail West Ridge

12400

East Fork Cebolla Creek

11600

11200

11000

RIO GRANDE NATIONAL FOREST

10600

To Lake City

149

P

85

Spring Creek Pass

To Creede

A lofty ridge connects four 13ers east of Spring Creek Pass on the Continental Divide.
PHOTO BY KEVIN BAKER

that line the exposed north rim of the ridge. From the trailhead at Spring Creek Pass, you'll bypass the Colorado Trail for some off-route hiking northeast to gain the west ridge on "Baldy no es Cinco" and continue along the ridge for all four peaks, then descend the Colorado Trail to Snow Mesa. Some mountaineers prefer to reverse this route, but it's nice to get the elevation out of the way early in the morning, on fresh legs, and then enjoy a leisurely hike out on the beautiful mesa and good trail. High-pointers can add unranked highpoint "Snow Mesa" on the hike back to the trailhead, by cutting off the trail about 1.4 miles past the lake, as the trail bends southwest, and going off-trail due west to the 12,393' highpoint (N37 56.34' / W107 6.384').

Miles and Directions

0.0 Begin at the trailhead (10,889') on the east side of CO 149 at Spring Creek Pass. Go northeast, cross the East Fork of Cebolla Creek, and gain the southwest ridge of the first peak. The ridge levels out at about 12,700', then climbs east to the summit.

2.9 Arrive at ranked 13,320' "Baldy no es Cinco." Continue to follow the ridge northeast, then descend east-southeast to a saddle, and climb to the next summit (N37 57.402' / W107 24. 6.900').

3.7 Arrive at ranked 13,390' Baldy Cinco. Continue southeast on the ridge. Descend northeast to a saddle and head east to the next highpoint (N37 57.330' / W107 6.182').

5.3 Arrive at ranked Point 13162. Continue east along the ridge, and drop just below the ridge crest to the right to pick up the trail (N37 57.222' / W107 4.752').

5.7 Join the Colorado Trail at 12,520' and follow it north. This will be your exit point for the descent, after the next peak (N37 57.267' / W107 4.325').

5.9 Leave the trail and head north to the next summit (N37 57.364' / W107 4.169').

6.7 Arrive at ranked Point 13510. Retreat south to the Colorado Trail and descend to the mesa, past a small lake and then west on the trail (N37 57.978' / W107 4.236').

13.7 Arrive back at the trailhead (N37 56.395' / W107 9.518').

86 Wolf Creek Pass Peak: Treasure Mountain C

Elevation: 11,910'
Distinction: P1K, Ranked 11er
Class: 2; Class 1 for 3.2 miles, Class 2 to summit
Difficulty and skill level: Moderate; Intermediate
Approximate moving time: 5 hours
Distance: 7.0 miles round-trip
Elevation trailhead to summit: 10,850' to 11,910' (+1,060'); about 2,500' round-trip
Terrain: Dirt trail, bushwhack, dirt and grass
Restrictions: No camping at trailhead
Amenities: Trailhead toilet and picnic tables; backcountry camping; campgrounds located along US 160; services in South Fork and Pagosa Springs
Trailhead: Wolf Creek Trailhead
Trails: Continental Divide National Scenic Trail, Treasure Mountain Trail #565, off-trail East Slope
Maps: DeLorme Page 88 A3, A4, Page 78 E4; USGS Wolf Creek Pass
County: Mineral
Land status: San Juan National Forest, (970) 247-4874, www.fs.usda.gov/sanjuan; Pagosa Ranger District, (970) 264-2268

Finding the trailhead: From South Fork, take US 160 West for 19 miles, or from Pagosa Springs, take US 160 East for 23 miles, to the top of Wolf Creek Pass. Park in the large lot on the south side of the road (GPS: N37 28.977' / W106 48.122').

The Peak

Treasure Mountain lies south of Wolf Creek Pass, in the Treasure Mountain Roadless Area. The roadless designation protects the plot of land between the Weminuche Wilderness to the north and the South San Juan Wilderness to the south. The pass is likely named for timber wolves that roamed the mountainside many years ago, now gone. Treasure Mountain is named for the legendary cache of gold, discovered and later buried in three locations by a French expedition that was commissioned by Napoléon Bonaparte in the 1700s. All but one member of the group were killed by Utes before they could retrieve the treasure. Many stories surround the mystery of the lost gold on Treasure Mountain, but it has never been recovered. You'll have excellent views of the South San Juan Mountains from the top of the peak.

The Climb

Wolf Creek Pass is open year-round, and the parking area at the summit is kept plowed through the winter for backcountry visitors who enjoy skiing, sledding, and snowshoeing the trails. The hike takes you south along the Continental Divide, then west at Treasure Pass, where you'll lose a lot of elevation before climbing back up to Treasure Mountain. Wolf Creek Pass Ski Area lies on the east side of the Divide, while the west side is crisscrossed with hiking trails and mountain biking paths.

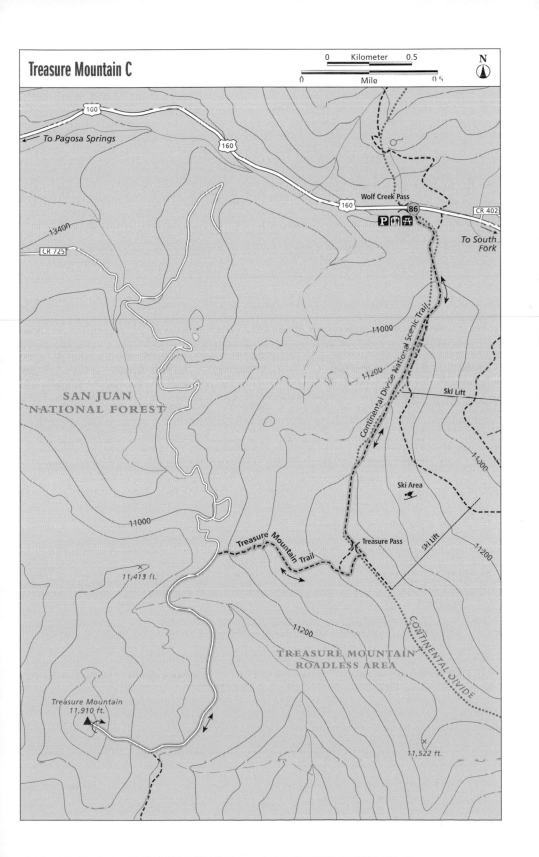

Treasure Mountain C

0   Kilometer   0.5

0   Mile   0.5

N

160

To Pagosa Springs

160

Wolf Creek Pass

86

CR 402

To South Fork

P

13400

CR 725

11000

11200

Continental Divide National Scenic Trail

Ski Lift

SAN JUAN NATIONAL FOREST

11300

Ski Area

11000

Treasure Mountain Trail

Treasure Pass

Ski Lift

11200

11,413 ft.

11200

TREASURE MOUNTAIN ROADLESS AREA

CONTINENTAL DIVIDE

Treasure Mountain 11,910 ft.

11,522 ft.

Grassy slopes lead up to the summit of Treasure Mountain C. PHOTO BY JOHN KIRK

Miles and Directions

0.0 Begin at the trailhead (10,850') and hike south on the Continental Divide Trail. Hike through the forest and past the ski area on the left, and bear right at the trail junction and over 11,742' Treasure Pass.

1.4 Turn right onto Treasure Mountain Trail and go west. The trail drops to about 10,900' and rises back up, then joins a dirt road and bends southwest (N37 27.886' / W106 48.323').

3.2 Depart the trail on the right and bushwhack northwest, up the slope to the summit (N37 27.260' / W106 49.180').

3.5 Arrive at ranked 11,910' Treasure Mountain. Return the way you came (N37 27.354' / W106 49.435').

7.0 Arrive back at the trailhead (N37 28.977' / W106 48.122').

87 South San Juan Mountains Highpoint: Summit Peak

Elevation: 13,300' (NAVD88 13,306')
Distinctions: South San Juan Mountains High-
point, Archuleta County Highpoint, South San
Juan Wilderness Highpoint, Prominence 100,
P2K, Ranked 13er
Class: 2; Class 1 for first 3.3 miles, Class 2
to summit
Difficulty and skill level: Moderate;
Intermediate
Approximate moving time: 5 hours
Distance: 7.4 miles round-trip
Elevation trailhead to summit: 10,900' to
13,306' (+2,406')
Terrain: Dirt trail, grass, and tundra;
creek crossing

Restrictions: No bicycles or motor vehicles
on trail; dogs must be on leash or under voice
command; follow wilderness regulations
Amenities: Campsites at nearby Stunner
Campground; backcountry camping; services
in Del Norte, Alamosa, and Pagosa Springs
Trailhead: Treasure Creek Trailhead
Trail: Treasure Creek Trail #710, Continental
Divide National Scenic Trail, off-trail South-
east Slope
Maps: DeLorme Page 89 B5; USGS Summit Peak
County: Archuleta
Land status: Rio Grande National Forest, (719)
852-5941, www.fs.usda.gov/riogrande; Conejos
Peak Ranger District, (719) 274-8971, South
San Juan Wilderness, www.wilderness.net

Finding the trailhead: From Del Norte, take US 160 West for 0.5 mile and turn left onto Pinos
Road. Drive 6.8 miles and join CR 14, then go 21.7 miles and turn left onto unpaved FR 380.
Go 7.7 miles on FR 380, to Lake De Nolda and Lake Annella, and turn right onto FR 243 (signed
"Dead End"), then continue 2.8 miles to the trailhead on the left side of the road. The trail starts
about 0.1 mile before the road dead-ends (GPS. N37 21.857' / W106 40.112').

The Peak

Summit Peak sits in the South San Juan Mountains, a spur of the San Juans proper
located in the South San Juan Wilderness. The range starts at Wolf Creek Pass and follows the backbone of the Continental Divide southeast to the New Mexico border
at Cumbres Pass. Other county highpoints in view from the top of Summit Peak
include ranked 13ers Conejos Peak, to the southeast in Conejos County, and Bennett
Peak, to the northeast in Rio Grande County.

The Climb

Access to Summit Peak may be limited seasonally by snow on the dirt road and
snowmelt at the creek crossing, so it's best to do this peak well after the spring thaw,
on dry roads and calm waters, and when high drifts have melted out of the forest. The
Treasure Creek Trail crosses the creek early on and heads south; however, there is a
waterfall located about 0.1 mile west of the end of FR 243, and a social trail lures hikers in that direction. Treasure Creek Falls is worth a visit, but if you choose to go that
way, be prepared for a creek crossing past the falls, and bushwhack southwest for 0.4

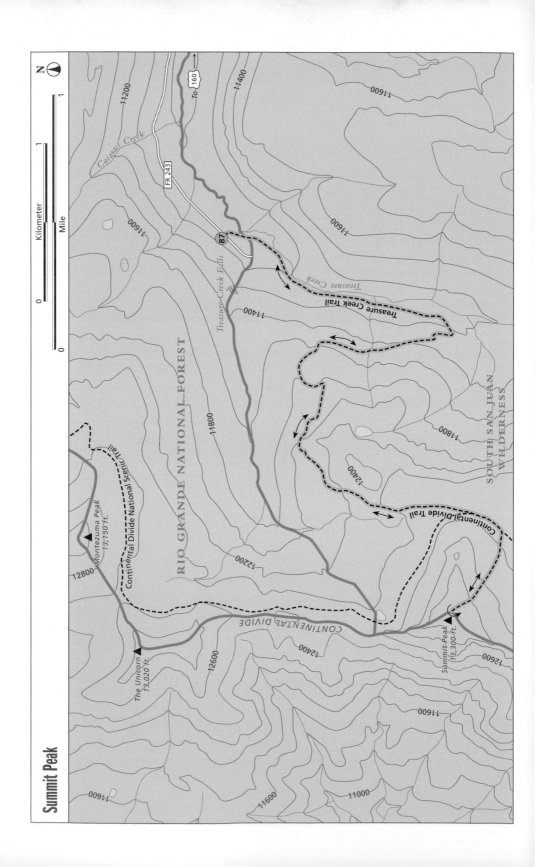

Summit Peak

To 160

To

11400

11600

11200

Cataract Creek

FR 243

11600

87

Treasure Creek Falls

11400

Treasure Creek Trail

Treasure Creek

11600

SOUTH SAN JUAN WILDERNESS

11800

12400

11800

Continental Divide Trail

RIO GRANDE NATIONAL FOREST

11800

12200

Continental Divide National Scenic Trail

Montezuma Peak
13,150 ft.

12800

The Unicorn
13,020 ft.

12600

12400

CONTINENTAL DIVIDE

12200

Summit Peak
13,300 ft.

12600

11600

11600

11600

11000

11400

0   Kilometer   1

0   Mile   1

N

The daunting northeast face of Summit Peak belies its gentler southeast access, in the South San Juan Mountains. PHOTO BY JOHN KIRK

mile to pick up the good trail. The falls, and the fact that this route cuts roughly 1.4 miles off your hike in each direction, make it an attractive alternative. A compromise is to take the official trail to the peak, then cut off to the waterfall on your return trip, at about 11,750' (N37 21.589' / W106 40.695'), take a break at Treasure Creek Falls (N37 21.813' / W106 40.330'), and then follow the creek east back to the road. If you're looking for more peaks to do in the area, the Continental Divide Trail sidles up alongside the east side of Summit Peak, and you can take it north to ranked 13ers "The Unicorn" and Montezuma Peak, and cut off the trail at about 1.5 miles and 2 miles, respectively, to head up to the summits of each peak.

Miles and Directions

0.0 Begin at the trailhead (10,900') and hike south. Cross Treasure Creek, then continue south-southwest on the trail.

1.1 Switchback north (right) at about 11,200'. Summit Peak is due west of this point, but if you stay on the trail north through the forest, you can avoid a very steep, direct ascent. The trail is faint and may be hard to follow, but continue until 11,600' where the trail bends to the northwest (N37 21.030' / W106 40.561').

1.9 Follow the trail as it curves west at 11,750', emerges from the trees, and then turns south. This is the cutoff point to Treasure Creek Falls, if you choose that route on your return. The daunting northeast face of Summit Peak comes into view ahead, but you will be accessing it via the easier southeast slopes (N37 21.589' / W106 40.695').

3.2 At the end of the Treasure Creek Trail, go south-southwest on the Continental Divide Trail (N37 20.965' / W106 41.365').

3.3 Depart the trail on the right at 12,560' and head up the grassy southeast slope of the peak (N37 20.856' / W106 41.441').

3.7 Arrive at ranked 13,306' Summit Peak. Return the way you came (N37 21.036' / W106 41.808').

7.4 Arrive back at the trailhead (N37 21.857' / W106 40.112').

88 Cimarron Range Highpoint: Coxcomb Peak

Elevation: 13,656' (NAVD88 13,662')
Distinctions: Cimarrron Range Highpoint, Bicentennial, Ranked 13er
Class: 5.6; Class 1 for first 3.5 miles, mixed Class 2, 3, 4, and 5 to summit, plus rappels
Difficulty and skill level: Very Strenuous; Advanced
Approximate moving time: 8 hours
Distance: 8.4 miles round-trip
Elevation trailhead to summit: 10,760' to 13,662' (+2,902'); about 3,800' round-trip
Terrain: Dirt trail, grass, scree, talus, and rock; creek crossings; exposure, risk of rockfall
Recommended extra gear: Backpack large enough to carry all gear, food, water, sports drink, extra clothing, plus your hiking shoes/boots; rock-climbing shoes, helmet, harness, personal anchor system (PAS) with locking carabiner, belay device (ATC) with locking carabiner, 165' (50 m) rope, set of wired stoppers, cams to 2½", 20' of webbing for belay anchor and rappels, rappel rings, and slings

Restrictions: Road closed seasonally; last 1.5 miles to trailhead may require high-clearance 4WD vehicle; trail closed to bicycles and motorized vehicles; follow wilderness regulations
Amenities: Seasonal camping at Beaver Lake, Big Cimarron, and Silver Jack Campgrounds; dispersed camping along FR 860 and at trailhead; backcountry camping; services in Gunnison, Montrose, and Ridgway
Trailhead: West Fork Trailhead
Trail: West Fork Trail #240, off-trail South Slope and West Ridge
Maps: DeLorme Page 67 E5, D5; USGS Wetterhorn Peak
Counties: Hinsdale, Ouray
Land status: Uncompahgre National Forest, (970) 874-6600, www.fs.usda.gov/gmug; Ouray Ranger District, (970) 240-5300; Uncompahgre Wilderness, www.wilderness.net

Finding the trailhead: From US 50, about 43 miles west of Gunnison and 21 miles east of Montrose, take Cimarron Road South for 17.6 miles, past Silver Jack Reservoir. Continue south on unpaved CR 858 for 8.9 miles, to Owl Creek Pass, then go 0.3 mile and turn right onto FR 860 / West Fork Road. Or from US 550 about 12 miles north of Ouray and 24 miles south of Montrose, take CR 10 / Owl Creek Road East for 14.9 miles to Owl Creek Pass, go 0.3 mile, and continue straight onto FR 860 / West Fork Road, then drive 3.3 miles on FR 860, to the trailhead. Note that the final 1.5 miles require a high-clearance vehicle to get over rocks and a stream crossing (GPS: N38 6.667' / W107 33.168').

The Peak

The Cimarron Range trends south from Owl Creek Pass to Wetterhorn Basin, along the West, Middle, and East Forks of the Cimarron River. Coxcomb Peak rises sharply above the range, a two-tiered fortress of stone, about 800' long from east to west, guarded by steep cliffs and cracked with chimneys that provide access to the summit.

Coxcomb Peak rises up like a fortress in the Cimarron Range. PHOTO BY KIEFER THOMAS

The peak was climbed by Henry Buchtel and a party of seven on August 16, 1929, after a failed attempt two days earlier by Dwight Lavender and Forrest Greenfield, who were not carrying a rope and were thwarted by the final notch to the summit. The name "Cimarron" is from the Spanish *cimarrón*, which means "wild or unruly," and the highpoint, Coxcomb Peak, is named for its resemblance to a rooster's crowning glory. From the summit, you will have views southeast, and turning clockwise, of ranked 14ers Uncompahgre Peak and Wetterhorn Peak, with ranked 13er Matterhorn Peak wedged between them; south across Wetterhorn Basin to ranked 13er Blackwall Mountain; southwest to ranked Point 12148; west to ranked 12er "U4"; northwest to unranked 12er "U5"; north to ranked 13ers Redcliff, "Fortress Peak," and Precipice Peak; and east to ranked 13ers "Heisshorn" and "El Punto."

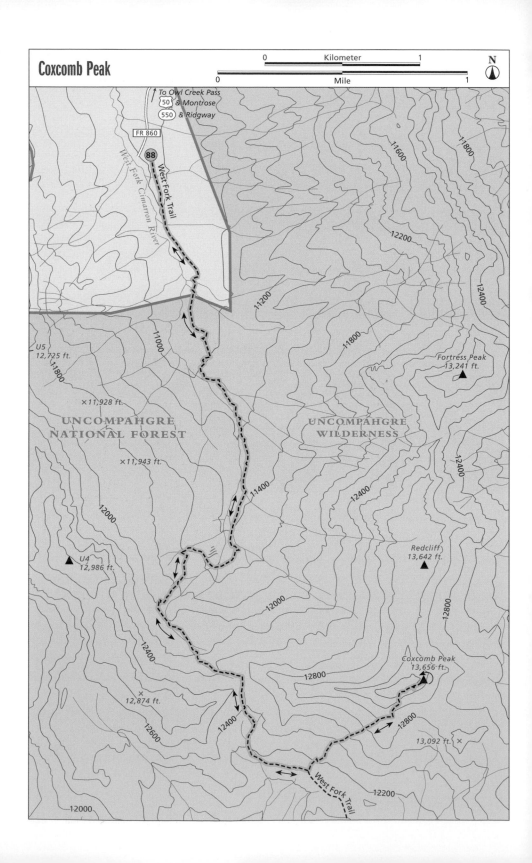

Coxcomb Peak

0   Kilometer   1

0   Mile   1

N

To Owl Creek Pass
50 & Montrose
550 & Ridgway

FR 860

88

West Fork Trail

West Fork Cimarron River

11,600

11,800

12,200

12,400

11,200

11,000

U5
12,725 ft.

11,800

11,800

×11,928 ft.

Fortress Peak
13,241 ft.

UNCOMPAHGRE
NATIONAL FOREST

UNCOMPAHGRE
WILDERNESS

×11,943 ft.

11,400

12,400

12,400

12,000

U4
12,986 ft.

Redcliff
13,642 ft.

12,000

12,800

12,400

×
12,874 ft.

Coxcomb Peak
13,656 ft.

12,800

12,800

13,092 ft. ×

12,600

12,400

West Fork Trail

12,200

12,000

The Climb

Coxcomb Peak is a technical climb, so you will need gear, skills, and—if you are not comfortable leading on trad—a solid climber or a guide to set up safe protection, top ropes, and rappels. The peak is best climbed in mid to late summer, when the chimney is most likely to be dry and free of ice. Most climbers reverse the route back to the trailhead, but alternatively, there is a rap station on the north side of the summit, requiring a steep descent on a loose, exposed Class 4 slope to the anchors. Be sure you have enough rope (you'll need a second 50 meter) and can locate the route before you pull your rope from the gap that you came up.

Miles and Directions

0.0 Begin at the trailhead (10,760') and hike south along the east banks of the West Fork of the Cimarron River, over a dry creek bed and across several creeks.

0.7 Enter the forest and continue south along the creek (N38 6.097' / W107 32.998').

2.0 Hike past a waterfall and cross to the west side of the creek. The route steepens and rises to a pass on Coxcomb's west ridge (N38 5.209' / W107 32.901').

3.0 Top out on the pass at 12,500'. Descend southeast into Wetterhorn Basin, below the south slopes of Coxcomb Peak (N38 4.773' / W107 32.783').

3.5 Depart the trail at about 12,100' and hike northeast on grass slopes toward the southwest ridge of the peak (N38 4.483' / W107 32.501').

3.9 At the top of the ridge, hike north over talus, toward the summit block. Scramble up Class 4 rocks for about 10' to an obvious chimney (N38 4.676' / W107 32.150').

4.0 Begin Class 5 climbing. Pitch 1: Climb the 50', Class 5 chimney, protecting with slings, cams, and nuts as needed. This section can be difficult if ice, snow, or any moisture exists. At the top, go north to exit the chimney, then east along the narrow ridge to an abrupt notch (N38 4.748' / W107 32.125').

4.1 Pitch 2: Sling rocks to set up a 20' rappel into the notch, rap down, and leave the rope as a top rope for the Class 5.6 return ascent on this section. Scramble up the other side of the notch and cross the exposed ridge to the summit (N38 4.786' / W107 32.059').

4.2 Arrive at ranked 13,662' Coxcomb Peak. Return the way you came, top-roping the Class 5.6, 20' climb out of the notch, and setting up your rope at the top of the chimney to protect the 50' downclimb on that section (N38 4.806' / W107 32.010').

8.4 Arrive back at the trailhead (N38 6.667' / W107 33.168').

89 San Juan Mountains Highpoint: Uncompahgre Peak

Elevation: 14,309' (NAVD88 14,315')
Distinctions: San Juan Mountains Highpoint, Hinsdale County Highpoint, Uncompahgre Wilderness Highpoint, Centennial, Prominence 100, P4K, Ranked 14er
Class: 2; Class 1 for first 3.3 miles, Class 2 to summit
Difficulty and skill level: Strenuous; Advanced
Approximate moving time: 5 hours
Distance: 7.4 miles round-trip (15.4 miles round-trip from lower trailhead)
Elevation trailhead to summit: 11,450' to 14,315' (+2,865'); about 3,000' round-trip
Terrain: Dirt trail, scree, and talus; risk of rockfall
Recommended extra gear: Helmet for rockfall; crampons or microspikes and ice axe if snow exists
Restrictions: Alpine Loop Scenic Byway is closed seasonally; access to upper trailhead requires high-clearance 4WD vehicle; 2 stream crossings exist on upper portions of road and may require very high clearance; trail closed to bicycles and motor vehicles; dogs must be on leash or under voice command; follow wilderness regulations
Amenities: Dispersed trailhead and backcountry camping; services in Lake City
Trailhead: Nellie Creek Trailhead
Trail: Nellie Creek Trail #877, off-trail South Ridge
Maps: DeLorme Page 67 E6; USGS Uncompahgre Peak
County: Hinsdale
Land status: Uncompahgre National Forest, (970) 874-6600, www.fs.usda.gov/gmug; Gunnison Ranger District–Lake City Office, (970) 641-0471 or (970) 944-2500; Uncompahgre Wilderness, www.wilderness.net

Finding the trailhead: From Lake City, take Gunnison Avenue / CO 149 South for 0.3 mile and turn right onto First Street, then go 0.1 mile and turn left onto CR 2/20. The road becomes the unpaved Alpine Loop Scenic Byway. Drive 5.1 miles and bear right at the sign for Nellie Creek, onto CR 2A/23. Low-clearance vehicles should park here (GPS: N38 1.231' / W107 24.046'), while other vehicles can continue. Go 2.3 miles and bear left to switchback south and stay on CR 2A/23, then go another 1.7 miles to the upper trailhead (GPS: N38 3.761' / W107 25.323').

The Peak

Uncompahgre Peak rises in the San Juan Mountains west of Lake City. The peak is named for the nearby Uncompahgre River, which was named by Ute natives, translated to mean "red lake." From the top of Uncompahgre, you'll be surrounded by San Juan summits, most notably the Cimarron Range northwest, ranked 13er Matterhorn Peak and ranked 14er Wetterhorn Peak west, and ranked 14ers Handies Peak, Redcloud Peak, and Sunshine Peak south.

The Climb

Like all Colorado 14ers, Uncompahgre Peak is climbed year-round, but winter snows require an extremely long approach, and winter gear and skills. In summer months,

A Colorado mountaineer takes in views from the summit of San Juan Mountains highpoint Uncompahgre Peak. PHOTO BY BILL MIDDLEBROOK

mountaineers flock to Lake City to climb the peak, along with other nearby 14ers Wetterhorn, Handies, Redcloud, and Sunshine Peaks, and Centennials Point 13832 and Point 13811. Since it is a long drive from major metro areas, you might want to reserve a motel room or cabin in town, or camp at the trailhead. The route described here begins at the upper trailhead; if you do not have a high-clearance vehicle, you'll have to park at the lower trailhead at 9,310', which will add 8 round-trip miles and 2,140' of elevation to your climb. Uncompahgre Peak is a step up from the typical 14,000' peak walk-up. Although there is a trail most of the way to the top, the terrain can be challenging, and there is a danger of rockfall on the steep west slope. Keep an eye on the weather on the hike back to the trailhead, where you're on open terrain with no protection from lightning for several miles. If storms do approach, spread your party out so that if anyone is struck, others can come to their aid. In good snow conditions, Uncompahgre may be climbed via West Face Couloirs.

Uncompahgre Peak

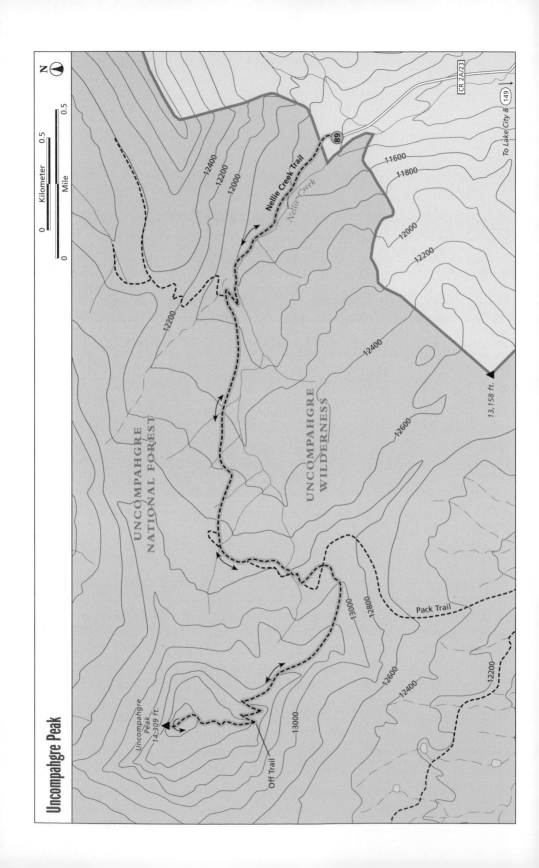

UNCOMPAHGRE NATIONAL FOREST

UNCOMPAHGRE WILDERNESS

Uncompahgre Peak 14,309 ft.

Off Trail

Pack Trail

Nellie Creek Trail

Nellie Creek

13,158 ft.

To Lake City & 149

CR 2A/23

89

N

Kilometer
0   0.5

Mile
0   0.5

11600
11800
12000
12200
12400
12600
12800
13000
13000
12600
12400
12200
12400
12200
12000

Miles and Directions

0.0   Begin at the upper trailhead (11,450') and hike northwest along Nellie Creek.

0.8   Switchback northeast on the trail (N38 4.074' / W107 26.005').

0.9   Switchback west at a trail junction, and continue west on the Nellie Creek Trail (N38 4.112' / W107 25.936').

1.9   The trail heads south, then northwest across the basin, with Uncompahgre Peak in view. Stay on the good trail as it sweeps gently up the southeast slopes (N38 4.128' / W107 27.004').

3.1   Start switchbacks to the south ridge of Uncompahgre Peak (N38 4.059' / W107 27.625').

3.3   Reach the crest of the south ridge at 13,800' and go north, curving around to the west face of the peak. The trail fades here and climbs steeply for about 150' on scree and talus (N38 4.028' / W107 27.715').

3.5   Top out on the steep slope and head north, then northeast, and finally northwest on easier terrain, toward the obvious summit ahead (N38 4.129' / W107 27.723').

3.7   Arrive at ranked 14,315' Uncompahgre Peak. Return the way you came (N38 4.301' / W107 27.723').

7.4   Arrive back at the trailhead (N38 3.761' / W107 25.323').

90 Sneffels Range Highpoint: Mount Sneffels

Elevation: 14,150' (NAVD88 14,156')
Distinctions: Sneffels Range Highpoint, Ouray County Highpoint, Mount Sneffels Wilderness Highpoint, Centennial, Prominence 100, P3K, Ranked 14er
Class: 2+; Class 1 for first 2.2 miles, mixed Class 2 and 2+ to summit
Difficulty and skill level: Strenuous; Advanced
Approximate moving time: 5 hours
Distance: 5.4 miles round-trip
Elevation trailhead to summit: 11,350' to 14,156' (+2,806')
Terrain: Dirt road, scree, and talus; exposure, risk of rockfall
Recommended extra gear: Helmet; crampons or microspikes and ice axe if snow exists
Restrictions: Camp Bird Road requires 4WD beyond fork at 7 miles and may be inaccessible in snow; Yankee Boy Basin Road is closed and gated seasonally and opens around May 1; trail closed to bicycles and motor vehicles; dogs must be on leash or under voice command; follow wilderness regulations
Amenities: Trailhead toilet; backcountry camping; services in Ouray
Trailhead: Yankee Boy Basin Lower Trailhead
Trails: Blue Lakes Trail #201, Mount Sneffels Trail #204, off-trail Lavender Col and Southeast Ridge
Maps: DeLorme Page 66 E3; USGS Mount Sneffels, Telluride
County: Ouray
Land status: Uncompahgre National Forest, (970) 874-6600, www.fs.usda.gov/gmug; Ouray Ranger District, (970) 240-5300; Mount Sneffels Wilderness, www.wilderness.net

Finding the trailhead: From Ouray, take US 550 South onto the Million Dollar Highway and turn right onto unpaved Camp Bird Road / CR 361. Go 4.7 miles and bear right onto Camp Bird Road / CR 26 / FR 853, and continue another 2.2 miles to a fork. If you are driving a passenger car, you will have to park here and hike up the road. Bear right onto 4WD Yankee Boy Basin Road / FR 853.1B, and continue for another 0.8 mile to the lower trailhead. Some vehicles can continue another 1.7 miles to more parking (GPS: N37 59.301' / W107 45.934').

The Peak

The Sneffels Range is a subrange of the San Juan Mountains located west of Ouray and visible from the Dallas Divide on CO 62, between Ridgway and Placerville, and along US 550, between Ridgway and Ouray. The highpoint, Mount Sneffels, was climbed by the Hayden Survey party on September 10, 1874. Its name is derived from *Snæfell*, an Icelandic volcano known to Jules Verne fans as the entrance to the earth's core in his novel *Journey to the Center of the Earth*. The standard route on Mount Sneffels is on the Mount Sneffels Trail, which climbs the steep, loose south slopes of the peak via Lavender Col, named for Dwight Lavender (1911–1934), Colorado mountaineer, author, and founder of the San Juan Mountaineers. From the top of Mount Sneffels, you can see as far west as the La Sals of Utah, but closer in, enjoy views clockwise, from the south, of ranked 13ers Mount Emma, Gilpin Peak, Dallas Peak, "T O," and "S 4"; north into Blaine Basin; and east of ranked 12er "Reconnoiter Peak" and ranked 13ers Mount Ridgway, Cirque Mountain, Teakettle Mountain, and Potosi Peak.

Mount Sneffels rises up in the Sneffels Range near Ouray. PHOTO BY BILL MIDDLEBROOK

The Climb

Mount Sneffels is usually climbed spring through fall, due to a very long approach and avalanche danger in winter snow. The standard route via the Mount Sneffels Trail and Lavender Col is steep, loose, and generally unpleasant as an ascent unless it's filled with consolidated late-spring snow, when avalanche danger is low, and enjoyed with the aid of crampons and ice axe. However, it's the easiest route and requires little route-finding. An alternate route to Mount Sneffels lies along the Southwest Ridge, gained with a hike to Blue Lakes Pass and a Class 3 ascent through a convoluted maze of rocky gullies. The Southwest Ridge demands good route-finding skills, so if you are a novice, find a more experienced climber to join you or hire a professional guide. Otherwise, take the standard route, described here. The Southwest Ridge may be accessed from the Yankee Boy Basin Trailhead or from the west on the Blue Lakes Trail (#201), beginning at a trailhead on East Dallas Creek Road (FR 851.3B). This trailhead is also the starting point for the Blaine Basin Trail (#203), leading to the north side of the peak. In consolidated snow, experienced mountaineers use this trail to access the Snake Couloir, the westernmost couloir on the north side of the peak, and technical climbers may access the North Buttress—located to the left of Snake Couloir—this way as well. Mount Sneffels' north-facing couloirs are extremely

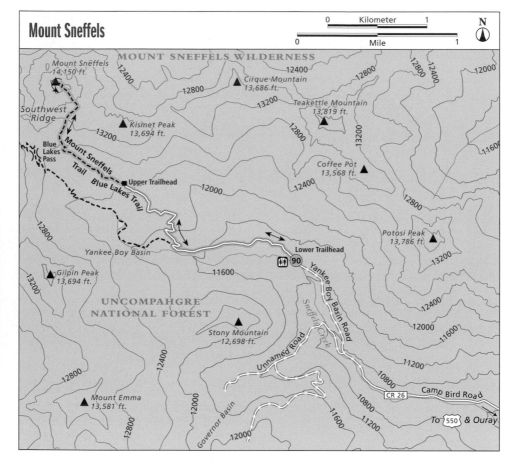

Mount Sneffels

dangerous in unconsolidated snow or when dry, and the North Buttress is loose and runout. Many of the lower peaks in this area are more technically difficult than Mount Sneffels, so do your homework if you plan on adding them to the agenda.

Miles and Directions

0.0 Begin at the lower parking area (11,350') and hike northwest on the 4WD road, bearing right at two junctions, at 0.1 and 0.4 mile, and continuing west and north on the road.

1.7 At the upper parking area (12,460'), take the Blue Lakes Trail northwest (N37 59.693' / W107 47.091').

2.1 Bear right at the junction to get on the Mount Sneffels Trail. The trail fades through talus, then climbs steeply north, then north-northeast up the Lavender Col to a gully high on the southeast slope (N37 59.842' / W107 47.416').

2.5 Just below the top of the gully, turn left and climb northwest through a rocky notch. Continue northwest toward the summit (N38 0.108' / W107 47.404').

2.7 Arrive at ranked 14,156' Mount Sneffels. Return the way you came (N38 0.227' / W107 47.540').

5.4 Arrive back at the trailhead (N37 59.301' / W107 45.934').

91 Ophir Pass Peak: Lookout Peak

Elevation: 13,661' (NAVD88 13,667')
Distinctions: Bicentennial, Ranked 13er
Class: 3; Class 2 to basin, mixed Class 2 and 3 to summit
Difficulty and skill level: Moderate; Advanced
Approximate moving time: 5 hours
Distance: 1.8 miles round-trip
Elevation trailhead to summit: 11,680' to 13,667' (+1,987')
Terrain: Dirt, grass, scree, talus, boulders, and slabs; exposure, risk of rockfall
Recommended extra gear: Helmet

Restrictions: Ophir Pass Road closed seasonally and may require high-clearance 4WD year-round
Amenities: Seasonal campgrounds along US 550; services in Silverton
Trailhead: Pullout on Ophir Pass Road
Trail: Off-trail South Slopes and South Ridge
Maps: DeLorme Page 76 B3; USGS Ophir
Counties: San Juan, San Miguel
Land status: San Juan National Forest, (970) 247-4874, www.fs.usda.gov/sanjuan; Columbine District–Silverton Public Lands Center, (970) 884-2512

Finding the trailhead: From Silverton, take US 550 North for 5 miles and turn left onto unpaved FR 679 / Ophir Pass Road. Go 3.2 miles and bear left to stay on Ophir Pass Road, then continue for 0.8 mile to a pullout on the right side of the road, 0.2 mile east of the top of the pass (GPS: N37 51.098' / W107 46.559').

The Peak

Lookout Peak sits south of Telluride, at Ophir Pass. The 11,814' pass lies along a scenic 4WD route connecting the Million Dollar Highway to the old mining town of Ophir, and Lookout Peak rises north of the pass. *Ophir* is a biblical reference to one source of King Solomon's treasures, and while you may not find any gold, silver, or precious gems on the peak, you will treasure the views from the summit. Looking south, and turning clockwise, ranked 13er South Lookout Peak lies on the other side of the pass, with the summits of Ice Lake Basin—most notably, Ulysses S. Grant ("U.S. Grant") Peak—beyond, to the southwest; the San Joaquin Ridge, Silver Mountain, and the Ophir Needles sprawl to the west, with the San Miguels and "the Wilsons" beyond; north, the peaks of Telluride rise above Bridal Veil Basin, with the Sneffels Range and Cimarrons beyond; east are the San Juan Mountains above Lake City; and the Grenadiers, Needle Mountains, and West Needles lie to the southwest.

The Climb

Lookout Peak is usually climbed in the summer months, when the route is dry and the road is open. Ophir Pass Road on the east side of the pass is navigable in a standard high clearance 4WD vehicle, but the west side is much more rugged, with an exposed half-mile section that narrows to a single lane. The climb to the peak is short

Lookout Peak stands north of Ophir Pass. PHOTO BY JOHN KIRK

but requires a lot of scrambling on loose rock that is exposed in places, and the route-finding will likely slow you down as well, so start early on a good-weather day, wear a helmet, and be prepared to take your time on this peak.

Miles and Directions

0.0 Begin at the pullout (11,680') and hike north on a steep climber's trail, past a small lake on the left, and into a basin east of the south ridge of the peak.

0.5 From the basin at 12,480', hike northwest on grassy slopes, staying left of loose scree and talus, to the south ridge. Don't be tempted to shortcut the route over scree and talus to the right of the grass, or you will be in for a tedious ascent (N37 51.462' / W107 46.689').

0.6 Scramble over rocks and up slabs to the ridge (12,600'), and head north on mixed Class 2 and 2+ terrain and over occasional exposed Class 3 sections, sticking to the ridge crest

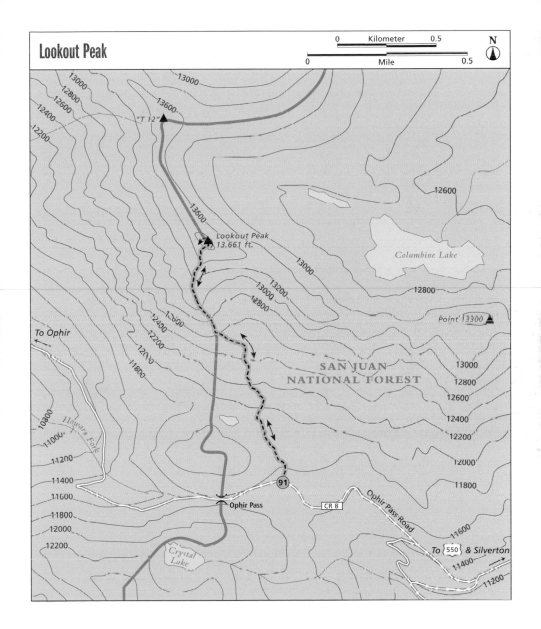

Lookout Peak

0 Kilometer 0.5

0 Mile 0.5

N

13000
12800
12600
12400
12200
13000
13600
"T 12"
12600
13600
Lookout Peak
13,661 ft.
13000
13200
13000
12800
12800
Columbine Lake
Point 13300
To Ophir
12400
12600
12200
12000
11800
SAN JUAN
NATIONAL FOREST
13000
12800
12600
12400
12200
12000
Howard Fork
10800
11000
11200
11400
11600
11800
12000
12200
91
Ophir Pass
CR 8
Ophir Pass Road
11800
11600
To 550 & Silverton
11400
11200
Crystal
Lake
11200

for the most solid rock. This is a very steep climb that eases at about 13,100', less than 0.25 mile from the summit, and with the most difficult section ahead. Veer to the right side of the summit block and carefully make your way up loose and exposed Class 3 ledges, and head west to the highpoint (N37 51.495' / W107 46.780').

0.9 Arrive at ranked 13,667' Lookout Peak. Return the way you came (N37 51.738' / W107 46.812').

1.8 Arrive back at the trailhead (N37 51.098' / W107 46.559').

92 Lizard Head Pass Peak: Black Face

Elevation: 12,147' (NAVD88 12,153')
Distinction: Ranked 12er
Class: 1
Difficulty and and skill level: Moderate; Beginner
Approximate moving time: 4 hours
Distance: 7.0 miles round-trip
Elevation trailhead to summit: 10,280' to 12,153' (+1,873'); about 2,200' round-trip
Terrain: Dirt and tundra
Restrictions: No bicycles or motor vehicles allowed on trail; follow wilderness regulations

Amenities: Trailhead toilet; backcountry camping; seasonal campgrounds along CO 145; services in Telluride
Trailhead: Lizard Head Trailhead
Trail: Lizard Head Trail #505
Maps: DeLorme Page 76 B2; USGS Mount Wilson
Counties: Dolores, San Miguel
Land status: Uncompahgre National Forest, (970) 874-6600, www.fs.usda.gov/gmug; Norwood Ranger District, (970) 327-4261; Lizard Head Wilderness, www.wilderness.net

Finding the trailhead: From Telluride, take CO 145 South for 15 miles to the top of Lizard Head Pass and turn right into the rest area. Continue another 0.1 mile, past the toilets, turning right and then left to trailhead parking (GPS: N37 48.753' / W107 54.508').

The Peak

Lizard Head Pass rises to 10,222' on the San Juan Skyway south of Telluride. The pass and the wilderness area are named for ranked peak Lizard Head, a rocky tower that sits northwest of the pass and is one of the most difficult 13ers in the state. A much easier destination, Black Face, lies between the pass and the peak, and a sweeping trail across the broad south slopes and east ridge ensures a pleasant hike to the top. Views from the San Miguel Mountains' Black Face are surprisingly good. The high San Miguels rise in the northwest, including 14ers El Diente, Mount Wilson, and Wilson Peak and 13er Gladstone Peak, while to the northeast, Lookout Peak and South Lookout Peak at Ophir Pass and the Sneffels Range at Ouray are in view. A spectacular array of summits line the eastern sky: the high peaks at Ice Lake Basin, including U.S. Grant Peak, Pilot Knob, Golden Horn, and Vermilion Peak.

The Climb

After you've summited Black Face, you can return the way you came up, or continue west on the trail for a closer look at Lizard Head. Make a loop of it by taking the Cross Trail south down to CO 145, where a railroad grade route parallels the highway, leading you back to your car at the top of the pass.

Black Face

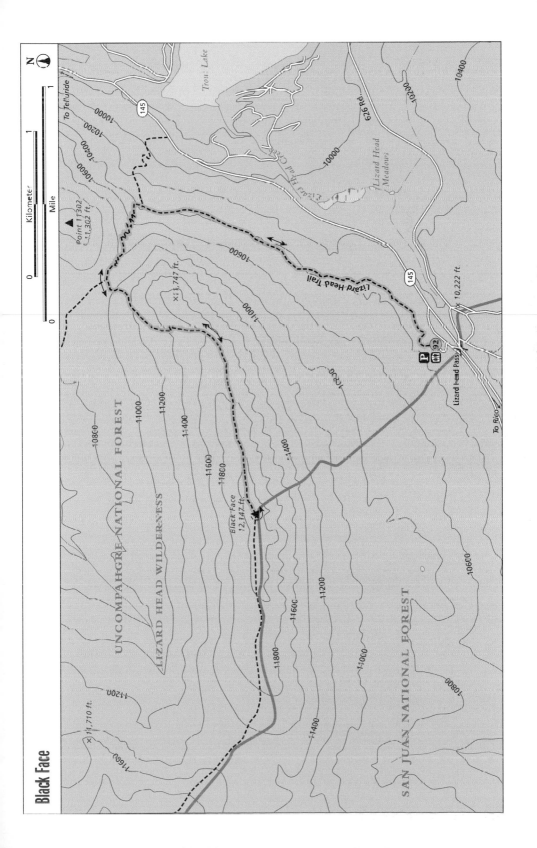

To Telluride ?

N

0   Kilometer   1

0   Mile   1

Trout Lake

145

10000

10200

10400

10600

Point 11302
11,302 ft.

626 Rd.

Lizard Head Meadows

10000

10200

10400

x 11,747 ft.

11000

10600

Lizard Head Trail

145

x 10,222 ft.

UNCOMPAHGRE NATIONAL FOREST

LIZARD HEAD WILDERNESS

10800

11000

11200

11400

11600

11800

Black Face
12,147 ft.

10800

11000

11200

11400

11600

11800

x 11,710 ft.

11600

11200

P

92

Lizard Head Pass

To Rico

SAN JUAN NATIONAL FOREST

10600

10800

10000

Black Face rises above Wilson Meadows at Lizard Head Pass, with views of the high peaks at Ice Lake Basin, east. PHOTO BY JOHN KIRK

Miles and Directions

0.0   Begin at the trailhead (10,280') and hike north-northeast across the south slopes of the peak.

1.6   At the trail junction (10,400'), start switchbacks west-northwest to the saddle southwest of ranked Point 11302 (N37 49.872' / W107 53.842').

2.1   Go left (west) at the junction with the Sheep Trail (10,850') to remain on the Lizard Head Trail, and go south-southwest up to the east ridge of the peak and west to the summit (N37 49.972' / W107 54.157').

3.5   Arrive at ranked 12,153' Black Face. Return the way you came (N37 49.432' / W107 55.293').

7.0   Arrive back at the trailhead (N37 48.753' / W107 54.508').

93 San Miguel Mountains Highpoint: Mount Wilson

Elevation: 14,246' (NAVD88 14,252')

Distinctions: San Miguel Mountains Highpoint, Dolores County Highpoint, Lizard Head Wilderness Highpoint, Centennial, Prominence 100, P4K, Ranked 14er

Class: 4; Class 1 for first 6.5 miles, mixed Class 2 and 3 to summit, with a few Class 4 moves the last 100 feet

Difficulty and skill level: Very Strenuous; Advanced

Approximate moving time: 10 hours

Distance: 14.8 miles round trip

Elevation trailhead to summit: 9,350' to 14,252' (+4,902'); about 5,500' round-trip

Terrain: Dirt trail, scree, talus, ledges, and boulders; creek crossing; exposure, risk of rockfall

Recommended extra gear: Helmet; crampons or microspikes and ice axe if snow exists; GPS; a short rope is recommended if you are uncomfortable with exposure

Restrictions: FR 535 is seasonal and closed far below the trailhead in winter, and may be blocked by snow into spring; no bicycles or motor vehicles allowed on trail; follow wilderness regulations

Amenities: Backcountry camping; seasonal campgrounds along CO 145; services in Telluride

Trailhead: Navajo Trailhead

Trail: Navajo Lake Trail #635, off-trail Northeast Ridge

Maps: DeLorme Page 76 B2, B1; USGS Mount Wilson, Dolores Peak

County: Dolores

Land status: San Juan National Forest, (970) 247-4874, www.fs.usda.gov/sanjuan; Dolores Public Lands Office, (970) 882-7296; Lizard Head Wilderness, www.wilderness.net

Finding the trailhead: From Telluride, take CO 145 South for 17.4 miles, over Lizard Head Pass, and turn right onto unpaved Dunton Road / CR 38 / FR 535. Drive 7.3 miles, past the Kilpacker Trailhead, and turn right toward the Navajo Trailhead. Continue 0.1 mile to a large parking area at the trailhead (GPS: N37 48.320' / W108 3.790').

The Peak

Mount Wilson is the highpoint of the San Miguel Mountains, located at the western edge of the San Juan Mountains near Lizard Head Pass. The peak is one of the most difficult 14,000' mountains in the state, due to a steep approach on talus slopes and some airy Class 4 moves near the top. The range is named for Saint Michael, a biblical archangel who is referred to as a "great prince who stands up for the children of your people." The peak is named for Hayden Survey topographer A. D. Wilson, who climbed it in 1874. You will have to stand up to a lot of loose rock, and a thrilling summit finish, to gain the highpoint of the mountain, where you will be treated to views of nearby San Miguel ranked 14er Wilson Peak; unranked 14ers El Diente Peak, "West Wilson," and "South Wilson"; and Centennial Gladstone Peak. The La Platas lie south, beyond the lowly Ricos, the Sneffels Range is north, and the Needles lie to the east.

Mount Wilson is one of the most technically demanding 14ers in Colorado.
PHOTO BY BILL MIDDLEBROOK

The Climb

Mount Wilson is best climbed from late spring to early fall, when the slopes are avalanche-free, the rock is dry, and the trailhead is accessible. Although the Class 4 finish tends to scare off some mountaineers, the real danger lies in the loose talus that you will have to climb through to get to the ridge. Wear a helmet and don't climb over other people, and bring an ice axe to cross snowfields that tend to linger here way too long. The good trail to Navajo Lake goes fast, and you should consider backpacking up to the lake and camping for the night at one of the many dispersed sites, saving the summit and descent back to the trailhead for day two. Summit day is tough, with a lot of elevation on rugged terrain. The crux of the climb is an exposed step, but even a short-legged person can make the stretch, with solid rock to hang onto on each side.

The Navajo Lake approach from the west, described here, is the most popular trail into the basin, but there are other options, including the Woods Lake approach from the northwest; the Rock of Ages approach from Silver Pick Basin, north; and the Kilpacker approach from the south. Keep in mind that all of these approaches require off-trail travel on difficult and dangerous terrain, and people have lost their lives on these peaks.

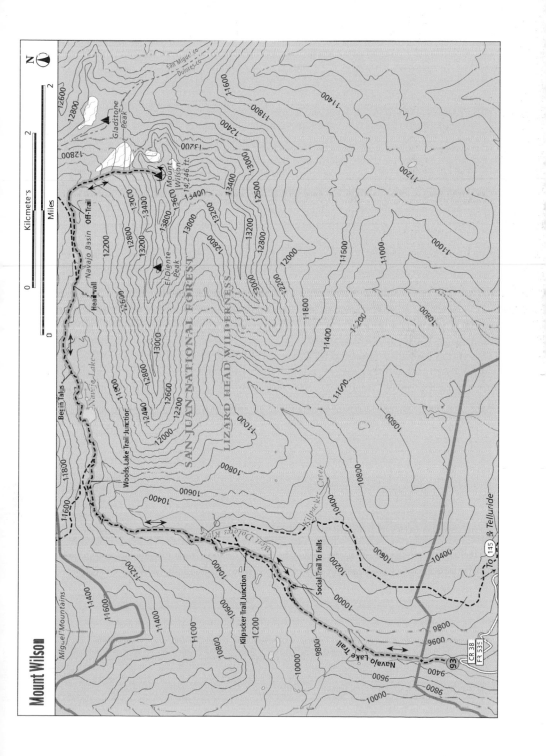

Mount Wilson

Miles and Directions

0.0 Begin at the trailhead (9,350') and hike north on the Navajo Lake Trail, past the first junction with the Groundhog Trail on your right.

0.2 Pass a bridge where the Groundhog Trail cuts off to your left, and continue north on the Navajo Lake Trail. Enter the Lizard Head Wilderness (N37 48.474' / W108 3.797').

0.8 Cross a bridge to the west side of the West Dolores River at 9,500', go up a short steep section, and continue north-northeast along the river and out of the trees. Dolores Peak appears to the west, and El Diente is in view to the north (N37 48.918' / W108 3.673').

1.7 Pass a social trail on the right (9,800') that leads down to West Dolores River Falls and Kilpacker Creek Falls. Continue on the Navajo Lake Trail (N37 49.408' / W108 3.111').

2.2 Pass the junction with the Kilpacker Trail, on the right, and head back into the trees. The Navajo Basin Falls appear in the cliffs to the right of the trail, and you will emerge from the forest again, go back into the trees, and come out again as the trail bends east (N37 49.746' / W108 2.800').

4.0 Pass the junction with the Woods Lake Trail, on the left at 11,200', and stay right to descend back into the forest (N37 50.844' / W108 2.194').

4.5 Meet the west edge of Navajo Lake (11,154'), with Gladstone and El Diente in view beyond. Follow the trail around the left (north) side of the lake (N37 50.856' / W108 1.700').

4.7 At the east end of the lake, continue east through the brush (N37 50.895' / W108 1.536').

5.0 Come out of the brush at 11,250' and begin climbing steeply on scree and talus, trending east toward a headwall (N37 50.959' / W108 1.253').

5.8 Reach the top of the headwall (11,900') and continue east on the talus trail (N37 50.958' / W108 0.477').

6.5 The trail continues, bending to the north at 12,280' toward Wilson Peak. Leave the trail here and head east, descending to the bottom of Navajo Basin. Cross the stream (N37 50.996' / W107 59.747').

6.6 Head south-southeast and ascend a rocky ridge that leads up toward the northeast ridge of the peak. Stay to the right of snowfields that may exist here year-round (N37 50.990' / W107 59.668').

7.0 Continue south along the right of the snowfield (13,050'). Gladstone Peak is due east of you, and El Diente is west (N37 50.677' / W107 59.470').

7.2 Reach a buttress and climb up (13,600'). The northeast ridge is in view directly ahead, but you will bear to the right and cross some rock ribs. Look for cairns in this section and don't climb too high, too soon. Look for the gully that leads up to the ridge (N37 50.521' / W107 59.459').

7.3 Climb up the talus gully and then follow the rocky crest of the ridge south. You will come to a very exposed section, and the crux of the climb. A huge boulder blocks the route, and you will have to hang on and step around it, to the left, to another rocky ledge with a lot of air under your feet. This is exposed, but not a big stretch. Once you are on the other side, scramble up some exciting Class 3 and 4 rock, and bear left to the summit.

7.4 Arrive at ranked 14,252' Mount Wilson. Return the way you came (N37 50.346' / W107 59.490').

14.8 Arrive back at the trailhead (N37 48.320' / W108 3.790').

94 Molas Pass Peak: Snowdon Peak

Elevation: 13,077' (NAVD88 13,082')
Distinctions: Prominence 300, P1K, Ranked 13er
Class: 3; Class 1 for first 2.3 miles, mixed Class 2 and 3 to summit
Difficulty and skill level: Moderate; Advanced
Approximate moving time: 4 hours
Distance: 6.0 miles round-trip
Elevation trailhead to summit: 10,760' to 13,082' (+2,322'); about 2,400' round-trip
Terrain: Dirt trail, scree, talus, boulders, and slabs; exposure, risk of rockfall
Recommended extra gear: Helmet
Restrictions: Andrews Lake Trailhead is closed seasonally, requiring a hike from a pullout on US 550 during snowy season; no bicycles or motorized vehicles allowed on trail; follow wilderness regulations
Amenities: Restrooms at trailhead; backcountry camping; seasonal campgrounds along US 550; services in Silverton and Durango
Trailhead: Andrews Lake Trailhead
Trails: Crater Lake Trail #623, unofficial "Snowdon Peak Trail," off-trail Northeast Ridge
Maps: DeLorme Page 76 C4; USGS Snowdon Peak
County: San Juan
Land status: San Juan National Forest, (970) 247-4874, www.fs.usda.gov/sanjuan; Columbine District–Silverton Public Lands Center, (970) 884-2512; Weminuche Wilderness, www.wilderness.net

Finding the trailhead: From Silverton, take US 550 South for 7 miles (0.9 mile past Molas Pass), or from Durango, take US 550 North for 40 miles (6.2 miles past Coal Bank Pass). On the east side of the road, turn south onto unpaved Andrews Lake Road and continue 1 mile to parking at the trailhead. If the lot is full or if you are camping, park in the upper lot on the left side of Andrews Lake Road and make the short hike to the lower lot near the lake, and the trailhead (GPS: N37 43.685' / W107 42.657').

The Peak

Red Mountain, Molas, and Coal Bank Passes rise up along the Million Dollar Highway on US 550 between Silverton and Durango. The northernmost pass is surrounded by Red Mountains 1, 2, and 3, but legal access to the peaks there is tricky due to private property in the Red Mountain Mining District. Molas and Coal Bank Passes have parking areas, trailheads, and short approaches to some wonderful San Juan Mountains. At Molas Pass, a recreation area at Andrews Lake provides easy access to the West Needle Mountains, a 9-mile-long stretch of high 12ers and low 13ers, wedged between the highway and the Animas River, in the Weminuche Wilderness. The West Needles line up in two groups, with unranked 12er "N 1," ranked 13ers Snowdon Peak and "N 2," and ranked 12er "N 3" in the northern group, east of Crater Lake, and ranked 13ers North Twilight Peak and Twilight Peak, unranked 13er South Twilight Peak, ranked 12er Point 12932, ranked 13er West Needle Mountain, and unranked 12er "N 4" situated south of the lake.

Snowdon Peak rises in the West Needle Mountains south of Molas Pass. PHOTO BY JOHN KIRK

Molas Pass is named for nearby Molas Lake, derived from the Spanish *mulas*, or mules. The origin of the name of the peak here is not known, although it may have been influenced by the more famous Mount Snowdon, the highpoint of Wales. From the top, you will have views of Jura Knob and Engineer Mountain to the west at Coal Bank Pass, while to the south and east, across the Animas River gorge, the Needle Mountains at Chicago Basin and the Grenadier Range line up in a towering delight of lofty summits.

The Climb

Mount Snowdon is climbed year-round, but exposure along the ridge makes a summer climb highly desirable and strongly recommended. You'll want a helmet and some experience on stiff Class 3 before attempting this peak. Climbers sometimes do the whole stretch of the northern group of the West Needle Mountains in one trip,

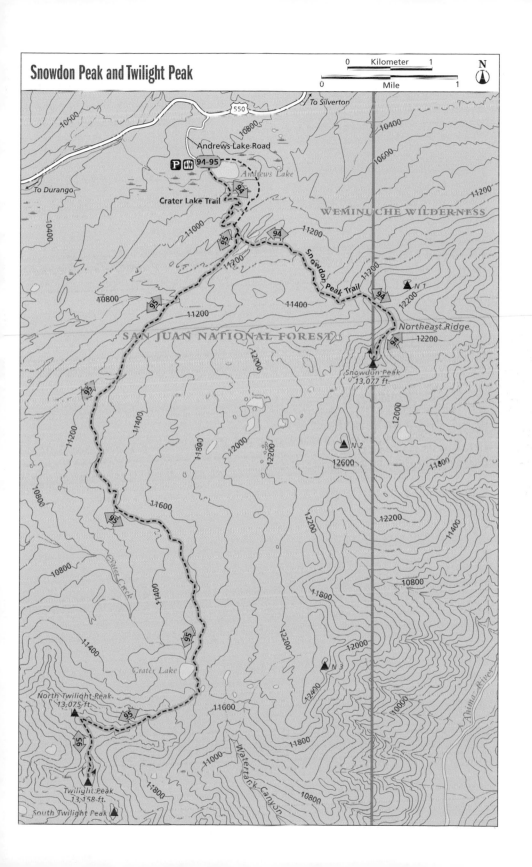

Snowdon Peak and Twilight Peak

0 Kilometer 1

0 Mile 1

N

To Silverton

550

Andrews Lake Road

94-95

Andrews Lake

94

Crater Lake Trail

To Durango

95

94

WEMINUCHE WILDERNESS

Snowdon Peak Trail

94

N 1

Northeast Ridge

94

SAN JUAN NATIONAL FOREST

95

95

Snowdon Peak
13,077 ft.

N 2

95

Otter Creek

95

Crater Lake

N 3

North Twilight Peak
13,075 ft.

95

95

Watertank Canyon

Twilight Peak
13,158 ft.

South Twilight Peak

Animas River

with a scrambly, mixed Class 3 and 4 traverse, dotted with stiff notches and exposed ridges, a descent to Crater Lake, and a hike back to the trailhead on the Crater Lake Trail. Be sure you are equipped with experience, route-finding skills, and good weather before attempting a traverse in the West Needles. Snowdon Peak may also be climbed on the west side via the Class 4 West Buttress or snow-climbed via "Naked Lady Couloir."

Miles and Directions

0.0 Begin at the trailhead (10,760') located at the southwest end of the parking area and hike south, bearing right to hike around the west side of Andrews Lake.

0.1 At the southwest end of the lake, hike southeast on the Crater Lake Trail.

1.1 Depart the trail on the left (11,200') and get onto the unofficial "Snowdon Peak Trail." Hike east across the meadow and between two lakes (N37 43.264' / W107 42.438').

1.5 Enter the forest and continue southeast on the trail (N37 43.182' / W107 42.032').

1.7 Hike south across a meadow.

1.9 Hike east through the forest (N37 42.908' / W107 41.782').

2.3 Hike southeast upslope (11,920') toward the Snowdon–"N 1" saddle.

2.6 Follow the climber's trail west of the ridge (12,520'), heading south to the northeast ridge (N37 42.747' / W107 41.185').

2.8 Gain the ridge (12,600') and go southwest on rocky and very exposed ledges along the east (left) side of the northeast ridge of the peak. The route narrows above Naked Lady Couloir on the west face, then eases to the summit (N37 42.654' / W107 41.159').

3.0 Arrive at ranked 13,082' Snowdon Peak. Return the way you came (N37 42.465' / W107 41.330').

6.0 Arrive back at the trailhead (N37 43.685' / W107 42.657').

95 West Needle Mountains Highpoint: Twilight Peak

See map on page 333.

Elevation: 13,158' (NAVD88 13,163') Twilight Peak; 13,075' North Twilight Peak

Distinctions: West Needle Mountains Highpoint, Prominence 100, P2K, Ranked 13er (Twilight Peak); Ranked 13er (North Twilight Peak)

Class: 3; Class 1 to Crater Lake, mixed Class 2 and 2+ to North Twilight Peak, mixed Class 2 and 3 to Twilight Peak

Difficulty and skill level: Very Strenuous; Advanced

Approximate moving time: 10 hours

Distance: 14.2 miles round-trip

Elevation trailhead to summit: 10,760' to 13,163' (+2,403'); about 4,200' round-trip

Terrain: Dirt trail, grass, scree, talus, crags, and ledges; exposure, risk of rockfall

Recommended extra gear: Helmet, ice axe, GPS

Restrictions: Andrews Lake Trailhead is closed seasonally, requiring a hike from a pullout on US 550; no bicycles or motorized vehicles allowed on trail; follow wilderness regulations

Amenities: Restrooms at trailhead; backcountry camping; seasonal campgrounds along US 550; services in Silverton and Durango

Trailhead: Andrews Lake Trailhead

Trail: Crater Lake Trail #623, off-trail East Ridge to North Twilight Peak and traverse on North Ridge of Twilight Peak

Maps: DeLorme Page 76 D4, C4; USGS Snowdon Peak

County: San Juan

Land status: San Juan National Forest, (970) 247-4874, www.fs.usda.gov/sanjuan; Columbine District–Silverton Public Lands Center, (970) 884-2512; Weminuche Wilderness, www.wilderness.net

Finding the trailhead: From Silverton, take US 550 South for 7 miles, or from Durango, take US 550 North for 40 miles. On the east side of the road, turn onto unpaved Andrews Lake Road and drive 1 mile to parking. If the lot is full, or if you are camping, park in the upper lot on the left side of Andrews Lake Road, and make the short hike to the trailhead at the southwest end of the lower parking area (GPS: N37 43.685' / W107 42.657').

The Peak

Twilight Peak tops the West Needle Mountains west of the Animas River between Silverton and Durango. From the summit, you'll have views east to the Grenadier Range, southeast to the Needle Mountains, northwest to the San Miguel Mountains, west to Engineer Mountain, and southwest to the La Plata Range.

The Climb

Twilight Peak is best climbed in summer when the trailhead is open and the rock is dry. In winter, ice and snow make the ridge traverse from North Twilight to Twilight difficult, so you'll need proper gear and skill, and you'll also want to avoid the steep, avalanche-prone north face of North Twilight Peak on your approach. For your descent from the top of Twilight Peak, you can return the way you came, or descend Twilight

The west ridge of North Twilight Peak is visible from Crater Lake near Molas Pass.
PHOTO BY JOHN KIRK

Peak's south ridge to unranked 13er South Twilight Peak, and take the southeast ridge to a saddle and talus slopes east off the peak. Unnamed couloirs on the north and east faces of the peaks from North Twilight to Point 12932 have been climbed in consolidated snow, with proper gear, skill, and a bit of scrambling to the rocky summits.

Miles and Directions

0.0 Begin at the 10,760' trailhead and hike around the west side of Andrews Lake, and southeast on the Crater Lake Trail.

1.1 Pass the unofficial "Snowdon Peak Trail" on the left at 11,200' and continue south on the Crater Lake Trail. Climb switchbacks in and out of the trees, past small ponds and marshy areas (N37 43.264' / W107 42.438').

5.3 Go around the left (east) side of Crater Lake at 11,620' and south on a faint trail, then angle southwest up grass slopes (N37 40.536' / W107 42.779').

6.0 At about 12,100', climb west to gain the rocky east ridge of North Twilight Peak (12,200'), and climb the ridge west-northwest to the summit (N37 40.174' / W107 43.132').

6.6 Arrive at ranked 13,075' North Twilight Peak. Descend southeast to a shallow saddle, then climb the ridge south toward Twilight Peak (N37 40.158' / W107 43.704').

7.0 The ridge cliffs out at a notch at about 13,000', the crux of your climb. Find a safe exit point to descend on the right, to the west side of the ridge, then climb up a gully, cross the gap, and climb up Class 3 rock to regain the ridge (N37 39.870' / W107 43.612').

7.1 Arrive at ranked 13,163' Twilight Peak. Return the way you came (N37 39.774' / W107 43.626').

14.2 Arrive back at the trailhead (N37 43.685' / W107 42.657').

96 Coal Bank Pass Peak: Engineer Mountain B

Elevation: 12,968' (NAVD88 12,973')

Distinctions: Prominence 200, P1K, Ranked 12er

Class: 3; Class 1 to Pass Creek Trail / Engineer Mountain Trail junction; mixed Class 2 and 3 to summit

Difficulty and skill level: Moderate; Advanced

Approximate moving time: 4 hours

Distance: 6.2 miles round-trip

Elevation trailhead to summit: 10,680' to 12,973' (+2,293')

Terrain: Dirt trail, scree, talus, boulders, and slabs; exposure, risk of rockfall

Recommended extra gear: Helmet

Restrictions: No bicycles or motor vehicles allowed on trail; dogs must be on leash or under voice command

Amenities: Restrooms are located 200' south of trailhead turnoff, on east side of US 550 at Coal Bank Pass rest area; backcountry camping; seasonal campgrounds along US 550; services in Silverton and Durango

Trailhead: Pass Creek Trailhead

Trails: Pass Creek Trail #500, off-trail Northeast Ridge

Maps: DeLorme Page 76 C3; USGS Engineer Mountain

County: San Juan

Land status: San Juan National Forest, (970) 247-4874, www.fs.usda.gov/sanjuan; Columbine District–Silverton Public Lands Center, (970) 884-2512

Finding the trailhead: From Silverton, take US 550 South for 14 miles, or from Durango, take US 550 North for 34 miles. Turn west at the signed dirt road for the Pass Creek Trail, to parking at the trailhead (GPS: N37 41.954' / W107 46.742').

The Peak

Engineer Mountain stands prominently above 10,640' Coal Bank Pass south of Silverton on the San Juan Skyway Scenic Byway, its east–west ridgeline rising up to pyramid-like summits at each end. "Coal Bank" references Colorado's mining history, and the peak was named for the Army Corps of Engineers, who surveyed the area in the late 1800s. You'll have views of surrounding San Juan Mountains from the top, including the West Needle Mountains to the east and the Rico Mountains to the west.

The Climb

Engineer Mountain affords easy access from US 550 and a well-worn approach trail. The craggy upper sections can be tricky in ice or snow, so use your best judgment and avoid wet or icy rock if you climb the peak out of season. Some climbers will want a spotter or a rope for protection on the Class 3 climb to the summit area and for the descent. Stay clear of the sheer north face and unstable rock glacier.

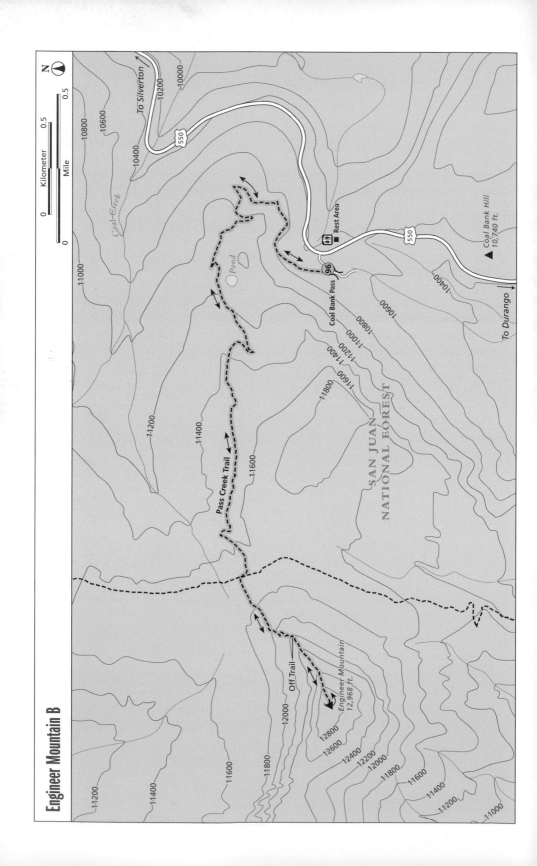

Engineer Mountain B

N

Kilometer
0   0.5

Mile
0   0.5

To Silverton

Coal Creek

550

10000
10200
10400
10600
10800
11000

Rest Area

96
Coal Bank Pass

550

Coal Bank Hill
10,740 ft.

To Durango

10400

10600
10800
11000
11200
11400
11600
11800

SAN JUAN
NATIONAL FOREST

Pond

11200

11400

11600

Pass Creek Trail

Off Trail

Engineer Mountain
12,968 ft.

11600

11800

12000

12800
12600
12400
12200
12000
11800
11600
11400
11200
11000

11200
11400

Engineer Mountain shows its sheer north face, west of Coal Bank Pass near Silverton.
PHOTO BY JOHN KIRK

Miles and Directions

0.0   Begin at the 10,680' trailhead located at the north end of the parking area and hike north, contour east, and follow switchbacks west across the grassy slopes and into the forest.

1.1   Pass a small lake to the left of the trail at 11,170', with Engineer Mountain in view above the trees (N37 42.302' / W107 46.786').

2.0   Emerge from the trees at 11,520' and cross the meadow (N37 42.253' / W107 47.564').

2.4   Meet the trail junction with the Engineer Mountain Trail, and the end of the official Pass Creek Trail (11,660'). Continue west-southwest on the use trail, toward the peak (N37 42.227' / W107 47.905').

2.5   Pass a large boulder at 11,800' and climb the steep scree and talus trail southwest toward the ridge (N37 42.190' / W107 48.015').

2.7   Continue up loose talus at 12,240' as the climber's trail narrows alongside the rocky lower rib of the northeast ridge (N37 42.072' / W107 48.131').

2.8   At 12,360', climb a Class 3, 10' crack section of rock and exit left, to the south side of the ridge. Locate the climber's trail over talus and scree, and hike west-southwest to the summit.

3.1   Arrive at ranked 12,973' Engineer Mountain. Return the way you came (N37 41.961' / W107 48.396').

6.2   Arrive back at the trailhead (N37 41.954' / W107 46.742').

97 Rico Mountains Highpoint: Blackhawk Mountain

Elevation: 12,681' (NAVD88 12,686')
Distinctions: Rico Mountains Highpoint, Prominence 200, P1K, Ranked 12er
Class: 2; Class 1 for most of route, Class 2 to summit
Difficulty and skill level: Strenuous; Intermediate
Approximate moving time: 8 hours
Distance: 13.8 miles round-trip from Celebration Lake (Bolam Pass); 11.6 miles round-trip from Hotel Draw Road; 12.7 miles from end to end with car shuttle
Elevation trailhead to summit: 11,100' to 12,686' (+1,586'), about 4,100' round-trip from Bolam Pass; 10,450' to 12,686' (+2,236'), about 3,300' round-trip from Hotel Draw Road; about 3,400' from Bolam Pass to Hotel Draw Road with car shuttle

Terrain: Dirt trail, grass, and tundra; creek crossings
Restrictions: Access to either trailhead requires high-clearance 4WD
Amenities: Backcountry camping; campsites at numerous campgrounds along Hermosa Park Road (east) and Barlow Creek Road (north); services in Durango, Silverton, and Rico
Trailheads: Bolam Pass, Hotel Draw Road
Trail: Colorado Trail Segment 26, off-trail East Slope
Maps: DeLorme Page 76 C2, D2; USGS Hermosa Peak
County: Dolores
Land status: San Juan National Forest, (970) 247-4874, www.fs.usda.gov/sanjuan; Columbine Ranger District–Silverton Public Lands Center, (970) 884-2512

Finding the trailhead: Since a car shuttle is recommended, two trailheads are described.

Bolam Pass / Celebration Lake: From Durango, take US 550 North for 26 miles, or from Silverton, take US 550 South for 22 miles, and turn west onto Purgatory Boulevard. Go 0.5 mile and bear right onto Hermosa Park Road, then go 3.2 miles and turn left onto FR 578 / Hermosa Park Road. Drive 13.3 more miles to a pullout at Celebration Lake (GPS: N37 42.784' / W107 54.220').

Hotel Draw Road: From Durango, take US 550 North for 26 miles, or from Silverton, take US 550 South for 22 miles, and turn west onto Purgatory Boulevard. Go 0.5 mile and bear right onto Hermosa Park Road, then go 3.2 miles and continue onto unpaved FR 578 / Hermosa Park Road. Drive 7.4 miles and turn left onto CR 40 / FR 550. Go another 4.8 miles to the trailhead on the right side of the road (GPS: N37 38.458' / W107 57.953').

The Peak

The Rico Mountains are situated between the San Miguels, to the north, and the La Platas, south, in the San Juan National Forest near Rico. The area is popular with hikers and mountain bikers but sees few peakbaggers, due to the low stature of the peaks here. *Rico* is Spanish for "rich," a name adopted after silver was discovered in the area in 1879, and Blackhawk is the name of an Indian chief. The Colorado Trail, a popular, 486-mile-long hiking path through Colorado's mountains, slices through the Ricos, climbing over Blackhawk Pass and providing access to an abundance of 12ers along the way.

Blackhawk Mountain tops the Rico Mountains at Blackhawk Pass in the San Juan National Forest. PHOTO BY JOHN KIRK

The Climb

The Colorado Trail is hiked year-round, but access to the trailheads at each end of Section 26 may be limited seasonally, so plan on a summer trip to Blackhawk Mountain. The route can be done as an out-and-back from either trailhead, but this is a good opportunity to hike a particularly scenic section of the Colorado Trail, Section 26 from Bolam Pass to Hotel Draw Road, and so a car shuttle is recommended. The trail is also open to mountain bikers, so expect to share it. If you start at Celebration Lake, just south of Bolam Pass, you can camp at a nearby campground or at the lake, then drive one vehicle to the lower trailhead in the evening or morning, and return to the lake to start your hike or bike. You'll climb steeply to Blackhawk Pass above the Hermosa Creek drainage on the Hermosa Creek Trail section of the Colorado Trail, passing by ranked 12ers Hermosa Peak and Section Point to the left of the trail. These peaks are optional Class 2 ascents, with the approach to Hermosa Peak along the bouldery west ridge, to a saddle north of the summit. At the top of the pass, ranked 12er "R 1" sits east of highpoint Blackhawk Mountain, on the left side of the trail, and you can add that as well. You'll leave the trail for barely half a mile to do Blackhawk Mountain, then descend and hike the trail to the southern trailhead and your second vehicle.

Miles and Directions

0.0 Begin at the trailhead at Celebration Lake (11,100') and hike southwest on the Colorado Trail (N37 42.784' / W107 54.220').

1.6 Stay left at the trail junction and continue southwest, contouring below Hermosa Peak (N37 42.966' / W107 55.498').

3.0 Bear right at the trail junction and go west toward Section Point (N37 42.368' / W107 56.609').

3.9 Contour around the north side of Section Point at about 11,800', then continue southwest (N37 42.289' / W107 57.464').

6.6 Depart the trail, right, at 11,900' Blackhawk Pass and ascend the east slopes of Blackhawk Mountain (N37 41.135' / W107 58.935').

6.9 Arrive at ranked 12,686' Blackhawk Mountain. You can turn around here and return the way you came, but the following directions assume a continuation of your hike to the south end of Segment 26. Descend back to the trail (N37 41.118' / W107 59.254').

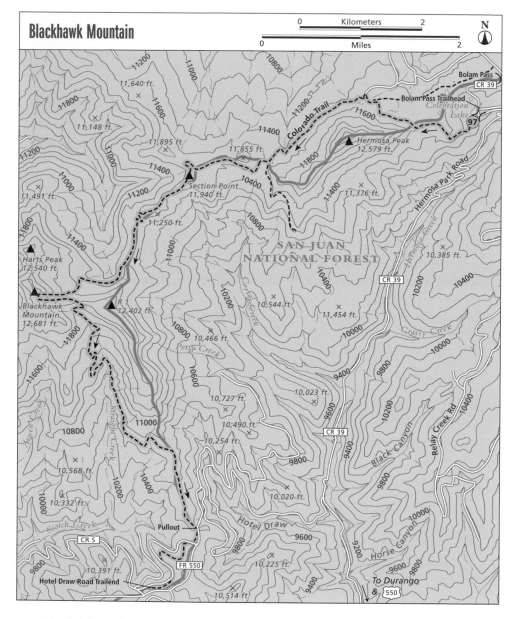

Blackhawk Mountain

0 — Kilometers — 2
0 — Miles — 2

N

Bolam Pass
CR 39
Bolam Pass Trailhead
Celebration Lake
97
11,640 ft.
11200
11000
10800
11,148 ft.
11800
11600
11400
Colorado Trail
11600
Hermosa Peak
12,579 ft.
11800
11,895 ft.
11,855 ft.
11200
11400
11400
11200
11000
Section Point
11,940 ft.
10400
10800
11,376 ft.
Hermosa Park Road
11,491 ft.
11000
11,250 ft.
11200
11000
10800
SAN JUAN
NATIONAL FOREST
10,385 ft.
CR 39
Harts Peak
12,540 ft.
11600
11400
R
12,402 ft.
Carriff Creek
10,544 ft.
11,454 ft.
10200
10400
Grassy Creek
10000
Blackhawk
Mountain
12,681 ft.
11800
10800
10,466 ft.
Petty Creek
10600
10,727 ft.
10,023 ft.
9400
9800
Relay Creek Rd
10400
11600
Aspen Creek
Straight Creek
11000
10800
10200
10,568 ft.
10400
10,490 ft.
10,254 ft.
9800
9600
CR 39
Black Canyon
10000
10,020 ft.
10000
9800
10,332 ft.
Scotch Creek
Pullout
Hotel Draw
9600
9200
Horse Canyon
9600
CR S
9800
FR 550
10,225 ft.
To Durango
& 550
10,391 ft.
Hotel Draw Road Trailend
10,514 ft.
9400

7.2 Rejoin the Colorado Trail and go south-southeast (N37 41.101' / W107 58.890').

8.0 Cross to the right (west) side of Straight Creek and hike south (N37 40.791' / W107 58.648').

8.9 Cross back to the east side of Straight Creek and hike south-southeast (N37 40.555' / W107 58.509').

11.4 The trail parallels Hotel Draw Road (FR 550) at 10,420' and passes a pullout on the road, then trends southwest (N37 38.987' / W107 57.414').

12.7 Arrive at the southern terminus of Segment 26 on Hotel Draw Road (N37 38.458' / W107 57.953').

342 The San Juan Mountains

98 Grenadier Range Highpoint: Vestal Peak

Elevation: 13,864' (NAVD88 13,870')
Distinctions: Grenadier Range Highpoint, Centennial, P1K, Ranked 13er
Class: 3; Class 1 to Vestal Basin, mixed Class 2 and 3 to summit
Difficulty and skill level: Very Strenuous, Advanced
Approximate moving time: 10 hours
Distance: 12.8 miles round-trip from train stop at Elk Park
Elevation trailhead to summit: 8,860' to 13,870' (+5,010'); about 5,600' round-trip
Terrain: Dirt trail, grass, scree, talus, ledges, and loose rock; creek crossings; exposure, risk of rockfall
Recommended extra gear: Helmet, GPS; cash or credit card for tickets and to buy snacks on train; exact train fare amount if you are hiking in and may be flagging train for ride out
Restrictions: Access to Elk Park Trailhead by train is seasonal, typically May–Oct, and requires a fee for you and your backpack; reservations are recommended; read all instructions on the Durango Train website for vital information on boarding times for backpackers;

train may be boarded in Durango, where there is a daily fee for parking your vehicle and no overnight camping at the parking lot, or you may board in Silverton and park your car several blocks from the train station, for free; alternate (free) access to trailhead is from Molas Park, adding 6.8 miles and 2,000' of elevation round-trip to your hike; no bicycles or motorized vehicles allowed on trail; follow wilderness regulations
Amenities: Restrooms and snack bar on train; backcountry camping; services in Durango
Trailhead: Elk Park Trailhead
Trails: Colorado Trail / Elk Creek Trail #503, unofficial "Vestal Creek Trail," off-trail South Face
Maps: DeLorme Page 77 C5, Page 76 C4; USGS Storm King Peak, Snowdon Peak
County: San Juan
Land status: San Juan National Forest, (970) 247-4874, www.fs.usda.gov/sanjuan; Columbine District–Silverton Public Lands Center, (970) 884-2512; Weminuche Wilderness, www.wilderness.net; Durango & Silverton Narrow Gauge Railroad, (970) 247-2733, www.durangotrain.com

Finding the trailhead: Take US 550 South or US 160 West to Durango and turn east onto W. College Drive, then go 0.1 mile and turn right onto Main Avenue and the train station on the left. Be sure to read all instructions for required early boarding times for backpackers on the Durango Train website to ensure you do not miss your train. Travel time to the Elk Park stop from Durango is about 3 hours (GPS: N37 43.925' / W107 39.562').

The Peak

The Grenadier Range lies east of the Animas River and north of the Needle Mountains, in the Weminuche Wilderness. The peaks here are like nothing you've seen in Colorado—stark blades of rock arched to the sky, running south-southeast from Garfield Mountain to The Guardian, and scattered north to Hunchback Pass. The highpoint, Vestal Peak, draws Centennial peakbaggers who come for the peak and stay for Arrow Peak, the Trinity Traverse, and other technical challenges hidden throughout the range.

The Climb

There are no roads into Vestal Basin, so a long backpack from Molas Pass, or a train ride from Durango or Silverton, is required. Call the railroad to make your train reservation, and let them know you will need to be on a train that stops at Elk Park. The north face of Vestal Peak, "Wham Ridge," is a popular Class 4 route, not described here. There are several options on the

The south face of Vestal Peak is accessed via the Vestal-Arrow saddle. PHOTO BY JOHN KIRK

Wham Ridge route, so if you prefer a more solid yet more difficult and exposed climb to the top of Vestal Peak, do your research first to get to the top, and follow the south face route described here for your descent. Vestal Peak is usually climbed in two days, with a train ride and hike in to the basin on the first day, and the climb, hike out, and train ride out on the second day. If you want to skip the train and backpack in from Molas Pass, you can camp at Molas Lake the night before and hike the Colorado Trail east down to the Animas River, which you'll cross on a bridge, then cross the tracks to pick up the trail to the Elk Park Trailhead. Molas Lake Park and Campground is located on US 550, south of Durango and just north of Molas Pass. There are lots of other great peaks in Vestal Basin, so if you have a few days, hang out and grab a few more summits. Just keep track of the time so you don't miss your train.

Miles and Directions

0.0 Begin at the Elk Park train stop (8,860') and locate the Colorado Trail on the east side of the tracks. Follow the good trail southeast.

0.6 Sign the Weminuche Wilderness register and continue southeast through the forest on Elk Creek Trail, along the north banks of Elk Creek (N37 43.612' / W107 39.120').

3.4 At the far (east) end of a large beaver pond (9,960'), locate a social trail that heads south, toward a large boulder. This is the cutoff to the unofficial "Vestal Creek Trail." Leave the Colorado Trail and head south, through some boulders (N37 43.247' / W107 36.457').

3.5 Pick up the Vestal Creek Trail and head south into the trees. The path becomes very faint and you may lose it in places, so a GPS helps to keep you on track (N37 43.172' / W107 36.450').

3.6 Cross Elk Creek at about 9,900'. The crossing can be difficult, and trekking poles are great for balance here. If you don't mind carrying the extra weight, a light pair of water shoes may also be useful (N37 43.083' / W107 36.380').

3.9 Emerge from the trees (10,250'), cross a stream, and head south back into the forest (N37 42.851' / W107 36.448').

4.9 Come back out of the trees and follow the creek southeast (N37 42.143' / W107 36.230').

5.1 Depart the Vestal Creek Trail (11,400') and go south on a climber's trail, and cross Vestal Creek. Hike south-southwest toward the Vestal-Arrow saddle, through talus and boulders (N37 42.028' / W107 36.006').

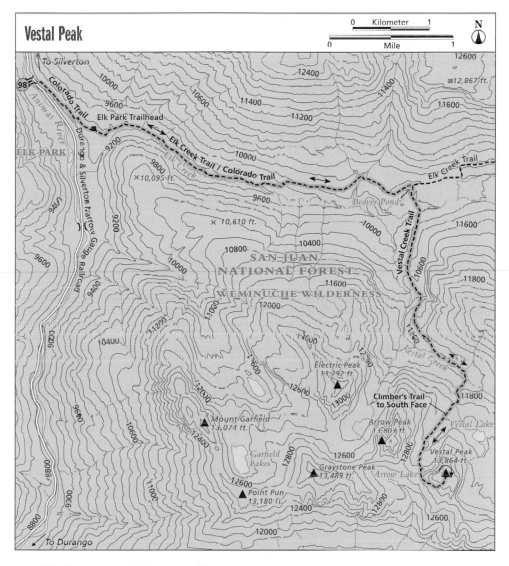

Vestal Peak

0 Kilometer 1

0 Mile 1

N

To Silverton

12600

12400

⊗12,867 ft.

Colorado Trail

Animas River

98

10000

10600

11400

11600

9600

Durango & Silverton Narrow Gauge Railroad

Elk Park Trailhead

11200

9200

Elk Creek Trail / Colorado Trail

10000

Elk Creek

Elk Creek Trail

ELK PARK

9800

×10,095 ft.

9400

9600

10000

9600

×10,610 ft.

Beaver Pond

10000

11600

Vestal Creek Trail

10400

10800

11800

10600

SAN JUAN
NATIONAL FOREST
WEMINUCHE WILDERNESS

11600

12000

10400

11200

11000

11600

Vestal Creek

11800

Electric Peak
13,292 ft.

Climber's Trail
to South Face

13000

12600

9600

12600

Mount Garfield
13,074 ft.

Arrow Peak
13,803 ft.

Vestal Lake

12800

10600

12800

Garfield
Lakes

Vestal Peak
13,864 ft.

12600

Graystone Peak
13,489 ft.

Arrow Lake

12800

12600

Point Pun
13,180 ft.

11000

12400

12600

9800

12000

To Durango

5.9 Continue south to the base of the scree slope.

6.0 Start the scree slope south.

6.1 Reach the 12,860' Vestal-Arrow saddle, and continue south-southeast to the south face. Begin the ascending traverse southeast on ledges (N37 41.358' / W107 36.369').

6.3 At about 13,200', climb steeply northeast on ledges toward a gully on the southeast face. Ascend north, following the line of the gully. There is serious danger of rockfall here, so avoid the loosest sections and climb to the left or right of the gully, on slightly more solid rock. At a ledge, go left and then up another short gully, then continue on rock northwest to the highpoint. Note your exit point here, so you can descend safely. A cairn is a good idea.

6.4 Arrive at ranked 13,870' Vestal Peak. Return the way you came (N37 41.362' / W107 36.168').

12.8 Arrive back at the trailhead (N37 43.925' / W107 39.562').

99 Needle Mountains Highpoint: Mount Eolus

Elevation: 14,083' (NAVD88 14,090')

Distinctions: Needle Mountains Highpoint, La Plata County Highpoint, Weminuche Wilderness Highpoint, Centennial, Prominence 100, P2K, Ranked 14er

Class: 3; Class 1 to Twin Lakes, mixed Class 2 and 3 to summit

Difficulty and skill level: Very Strenuous; Advanced

Approximate moving time: 12 hours

Distance: 17.4 miles round-trip

Elevation trailhead to summit: 8,200' to 14,090' (+5,890'); about 6,100' round-trip

Terrain: Dirt trail, grass, scree, talus, slabs, and ledges; creek crossings; exposure, risk of rockfall

Recommended extra gear: Helmet; crampons or microspikes and ice axe if snow exists; GPS; cash or credit card for tickets and to buy snacks on train; exact train fare amount if you are hiking in and may be flagging train for ride out

Restrictions: Access to Needleton by train is seasonal, typically May–Oct, and requires reservations and fee for you and your backpack; reservations are recommended, especially if you plan on boarding the train in Durango; read all instructions on the Durango Train website for vital information on boarding times for backpackers; train may be boarded in Durango, where there is a daily fee for parking your vehicle and no overnight camping at the parking lot, or you may board in Silverton and park your car several blocks from the train station, for free; alternate (free) access to trailhead is from Animas River Trail, adding much distance and elevation to your hike; no bicycles or motorized vehicles allowed on trail; fires not allowed in Chicago Basin; follow wilderness regulations

Amenities: Restrooms and snack bar on train; backcountry camping; services in Durango

Trailhead: Needleton

Trails: Needle Creek Trail #504, unofficial "Twin Lakes Trail," unofficial "Mount Eolus Trail," off-trail Northeast Ridge

Maps: DeLorme Page 77 D5, Page 76 D4; USGS Columbine Pass, Mountain View Crest, Snowdon Peak

County: La Plata

Land status: San Juan National Forest, (970) 247-4874, www.fs.usda.gov/sanjuan; Columbine District–Silverton Public Lands Center, (970) 884-2512; Weminuche Wilderness, www.wilderness.net; Durango & Silverton Narrow Gauge Railroad, (970) 247-2733, www.durangotrain.com

Finding the trailhead: Take US 550 South or US 160 West to Durango and turn east onto W. College Drive, then go 0.1 mile and turn right onto Main Avenue and the train station on the left. Be sure to read all instructions for required early boarding times for backpackers on the Durango Train website to ensure you do not miss your train. Travel time to the Needleton stop from Durango is about 2.5 hours (GPS: N37 38.012' / W107 41.568').

The Peak

The Needle Mountains lie east of the Animas River and south of the Grenadier Range, in the Weminuche Wilderness. There are no roads into the Needles, so climbers make long treks over mountain passes to reach the peaks here, or take the train from Silverton or Durango. The Needleton stop is popular with mountaineers as the access point to Chicago Basin, an alpine valley surrounded by numerous 13ers and some of the best 14,000' peaks in the state. Mount Eolus, the highpoint of the Needles, was named by the Hayden Survey for Aeolus, the Greek god of the winds. You won't want to climb Eolus on a windy day or in inclement weather, as the route from the saddle to the summit is exposed and a hasty retreat would be difficult. From the top, you'll have spectacular views of ranked 14ers Sunlight Peak and Windom Peak to the east; unranked 14er North Eolus to the north; the Needles at Ruby Basin to the northwest, including Centennial peaks Pigeon and Turret; and a string of 13ers to the south.

Mount Eolus stands high above Chicago Basin in the Weminuche Wilderness.
PHOTO BY BILL MIDDLEBROOK

The Climb

Mount Eolus isn't the hardest 14er in Colorado, but it is challenging, and if you enjoy Class 3 scrambling, it may become one of your favorites. If you're taking the train to the trailhead, you'll be doing the peak in the summertime. Mount Eolus is usually done in two days, with a train ride and camp on the first day, and the summit and hike back to the trailhead, and the train ride out, on the second. Be sure to call the railroad to make your train reservation, and let them know you will need to be on a train that stops at Needleton. Most climbers make a three-day or longer weekend of it, and summit Mount Eolus and North Eolus on one day and Windom and Sunlight on another. If you don't want to take the train, you can hike in via the Purgatory Trail and Animas River Trail, beginning at the old Purgatory Campground north of Durango. The route from Needleton is straightforward into Chicago Basin, where you should locate a campsite for the night, then scout out the trail ahead so you can find it in the morning, by headlamp. Goats and marmots are especially common and daring in Chicago Basin, so don't leave any food or soft items—boots, packs, or trekking poles with soft handles or straps—unattended, or they will get thoroughly chewed, and perhaps eaten.

At the far end of the basin you'll leave the Needle Creek Trail, which continues to Columbine Lake, and hike north up to Twin Lakes instead. Some climbers prefer to camp near the lakes (> 200'), rather than in the basin, for a shorter summit bid the next day. West of Twin Lakes, the climb gets a lot more exciting, with lots of scrambling, a rocky slab ramp, a catwalk, and a tangle of ledges to the airy summit. In good spring snow, the peak may also be climbed via the East, or "E," Couloir.

Mount Eolus

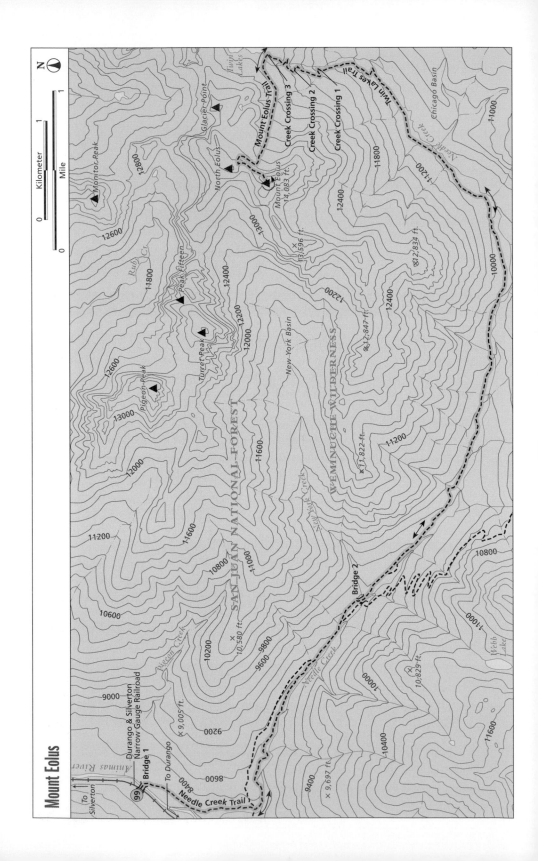

Miles and Directions

0.0 Depart the train, grab your pack as it is unloaded, and cross the bridge over the Animas River (8,200'). Turn right onto the Needle Creek Trail, and hike south along Needle Creek.

0.8 Turn left at the trail junction, signed for Needle Creek Trail. Enter the Weminuche Wilderness and sign the register, then hike southeast through the forest on the good trail.

2.5 Cross a footbridge over New York Creek (9,150') and continue southeast, then east on the trail (N37 36.793' / W107 40.256').

5.4 Emerge from the trees and enter Chicago Basin. As the trail curves to the northeast at about 10,850', look for a place to camp. You'll want access to water for cooking and to fill up for the next day's climb, but stay at least 200' from the creek, and even further away from the creek to go to the bathroom, so as not to sully the water for other campers. Once you've set up camp, scout out the next trail junction so you know where you're going in the dark the next morning. There are a lot of side trails leading to dispersed camping, but you'll stay west of the creek on the main trail for your ascent (N37 36.111' / W107 37.473').

6.5 Go left at the signed trail junction for Twin Lakes (11,200'). Hike north through the forest and over slabs, staying left of Needle Creek (N37 36.723' / W107 36.589').

6.9 The creek splits ahead, forking to the west and north. Cross to the north side of the west fork at 11,700' and continue north on steep terrain (N37 36.989' / W107 36.600').

7.3 Cross to the east side of the north fork of the creek (12,280') and continue north toward Twin Lakes (N37 37.197' / W107 36.579').

7.5 At Twin Lakes (12,500'), turn left and cross to the north side of the creek. You can see Mount Eolus from here, to the west. Get on the faint trail that heads northwest to the cliff ahead (N37 37.311' / W107 36.504').

7.6 The trail is stronger below the cliff, where it bends southwest into a nice grassy area (N37 37.328' / W107 36.580').

7.8 The trail bends west (12,600'), then west-northwest, and you can start to see the rest of the route. Look for a ramp ahead that angles up to the right. You are aiming for the bottom of the ramp. Continue to climb steeply, gaining about 800' in less than half a mile.

8.2 Continue west-northwest on rockier terrain and over slabs (N37 37.351' / W107 37.193').

8.3 The trail ends at the bottom of the rocky ramp (13,600'). Turn right and go northeast up the ramp. The rock angles off a bit to the right, so stay off downsloping wet or icy rock and avoid a tumble. At the top of the ramp, the trail bends left (north) and then northwest toward the Eolus–North Eolus saddle (N37 37.374' / W107 37.251').

8.4 Reach a flat area on the top of the ramp (13,700'). Go left and scramble up mixed Class 2 and 3 rock to a notch on the ridge ahead (N37 37.463' / W107 37.192').

8.5 From the notch (13,880'), turn left and follow the ridge south across the "catwalk." This is very exposed and requires a few easy Class 3 moves. The obvious route stays at ridgeline, then bends to the left of the vertical ridge ahead (N37 37.466' / W107 37.244').

8.6 Exit the catwalk and head to the left (east) face of the ridge, and under a very steep section of rock on the face. There is no defined route to the summit from here, but there are cairns and sections of trail that zigzag up through the ledges to a point on the ridge just south (left) of the highpoint. Climb mixed Class 2 and 3 rock to the top. On the ridge, turn right up a rocky ramp to reach the tiny summit.

8.7 Arrive at ranked 14,090' Mount Eolus. Return the way you came (N37 37.310' / W107 37.360').

17.4 Arrive back at the trailhead (N37 38.012' / W107 41.568').

100 La Plata Mountains Highpoint: Hesperus Mountain

Elevation: 13,232' (NAVD88 13,237')
Distinctions: La Plata Mountains Highpoint, Montezuma County Highpoint, Prominence 100, P2K, Ranked 13er
Class: 2+; Class 1 for first 0.8 mile, mixed Class 2 and 2+ to summit
Difficulty and skill level: Strenuous; Advanced
Approximate moving time: 5 hours
Distance: 4.2 miles round-trip
Elevation trailhead to summit: 10,900' to 13,237' (+2,337'); about 3,000' round-trip
Terrain: Dirt trail, bushwhack, grass, scree, talus, and boulders; creek crossing; risk of rockfall
Recommended extra gear: Helmet

Restrictions: Access to Sharkstooth Trailhead may require high-clearance 4WD, depending on conditions; no camping within 300' of the trailhead
Amenities: Camping and toilets seasonally at nearby Transfer Campground; backcountry camping; services in Mancos
Trailhead: Sharkstooth Trailhead
Trail: West Mancos Trail #621, off-trail West Ridge
Maps: DeLorme Page 86 A1; USGS La Plata
County: Montezuma
Land status: San Juan National Forest, (970) 247-4874, www.fs.usda.gov/sanjuan; Dolores Ranger District, (970) 882-7296

Finding the trailhead: From US 160 in Mancos, go north on CO 184 West for 0.3 mile and turn right onto CO 42. After 5.3 miles the road becomes unpaved FR 561. Continue for another 6.5 miles, past Transfer Campground, and turn right onto FR 350. Go 6.4 miles and bear right onto FR 346 / Aspen Loop Trail, then continue 1.5 miles, past Twin Lakes, and to the trailhead (GPS: N37 27.711' / W108 5.703').

The Peak

The La Plata Mountains are a spur of the San Juan Mountains located west of the Animas River and south of the Rico Mountains. Hesperus Mountain attracts county highpointers and P2K peakbaggers, and is a great excuse to visit the loose and rugged La Platas in the southwest part of the state. *La Plata* means "the silver," referring to ore discovered nearby in the 1700s, and *Hesperus* is Navajo for "big sheep," for the bighorn sheep that roam the peak's rocky slopes. The peak is the northernmost of the four corners of the Navajo *Dinétah*, or native homeland, but lies on public lands in the San Juan National Forest. The summit provides views southeast of nearby ranked 13ers Lavender Peak and Babcock Peak, and many more challenging summits.

The Climb

This is a short climb, but the ridge demands slow progress on boulders, talus, and ledges. Be sure to get on the right trail: The well-worn Sharkstooth Trail goes east to Sharkstooth Pass, but you will want to go south on the West Mancos Trail. Descend to the North Fork of the West Mancos River, cross the footbridge, and go west along the south side of the river, then bushwhack south toward the peak. There is no official

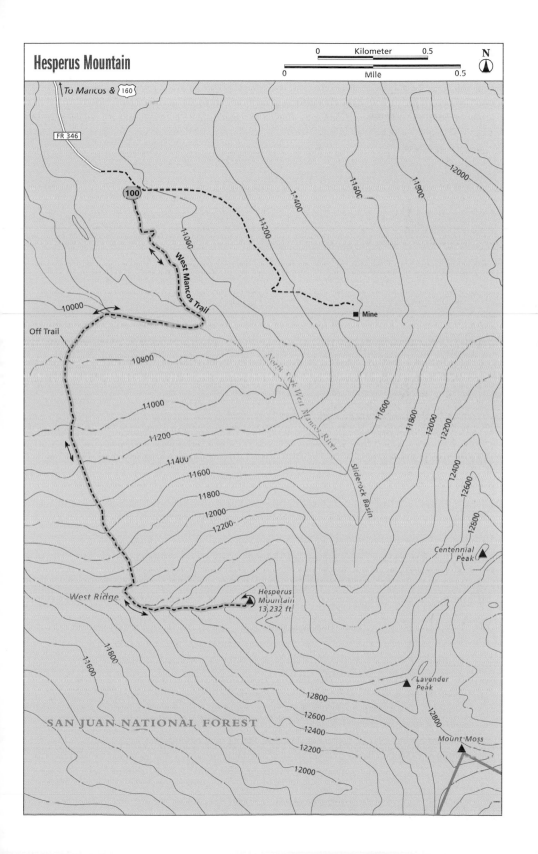

Hesperus Mountain

0   Kilometer   0.5

0   Mile   0.5

N

To Mancos & 160

FR 346

100

West Mancos Trail

11000

11200

11400

11600

11800

12000

11500

Mine

10000

Off Trail

10800

11000

11200

11400

11600

11800

12000

12200

North Fork West Mancos River

Sliderock Basin

11600

11800

12000

12200

12400

12600

12800

Centennial Peak

Hesperus Mountain 13,232 ft.

West Ridge

11800

11600

Lavender Peak

12800

12600

12400

12200

12000

12800

Mount Moss

SAN JUAN NATIONAL FOREST

Hesperus Mountain tops the La Plata Mountains in the San Juan National Forest near Mancos.
PHOTO BY JOHN KIRK

trail after you leave the river, but faint climber's trails and steep gullies make the route up the north face obvious from below. Choose the easiest path and head up to a saddle on the ridge, and east to the summit.

Miles and Directions

0.0 Begin at the trailhead (10,900') and hike south on the West Mancos Trail, descending into the North Fork of the West Mancos River drainage.

0.5 Cross the river (10,700') and turn right to go west on the trail. After about 0.25 mile depart the trail, left, and bushwhack south through deadfall. At treeline, locate a black gully leading up to the west ridge of the peak, and start the steep climb up to the saddle at the top (N37 27.382' / W108 5.494').

1.7 Gain the west ridge (12,300') and turn left to start the mixed Class 2 and 2+ climb on loose talus and boulders. A faint climber's trail and cairns mark the way along the south side of the ridge, angling up to the summit (N37 26.726' / W108 5.728').

2.1 Arrive at ranked 13,237' Hesperus Mountain. Return the way you came (N37 26.700' / W108 5.337').

4.2 Arrive back at the trailhead (N37 27.711' / W108 5.703').

Appendix A: References and Resources

Books

Bright, William. *Colorado Place Names* (3rd edition). Boulder, CO: Johnson Books, 2004.

Conners, Ben, and Brian Miller. *Climbing and Skiing Colorado's Mountains: 50 Select Ski Descents.* Guilford, CT: FalconGuides, 2014.

Covill, Dave, and John Drew Mitchler. *Hiking Colorado's Summits: A Guide to Exploring the County Highpoints.* Guilford, CT. Globe Pequot, 2002.

Dawson, Louis W., II. *Dawson's Guide to Colorado's Fourteeners, Vol. 1: The Northern Peaks.* Colorado Springs, CO: Blue Clover, 1994.

———. *Dawson's Guide to Colorado's Fourteeners, Vol. 2: The Southern Peaks.* Colorado Springs, CO: Blue Clover, 1996.

DeLorme Mapping Editor. *Colorado Atlas & Gazetteer.* Yarmouth, ME: DeLorme Mapping, 2011.

Fredston, Jill, and Doug Fesler. *Snow Sense: A Guide to Evaluating Snow Avalanche Hazard* (5th edition). Anchorage, AK: Alaska Mountain Safety Center, 2011.

Garratt, Mike, and Bob Martin. *Colorado's High Thirteeners: A Climbing & Hiking Guide* (3rd edition). Boulder, CO: Johnson Books, 2002.

Green, Stewart M. *Rock Climbing Colorado: A Guide to More Than 1,800 Routes* (2nd edition). Guilford, CT: FalconGuides / Globe Pequot, 2010.

———. *Scenic Routes & Byways Colorado.* Guilford, CT: Globe Pequot, 2013.

Jacobs, Randy, and The Colorado Mountain Club with Robert M. Ormes. *Guide to the Colorado Mountains* (9th edition). Boulder, CO: Johnson Books, 1992.

Jacobson, Cliff, and Lon Levin. *Basic Illustrated Map and Compass.* Guilford, CT: FalconGuides / Globe Pequot, 2008.

Mountaineers. *Mountaineering: Freedom of the Hills* (8th edition). Seattle, WA: Mountaineers Books, 2010.

Reed, Jack, and Gene Ellis. *Rocks Above the Clouds: A Hiker's and Climber's Guide to Colorado Mountain Geology.* Golden, CO: Colorado Mountain Club Press, 2009.

Rennicke, Jeff. *Colorado Mountain Ranges.* Helena and Billings, MT: Falcon, 1986.

Roach, Gerry. *Colorado's Fourteeners: From Hikes to Climbs* (3rd edition). Golden, CO: Fulcrum, 2011.

Roach, Gerry, and Jennifer Roach. *Colorado's Thirteeners: From Hikes to Climbs.* Golden, CO: Fulcrum, 2001.

Spitzer, Rick. *Colorado Mountain Passes: The State's Most Accessible High Country Roadways.* Boulder, CO: Westcliffe, 2009.

Websites

America the Beautiful National Parks and Federal Recreational Lands Annual Pass: www.nps
.gov/findapark/passes.htm

Barr Camp: www.barrcamp.com

Colorado Department of Transportation: www. cotrip.com

Colorado Fourteeners Initiative: www.14ers.org

Colorado Mountain Club: www.cmc.org

Colorado Outdoor Recreation Search and Rescue Card: www.dola.colorado.gov/sar/order
Instructions.jsf

Colorado Search and Rescue Board: www.coloradosarboard.org

Colorado State Parks Pass: www.cpw.state.co.us/buyapply/Pages/ParksPassInfo.aspx

Fourteeners: www.14ers.com

Free Campsites: www.freecampsites.net

Friends of Berthoud Pass: www.berthoudpass.org

Leave No Trace: www.lnt.org

Lists of John: www.listsofjohn.com

National Oceanic and Atmospheric Administration: www.noaa.gov

National Operational Hydrologic Remote Sensing Center: www.nohrsc.noaa.gov

Open Snow: www.opensnow.com

Peakbagger: www.peakbagger.com

PeakFinder: www.peakfinder.org

Pikes Peak Cog Railway: www.cograilway.com

SummitPost: www.summitpost.org

Thirteeners: www.13ers.com

USGS Map Locator and Downloader: www. store.usgs.gov

Appendix B: Land-Use Contact Information

Bureau of Land Management Field Offices

Badger Creek State Trust and Waugh Mountain State Trust Land Management Areas
State Land Board, South Central District
(719) 543-7403
www.trustlands.state.co.us/Districts/Pages/SouthCentral.aspx

Colorado River Valley Field Office
2300 River Frontage Road
Silt, CO 81652
(970) 876-9000
www.blm.gov/co/st/en/fo/crvfo.html

Colorado State Land Board
www.trustlands.state.co.us

Grand Junction Field Office
2815 H Road
Grand Junction, CO 81506
(970) 244-3000
www.blm.gov/co/st/en/fo/gjfo.html

Royal Gorge Field Office
3028 E. Main Street
Cañon City, CO 81212
(719) 269-8500
www.blm.gov/co/st/en/fo/rgfo.html

San Luis Valley Field Office
46525 Highway 114
Saguache, Colorado 81149
(719) 655-2547
www.blm.gov/co/st/en/fo/slvfo.html

Campgrounds

Recreation.gov
(877) 444-6777
www.recreation.gov

City, County, State, and National Monuments, Open Spaces, Parklands, Parks, and Recreation Areas

City of Boulder Open Space & Mountain Parks
PO Box 791
Boulder, CO 80306
(303) 441-3440
www.bouldercolorado.gov

Great Sand Dunes National Park and Preserve
11500 Highway 150
Mosca, CO 81146-9798
(719) 378-6300
www.nps.gov/grsa/index.htm

Larimer County Department of Natural Resources
1800 S. CR 31
Loveland, CO 80537
(970) 679-4570
www.co.larimer.co.us/naturalresources

Rocky Mountain National Park
1000 Highway 36
Estes Park, CO 80517-8397
(970) 586-1206
www.nps.gov/romo

Royal Gorge Park, City of Cañon City
Parks Division
221 Griffin Avenue
Cañon City, CO 81212

(719) 269-9028
www.canoncity.org/Parks_Forestry_Cemetery/Parks/Parks_Division.htm

National Forests

Arapaho National Forest
2150 Centre Avenue, Building E
Fort Collins, CO 80526
(970) 295-6600
www.fs.usda.gov/arp

Grand Mesa National Forest
2250 Highway 50
Delta, CO 81416
(970) 874-6600
www.fs.usda.gov/gmug

Gunnison National Forest
2250 Highway 50
Delta, CO 81416
(970) 874-6600
www.fs.usda.gov/gmug

Pike National Forest
2840 Kachina Drive
Pueblo, CO 81008
(719) 553-1400
www.fs.usda.gov/psicc

Rio Grande National Forest
1803 W. Highway 160
Monte Vista, CO 81144
(719) 852-5941
www.fs.usda.gov/riogrande

Roosevelt National Forest
2150 Centre Avenue, Building E
Fort Collins, CO 80526
(970) 295-6600
www.fs.usda.gov/arp

Routt National Forest
2468 Jackson Street
Laramie, WY 82070

(307) 745-2300
www.fs.usda.gov/mbr

San Isabel National Forest
2840 Kachina Drive
Pueblo, CO 81008
(719) 553-1400
www.fs.usda.gov/psicc

San Juan National Forest
15 Burnett Court
Durango, CO 81301
(970) 247-4874
www.fs.usda.gov/sanjuan

Uncompahgre National Forest
2250 Highway 50
Delta, CO 81416
(970) 874-6600
www.fs.usda.gov/gmug

White River National Forest
900 Grand Avenue
Glenwood Springs, CO 81601
(970) 945-2521
www.fs.usda.gov/whiteriver

Private Lands
Cielo Vista Ranch
www.cielovistaranchco.com

Durango & Silverton Narrow Gauge
Railroad
479 Main Avenue
Durango, CO 81301
(970) 247-2733
www.durangotrain.com

Ranger Districts

Aspen-Sopris Ranger District
806 W. Hallam Street
Aspen, CO 81611
(970) 925-3445

Boulder Ranger District
2140 Yarmouth Avenue
Boulder, CO 80301
(303) 541-2500

Canyon Lakes Ranger District
2150 Centre Avenue, Building E
Fort Collins, CO 80526
(970) 295-6700

Clear Creek Ranger District
101 Highway 103
PO Box 3307
Idaho Springs, CO 80452
(303) 567-3000

Columbine Ranger District–Silverton Pub
lic Lands Center
1468 Greene Street
PO Box 709
Silverton, CO 81433
(970) 884-2512

Conejos Peak Ranger District
15571 CR T5
La Jara, CO 81140
(719) 274-8971

Dillon Ranger District
680 Blue River Parkway
Silverthorne, CO 80498
(970) 468-5400

Divide Ranger District–Creede Office
304 S. Main Street
PO Box 270
Creede, CO 81130
(719) 658-2556

Dolores Public Lands Office
29211 Highway 184
Dolores, CO 81323
(970) 882-7296

Dolores Ranger District / Tres Rios BLM
Field Office
29211 Highway 184
Dolores, CO 81323-9308
(970) 882-7296

Eagle–Holy Cross Ranger District
24747 Highway 24
Minturn, CO 81645
(970) 827-5715

Grand Valley Ranger District
2777 Crossroads Boulevard, Suite 1
Grand Junction, CO 81506
(970) 242-8211

Gunnison Ranger District
216 N. Colorado Street
Gunnison, CO 81230
(970) 641-0471

Gunnison Ranger District–Lake City Office
PO Box 483
Lake City, CO 81235
(970) 641-0471 or (970) 944-2500

Hahns Peak / Bears Ears Ranger District
925 Weiss Drive
Steamboat Springs, CO 80487-9315
(970) 870-2299

Leadville Ranger District
810 Front Street
Leadville, CO 80461
(719) 486-0749

Norwood Ranger District
1150 Forest Street
PO Box 388

Norwood, CO 81423
(970) 327-4261

Ouray Ranger District
2505 S. Townsend Avenue
Montrose, CO 81401
(970) 240-5300

Pagosa Ranger District
180 Pagosa Street
PO Box 310
Pagosa Springs, CO 81147
(970) 264-2268

Paonia Ranger District
N. Rio Grande Avenue
PO Box 1030
Paonia, CO 81428
(970) 527-4131

Parks Ranger District
(970) 723-2700

Pikes Peak Ranger District
601 S. Weber Street
Colorado Springs, CO 80903
(719) 636-1602

Rifle Ranger District
0094 CR 244
Rifle, CO 81650
(970) 625-2371

Saguache Ranger District
(719) 655-2547

Salida Ranger District
5575 Cleora Road
Salida, CO 81201
(719) 539-3591

San Carlos Ranger District
3028 E. Main Street
Cañon City, CO 81212
(719) 269-8500

South Park Ranger District
320 Highway 285
PO Box 219
Fairplay, CO 80440
(719) 836-2031

South Platte Ranger District
19316 Goddard Ranch Court
Morrison, CO 80465
(303) 275-5610

Sulphur Ranger District
9 Ten Mile Drive
Granby, CO 80446
(970) 887-4100

Yampa Ranger District
300 Roselawn Street
Yampa, CO 80483
(970) 638-4516

State Division of Wildlife

Colorado Division of Wildlife,
Colorado Parks & Wildlife
(303) 297-1192
www.cpw.state.co.us

Wilderness Areas

Buffalo Peaks Wilderness
Collegiate Peaks Wilderness
Eagles Nest Wilderness
Flat Tops Wilderness
Great Sand Dunes Wilderness
Greenhorn Mountain Wilderness
Hunter-Fryingpan Wilderness
Holy Cross Wilderness
Indian Peaks Wilderness
La Garita Wilderness
Lizard Head Wilderness
Lost Creek Wilderness
Maroon Bells–Snowmass Wilderness
Mount Massive Wilderness
Mount Sneffels Wilderness

Mount Zirkel Wilderness
Ptarmigan Peak Wilderness
Raggeds Wilderness
Rawah Wilderness
Rocky Mountain National Park
Wilderness
Sangre de Cristo Wilderness
South San Juan Wilderness
Spanish Peaks Wilderness
Uncompahgre Wilderness
Vasquez Peak Wilderness
Weminuche Wilderness
West Elk Wilderness
Contact the local Ranger District or go to
www.wilderness.net

Wildlife Areas and Offices

Colorado Parks & Wildlife, Southeast
Office–Pueblo
600 Reservoir Road
Pueblo, CO 81005
(719) 561-5300

Lake Dorothey State Wildlife Area and
James M. John State Wildlife Area
www.cpw.state.co.us

Wildlife Management Areas, Colorado
Division of Wildlife
(303) 297-1192
www.cpw.state.co.us

About the Author

Susan Joy Paul has hiked, climbed, snow-shoed, rappelled, and at times—when the winds above 14,000' were screaming—crawled across the state of Colorado, reaching the summits of more than 600 mountains along the way. She has climbed all the ranked 14,000' peaks in the state, and is the only woman to have summited all the ranked peaks in Teller County and in El Paso County. In her first book, *Touring Colorado Hot Springs*, Susan took a break to relax and revitalize at 32 of the state's hot springs, and in *Hiking Waterfalls in Colorado* she hit the trail, visiting 150 of the state's waterfalls. Now, in *Climbing Colorado's Mountains*, Susan returns to the peaks, and is happy to present this com-

Author Susan Joy Paul
PHOTO BY STEWART M. GREEN

pilation of her mountaineering experience and research—along with descriptions, maps, and photographs of 100 Colorado mountain adventures—to anyone who loves the mountains as much as she does. Susan lives in Colorado Springs, Colorado.